Law, Lawyers and Justice

This book engages with the place of law and legality within Australia's distinctive contribution to global televisual culture.

Australian popular culture has created a lasting legacy – for good or bad – of representations of law, lawyers and justice 'down under'. Within films and television of striking landscapes, peopled with heroes, antiheroes, survivors and jokers, there is a fixation on law, conflicts between legal orders, brutal violence and survival. Deeply compromised by the ongoing violence against the lives and laws of First Nation Australians, Australian film and television has sharply illuminated what it means to live with a 'rule of law' that rules with a legacy, and a reality, of deep injustice. This book is the first to bring together scholars to reflect on, and critically engage with, the representations and global implications of law, lawyers and justice captured through the lenses of Australian film, television and social media.

Exploring how distinctively Australian lenses capture uniquely Australian images and narratives, the book nevertheless engages these in order to provide broader insights into the contemporary translations and transmogrifications of law and justice.

Kim D. Weinert is a PhD candidate at Griffith Law School, Griffith University.

Karen Crawley is a senior lecturer at Griffith Law School, Griffith University.

Kieran Tranter is Chair of Law, Technology and Future in the School of Law, Queensland University of Technology.

Law, Lawyers and Justice

Through Australian Lenses

Edited by Kim D. Weinert, Karen Crawley and Kieran Tranter

Routledge
Taylor & Francis Group
LONDON AND NEW YORK

First published 2020
by Routledge
2 Park Square, Milton Park, Abingdon, Oxon OX14 4RN

and by Routledge
605 Third Avenue, New York, NY 10017

First issued in paperback 2021

Routledge is an imprint of the Taylor & Francis Group, an informa business

A Glasshouse book

Publisher's Note
The publisher has gone to great lengths to ensure the quality of this reprint but points out that some imperfections in the original copies may be apparent.

British Library Cataloguing-in-Publication Data
A catalogue record for this book is available from the British Library

Library of Congress Cataloging-in-Publication Data
Names: Weinert, Kim D., editor. | Crawley, Karen, editor. | Tranter, Kieran, editor.
Title: Law, lawyers and justice : through Australian lenses / Kim D. Weinert, Karen Crawley, Kieran Tranter [editors].
Description: London ; New York : Routledge, 2020. | Includes bibliographical references and index.
Identifiers: LCCN 2019053708 (print) | LCCN 2019053709 (ebook) | ISBN 9780367210458 (hardback) | ISBN 9780429288128 (ebook)
Subjects: LCSH: Justice, Administration of, in motion pictures. | Lawyers in motion pictures. | Law in motion pictures. | Motion pictures–Australia–History and criticism. | Legal television programs–Australia–History and criticism. | Justice, Administration of, on television. | Lawyers on television. | Social media–Australia.
Classification: LCC PN1995.9.J8 L39 2020 (print) | LCC PN1995.9.J8 (ebook) | DDC 791.43/653–dc23
LC record available at https://lccn.loc.gov/2019053708
LC ebook record available at https://lccn.loc.gov/2019053709

Typeset in Times New Roman
by Apex CoVantage, LLC

ISBN 13: 978-1-03-223723-7 (pbk)
ISBN 13: 978-0-367-21045-8 (hbk)

Contents

Preface

> Jingeri
> Yugambeh for 'Hello'
> The Yugambeh are the First Nation people of the southeast of what the British called Queensland. Their country includes the cities and towns of the Gold Coast, Logan and Beaudesert. We acknowledge their elders past, present and future.

'Australians all let us rejoice, For we are young and free': these are the opening lines of a nationalistic ditty that was adopted as the Australian national anthem in 1984, replacing 'God Save the Queen'. Reflective of a confident white society debuting on the world stage, the very lyrics are divisive. For the First Nations people of the land and nearby islands that the North has now called Australia, to sing of youth (in the context of 65,000 years of continuous cultural habitation) and freedom (in the context of the settler state and its continual practices of 'interventions', removals from country and killings) is a sad irony. The positive projections of the lyrics and the jaunty musicality of the anthem are undercut by a cruel reality.

For lawyers interested in the processes by which culture, materiality and power build, maintain and contest relationships and realities, it is highly provocative to live, teach and research in Australia. These processes seem immediate and obvious, and the high stakes of their playing out on the lives and bodies of Australians and those caught in its governmental orbit – like the feared boat-arriving asylum seekers – are witnessed continually in the media, storytelling and cultural artefacts emanating from Australia.

Yet what this says about law, lawyers and justice has not been strongly explored from the location of popular culture and law. There is a sense of injustice felt deep in the soul and seen in the land that is almost too painful to address. This is the motivation for this book. It is a beginning, not an end, reflecting a desire to bring to words what is felt and seen. We do not present it as a definitive work – such a claim implies that the object of study is entombed in history, discrete and knowable. Rather, we are each living and working (and watching and consuming visual culture) in a present Australia that *is* its colonial past, over-determined by the indefatigable legalities of the settler state. Yet we can hope for the future. We commit this book to the shared struggle for a future filled with hope that lies beyond the settler state and its legalities of violence.

Nothing ever comes from nothing. The catalyst for this book was Kim arriving at Griffith Law School at Griffith University to pursue a doctorate with Kieran and Karen, which engaged more fully with the law and legalities of speech projected by Australian film. Her project inspired a workshop at Griffith funded by the Law Futures Centre, and this volume emerged from the papers presented. Our thanks to Melinda Davis from the Centre for organizing the workshop and for the support and encouragement of the Centre's inaugural director, Professor John Flood, and his successor, Professor Don Anton. A special thanks to our esteemed colleagues, Professor Charles Lawson and Dr Edwin Bikundo, who attended the workshop and, as always, provided thoughtful and engaging feedback on the draft papers.

We would especially like to thank members of the Australian and international academies who committed to and supported this project through undertaking blind reviews of the draft chapters. These chapters are more rigorous and better located because of their generosity and expertise. In no particular order, our thanks go to Professor Julian Webb, Professor Peter Robson, Dr Linda Haller, Associate Professor Catriona Elder, Associate Professor Francesca Bartlett, Professor Rebecca Johnson, Professor Simon Rice, Associate Professor Felicity Collins, Professor Bridget Griffen-Foley, Associate Professor Rebecca Johinke, Dr Victoria Herche, Professor Sue Turnbull, Dr Chris Butler, Dr Poppy De Souza and Professor Jon Stratton. A very special thank you to Susan Jarvis, who copy-edited the chapters for us.

Finally, this book is dedicated to Rémy Sébastien, who was born on 9 September 2019 as the final parts of the book were being arranged. May he grow into that future Australia filled with hope.

Kieran Tranter, Kim D. Weinert and Karen Crawley
Written in Yugambeh Country, 20 September 2019

Notes on contributors

Thalia Anthony is an associate professor in law at the University of Technology Sydney. Her expertise is in the areas of criminal law, procedure and incarceration as it affects Aboriginal and Torres Strait Islander people, with a particular focus on the experiences of Indigenous women and young people. Her research relies on collaborations with Indigenous organizations in Australia and overseas, and she expresses her ongoing gratitude for their contributions to joint projects. Thalia's major books include *Indigenous People, Crime and Punishment* (Routledge, 2013) and *Decolonising Criminology* (Palgrave Macmillan, 2019).

Bruce Baer Arnold is an assistant professor at the Canberra Law School, University of Canberra, where he teaches technology law. His chapter reflects his doctorate on the construction of legal identity and writing about LGBTIQ people within the justice system.

Karen Crawley is a senior lecturer at the Griffith Law School and a managing editor of the *Australian Feminist Law Journal*. Karen researches in law and the humanities, with a particular interest in literary, visual and critical feminist approaches to law and justice. She is a graduate of the University of Sydney, with honours in English Literature and Law, and did her postgraduate study at McGill University (LLM and PhD). She is a member of the Law, Literature and Humanities Association of Australasia.

Penny Crofts is an associate professor in the faculty of law, University of Technology Sydney, Australia. She researches in the area of socio-legal studies, focusing on issues of justice in criminal law in practice and theory, and makes a distinctive contribution to critical evaluations of criminal legal models of culpability and enforcement. Her analysis of criminal legal models of wickedness has contributed to a jurisprudence of blameworthiness. Penny is currently researching a project entitled 'Rethinking Institutional Culpability: Criminal Law, Philosophy and Horror'.

Chris Cunneen is Professor of Criminology at Jumbunna Institute for Indigenous Education and Research, University of Technology Sydney. He researches criminal justice issues in the context of colonialism.

Kirsty Duncanson is a senior lecturer in the Department of Social Inquiry at La Trobe University, where she teaches subjects about power and justice, policy and community and crime and justice on screens (in art and podcasts) with the wonderful Maria Elander. She researches thinking about film and television through the lens of cultural legal studies. At present, she is preoccupied by *Fifty Shades of Grey*, *House of Cards*, *Cleverman* and *Doctor Who*. With Emma Henderson, she has been interviewing barristers to find out how they are trained for, prepare for and deliver in sexual assault trials.

John Flood is Professor of Law and Society at Griffith University. He researches professions and globalization and is now examining the role of technology in law. He tweets at @JohnAFlood.

Laura Joseph is a senior learning designer for TAFE NSW. She received her PhD in English and Gender Studies from the University of New South Wales. Her research focuses on the relationship between the trope of hell and antipodean colonial identity from pre-modern literature to contemporary Australian and New Zealand representations.

Pauline Klippmark is a lawyer, honours graduate and research assistant with Griffith Law School. She has published in *Social & Legal Studies*, worked as a research assistant in the fields of international criminal law and international human rights law, and tutored law students in Griffith University's Indigenous Tutorial Assistance Scheme. She hopes to research at the intersection of law and culture while working close to the law.

Julian R. Murphy is a lawyer and a PhD student in the School of Law at the University of Melbourne. Julian's writing about Indigenous legal issues has been published in the *Indigenous Law Bulletin*, the *Australian Law Journal*, the *Northern Territory Law Journal* and mainstream media outlets, including *The Guardian* and the *Sydney Morning Herald.*

Lili Pâquet is a lecturer at the University of New England. She teaches and publishes on rhetoric, writing, law and literature and crime fiction. Lili's book, *Crime Fiction from a Professional Eye: Women Writers with Law Enforcement and Justice Experience*, was published in 2018 by McFarland.

Jack Quirk is a PhD student in the English Department at Brown University in Providence, Rhode Island, United States. His work maintains the indispensability of literary and cultural critique to our understanding of how law functions in the world. Before graduate school, he worked as a lawyer in Australia.

Honni van Rijswijk is a senior lecturer in the Faculty of Law, University of Technology Sydney, Australia. She received her PhD from the University of Washington, where she was a fellow in the Society of Scholars at the Simpson Center for the Humanities. She has published on feminist theories of harm, formulations of responsibility in law and literature, the role of history in the common law and questions of justice relating to the Stolen Generations. Honni is currently writing a monograph, *Law and the Girl: Gender, Genre, Violence.*

Sophie Russell is a PhD candidate in the Faculty of Law, University of Technology Sydney and a research associate in the Faculty of Law, University of New South Wales. Sophie's research focuses on the policy and practice of punishment and reintegration.

Cassandra Sharp is an associate professor in the School of Law at the University of Wollongong and the managing editor of *Law Text Culture*. She is also a member of the university's Legal Intersections Research Centre. Recent publications include the edited collection *Cultural Legal Studies* (with Marett Leiboff, Routledge, 2015) and articles in the *Griffith Law Review*, *Law & Literature* and the *International Journal for the Semiotics of Law*.

Kieran Tranter is the Chair of Law, Technology and Future in the School of Law, Queensland University of Technology. He researches projections of law and technology within the cultural imaginary. His latest book, *Living in Technical Legality: Science Fiction and Law as Technology*, was published by Edinburgh University Press in 2018.

Kim D. Weinert is a PhD candidate at Griffith University, Queensland, where her PhD is focused on examining Australia's representations of speech in Australian film from the 1970s to the 2000s. Kim is supported by an Australian Government Research Training Programme (RTP) Scholarship and is a member of Griffith University's Future Centre. Kim teaches torts law online at the University of the South Pacific and has published previously in the areas of not-for-profit law and cultural legal studies.

Part I

The unsettled law and justice of Australia

Chapter 1

Australian lenses on law, lawyers and justice

Kim D. Weinert, Karen Crawley and Kieran Tranter

THE NIGHTINGALE

In 2019, Jennifer Kent's *The Nightingale*,[1] the follow-up film to her well-received genre horror first film *The Babadook*,[2] caused controversy at the Sydney Film Festival. Set in 1825 in the British penal colony of Van Diemen's Land, the film tells a highly graphic story of rapes, murders and revenge that some audience members were unable to sit through.[3]

The Nightingale is an Australian story. It is an Australian production and has an Australian director. It was filmed on location in the haunting Gothic forests of Tasmania, and it is set during the period of Australian colonial penal history. Many of the cast are Australian actors. But its Australianness is more than the nationalities of its production, personnel and setting. *The Nightingale* projects something deeply insidious and horrifying about law and justice within Australia. Those who enact the law in the film – the British military and its governing regime – were the abusers of the young Irish convict Clare (Aisling Franciosi) and the murderers of her husband and young child. Their law was a law of rights – of ownership of this woman and her body – that was promoted and protected by the overarching legality of the penal regime. Law and justice are in opposition in *The Nightingale*. The rule of law is revealed as a naked exercise of biopower in the furtherance of colonial occupation. As the film descends into a vengeance chase by Clare and her reluctant Aboriginal tracker Billy/Mangala (Baykali Ganambarr), film-goers become witnesses to the genocide of Tasmania's Aboriginal people in what is now recognized as the Black War.[4] Through Kent's lens, this violence is shown as a pogrom, as racial violence emanating from careless anger and utter dehumanization. *The Nightingale* projects law and justice in Australia as a bloody mess composed of gender, race, bodies and land ground together by pure violence. This is an unflinching and unsettling representation of law and justice – something that would be easier to walk away from than to watch and deal with.

This book gathers chapters on law, lawyers and justice through Australian lenses. Like *The Nightingale*, what is revealed has an unsettled nature. It would be easy to walk away; it would be easy to historicize and – like a certain Australian prime minister – to refuse to say 'Sorry' and to place the trauma of Australia into a distant colonial past.[5] The contributors to this volume certainly do not do this. Engaging with law and justice through Australian lenses reveals that its violent legality is profoundly unjust, that cherished notions from the jurisprudence of the North – the rule of law, sovereignty, rights – function as weapons of the settler state and that the actual site of law is not the institutions of courts, law offices and parliaments, but always bodies and the land.

This book emerges from a lacuna in the ever-developing field of law and popular culture,[6] which has found a diverse and growing audience among scholars and students of law. There is something liberating in seeing law beyond the posited rules and institutions of the legal system. The field of law and legality is pervasive: it does not just manifest in formal texts, officers and practices, but inundates all cultural life; it is animated, demonstrated and critiqued through cultural artefacts. In recent years, law and popular culture has become an expansive field of study, building upon more established 'law and literature' media of fiction and film to embrace television,[7] video games,[8] street art,[9] music,[10] comics,[11] visual art[12] and the multimodalities of fan prosuming.[13]

A core location for law and popular culture – especially in its seeking out law in non-traditional mediums – has been the Australian legal academy. Australian scholars have made substantial contributions to the foundational theorizing and practice of law and popular culture, exemplified by the work of Margaret Thornton,[14] Desmond Manderson,[15] William P. MacNeil[16] and Alison Young.[17] Following these founding contributions, a range of Australia-based scholars have forged important contributions within law and popular culture, often called 'cultural legal studies'; they include Edwin Bikundo, Karen Crawley, Penny Crofts, Kirsty Duncanson, Marett Leiboff, Edward Mussawir, Timothy D. Peters, Honni van Rijswijk, Cassandra Sharp and Kieran Tranter.

This Australian law and popular culture movement has an interesting dimension. Often these scholars' engagement is with global texts and franchises – in a globalized media space and a globalized academy, such examinations and critiques are both needed and vitally important. There cannot be a sort of Trump trade war nationalism where only scholars who share the nationality of the cultural text have legitimacy in its legal exegesis. Australian popular culture is particularly awash with cultural products from the United States, the United Kingdom, Japan and Korea. As a settler state, Australia's importation of culture is a defining characteristic; however, this international, global focus of analysis could be seen as disconnecting the scholar from their own life and land. As shown by *The Nightingale*, Australia's colonial history, geography and economy, as well as its past and present social anxieties, have had a particular legacy in law, legality and governing that is written in and through Australia's own cultural artefacts. So, while Tranter might write repeatedly about the legalities of time and memory that materialize through the very British science fiction series *Doctor Who*, that does connect with Australian concerns as living legal subjects, caught in a vortex of imagined pasts and projected futures, it is worked through denotations of the 'Sceptred Isle', aliens speaking perfect BBC English, bow-ties, memories of Empire and London Metropolitan police boxes.[18]

This does not mean that Australian law and popular culture scholars are purely cultural expats, watching, writing and yearning for representations of living from another hemisphere. In the foundational *Lex Populi*, William P. MacNeil spends some time with the Kerrigans from *The Castle*,[19] seeing in the film a complex set of projections around particular Australian concerns with class, race, land and ownership against the background of the common law *Mabo* and *Wik* native title decisions.[20] That legal reworkings of the foundational myths of the settler state in the *Mabo* decision go to the core of Australian culture is the premise of Felicity Collins and Therese Davis's *Australian Cinema After Mabo*.[21] Like MacNeil's exploration of *The Castle*, these authors identify a distinct inversion of earlier settler state social imaginaries in Australian films from the late 1990s through to the early 2000s,[22] showing how Australian law and its legal preoccupations manifest in culture.

The legalities, violence and trauma of the settler state projected through Australian cultural artefacts have been identified by other law and popular culture scholars. When he is not out of this world via various non-Australian science fiction franchises, Kieran Tranter has engaged with George Miller's violent *Mad Max* films[23] as projecting a distinctly Australian integration of the motor vehicle into the imagining and structuring of governing regimes.[24] Honni van Rijswijk has drawn upon First Nation Australian author Alexis Wright's fantastic, dystopian novel *The Swan Book*[25] to emphasize the interconnectedness of suffering, law and violence. The novel is set in a future of cataclysmic climate change where the Northern Territory Intervention has endured and intensified; van Rijswijk writes that, to understand the protagonist's suffering,

> means to mourn land and animals, laws, language and culture, and also to understand that land, animals and laws mourn. The argument of *The Swan Book* is that these harms cannot be isolated: the rape of women and children is connected to state practices of incarceration and punishment, to poverty, abuse of the rule of law, and to forced assimilation. The failure of law to register the interconnectedness of these harms in law's archive is part of law's violence.[26]

Manderson's *Kangaroo Courts and the Rule of Law*[27] explores D. H. Lawrence's 1922 novel *Kangaroo*,[28] about the sojourn to Australia of an English author and his wife and their interaction with a group of ex-Diggers galvanizing towards fascism. Paralleling Lawrence's feverish imagined Australia with Carl Schmitt's Weimar concerns with the terminal decline of the West due to the 'neutrality' of positivism and liberalism, Manderson begins to articulate the dilemmas of modernism – the dreams turned nightmares of both rationalism and romanticism that intensified in literature, philosophy and law after the Great War. For Manderson, Lawrence's Australia becomes a site where the literal instrumentalism of the rule of law is polarized by romance for a society ruled by law. Manderson draws out from Lawrence's Australia a site where the tensions of various Northern projects

– the state, the rule of law, Western civilization – are exposed raw and revealed in their conflicted polarity.

This was the motivation for this edited volume: a deep sense that examining law, lawyers and justice through Australian lenses – that is, through stories and cultural artefacts emanating from the particular antipodean place now known as Australia – is an exercise that is both potent and unique to bring Australian-located stories about law, lawyers and justice to a wider audience and through calling into question the comfortable and accepted understandings of law, lawyers and justice projected by the global North onto this land and its inhabitants. In the next section, we contextualize the idea of an Australian lens, providing an orientation to the historic and institutional practices that support and sustain Australian film, television and social media. In the final section, we outline the chapters to follow.

Through Australian lenses

This book concerns law, lawyers and justice through Australian lenses. This idea requires explanation. Following law and popular culture's expansive approach to media, we did not want to limit the analysis to old forms of media. The idea of a lens was important. Lenses, of course, suggest the technical apparatus of the camera, immediately suggesting film and television as cultural artefacts in which lenses are integral to production. Yet the idea of a lens, and especially the idiom 'through a lens', exceeds this denotation. The phrase has connotations regarding the origins of technoscience in the lensed apparatuses of the telescope and microscope – instruments that reveal what is unseen to the unassisted sight of the naked eye. The deployment of the phrase to signpost critique is common in scholarly titles.[29] Within this context, our use of 'through' and 'lenses' is thoughtful – suggesting a focus on the technical capturing of the image and also suggesting the idiom's connotations of revealing and critique. Here, though, we complicate this notion of lenses by suggesting a national focus: the lenses of this book are Australian.

When considering *The Nightingale*, some elements of what we consider to be an Australian lens were revealed. In a globalized media and culture environment, the ascription of nationality to a specific artefact is problematic. *The Nightingale* had an Australian director and producers, was filmed in Australia, was funded by Screen Australia and told a particular story located in a specific and brutal colonial history of penal transportation and racial extermination. Despite this, its lead was an Irish actor, it was co-produced by the Canadian production company Bron Studios and its launch strategy deliberately targeted international film festivals.[30] To be uniquely and definitively Australian – even in such obvious ways as manifested in *The Nightingale* – does not preclude wider global engagement in both production and impact.[31]

Like *The Nightingale*, all the artefacts considered by this book are Australian in multiple registries. Foremost, and tellingly, the landscapes, stories and people captured on the camera lenses are distinctly Australian: from the rapscallion lawyer rogue Cleaver Green in the Australian Broadcasting Corporation (ABC)'s dark comedy *Rake*[32] to consideration of the filmic and television iterations of *Picnic at Hanging Rock*[33] to the image-based content about race, crime and vigilantism shared by Australian social media users. These are Australian stories in Australian landscapes being told by Australians, predominately for Australians.

Further, in planning this book, we were not against the notion of a lens extending beyond its association with the technologies of visual recording; Alexis Wright's *The Swan Book*, as shown by Honni van Rijswijk, is itself a highly focused lens, exposing and revealing the modalities of the Australian settler state. However, the lenses deployed by the chapters in the book are more within the core understanding of the term as ocular and imagistic. The chapters focus on, expose and reveal dimensions of law, lawyers and justice through Australian film, television and social media.

This claim in turn requires some further location. Australian films and filmmaking have an ebbed history. Film is a complex, political and technological system that is clearly associated with global projections of Western cultural values.[34] The history of film in Australia can be seen as mostly the history of cultural importation from the United Kingdom and then the United States. The agreed-upon 'first' Australian films were produced by the Salvation Army in Melbourne from 1897 to 1900,[35] and there was a pioneering period of Australian film prior to World War I, with a succession of long story films telling and celebrating well-regarded narratives from within mainstream white settler society, particularly *The Story of the Kelly Gang*,[36] *Eureka Stockade*[37] and *Robbery Under Arms*.[38] These films connected to an indigenous (but distinctly *not* Indigenous) white nationalism defining itself in contrast to the hierarchies and stagnation of the 'Old Country'.

World War I effectively killed the nascent Australian film industry, and Australian audiences through to the 1960s were screened British and American films. A turning point was 20th Century Fox's 1952 production of *Kangaroo*[39] – unconnected to Lawrence's tale – that filmed a technicolour Western with actors from the United States as leads around Port Augusta. The popular and critical reaction against the representations of Australia in *Kangaroo* led to growing calls for a dedicated Australian film industry reflecting 'Australia', understood as coterminous with mainstream white culture, values, dreams and sensibilities.[40]

The beginning of television broadcasting in 1956 also highlighted the need for Australian content on the rapidly growing number of Australian screens.[41] Yet meaningful government intervention in the Australian film and television industry did not occur until the late 1960s, with the establishment of the Australian Council for the Arts, the Experimental Film Fund, the Australian Film Development Corporation and a national film and television school.[42] Driving this public investment in Australian lenses was a growing awareness of the need to explore and foster a distinctive 'Australian culture' within a changing world.[43]

The 1970s saw the emergence of a distinctly Australian cinema and style: the Ocker film, screening a 'larger-than-life' exaggeration of mainstream white Australian culture,[44] with thick accents, slang and bad-manners[45] in the everyday contexts of suburbia[46] and the beach.[47] The commercial viability of these films gave a boost of confidence to both the emerging Australian film industry and the government to pursue more diverse and challenging storytelling.[48] As discussed by Cassandra Sharp in her chapter, the 1970s also saw the emergence of a unique Australian television industry: from slow beginnings in the 1960s with games, variety and news/current affair shows to genre police shows, the 1970s saw some brazen and ground-breaking television, such as *Number 96*,[49] a weekly soap/sitcom that had the first leading openly gay character in a mainstream weekly show and overt, censor-baiting nudity, together with the global cult women's prison soap/drama *Prisoner*.[50]

Australian film found global recognition in the 1980s with the *Mad Max* franchise and particularly with the unexpected success of the comedy *Crocodile Dundee*.[51] With this international awareness came local concerns about the Hollywood-ization of Australian film, which overlooked the nurturing of unique Australian voices and stories in the pursuit of global sales.[52] Tom O'Regan[53] suggests that this led filmmakers to search for a 'new Australianness', telling more inclusive stories about interpersonal struggles relating to gender, sexual orientation, race and ableist identities.[54] In this, *Crocodile Dundee* could be seen as a last hurrah for the Ocker sensibility of 'knockabout' white Australian masculinity, soon to be replaced in the bush by *The Adventures of Priscilla, Queen of the Desert*.[55]

Australian television produced many notable shows during and after the 1980s, but none has had the same kind of international breakthrough success as *Crocodile Dundee*. Notable lingering successes have been the soaps *Neighbours* and *Home and Away* in the UK market.[56] This does not mean, however, that Australian television has not found a broader international market. A recent study of law and justice television beamed to various national audiences found that often Australia content was ranked fourth after content from the United States, United Kingdom and national productions.[57] Fast forward to the present century and Australia has an active and vibrant film and television industry, producing distinctly Australian films like *The Nightingale* and also hosting large Hollywood franchise productions such as two of the Star Wars prequel films[58] and *Thor: Ragnarok* from the Marvel Cinematic Universe.[59] In 2015 it was suggested that the sector made a direct contribution of $4.8 billion to the Australian economy, supporting 39,000 full-time jobs,[60] and several Australian actors such as Nicole Kidman, Cate Blanchett, Geoffrey Rush, Hugh Jackman, Margot Robbie and the Hemsworth brothers have reached global stardom.

Yet this account of film and television production does not exhaust the lenses in this book. Australians – notwithstanding national debates on investment in infrastructure and notorious low bandwidth speeds[61] – are very connected contributors to new media. Contemporary statistics suggest that Australians are highly engaged with digital platforms, with recent studies indicating that 83 per cent of Australians actively use a social media account, and 34 per cent engage with social media more than five times a day.[62] Australian governments are also highly visible users of social media,[63] and even Australian courts have established social media strategies.[64] Following global patterns, Australian social media activity is dominated by the market-leading US platforms Facebook, Instagram, Snapchat and a declining use of Twitter.[65] There is yet to be an Australian social media platform; even the digital marketplace Gumtree, which is widely used in Australia, originated and is headquartered in the United Kingdom.[66] This digital activity is producing a vast archive of online material by Australians and Australian institutions about Australia. Not only are elements of the archive available to government decision-makers when making decisions under Australian law,[67] but, as Cassandra Sharp has recently explored, social media archives can be read to explore Australians' affective articulations and representations of law and justice during terrorist events.[68] The idea of law, lawyers and justice through Australian lenses in this book also extends to a lens formed by the images, emojis and text on Australian social media accounts.

Lenses refract light, bending and focusing it. Lenses also disperse light, splitting white light into the colour spectrum. Lenses are not mirrors, though: mirrors merely reflect, while refraction and dispersion are more revealing. In the chapters of this book, the exposure of law, lawyers and justice to Australian lenses – film, television and social media – is quite revealing, uncovering the illusions of Northern legality, the brutality of law and the contestability of justice in Australia.

Chapters

The chapters in this book are organized in two parts. The first part concerns the unsettled law and justice in Australia. It refracts the legalities of the North through the practices, legacies and lives of the Australian settler state. Central to this part are the legacy and lingering injustices experienced by First Nations people. The second part focuses on bodies, gender and justice, bringing a lens to the intersections of Australian gendered identities and law.

Part I: The unsettled law and justice of Australia

The chapters in this part are unified through concerns with the settler state, its penal origins and predictions, its genocidal activities and its contested sovereignty. Through the lenses deployed in this chapter, the legalities that sustain the settler state are revealed along with the possibilities and cultures of future justice.

The opening chapter is Cassandra Sharp's examination of 'law and justice'–themed television shows produced in Australia over the past 60 years. Focusing on the lawyer, crime and prison shows, Sharp reveals the profound interest shown by Australians (and their cultural caretakers) in law and crime storytelling. From relocations of the US-style police show to Australian contexts in the 1960s and 1970s to the boom in reality and 'true crime' television since 2000, Australian-produced and voiced lawyer, crime and prison shows have been an enduring feature of Australian television broadcasting. Sharp concludes that this national storytelling about law and justice – particularly criminal justice – has colonial roots. The Australian settler state emerges from the penal enterprise of transportation. Australia is a nation where law and injustice, crime and punishment are deeply mythologized. When Australian commercial television stations screen the latest crime production, they are engaged in a process of constituting and reconstituting the Australian settler state.

In their chapter, Jack Quirk and Julian R. Murphy consider two recent Australian films that engage directly with the legalities of the settler state for First Nations people: *Sweet Country*[69] and *Charlie's Country*.[70] Through their examination of *Sweet Country*, they identify an illusory rule of law on the frontier. This combination of illusion, rule of law and the frontier is then explored through *Charlie's Country*, where Charlie's attempt at attaining self-sovereignty in the context of the Northern Territory Intervention[71] is cut through and undermined by settler legality that is both absolute and ludicrously implemented by Kafkaesque officials. The rule of law cuts through both films. In *Sweet Country*, it impotently allows mob justice; in *Charlie's Country*, the micro-complexity of the regulatory state – applied with renewed zealotry in the Intervention – reveals the rule of law as a maze that First Nation Australians cannot escape.

The idea of escape is central to the chapter by Thalia Anthony and Kieran Tranter. They focus on the consistent settler state trope of the chase: the pursuit of First Nations people by the officials of the settler state. They identify the core tropes of the Australian chase through the films *Jedda*,[72] *The Chant of Jimmie Blacksmith*,[73] *Backroads*[74] and *Rabbit-Proof Fence*,[75] before showing how the structure of a young First Nations person being chased by the angry embodiment of white law, ending in the death of the First Nations person, repeats on Country. They identify how settler state law continues to structure and condone the chasing and killing of First Nations children and young people.

A key lens that Anthony and Tranter explore in the complicities of settler state legality in the chasing and killing of First Nations people is Australian social media. They identify that the chase and death of 14-year-old Elijah Doughty at Kalgoorlie-Boulder in 2016 occurred in a context of highly venomous racist hate directed at young First Nations people, emanating from local and well-subscribed 'law and order' Facebook sites. This talk by white Australians was accompanied by posts of images of young First Nations people and exhortations for extra-judicial violence and killing. The social media lens as a focus for the articulation of resurgent racism and hate speech in Australia is the subject of the chapter by Chris Cunneen and Sophie Russell. Examining threads from the Kalgoorlie-Boulder sites and also from similar sites in other Australian locations and towns, the authors show a pervasive dehumanization of First Nations people and complicity by the Australian settler state, its laws and the platforms in not preventing and taking down this material.

The chapter by Penny Crofts and Honni van Rijswijk takes the examination of the settler state in a different direction. They revisit the celebrated book and film *Picnic at Hanging Rock*,[76] particularly their recent Australian reimagining as a television series.[77] They locate the film and series within the brutal context of

Australian institutions, particularly as made public in the recent Royal Commission into Institutional Child Abuse.[78] For van Rijswijk and Crofts, the story of disappearing children, land and the enclosed legality of total institutions – such as boarding schools – becomes an exploration of the Gothic and its manifestation in Australian institutions, where fear and violence turn inwards when seeing only an incomprehensible land and absent First Nations people.

Pauline Klippmark's chapter focuses on the trauma of absence of First Nations people within the Australian settler state. She looks closely at Kent's *The Babadook*, identifying in this peculiar horror film and its generic first-world urban environments a particular Australian sensibility. Drawing on conceptualizations of the spectre and haunting, Klippmark sees the Babadook as an embodiment of the trauma of dispossession and denial at the core of the settler state. She also sees in the unusual conclusion of the film, with the protagonist coming to a degree of uncomfortable acceptance and care towards the Babadook, a possibility for Australians to begin to renegotiate the founding myths and violent articulations of the settler state.

A strong step towards this renegotiation can be seen in Kristy Duncanson's chapter, which takes as its inspiration the recent song and music video 'Native Tongue' by First Nations performer Mojo Juju.[79] Through a gentle and patient reading of the lyrics, costumes, staging and choreography, Duncanson brings to the forefront Mojo Juju's proud and nuanced articulation of belonging, identity and sovereignty, notwithstanding the past and contemporary actions of the settler state. Whereas the previous chapters map and expose the legal complicities and illusions that insubstantially hide the genocidal violence of the settler state, Duncanson's reading of Mojo Juju presents survival, empowerment and a possibility for empathy and pleasure. In this, a future justice beyond the white patriarchies of the settler state can be glimpsed.

Part II: Australian gendered identities and law

A recurring feature of Australian cultural artefacts has been an emphasis on men and a certain form of masculinity. The perceived necessities of the settler state, its convict and penal origins, a landscape as 'other', a geo-political legacy of fighting in the North for colonial powers – all of this called forth an ideal of the stoic man engaged in struggle. Australian (white) men were rough and ready, inventive, irreverent and, in the enshrining of 'mateship', highly homosocial.[80] In this part, the old myths of the white Australian male as 'battler' or 'larrikin' are placed in relation to law and lawyers. Furthermore, possibilities of justice for gendered identities in Australia that exceed hegemonic masculinities[81] are explored.

The first two chapters in this part look directly at the transmission of the larrikin into law by the television show *Rake*. John Flood's concern is with national representations of lawyering, comparing the mostly establishment figure of celebrated English fictional barrister Horace Rumpole (made iconic by the Australian actor Leo McKern in the long-running Thames Television series) with the rakish Cleaver Greene (Richard Roxburgh). For Flood, the popular enjoyment in the representations of lawyering in *Rake* simultaneously reflects cynicism about government and legal institutions and 'democratic' ideas of justice and victories for the individual against structured power. Lili Pâquet is more critical of *Rake*. For her, the larrikin dimensions to Greene allow a highly problematic masculinity to be rendered charming. The fact that Greene, the privileged white male, and his privileged white male clients manage to triumph shows gendered tensions within the articulation of liberal legalism in Australia.

Whereas Flood and Paquet see some redemption in Australian larrikin masculinity as it informs lawyering, Bruce Arnold sees toxicity. Arnold focuses on the scenes of male rape in *Mad Max*,[82] the *Chant of Jimmie Blacksmith*, *Wake in Fright*[83] and *Ghosts . . . of the Civil Dead*.[84] He identifies a strong connection between male rape represented in Australian film, dominant articulations of Australian masculinity and Australian law's slow accounting for this violence. Violence is also a central theme in Kim D. Weinert's chapter, which focuses on the film *Romper Stomper*.[85] This film about neo-Nazi skinheads in Melbourne during the 1990s can be seen as prefiguring contemporary concerns with the rise of the alt-right in Australian and other nations. While acknowledging this, Weinert situates *Romper Stomper* in its specific socio-political milieu. She sees in the film a presentation and a reaction to the first waves of neoliberal governmental reforms at the time. The film makes various speech acts – there are the representations of hate speech and racial violence by Hando (Russell Crowe) – but it also speaks to the elements of neoliberalism, the competitive individual, the market and an absent state. The film testifies to the futility of extreme right ideology (in the form of Hando's attraction to the aesthetics of Nazism) and less extreme right ideologies (in the form of neoliberalism) to provide for a social future.

The future is the focus of Kieran Tranter's revisiting of the *Mad Max* franchise, taking the 2015 film *Mad Max: Fury Road*[86] as an opportunity to return to and reconsider the franchise. While the future is the focus, Tranter spends significant time in the past – the past of the *Mad Max* franchise and the past of white settler state 'combustion' masculinity. He reviews how the earlier films drove on a precipice between a celebration and a critique of marauding men in machines; that focus, however, is not present in *Fury Road*. In the new film, men do not save and do not lead the next wave of colonialists to claim an empty land and start the cycle of domination again; rather, it is women, manifesting a very different set of commitments to land and to technology, who return to the origin to build something new.

Tranter's conclusions on Australia, women and the possibility of justice are also the overarching themes in the chapter by van Rijswijk and Laura Joseph, which examines the contemporary remake of *Prisoner*, titled *Wentworth*.[87] In their chapter, *Wentworth* is a lens with multiple foci. The first views it as a katabasis narrative – a story of descent to the underworld – creating a telling account of the Australian carceral imaginary where transportation sent convicts down to New South Wales and the everyday experience of serving prison time as a journey through hell. However, as the authors emphasize, the structured hell of the prison is also a place for agency and connection. In the rise and then suicide of Bea Smith (Danielle Cormack) across its first four seasons, the show presents the impossibility of justice at the core of liberal legality, particularly because of its grounding in bodily violence. While *The Nightingale* ends with the mortally wounded Billy and the avenged Clare free in the bush, and *Fury Road* has the women disposing of the violent men to return to liberate the citadel, *Wentworth* shows the indefatigable nature of the settler state in its gender violence and in taking, sequestering, rendering vulnerable and hurting bodies.

This contestation of conclusions is a particular message that emerges when considering law, lawyers and justice through Australian lenses. The settler state in its material, thanological practices looms large. Forms of legality from the North that are supposed to save – the rule of law, individual rights and freedoms, protective institutions – are inverted into perverse projects of removal, incarceration and undisguised violence. Like *The Nightingale*, this is difficult to watch. It is also difficult to know how to respond and resist. Australian lenses present various responses to Australian law and justice. Cleaver Greene is compromised and complicit – like Max (Mel Gibson/Tom Hardy) from the *Mad Max* franchise, his position and projection of masculinity only reinscribes core elements of the settler state. Hando's extreme projections of white masculinity simply implode; the hierarchy and violence that transposes mateship to male-on-male sexual assault essentially combusts. And Bea is eventually ground down by the carceral condition.

The Nightingale concludes with Clare performing a hybrid expression of release, singing an Irish-style folk song to Billy in his warrior paint as the sun rises. This tender moment after a film of direct, unflinching violence could be significant. Mojo Juju, proud and vulnerable, sings of the trauma of the past and declares uncertain belongings. However, this is accompanied by the certainty of birth under a Southern sun and the certainty of living in 'this skin';[88] she is from Australia and the settler state, but she is not. Hers is a declaration of an identity and a location of resistance that must be nurtured. We dream that a future issue of law, lawyers and justice through Australian lenses will tell of a nation and a legality that has unsettled the settler state; locked away its governmental forms, toxicity and subjectivities and is working towards a justice of healing and hope.

Notes

1 Kent, *The Nightingale* (2019).
2 Kent, *The Babadook* (2014).
3 Thomas (2019).
4 Clements (2014).
5 Barta (2008), p 203.
6 On the development of law and popular culture, see Crawley and Peters (2018).
7 See, for example, Robson and Schulz (2016); Robson and Silbey (2012).
8 See, for example, Pearson and Tranter (2015); Skyes (2017).
9 See, for example, Young (2013).

10 Ondrich (2018); Skyes and Tranter (2018).
11 See, for example, Giddens (2018).
12 See, for example, Crawley and Tranter (2019); Manderson (2019).
13 See, for example, Pearson (2019).
14 Thornton (2002).
15 Manderson (2000).
16 MacNeil (2007, 2012).
17 Young (1996, 2009).
18 Tranter (2013a, 2013b, 2015, 2017, 2018b).
19 Sitch, *The Castle* (1997).
20 *Mabo v Queensland (No. 2)* (1992) 175 CLR 1; *Wik Peoples v Queensland* (1996) 187 CLR 1; MacNeil (2007), pp 116–31.
21 Collins (2004), pp 51–69.
22 Collins and Davis (2004), pp 5–7.
23 Miller, *Mad Max* (1979); Miller, *Mad Max 2: The Road Warrior* (1981); Miller and Ogilvie, *Mad Max: Beyond Thunderdome* (1985).
24 Tranter (2003).
25 Wright (2013).
26 van Rijswijk (2017), p 327.
27 Manderson (2012).
28 Lawrence (2002).
29 See, for example Forde-Mazrui (2005); Lim (2018); Redlich, Wilford and Bushway (2017).
30 Bizzaca (2019).
31 Collins and Davis (2004), p 7.
32 *Rake* (2010–18), S1–5.
33 *Picnic at Hanging Rock* (2018–), S1– .
34 Kittler (1999).
35 Bertrand and Routt (1989); Garlick (1965).
36 Tait Brothers (1906).
37 Australasian Films (1907).
38 MacMahon's Exquisite Pictures (1907).
39 Milestone, *Kangaroo* (1952).
40 Hassam (2006).
41 Moran (1989), p 26.
42 Bertrand and Collins (1981).
43 Bertrand and Collins (1981), pp 149–58; O'Regan (1996), p 28.
44 Genres included horror (*The Cars That Ate Paris*, 1974); comedy (*Salute to the Great McCarthy*, 1975; *Stork*, 1971; *Alvin Purple*, 1973; *The Adventures of Barry McKenzie*, 1972); period (*Picnic at Hanging Rock*, 1975); art house (*Libido*, 1973) and pornography (*An Essay on Pornography*, 1973). See O'Regan (1989a), p 75.
45 O'Regan (1989a), p 76.
46 For example, *Don's Party* (1976); *Alvin Purple* (1973).
47 *Palm Beach* (1979).
48 Films such as *Picnic at Hanging Rock* (Weir, 1975) and *My Brilliant Career* (Armstrong, 1979). Tom O'Regan (1989a), p 95.
49 *Number 69* (1972–77), S1–6.
50 *Prisoner* (1979–86), S1–8.
51 Rimfire Films, 1986.
52 O'Regan (1989b), pp 129–30.
53 O'Regan (1989b), p 130.
54 Craven (2001), pp 6, 20.
55 Elliot (1994).

56 Dunleavy (2005).
57 See Tranter (2018a), p 666, referring to Robson and Schulz (2016).
58 Lucas, *Star Wars: Attack of the Clones* (2002); Lucas, *Star Wars: Revenge of the Sith* (2005).
59 Waititi, *Thor: Ragnarok* (2017).
60 Australian Screen Association (2015), p 4.
61 Wilken et al. (2015).
62 Yellow (2018), p 10.
63 Abedin and Babar (2018); Evans et al. (2019).
64 Henderson (2018).
65 Yellow (2018), p 15.
66 Roy Morgan (2018).
67 Sleep and Tranter (2018).
68 Sharp (2018a, 2018b).
69 Thornton, *Sweet Country* (2018).
70 de Heer, *Charlie's Country* (2013).
71 On the legalities of the Northern Territory Intervention, see Anthony (2009); Anthony and Blagg (2012).
72 Chauvel, *Jedda* (1955).
73 Schepisi, *The Chant of Jimmie Blacksmith* (1978).
74 Noyce, *Backroads* (1977).
75 Noyce, *Rabbit-Proof Fence* (2002).
76 Weir, *Picnic at Hanging Rock* (1975).
77 *Picnic at Hanging Rock* (2018), S1– .
78 Royal Commission into Institutional Responses to Child Sexual Abuse (2017).
79 Juju (2018) 'Native Tongue'.
80 See, for example, Murrie (1998); Pease (2001).
81 Connell (2005), p 77.
82 Miller, *Mad Max* (1979).
83 Kotcheff, *Wake in Fright* (1979).
84 Hillcoat, *Ghosts . . . of the Civil Dead* (1988).
85 Wright, *Romper Stomper* (1992).
86 Miller, *Mad Max: Fury Road* (2015).
87 *Wentworth* (FremantleMedia Australia, 2012–17), S1–6.
88 Juju (2018) 'Native Tongue'.

References

Secondary sources

Babak Abedin and Abdul Babar (2018) 'Institutional vs Non-Institutional Use of Social Media During Emergency Response: A Case of Twitter in 2014 Australian Bush Fire' 20 *Information Systems Frontiers* 729.

Thalia Anthony (2009) 'Governing Crime in the Northern Territory Intervention' 27 *Law in Context* 90.

Thalia Anthony and Harry Blagg (2012) *Addressing the 'Crime Problem' of the Northern Territory Intervention: Alternate Paths to Regulating Minor Driving Offences in Remote Indigenous Communities*, Criminology Research Council.

Australian Government (2017) *Royal Commission Into Institutional Responses to Child Sexual Abuse*.

Australian Screen Association (2015) *Economic Contribution of the Film and Television Industry in Australia*, Australian Screen Association.

Tony Barta (2008) 'Sorry, and Not Sorry, in Australia: How the Apology to the Stolen Generations Buried a History of Genocide' 10 *Journal of Genocide Research* 201.

Ina Bertrand and Diane Collins (1981) *Government and Film in Australia*, Currency Press 145.

Ina Bertrand and William Routt (1989) 'The Big Bad Combine: Some Aspects of National Aspirations and International Constraints', in Albert Moran and Tom O'Regan (eds), *The Australian Screen*, Penguin.

Caris Bizzaca (2019) '*The Babadook* to *The Nightingale*: Festival Release Strategies', *Screen Australia*, www.screenaustralia.gov.au/sa/screen-news/2019/06-11-festival-release-strategies.

Nicholas Clements (2014) *The Black War: Fear, Sex and Resistance in Tasmania*, University of Queensland Press.

Felicity Collins and Therese Davis (2004) *Australian Cinema After Mabo*, Cambridge University Press.

R.W. Connell (2005) *Masculinities* (2nd ed.), Polity Press.

Ian Craven (2001) *Australia Cinema in the 1900s*, Frank Cass.

Karen Crawley and Timothy D. Peters (2018) 'Introduction: "Representational Legality"', in Timothy D. Peters and Karen Crawley (eds), *Envisioning Legality: Law, Culture and Representation*, Routledge.

Karen Crawley and Kieran Tranter (2019) 'A Maelstrom of Bodies and Emotions and Things: Spectatorial Encounters with the Trial' 32 *International Journal for the Semiotics of Law* 621.

Trisha Dunleavy (2005) '*Coronation Street, Neighbours, Shortland Street*: Localness and Universality in the Primetime Soap' 6 *Television & New Media* 370.

Mark Evans, Patrick Dunleavy, Carmel McGregor and Max Halupka (2019) 'Towards Digital Era Governance: Lessons from the Australian Experience', in Andrew Massey (ed.), *A Research Agenda for Public Administration*, Edward Elgar.

Kim Forde-Mazrui (2005) 'Learning Law Through the Lens of Race' 21 *Journal of Law and Politics* 1.

Robert Garlick (1965) 'Australian Film Production' 37 *The Australian Quarterly* 62.

Thomas Giddens (2018) *On Comics and Legal Aesthetics: Multimodality and the Haunted Mask of Knowing*, Routledge.

Andrew Hassam (2006) 'From *Kangaroo* to *Salaam Namaste*: Australia as an Exotic Film Location' 12 *Hungarian Journal of England and American Studies* 19.

Andrew Henderson (2018) 'The High Court and the Cocktail Party from Hell: Can Social Media Improve Community Engagement with the Courts?', in Tania Sourdin and Archie Zariski (eds), *The Responsive Judge*, Springer.

Friedrich A. Kittler (1999) *Gramophone, Film, Typewriter*, Stanford University Press.

Yaner Lim (2018) 'Understanding the War on Drugs in America Through the Lens of Critical Race Theory' 5 *Bristol Law Review* 156.

William P. MacNeil (2007) *Lex Populi: The Jurisprudence of Popular Culture*, Stanford University Press.

——— (2012) *Novel Judgements: Legal Theory as Fiction*, Routledge.

Desmond Manderson (2000) *Songs Without Music: Aesthetic Dimensions of Law and Justice*, University of California Press.

——— (2012) *Kangaroo Courts and the Rule of Law: The Legacy of Modernism*, Routledge.

——— (2019) *Danse Macabre: Temporalities of Law in the Visual Arts*, Cambridge University Press.

Albert Moran (1989) 'Three Stages of Australian Television', in John Tulloch and Graeme Turner (eds), *Television: Programs, Pleasure and Politics*, Allen & Unwin.

Roy Morgan (2018) 'eBay King of Online Shopping Ahead of Gumtree, Amazon, Kogan & Groupon', www.roymorgan.com/findings/7623-top-online-shopping-auctions-websites-march-2018-201806180044.

Linzi Murrie (1998) 'The Australian Legend: Writing Australian Masculinity/Writing "Australian" Masculine' 22 *Journal of Australian Studies* 68.

Rudolf Michael Ondrich (2018) 'Reading Wilhelm Furtwängler Jurisprudentially: Furtwängler's Music Making in the Light of Legal Philosophy' 31 *International Journal for the Semiotics of Law* 349.

Tom O'Regan (1996) *Australian National Cinema*, Taylor & Francis.

——— (1989a) 'Cinema Oz: The Ocker Film', in Albert Moran and Tom O'Regan (eds), *The Australian Screen*, Penguin.

——— (1989b) 'The Enchantment with Cinema – Film in the 1980s', in Albert Moran and Tom O'Regan (eds), *The Australian Screen*, Penguin.

Ashley Pearson (2019) 'Legal Personhood in Video Games, Canonical Media and Fandom', PhD thesis, Griffith Law School.

Ashley Pearson and Kieran Tranter (2015) 'Code, Nintendo's Super Mario and Digital Legality' 28 *International Journal for the Semiotics of Law* 825.

Bob Pease (2001) 'Moving Beyond Mateship: Reconstructing Australian Men's Practices', in Bob Pease and Keith Pringle (eds), *A Man's World: Changing Men's Practice in a Globalized World*, Zed Books.

Allison D. Redlich, Miko M. Wilford and Shawn Bushway (2017) 'Understanding Guilty Pleas Through the Lens of Social Science' 23 *Psychology, Public Policy, and Law* 458.

Peter Robson and Jennifer L. Schulz (eds) (2016) *A Transnational Study of Law and Justice on TV*, Hart.

Peter Robson and Jessica Silbey (eds) (2012) *Law and Justice on the Small Screen*, Hart.

Cassandra Sharp (2018a) '#fear&loathing in Sydney: Law, Justice and the Experience of Fear in a Hashtag World' 30 *Law and Literature* 29.

——— (2018b) '#Vulnerability – Expectations of Justice Through Accounts of Terror on Twitter' *Journal of Oxford Centre for Socio-Legal Studies* 1.

Robbie Skyes (2017) '"Those Chosen by the Planet": *Final Fantasy VII* and Earth Jurisprudence' 30 *International Journal for the Semiotics of Law* 455.

Robbie Skyes and Kieran Tranter (2018) 'The Rise and Fall of Ziggy Stardust and Natural Law' 31 *International Journal for the Semiotics of Law* 325.

Lyndal Sleep and Kieran Tranter (2018) 'Social Media in Social Security Decision Making in Australia: An Archive of Truth?' 22 *Media Arts and Law Review* 442.

Sarah Thomas (2019) '"I'm Not Watching This": Film's Brutal Account of Australia's Colonial History Sparks Walkout', *ABC News*, 6 November, www.abc.net.au/news/2019-06-11/sydney-film-festival-the-nightingale-premiere-sparks-controversy/11198288.

Margaret Thornton (2002) *Romancing the Tomes: Popular Culture Law and Feminism*, Cavendish.

Kieran Tranter (2003) 'Mad Max: The Car and Australian Governance' 5 *National Identities* 67.

——— (2013a) '"Her Brain Was Full of Superstitious Nonsense": Modernism and the Failure of the Divine in *Doctor Who*', in Andrew Crome and James McGrath (eds), *Time and Relative Dimensions in Faith: Doctor Who and Religion*, Darton, Longman and Todd.

——— (2013b) 'In and Out of Time: Memory and Chronology of *Doctor Who*', in Gillian Leitch (ed.), *Doctor Who in Time and Space*, McFarland.

——— (2015) 'Narrative and Paradoxes in *Doctor Who* "Time Loop" Stories', in Sherry Ginn and Gillian Leitch (eds), *The Past from the Present, the Future from the Past: Television Explores Time Travel*, Rowman and Littlefield.

——— (2017) 'Law, the Digital and Time: The Legal Emblems of *Doctor Who*' 30 *International Journal for the Semiotics of Law* 515.

——— (2018a) 'Book Review: *A Transnational Study of Law and Justice on TV*' 27 *Social & Legal Studies* 665.

——— (2018b) *Living in Technical Legality: Science Fiction and Law as Technology*, University of Edinburgh Press.

Honni van Rijswijk (2017) 'Encountering Aboriginal Legalities Through a Literary Jurisprudence of Suffering', in Susan Petrilli (ed.), *Challenges to Living Together: Transculturalism, Migration, Exploitation for a Semioethics of Human Relations*, Mimesis International.

Rowan Wilken, Jenny Kennedy, Michael Arnold, Martin Gibbs and Bjorn Nansen (2015) 'Framing the NBN: An Analysis of Newspaper Representations' 47 *Communication, Politics and Culture* 55.

Yellow (2018) *Yellow Social Media Report 2018 – Consumers*, www.yellow.com.au/wp-content/uploads/2018/06/Yellow-Social-Media-Report-2018-Consumer.pdf.

Alison Young (1996) *Imagining Crime*, Sage.

——— (2009) *The Scene of Violence: Cinema, Crime, Affect*, Routledge-Cavendish.

——— (2013) *Street Art, Public City: Law, Crime and the Urban Imagination*, Routledge.

Primary legal sources

Mabo v Queensland (No. 2) (1992) 175 CLR 1.

Wik Peoples v Queensland (1996) 187 CLR 1.

Primary literature, films and media

Gillian Armstrong (1979) *My Brilliant Career*, Margaret Fink.

Bruce Beresford (1976) *Don's Party*, Double Head Productions.

Tim Burstall (1973) *Alvin Purple*, Hexagon Productions.

Charles Chauvel (1955) *Jedda*, Columbia Pictures.

Rolf de Heer (2013) *Charlie's Country*, Bula'bula Arts and Vertigo Productions.

Stephan Elliott (1994) *The Adventures of Priscilla, Queen of the Desert*, Polygram Filmed Entertainment.

John Hillcoat (1988) *Ghosts . . . of the Civil Dead*, NLT Productions.

Mojo Juju (2018) 'Native Tongue', video, www.youtube.com/watch?v=JLQ4by3lUJo.

Jennifer Kent (2014) *The Babadook*, Entertainment One, Umbrella Entertainment.

——— (2019) *The Nightingale*, Transmission Films.

Ted Kotcheff, *Wake in Fright* (1979) Group W Films and NLT Productions.

D.H. Lawrence (2002) *Kangaroo*, Cambridge University Press.
George Lucas (2002) *Star Wars: Attack of the Clones*, 20th Century Fox.
——— (2005) *Revenge of the Sith*, Star Wars 20th Century Fox.
Lewis Milestone (1952) *Kangaroo*, 20th Century Fox.
George Miller (1979) *Mad Max*, Roadshow Film Distributors.
——— (1981) *Mad Max 2: The Road Warrior*, Warner Bros.
——— (2015) *Mad Max: Fury Road*, Warner Bros.
George Miller and George Ogilvie (1985) *Mad Max: Beyond Thunderdome*, Warner Bros.
Phillip Noyce (1977) *Backroads*, Backroads Production.
——— (2002) *Rabbit-Proof Fence*, Becker Entertainment.
Picnic at Hanging Rock (2018) FremantleMedia Australia, S1–.
Fred Schepisi (1978) *The Chant of Jimmie Blacksmith*, Hoyts.
Rob Sitch (1997) *The Castle*, Working Dog.
Albie Thoms (1979) *Palm Beach*, Albie Thoms Productions.
Warwick Thornton (2017) *Sweet Country*, Transmission Films.
Taika Waititi (2017) *Thor: Ragnarok*, Walt Disney Studios.
Peter Weir (1975) *Picnic at Hanging Rock*, McElroy & McElroy and Picnic Productions.
Alexis Wright (2013) *The Swan Book*, Giramondo.
Geoffrey Wright (1992) *Romper Stomper*, Film Victoria.

Chapter 2

Crime drama and national identity on Australian television, 1960–2019

Cassandra Sharp

Introduction

In 2016, Australia celebrated the 60th anniversary of television broadcasting. For over six decades, Australians have been tuning in regularly to be informed, entertained, challenged and comforted by the various products of the small-screen industry. Despite changing political landscapes, advancements in technology and disruptions of distribution by new competitors, Australian television has attempted to adapt and evolve to the new opportunities of the 21st century. Contrary to historical predictions, television is far from dead;[1] instead, the television industry is currently flourishing in a world that demands high-quality storytelling and content. Viewing options are endless, and with the availability and popularity of on-demand services in addition to programmed free-to-air platforms, Australians have far greater access to both local and global content than ever before.

While charting the development of Australian television, with a particular focus on crime and justice, this chapter seeks to elucidate the elements that have engaged the hearts and minds of Australian viewers. The television crime drama series remains a persistent and resilient narrative framework through which to deal with issues of social and cultural relevance.[2] In this chapter, the direction of our critical gaze within this genre is on those Australian dramas that portray the detection, regulation and punishment of crime. The first part of the chapter outlines the development of the television landscape within a post-war Australian setting and explores the impact of a political push for visual representations of national identity. The second part identifies how this Australian television landscape became the petri dish within which crime drama series proliferated and describes several key productions that use the police procedural formula and 'real-life' crime stories as vehicles for social and cultural commentaries. The chapter then directs our attention to the representation of women in all aspects of the criminal justice process – from litigator to prisoner – and observes that the common theme of overcoming adversity, particularly as a legal subject, reflects one aspect of an Australian consciousness. By bringing national identity and cultural history to the fore, the chapter concludes with a brief comment on the elements of an Australian 'identity' that have been utilized in Australian crime drama representations.

The development of Australian television

In 1956, the year of the introduction of broadcasting in Australia, a mere 5 per cent of Melbourne households and 1 per cent of those in Sydney owned a television set.[3] In the years that followed, families would gather together around the single unit to watch scheduled programming. Of course, today, technologies of production have changed, so while televisions still seem to dominate the Australian living room (and other rooms in the house) with ever-larger screens, advances in technology now also enable individual viewing from even the smallest of handheld screens.[4] Furthermore, modes of viewing have diversified significantly across devices, producers, platform content and locations of viewing. Indeed, recent surveys indicate that 72 per cent of Australians 'binge watch' television – watching three or more episodes in one sitting[5] – and that most people (91 per cent) multitask across devices and activities while watching television.[6] This is a far cry from the post-war setting in which Australian television began.

Historically, the Australian television landscape has been dominated by three free-to-air commercial networks – Seven, Nine and Ten, broadcasting out of the major capital cities – and three national public broadcasters – the Australian Broadcasting Corporation (ABC), the Special Broadcasting Service (SBS) and National Indigenous Television (NITV).[7] Yet the development and expansion of television in Australia had somewhat slow beginnings, having been significantly delayed by World War II. Although experimental transmissions using the Radiovision system[8] had been conducted in the 1920s and 1930s, it wasn't until 1953 that the Menzies government (which came to power in 1949) established a Royal Commission[9] to report on methods that would elicit the best use of television broadcasting in the public interest.

The Royal Commission's report was 'optimistic about the cultural role of television',[10] and recommended that television services should be introduced gradually.[11] As a result, the government amended the *Australian Broadcasting Act 1948* (Cth) to allow for the granting of commercial licences. The consequent *Broadcasting and Television Act 1956* (Cth) provided 'the legislative framework for a dual system of TV ownership',[12] with a national government-funded TV network run by the ABC operating alongside privately owned commercial stations.

In addition, the government established the Australian Broadcasting Control Board (ABCB), an agency responsible for the regulation of broadcasting standards and practices. The ABCB conducted public hearings into the allocation of TV licences for Sydney and Melbourne, but only if they could ensure that the licence would be 'conducted in this country as an Australian enterprise; one of its main purposes being to develop a sound Australian sentiment and the beliefs and standards which will help to make Australia a great country'.[13] Importantly, the granting of various commercial licences laid the groundwork for the launch of full-scale television broadcasting on 16 September 1956, which was famously introduced on station TCN-9 Sydney[14] by Bruce Gyngell with the words 'Good evening, and welcome to television'.[15]

'Marching into colour' and the run towards digital TV

From the late 1950s through to the early 1970s, television was a warmly received technological advance in Australian culture and fast became a growth industry as the main form of entertainment and information for most Australians, supplanting radio, cinema, newspapers and magazines.[16] Some highlights of Australian television development during this time included:

- In 1966, being able to receive daily news reports via satellite;
- In 1969, along with the rest of the world, being able to watch the live broadcast coverage of the Apollo 11 moon landing; and
- In 1970, the official opening of a microwave link between the east and west coasts, enabling transmission of material across the country. This fostered a sense of national unity following the devastating effects of Cyclone Tracy, most evident in a 28-hour telethon broadcast across the country on 31 December 1974 by the Nine Network and News Limited to raise money for the Cyclone Tracy relief appeal.

Moving faster with technological developments, in 1972 the Australian government announced that all stations would convert to colour on 1 March 1975.[17] With 'March First into Colour' as the key advertising slogan, the Australian public is said to have had one of the fastest changeovers to colour television in the world, and so by 1980, almost 80 per cent of homes owned a colour television set.[18] The changing social and political landscape that was characteristic of the 1970s and 1980s was also reflected in the vision that was being broadcast on Australian television during that period, which particularly impacted the developing multicultural population. The launch in 1980 of Australia's second national public broadcaster, SBS, prioritized subtitled and foreign-language content and 'emphasized what was seen as the lack of responsiveness among Australia's media institutions to an increasingly culturally diverse society'.[19] Although the 1990s unfortunately began with the nation in a recession, impacting the budgets of TV networks and affecting the profitability of local production,[20] this decade also ushered in the era of 24-hour transmission (starting with the ABC in 1993) and pay TV, or subscription television (in 1995, with Galaxy, Optus Vision, AUSTAR and Foxtel the prime competitors).

The turn of the millennium not only witnessed the emergence of community television stations (including NITV in 2007), but also introduced the possibilities of digital television and the options of widescreen, standard definition and high-definition (HD) production. At the start of the 21st century, the ABC, commercial networks and pay TV began transmitting in HD digital, with several networks operating a second standard-definition digital channel. Over the last ten years, Australian television has seen the complete shutdown of all analogue services, the introduction of 3D test transmissions (Foxtel, Nine Network and SBS) and the availability of services that provide TV on demand – either by subscription or by free-to-air TV – to catch up on missed episodes.

The television lens within a developing national identity

In the early years of Australian television, following the first issue of TV licences, there was no enforcement of local content quotas by the government or the ABCB, so US and UK imports were the dominant products shown on air.[21] This was particularly the case with drama, with nearly all dramas scheduled on the commercial networks being produced in the United States (*Perry Mason* was a favourite) and British programmes dominating the ABC. Because it wasn't convenient or cost-effective for networks to produce local content at this time, only the most basic shows in the variety or quiz format were produced in Australia, and these were usually developed by the ABC. By the end of the 1950s, at least 80 per cent of all Australian TV content was sourced from the United States,[22] and demands were increasing for the Australian government to foster an Australian perspective on television.[23] In 1960, the first Australian content regulations for television were introduced yet they were resisted and barely complied with.[24] As a result, Hector Crawford (head of Crawford Productions) aggressively pursued an agenda to increase Australian content as a 'moral necessity'. In a self-produced pamphlet published in 1959, he questions the value to the Australian people of imported content:

> Do these programmes stimulate among Australians a consciousness of national identity and pride in our nation for our own cultural ideas and patterns? Do they typify Australian attitudes and institutions, Australian habits and customs, Australian manners, speech and dress? . . . Do they stimulate the life of the nation by offering opportunities for the artistic and creative abilities of Australians? . . . Do they enlighten Australia as to their own country's history and traditions, its national life and the achievement of their fellow-Australians?[25]

At the same time, other concerns were raised about the political and financial entanglements of cross-media ownership. A snapshot from 1960 shows the Packer family's Consolidated Press group controlling the Nine Network, the Herald and Times newspaper group controlling HSV-7 in Melbourne and John Fairfax's newspaper group controlling ATN-7 in Sydney:

> A pattern of high-level political allegiances between the commercial broadcasters and Liberal-Country Party Coalition governments emerged. . . . As a consequence, the Australian Broadcasting Control Board (ABCB), the principal broadcasting regulator, was left very weak and uncertain of its capacity to control broadcaster conduct.[26]

The combination of these concerns surrounding 'content' and 'ownership' eventually led the federal government to commission a report into the production of television material in 1963. Chaired by Senator Victor Vincent, the so-called Vincent Report identified that 97 per cent of television drama content was imported from the United States.[27] This was especially egregious because the *Broadcasting and Television Act 1956* had required licensees to 'as far as possible, use the services of Australians in the production and presentation of radio and television programs'[28] and had stipulated a minimum 5 per cent broadcasting of Australian-produced material.[29] Although the committee recommended a number of reforms, none was actually implemented by the Menzies government at that time. Eventually, in 1970, the ABCB introduced regulations that imposed a significantly greater local content quota (45 per cent of evening programmes had to be produced within Australia)[30] in order to prevent the television industry from being overly 'Americanized'.[31] The Vincent Report articulated a strong desire to combat undesirable sociological and cultural consequences for the next generation as a result of continuing this state of affairs:

> Perhaps the greatest danger lies in its effect upon the rising generation . . . who, day by day, are not only receiving anything but the most inadequate picture of Australia, her national traditions, culture and way of life, but in its place are recipients of a highly coloured and exaggerated picture of the way of life and morals of other countries (mainly the USA).[32]

As a result of the amended legislation and the increased local content quota, the capacity of television to impact audiences was harnessed to produce content that was 'distinctively Australian in program character' and 'in the best interests of the nation'.[33] This meant that while faces on our TV screens were still largely imported, an Australian identity was proactively and progressively being pursued, with shows such as *Bandstand, Homicide* and *The Mavis Bramston Show* forming a big part of Australian popular culture.[34]

In 1976–77, the ABCB was superseded by the Australian Broadcasting Tribunal (ABT); since that time, although quotas for Australian content have increased to 55 per cent,[35] many 'still believe that the bar for Australian content has been set too low'.[36] Nevertheless, the local content quota did enable the expansion of locally produced Australian drama series in the 1970s and 1980s, and the nation has produced numerous notable television series and mini-series.

This historical recount of the introduction and progression of Australian television over the last 60 years frames an exploration in the next section of the nature of crime and justice TV shows produced locally during this time. Interestingly, in the desire to foster, promote and express an Australian culture and outlook within local television content, a prominent manifestation arose within the dramatic genre, with popularly received programmes often framed around issues of crime, policing and justice. In the context of a nation that was building cultural identity, the next section of the chapter reflects on the manner in which local content production contributed to the representation of law, crime and justice on Australian television. It does so by outlining an historical trajectory of Australian television crime story production with a particular focus on the police procedural and portrayals of 'real-life' crime.

Police dramas and 'real-life' crime

Although, in law, crime and punishment incorporate not only the elements of policing but also those of adjudication and punishment, in many television crime series, these latter domains are usually peripheral or absent.[37] Police procedurals and associated 'based in reality' crime narratives often highlight only those complexities of social order, law and criminality that relate to the identification, pursuit and capture of criminals.[38] This section highlights the chronological progression of fictional depictions of crime on Australian television.

The 1960s and 1970s

One of the earliest and most famous Australian police drama series was *Homicide*, produced by Crawford Productions for the Seven Network between 1964 and 1977. Widely known for changing the landscape of Australian TV and for constituting a 'major stimulus to local TV production',[39] *Homicide* was an immediate and profitable success story for the Seven Network primarily because 'viewers enjoyed seeing stories played out in their own familiar suburban backdrops and without an American or English accent'.[40] The series was set in a real location – Melbourne's Russell Street police headquarters – and although it followed a fictional homicide squad, many episodes were based directly on real cases. For the local production industry as well as cultural nationalists, the success of local programming was indicative of the impact of self-recognition – when Australian audiences were 'confronted by culturally familiar locales and modes of behaviour'.[41] The success of the series (which holds the record as one of the two longest-running Australian drama series)[42] demonstrated that there was indeed a market for locally produced dramas in these early days of Australian television. This was, of course, music to the ears of Hector Crawford, who was striving to ensure that television programmes stimulated a 'consciousness of Australian identity, a sense of national pride, and a regard for national cultural ideas and patterns'.[43]

One key aspect of the ground-breaking nature of *Homicide* was that it pioneered the use of voiceovers as a mechanism for conveying crucial information and context to the audience. It has been argued that this aspect 'established the key selling point of all subsequent Australian television crime drama: realism'.[44] This desire to produce distinctly Australian content acknowledged the sociological importance of fostering national identity, and such a conviction to realistically 'typify Australian attitudes, institutions, habits, customs, manners, speech and dress'[45] inspired the Crawfords to follow *Homicide* with two more police dramas: *Division 4* (1969–75) for the rival Nine network and *Matlock Police* (1971–76) for Ten. *Division 4* was a melodrama set in Yarra Central, a fictitious inner Melbourne suburb with a broad demographic and, in a similar fashion to *Homicide*, presented the inner workings of a police station dramatized with realism and authenticity.[46] *Matlock Police*, however, differentiated itself from its predecessors by focusing on the drama-filled personal lives of the police officers working in the fictional small country town of Matlock.

This trend towards a 'soap opera' element, with an increased emphasis on personal relationships within the police force, enabled the Crawfords to have further production success with *Cop Shop* (1977–83) on the Seven Network. Exploring the nature of social and romantic relationships at a time of significant social transformation, *Cop Shop* took viewers twice a week into the lives and homes of both uniformed police officers and the plain-clothes detectives of the fictional Riverside Police.[47] In each of these series, the police were (for the most part) portrayed extremely positively, and writers were often assisted by members of the Victorian Police Force.

The 1980s

The positive portrayal of police officers and their relationship with Australia began to change with the advent of more edgy programming in the 1980s. For example, in 1983 the ABC produced *Scales of Justice*, a series of three self-contained, character-linked dramas that painted a less positive picture of Australian law enforcement than its predecessors on the commercial stations. Arguably one of the more controversial Australian mini-series ever produced, the series attracted criticism (from the police and commentators alike) for its portrayal of entrenched, systemic corruption at all levels of law enforcement and for its observational, 'docudrama' style. The concern was that its realism would confuse audiences who were not capable of distinguishing fiction from fact. One journalist asked, 'To what extent can the community be expected to perceive the difference between documentary and docudrama?'[48] Despite the criticism, the 'authentic' style of *Scales* and its blurring of boundaries between real-life events and fictional accounts contributed in the late 1980s and early 1990s to Australian audiences increasing their appetite for stories based on 'real-life' events and true crime. The ABC obliged in 1989 by recreating the Fitzgerald Inquiry[49] for the small screen in *Police State*, a programme based largely on transcripts of the inquiry itself.[50] This was quickly followed by *Phoenix* (1992–93), which recounted the investigation of the bombing of the Victorian state police headquarters, loosely based on the real-life circumstances of the Russell Street bombing in 1986. These two series used documentary-style cinematography and were received favourably by the critics.[51]

The 1990s

In the mid-1990s, the ABC continued the emphasis on 'real-life' storytelling with *Blue Murder* (1995), a mini-series that portrayed the relationship between controversial NSW Detective Roger 'the Dodger' Rogerson and notorious criminal Arthur 'Neddy' Smith. The series presented 'a world where co-dependence and cooperation between cops and criminals is a normal part of police culture'.[52] Again using voiceover narration by the major characters, *Blue Murder* featured the naturalistic style and the observational camera techniques that had flavoured earlier ABC productions. It particularly tapped into the public's apparent enthusiasm for stories that mirrored real-life events,[53] which could be 'recognized as part of the criminal world on the edges of their consciousness'.[54]

Interestingly, this mini-series was completed while its real-life counterparts were very much a part of the Australian criminal landscape – Neddy Smith was facing murder charges at the time, and an injunction was granted to postpone the broadcast of the series until after the trial as a way of mitigating possible prejudice and subjectivity in the outcome. To add further intersection between fact and fiction, this was also the time when police corruption was a key subject of public debate, and the Wood Royal Commission of New South Wales (1994–97) was tasked with investigating the existence and extent of corruption in the NSW Police Service. The claims were substantiated, and the series eventually aired in 2001.

Ironically, it might be argued that both *Scales of Justice* and *Blue Murder* provided a level of critique concerning an Australian 'consciousness' and 'identity' and in some ways effected a provocation of the shiny veneer of what it means to be Australian. As Susan Lever argues, the interaction of police and criminals in *Blue Murder* in some ways perverted the concept of Australian mateship:

> It shows that men displaying all the Australian qualities of mateship, dry humour and commitment to family life could act as a law unto themselves. It asks its audiences to reflect on this suburban culture and the violent underside of its cheery mateship.[55]

In addition to the shows aired on the ABC, the late 1990s saw a boom in Australian-made crime drama series on commercial television. Some of these shows included the Nine Network productions *Stingers* (1998–2004) and *Water Rats* (1996–2001) and the long-running Seven Network police drama *Blue Heelers* (1993–2006). *Stingers* was a brisk, gritty series that followed agents in a police undercover unit who created false identities to get close to their targets, while *Water Rats* differentiated itself by uniquely focusing on the Sydney Water Police as they investigated crimes around aesthetically stunning Sydney Harbour locations. *Blue Heelers* was by far the audience favourite for many years and equalled the record set by *Homicide* for longest-running series. It followed in the early tradition of *Matlock Police* by depicting events in the fictional rural Victorian setting of Mount Thomas and regularly secured awards, including 14 TV Week Gold Logies for its main actors.

The turn of the millennium

The success of *Blue Heelers* sparked a flurry of production of police-driven crime series in the new millennium, including *Young Lions* (2002) on Nine, *White Collar Blue* (2002–03) and *Rush* (2008–11) on Ten and *City Homicide* (2007–11) on Seven. SBS also eventually found success with the production of police and crime dramas with two variations on the traditional police format. As an additional national broadcaster with the specific mandate to 'reflect Australia's multicultural society',[56] the police drama *East West 101* seemed to provide SBS with a 'fitting means for producing multicultural stories'.[57] Premiering in 2007, this series redeployed techniques of gritty naturalism using dream and flashback sequences to provide a fresh take on criminal activities occurring in Sydney's multicultural west. By tackling the complex and nuanced issue of race relations surrounding the police force, SBS was seen as successfully adopting a 'leadership role in familiarizing Australians with their own real diversity'.[58] With its second production series *Carla Cametti PD* (2009), SBS took a different approach to the police genre by basing the story on an Italian-Australian female police detective who was descended from the mafia and found herself investigating her own gangster family. It was unfortunately short-lived, however, with only six episodes produced.

In the late 2000s, the popularity of 'real-life' crime depictions reached fever pitch with the Nine Network's *Underbelly* franchise (beginning in 2008), which was based on tales drawn directly from the Australian criminal underworld. The first series, dramatizing Melbourne's 'gangland wars', was stylized heavily on the US drama series *The Sopranos*[59] and was favourably received by audiences and critics alike. *Underbelly* was a massive ratings success for Channel Nine[60] and was hailed as 'Australia's best ever crime drama'[61] and the '*Blue Murder* of its time'.[62] Ironically, though, reminiscent of the legal circumstances surrounding *Blue Murder*, an injunction was filed against the screening of *Underbelly* in Victoria. Key underworld figures involved in these gangland wars were about to begin criminal trials, and the concern was that the fictionalized re-enactments of several events and characters would be unfair to those accused.[63] As a result, *Underbelly* began screening on 13 February 2008 on the Nine Network in all parts of Australia *except* Victoria. An edited version of the series with only the first five episodes premiered in Victoria on 14 September 2008 after the injunction was partially lifted, but it wasn't until 2011 that the series could finally be screened in Victoria as *Underbelly: Uncut*.[64]

The *Underbelly* series has continued to enjoy ratings success with the production of five more seasons in recent years – each one covering a different time period in Australia's sordid criminal history.[65] Importantly, the popularity of the *Underbelly* series continues to demonstrate an almost insatiable public appetite for the 'real-life' crime storytelling that has fuelled the production of local drama series over the last 60 years.

The trend of fictionalizing 'real-life' crime, or at the very least portraying authentic Australian crime stories, has continued well into this last decade. With more recent series such as *The Circuit*, *The Kettering Incident* and *Secret City*, audiences have demonstrated a pervasive local interest in viewing crime stories that represent a familiar social landscape while also addressing contemporary issues of concern, both nationally and internationally.

Mystery Road (2018),[66] produced by the ABC, is one such contemporary example that demonstrates the possibility of the Australian television industry finding an audience in a changing global television market while still reflecting national concerns. Set in the chronological space between the Bunya Productions films *Mystery Road* (2013) and *Goldstone* (2016), this six-part television series tells the story of Aboriginal Detective Jay Swan (Aaron Pedersen),[67] who works with local police sergeant Emma James (Judy Davis) to investigate the mysterious disappearance of two young farmhands on an outback cattle station, one a local Aboriginal football star and the other a white Australian backpacker with a dubious past. Filmed in Kununurra and Wyndham in far north Western Australia, it is a series that reflects a tangible historical friction concerning two competing cultural identities in a small Australian country town. *Mystery Road* continues from its filmic origins to pull on the thread of fractured identities and explore how these two cultures collide over a story of crime amid small-town politics and community relationships. In reframing the familiar cultural trope of the Indigenous person '"caught between two cultures" [and] rendering that figure as an active bicultural negotiator',[68] *Mystery Road* leaves open broader questions about how history haunts all Australians, whatever their colour.[69] As Aaron Pederson has commented about his character, Jay Swan:

> He's smack in the middle of the line Australia walks. . . . And being a copper, dealing with family . . . he's so human. I believe this character is so important for Australian storytelling and Australian identity.[70]

Reflecting more than ever that Australian crime dramas deploy society's most pressing economic, cultural and political concerns to create gripping drama and thought-provoking storytelling, *Mystery Road* underscores the history of race relations in Australia.

A contemporary fascination with reality Australian policing

In addition to reality-based crime and police dramas, over the last decade or so, Australian television audiences have demonstrated a distinct penchant for reality-style programming that depicts police undertaking their duties. Four series in particular – *Gold Coast Cops*, *Territory Cops*, *Highway Patrol* and *Crash Investigation Unit* – form the core group of reality-based shows that lead Australian-produced prime-time viewing over several nights of the week during non-ratings periods across the year. The 'ride-along' format provides viewers with a behind-the-scenes glimpse of the inner workings of the police and the capacity to feel part of the process.

Both *Crash Investigation Unit* (2008–11) and *Highway Patrol* (2009–18), produced by the Seven Network, focused on road crimes and serious traffic incidents. Depicting the investigations into serious traffic offences and incidents that occur on our major roads, including high-speed police chases, attending major road accidents and confronting out-of-control drunk drivers, these series follow a documentary-style presentation designed to demonstrate 'real-time' police activity.

The fascination that Australian audiences have with the 'real-life' work of police officers continued with *Territory Cops* (2012). Following police officers in the Northern Territory (described in one episode as 'one of the last frontiers'), the unique criminal problems of that area are highlighted: issues with alcohol and drugs in more remote communities, the large distances between towns in the outback and the native wildlife. *Gold Coast Cops* (2014–15), also airing on the Ten Network in the timeslot prior to *Territory Cops*, mirrors a similar pattern to its prime-time bedfellow: it follows the daily activities of police officers from the newly created Rapid Action & Patrols Group (RAP) on Queensland's Gold Coast. Giving unprecedented access[71] to what is described as an 'elite' taskforce responsible for 'policing everything from bikie gangs and street violence to drug heists and organized crime', the media release suggested the series would give 'viewers a compelling insight into the RAP and the men and women fighting crime on the Gold Coast'.[72] Interestingly, despite its popularity, *Gold Coast Cops* attracted significant attention in social media for the disunity it provoked within the police force. Many police officers external to the RAP unit have taken umbrage at the use of the term 'elite' as a descriptor for this taskforce and have argued that RAP alone is not responsible for the success of the Queensland Police Force.[73]

It is worth noting the 'Australianness' in these series. Australian slang ('fair dinkum') and the Aussie tradition of assigning nicknames ('Wombat', 'Macca') are especially emphasized, as is the stereotypical Australian laid-back casual attitude evident in the police officers' interactions with suspects. The ongoing success of reality policing reflects that a virtual 'ride-along' is a voyeuristic pleasure that viewers appreciate on Australian television.

The female lens

The most prominent and successful series developed in Australia within the genre of crime dramas have often revolved around key female figures. In the early 1980s, *Prisoner* (1979–86) was a powerful, transgressive and unique drama series based around the lives of the inmates and staff of the maximum-security Wentworth Detention Centre. As the only Australian television series (at the time) to really deal with incarceration, the opening scenes were charged with emotion and gritty realism as two terrified new inmates entered the prison. The premise was that as women from diverse backgrounds are confronted by life in a prison cell, the rules and boundaries that keep the isolated community together are pushed to extremes. As a result, the struggles for power, for friendship and for rehabilitation became dominant storylines. The 'unglamorous'[74] women of *Prisoner* were particularly admired for their shrewdness, lack of respect for authority and strong female agency. *Prisoner* was one of Australia's most popular series and has become a cult classic, surviving as an important part of Australian television history and culture.

During the time *Prisoner* was on the air, other female legal characters were being conceived. Known primarily for its successful and popularly received police dramas, Crawford Productions again struck gold in the early 1980s with its dramatic soap opera construction of law and justice in *Carson's Law* (1983–84). Produced for the Ten Network, *Carson's Law* was a period piece set in the 1920s, and its protagonist was an independent 'progressive' lawyer and mother of three who had to constantly fight prejudice within a male-dominated legal world. The series progressively tells the story of Jennifer Carson (played by Lorraine Bayly in a part created for her), who marries into an influential law firm but quickly has to deal with the intrigue, prejudice and stubbornness of the family patriarch when her husband suddenly dies. It was critically acclaimed for its attention to period detail and high technical standard; however, the series was subject to significant criticism for

> the scant regard paid to real life legal practice. . . . Jennifer acted as a criminal solicitor doing the main interviewing and investigating work, before switching over to act as barrister, presenting the same case in court.[75]

Despite this, *Carson's Law* successfully depicted the everyday (and timeless) struggle of female lawyers with regard to fighting prejudice and stereotypes. Since then, several other popular Australian female characters have found their place within the fictional law firm or courtroom, and it was the portrayal of Jennifer Carson's struggles that was echoed in the ABC's late 1990s production of *SeaChange* – the next series to demonstrate the complexities of juggling motherhood and a professional legal career.

In *SeaChange* (1998–2000), Laura Gibson is a successful city corporate lawyer with an all-consuming career whose world suddenly implodes. After she loses a partnership at work, then discovers that her husband has not only been arrested on fraud but also been having an affair with her sister, she packs up her life and looks for a change. On a whim, and with her two children in tow, Laura takes up a position as a local magistrate in the small and sleepy coastal town of Pearl Bay, where she hears many eccentric cases. Attracting record-breaking audiences for a non-commercial drama, it was the most popular Australian series on air at the time.[76] Part of its appeal was the focus on the characters' struggles with what is actually required to live a meaningful life. Interestingly, Laura's courtroom provides the perfect venue for a small town to balance the relationship between the rule of law and the rules of community and friendship, by reasserting 'the value of detached legal judgment . . . and pos[ing] questions about taking the desire to belong too far'.[77] *SeaChange* was a whimsical series with quirky characters that attracted popular attention because of its anti-materialistic, small-town message, and it popularized the idea of city dwellers moving to a more relaxed coastal lifestyle.[78] In a beguiling way, this series demonstrated the difficulties female lawyers/judges face in a traditionally male-dominated arena[79] and again echoed the Australian mythology of overcoming adversity.

The ABC series *Crownies* (2011), on the other hand, follows five young solicitors fresh out of law school (three of whom are women) as they begin work at the Crown Prosecutor's Office and make decisions about the prosecution of alleged wrongdoers. As is seemingly a tradition in ABC legally themed dramatic productions, the series is based on the real-life NSW Office of the Director of Public Prosecutions (DPP) – a frantic workplace where discussion of murders, political corruption and sexual abuse of minors is not only commonplace, but mandatory.[80] The series thus highlights the moral dilemmas facing public prosecutors in a world that craves retributive justice, and the storylines show these young men and women attempting to negotiate the pressures of balancing (at times) conflicting personal values and legal principles. With strong female characters becoming more prevalent on television in contemporary times, the ABC introduced us to several interesting and complex female characters in *Crownies*, particularly Senior Crown Prosecutor Janet King (Marta Dusseldorp), who inspired the spin-off production *Janet King* (2014–17). An eight-hour legal/political thriller, the first season of the series explores the dilemmas of this fiercely independent woman who returns to work after maternity leave[81] and is flung into a shocking prosecution that involves intrigue, twists and revelations that have a huge impact on her life. The portrayal of Janet King in both these series demonstrates that Australian audiences are extremely receptive to storylines involving complicated yet professional and highly competent female lawyers.

It is interesting to note that another ABC production, *Rake* (2010–18), uses the unprofessionalism of a male criminal defence barrister to serve as stark comparison. The main character, Cleaver Greene, is a brilliant barrister whose life is spiralling out of control. At once charismatic and self-destructive, he is a gambler in serious debt, he participates in many questionable activities and he defends the indefensible: from bigamists to cannibals, drug lords to murderers, and somehow still seems to keep his career afloat. The series gained popularity for the way his character was portrayed and acted by Richard Roxburgh – simultaneously charming, garish, colourful and exasperating. Rather than the usual legal drama, which is procedural and formulaic, *Rake* thrives and survives on the sometimes-shocking overlap between Greene's personal and professional lives. The show has had further success in other jurisdictions: for example, airing on Netflix in the United States, the United Kingdom and Canada.[82]

Television's most recent success, capitalizing on the popularity of the carceral gaze of *Prisoner*, is the contemporary Australian drama *Wentworth* (2012–), now in its seventh season, which is produced by Foxtel. Conceived as a reimagining of *Prisoner*, the series was devised to be a 'dynamic and very confronting drama series' that would 'push all boundaries and honestly depict life on the inside'.[83] Again set in a modern-day women's prison and exploring the politics and shifting hierarchies of incarcerated women, the first episode became the most watched Australian drama series premiere in Foxtel history.[84] Interestingly, returning to the drive to push Australian culture on our small screens, the series producer indicated that Australian identity remains at the heart of creating local content: 'It's a drama series built on the great Australian tradition of overcoming the odds to find mateship and belonging in the most unlikely circumstances'.[85] It is this recurring concept of framing a so-called 'Australian identity' that the next section of the chapter problematizes within the genre of television crime dramas.

Conclusions: colonial heritage, national identity and crime

The foregoing discussion of the history of Australian television production to date indicates that home-grown dramas based on issues surrounding crime detection, police activity and incarceration continue to be well received by the Australian public. Of course, this public appetite for crime stories is not unique to Australia. As the recent transnational success of the Scandinavian-noir crime series *The Killing [Forbrydelsen]* (2007–12) and *The Bridge* (2011–18) has demonstrated, small-screen criminal storytelling is very much a part of our global contemporary daily life and naturally echoes familiar global concerns about issues of safety, order, power and authority. In this sense, crime dramas play a 'critical role in bringing current social issues and anxieties into the public domain' and have the capacity to create emotional connections, insight and identity. Given that Australians not only spend more than 24 hours a week watching television,[86] but also seek and prioritize local content,[87] it is important to consider what is being reflected in Australian television crime stories.

In this chapter, I have argued that television has functioned historically as 'an important source of the sense of nationhood',[88] and I have pointed to the national identity project at work within the politicized creation, production and reception of Australian content on television. It is therefore critical to ask exactly what Australian identity or culture has been privileged as content has been produced. What is the essence of being Australian that is portrayed? Recognizing our post-colonial context, this last section reflects briefly on the Australian mythologies related to national identity that are iterated within Australian crime stories.

It is true that 'there is no singular, irreducible, national narrative, no essentialist "national identity"',[89] and that the Australian 'mythscape' is being negotiated and restructured frequently.[90] However, it is generally acknowledged that an Australian identity includes British colonization, 'white' settlement and convict transportation.[91] It has therefore been argued that Australia's distinctive character is 'rooted in the colonial project that lies deep at the heart of Australia's becoming and is therefore intrinsic to an Australian sense of identity'.[92] Interestingly, while our convict heritage was once regarded as a shameful 'stain' on a family tree,[93] it is now increasingly being viewed as having been necessary for national character-building and is a source of pride.[94] Prevailing foundation myths such as 'the great Aussie battler', 'mateship' and the mythologized bush landscape have more recently played into the dominant political and cultural shaping of our national identity. This convict ancestry

> is developed and transformed in terms of a robust mythology, literature and drama of inversion involving prisoners and authority, convict and officer, bush worker and squatter, bushranger and police.[95]

Yet this colonial heritage has also left a deep psychological scar – the formation of Australia through violence, dispossession and the legal fiction of *terra nullius* has bequeathed 'significant contemporary implications' to successive generations.[96] Such implications both create suspicion of institutionalized colonizing behaviours and lead to disrespect for authority and inspire the fight for a 'fair go' or the willingness to struggle against injustices at the hands of corrupt authorities.[97]

Undoubtedly our contemporary Australian attitudes and values partly reflect our colonial heritage and, just as the Australian television industry has developed over the last six decades, so too representations of an Australian national identity have emerged that embrace anti-authoritarian struggles for freedom, egalitarianism, resilience and overcoming adversity in the face of injustice. It is these themes that have been prevalent in many of the crime dramas discussed in this chapter, with each series, in its own way, weaving the essence of being Australian into the fabric of crime storytelling. Drawing on recognizable versions of everyday locations and emphasizing the importance of communities, Australian crime series have negotiated the boundaries between a familiar predictable world and the uncertainties and often arbitrary dangers of crime, which act as a disruption to the equilibrium of the everyday. Whether the focus has been on police, criminals, lawyers or 'real-life' participants, Australian television crime drama series have historically provided an opportunity to mirror and critique discourses of local or national cultural identities and to build cohesion and understanding across Australia's diverse communities. May this continue in the decades to come.

Notes

1. Harrington (2014), p 173.
2. Sue Turnbull (2014, p 11) writes that, 'Sweeping generalisations about the television crime drama series still abound and should be avoided, since for every claim that is made about the genre, an example can be found that contradicts it'. While much has been written about the multifarious nature of the 'crime drama' genre and how to effectively delineate its texts, there is not sufficient space in this chapter to elucidate all aspects of the genre. The focus in this chapter is on the aspects of 'crime drama' that involve detection, regulation and punishment of crime.
3. Televisionau.com, 'The History of Australian Television – 1950–59'.
4. Some 81 per cent of Australians own a smartphone and 63 per cent own a tablet (Deloitte 2014).
5. Deloitte (2014).
6. We Are Social (2019).

7 Regional television in Australia is made possible by the affiliation of independently owned networks with metropolitan stations (these include WIN Television, Southern Cross Ten and Prime Television). Multiple on-demand platforms are now available and include subscription on demand video (SVOD – for example, Netflix, Stan); broadcast video on demand (BVOD – for example, catch-up services iView, TenPlay) and transactional video on demand (TVOD – for example, iTunes, GooglePlay, BigPond).
8 Beilby (1981), p 173; Luck (2006), p 15.
9 Australian Government (1954).
10 Armstrong (2014), p 41.
11 Australian Government (1954), p 102.
12 In line with what already held in radio: Curthoys (1991), p 155.
13 Australian Broadcasting Control Board Report and Recommendations to the Postmaster General pursuant to the *Television Act 1953*, p 20, para 36, cited in Horgan (2006), p 11.
14 This was timed well to enable coverage of the Melbourne Olympics, which was held in November 1956. See also Harrington (2014), p 173.
15 McWhirter (2006). Interestingly, an interview with Dame Edna Everage (a comic character created and performed by Barry Humphries) was one of the programmes screened on HSV-7's first day of programming in 1956. The character went on to enjoy great success in the United Kingdom and later the United States.
16 Free TV Australia (n.d.).
17 Again, this was to align with the Olympics – this time the Montreal 1976 Olympics.
18 The conversion to colour TV cost the ABC about $46 million and the commercial sector $70 million: Televisionau.com, 'The History of Australian Television – 1970–79'. It might be argued, however, that for the commercial sector this was easily offset by the revenue raised through advertising because by 1980, commercial television in Australia became the main advertising medium and accounted for 33 per cent of all mainstream advertising (a figure that had more than doubled since 1960, when it accounted for only 15 per cent of advertising revenue): Free TV Australia (n.d.).
19 Cunningham and Turner (2010), p 156.
20 For example, Seven and Ten began the decade in receivership, and tight budgets and cost cutting were common: Televisionau.com, 'The History of Australian Television – 1990–99'.
21 See Moran (1985), pp 27–8; Harrington (2014), p 175.
22 Skwirk.com.au; see also McKee (2001).
23 O'Regan (1989).
24 O'Regan (1989).
25 Crawford (1959).
26 Cunningham and Turner (2010), p 157.
27 Australian Government (1963). See more information in Cunningham and Turner (2010), p 157.
28 *Broadcasting and Television Act 1956* (Cth), s 88(1).
29 *Broadcasting and Television Act 1956* (Cth), s 88(2).
30 Three years later, in 1973, the ABCB changed Australian content requirements from a quantitative to a qualitative 'points system' to encourage the televising of Australian variety, news, current affairs and drama programmes: Australian National Film and Sound Archive (n.d.). See also Cunningham and Turner (2010), p 175.
31 'Many Australians, particularly young Australians, already prefer American drama to Australian productions of equivalent artistic merit because they have by now accepted American values and a preference for that particular form of the American way of life which is depicted by American TV programs. Further, evidence of this is discernible

in the pronounced American accents sometimes affected by Australian radio and TV announcers'. See Australian Government (1963), p 16.
32 Australian Government (1963), p 16.
33 O'Regan (1989).
34 Televisionau.com, 'The History of Australian Television – 1970–79'.
35 Mandated by the Broadcasting Services (Australian Content Standard) 2005, created under the *Broadcasting Services Act1992* (Cth) and regulated by the Australian Communication and Media Authority (ACMA).
36 *Australian National Film and Sound Archive*, 'Digital Learning TV and Family Life'. See also Cunningham and Turner (2010), p 175.
37 Moran (1985), p 162.
38 Albert (1985), p 162.
39 Cunningham and Turner (2010), p 157.
40 Televisionau.com, 'Cop Shows'. The series even managed to sell overseas.
41 Harrington (2014), p 175.
42 *Blue Heelers* was allowed to produce its final episode at 510 – the same number of episodes as *Homicide*.
43 McKee (2001), p 52, cited in Rogers (2008), p 83.
44 Nette (2015), p 52.
45 McKee (2001), p 52, cited in Rogers (2008), p 83.
46 'Division 4', *Classic Australian Television*.
47 Other less successful attempts at police dramas during this time included Ten's *Bellamy* (1981) and *Special Squad* (1984) and Nine's soap opera drama *Waterloo Station* (1983).
48 Helenn Thomas writing in 1983 in the Age quoted in Matthews (n.d.a).
49 This was a Commission of Inquiry into Possible Illegal Activities and Associated Police Misconduct from 1987 through 1989, which examined corruption in the Queensland police force. It was presided over by Tony Fitzgerald QC and resulted in the deposition of a premier and the incarceration of three former ministers and a police commissioner.
50 Kate Mathews reports that, 'In one curious sequence that further complicates the distinction between real and represented events, Sergeant Colin Dillon plays himself, delivering his own testimony once more for the screen': Matthews, 'Reality and TV Crime'.
51 Matthews (n.d.a).
52 Matthews (n.d.a).
53 The key taglines for the series were 'one of the most shocking characters in the history of law enforcement – a true story' and 'the best police force money can buy'.
54 Lever (2001), p 60.
55 Lever (2001), p 60.
56 *Special Broadcasting Act 1991* (Cth), s 6.
57 Nicholls (2011), p 574.
58 Ang, Hawkins and Dabboussy (2008).
59 Turnbull (2014), p 4.
60 It was such a ratings success that the Ten Network attempted production of its own version *Bikie Wars: Brothers in Arms* in 2012: see http://televisionau.com/feature-articles/cop-shows.
61 Casey (2008); Ziffer (2008).
62 Idato (2008).
63 Interestingly, the screening of *Underbelly* (and its potential to produce bias) was used by one of the underworld criminals, Tony Mokbel, as justification to fight his extradition from Greece. It was also suggested that another major criminal featured in the series, Carl Williams, could have his appeal jeopardized on the basis of unfair prejudice: www.australiantelevision.net/underbelly/legal.html.

64 For a quick, concise summary of the legal issues surrounding this series, see 'Australian Television', www.australiantelevision.net/underbelly/legal.html.
65 *Underbelly: A Tale of Two Cities* takes us back to 1976; *Underbelly: The Golden Mile* is set in Sydney's King Cross in 1988–99; *Underbelly: Razor* is set in the 1920s; *Underbelly: Badness* takes place in Sydney from 2001–12; *Underbelly: Squizzy* spans the years 1915–27.
66 At the time of writing, this had just aired on Australian screens. The series is a spin-off of Ivan Sen's films *Mystery Road* (Bunya Productions, 2013) and *Goldstone* (Bunya Productions, 2016).
67 Pedersen also portrayed an Aboriginal lawyer in *The Circuit*, where he works for the Aboriginal Legal Service and attempts to bridge the gap between the white legal system and the Aboriginal community in Broome, Australia.
68 Rutherford (2015).
69 Behrendt (2018).
70 Johnson (2018).
71 'Our crews have been granted full access to the operations of this elite team who are first on the scene when the action happens. The vision we have captured so far is extraordinary': Eyeworks Australia Managing Director, John McAvoy, Network Ten Promotional online material for *Gold Coast Cops*, http://tenplay.com.au/channel-ten/gold-coast-cops/about.
72 Network Ten Chief Programming Officer Beverley McGarvey, Network Ten Promotional online material for *Gold Coast Cops*, http://tenplay.com.au/channel-ten/gold-coast-cops/about.
73 Remeikis (2014). This is, of course, despite the unit stimulating an increased level of successful public 'tip-offs' since *Gold Coast Cops* started airing: Cartwright (2015).
74 McKee (2001), pp 176–7.
75 Aussie Soap Archives.
76 Matthews (n.d.b): 'With audiences that sometimes topped two million, *SeaChange* knocked current affairs show *60 Minutes* (1979–) from its previously comfortable perch atop the ratings in the Sunday night 7.30 pm family viewing timeslot'.
77 Matthews (n.d.b).
78 Murphy (2002).
79 As an interesting aside, at the time of writing, *SeaChange* is currently being revived for the Nine network with Sigrid Thornton reprising her role more than 20 years after its first creation.
80 Blundell (2011).
81 The character of Janet King is in a same-sex relationship and has a child through IVF.
82 Interestingly, the Fox Network in the United States has produced a US version starring Greg Kinnear as the lead character.
83 Dallas (2012).
84 Hardie (2013).
85 Jo Porter, quoted in *Dallas* (2012).
86 Deloitte (2019).
87 Some 58 per cent feel local content on streaming services is important – Deloitte (2019).
88 Smith (1998), p 3.
89 Bell (2003), p 73.
90 Bell (2003), p 73.
91 Tranter and Donoghue (2007), p 168.
92 Heron (2016), p 91.
93 Tranter and Donoghue (2003), p 555.
94 'It became increasingly fashionable to uncover a convict ancestor': Tranter and Donoghue (2003), p 556.

95 Curthoys and Docker (1989), p 57.
96 Maddison (2012), p 696.
97 Tranter and Donoghue (2003), p 555.

References

Secondary sources

'American and British Cultural Influence', *Skwirk.com.au*, www.skwirk.com.au/skwirk/uploadFiles/content/database/files/chapter.1880.body.html.

Ien Ang, Gay Hawkins and Lamia Dabboussy (2008) *The SBS Story: The Challenge of Diversity*, UNSW Press.

Mark Armstrong (2014) 'Australian Broadcasting Control Board', in Bridget Griffen-Foley (ed.), *A Companion to the Australian Media*, Australian Scholarly Publishing.

Aussie Soap Archives, http://members.ozemail.com.au/~fangora/index.html.

Australian Government (1954) *Royal Commission into Television Report*.

——— (1963) *Report from the Select Committee on the Encouragement of Australian Production for TV*, Australian Government.

Australian National Film and Sound Archive (n.d.) 'Digital Learning TV and Family Life', n.p.

Larissa Behrendt (2018) '*Mystery Road* Review – TV Spin-off Unearths Ambitious Tale of Small-Town Secret', *The Guardian*, 4 June, www.theguardian.com/tv-and-radio/2018/jun/03/mystery-road-review-tv-spin-off-unearths-ambitious-tale-of-small-town-secrets.

Peter Beilby (1981) *Australian TV – The First 25 Years*, Nelson.

Duncan Bell (2003) 'Mythscapes: Memory, Mythology, and National Identity' 54 *British Journal of Sociology* 63.

Graeme Blundell (2011) 'DPP Lawyer Drama a Crownie Achievement for ABC', *The Australian*, 9 July.

Darren Cartwright (2015) 'Gold Coast Cops Attracts Public Tip-Offs', *News.com.au*, 16 March, www.news.com.au/national/queensland/gold-coast-cops-attracts-public-tip-offs/story-fnk7yze2-1227264927373.

Marcus Casey (2008) 'Butterflies in the Underbelly for Gang Show on Channel Nine', *Daily Telegraph*, 31 January.

Hector Crawford (1959) 'Commercial Television Programs in Australia', quoted in Alan McKee (2001) *Australian Television: A Genealogy of Great Moments*, Oxford University Press.

Stuart Cunningham and Graeme Turner (eds) (2010) *The Media and Communications in Australia* (3rd ed.), Allen & Unwin.

Ann Curthoys (1991) 'Television Before Television' 4 *Continuum: Journal of Media & Cultural Studies* 152.

Ann Curthoys and John Docker (1989) 'In Praise of *Prisoner*', in John Tulloch and Graeme Turner (eds), *Australian Television Programs, Pleasure and Politics*, Allen & Unwin.

Sam Dallas (2012) 'Foxtel Commissions New Prisoner Series, Titled *Wentworth*', *If Magazine*, 5 March, www.if.com.au/foxtel-commissions-new-prisoner-series-titled-wentworth.

Deloitte (2014) *Media Consumer Survey*, www2.deloitte.com/au/en/pages/technology-media-and-telecommunications/articles/media-consumer-survey-2014.html.

——— (2019) *Media Consumer Survey*, www2.deloitte.com/au/en/pages/technology-media-and-telecommunications/articles/media-consumer-survey-2019.html.

Digital Learning (n.d.) 'TV and Family Life', *Australian National Film and Sound Archive*, http://dl.nfsa.gov.au/module/645.

'*Division 4*' (n.d.) *Classic Australian Television*, www.classicaustraliantv.com/div4.htm.

'Feature Articles – Cop Shows' (n.d.) Televisionau.com, http://televisionau.com/feature-articles/cop-shows.

Free TV Australia (n.d.) 'Inside the Industry – History of TV', *Free TV Australia*, www.freetv.com.au/content_common/pg-inside-the-industry.seo.

Giles Hardie (2013) '*Wentworth* Breaks Out with a Bang as Arrow Strikes for Nine', *Sydney Morning Herald*, 2 May.

Stephen Harrington (2014) 'Television', in Stuart Cunningham and Sue Turnbull (eds), *The Media & Communications in Australia* (4th ed.), Allen & Unwin.

Janie Heron (2016) 'A *Glitch* in the Script: Fantasy, Realism and the Australian Imagination' 18 *Coolabah* 85.

'The History of Australian Television – 1970–79, Timeline' (n.d.) Televisionau.com, http://televisionau.com/timeline/1970-1979.

'The History of Australian Television – 1990–99, Timeline' (n.d.) Televisionau.com, http://televisionau.com/timeline/1990-1999.

Brendan Horgan (2006) *Radio with Pictures: 50 Years of Australian Television*, Lothian.

Michael Idato (2008) 'Pick and Mix', *Sydney Morning Herald*, 3 January.

Neala Johnson (2018) 'Indigenous Actor Aaron Pedersen is After Presence, Not Fame', *The Advertiser*, 18 May.

Susan Lever (2001) 'Dramatic Interpretation and Documentary Fact: Ian David's Writing for Television' 126 *Metro Magazine: Media & Education Magazine* 56.

Peter Luck (2000) *50 Years of Australian TV – An Insider's View 1956–2006*, New Holland.

Sarah Maddison (2012) 'Postcolonial Guilt and National Identity: Historical Injustice and the Australian Settler State' 18(6) *Social Identities* 695.

Kate Matthews (n.d.a) 'Reality and TV Crime', *Australian Screen, Australian National Film and Sound Archive*, http://aso.gov.au/titles/series/homicide.

——— (n.d.b) '*SeaChange* – One of the Gang', *Curator's Notes: Australian Screen Australian National Film and Sound Archive*, http://aso.gov.au/titles/tv/seachange-one-of-the-gang/notes.

Beverley McGarvey (n.d.) 'Promotional Online Material – *Gold Coast Cops*', *Network Ten*, http://tenplay.com.au/channel-ten/gold-coast-cops/about.

Alan McKee (2001) *Australian Television: A Genealogy of Great Moments*, Oxford University Press.

Erin McWhirter (2006) 'Australia Celebrates 50 Years of Television', *News Limited*, www.news.com.au/entertainment/story/0,23663,20357015-5007183,00.html.

Albert Moran (1985) *Images & Industry: Television Drama Production in Australia*, Currency Press.

Peter Murphy (2002) '*SeaChange*: Re-Inventing Rural and Regional Australia' 2 *Transformations*, http://citeseerx.ist.psu.edu/viewdoc/download?doi=10.1.1.732.5116&rep=rep1&type=pdf.

Andrew Nette (2015) 'Crime Pays: *Underbelly*, *Homicide* and *Blue Murder*' 186 *Metro Magazine* 50.

Brett Nicholls (2011) '*East West 101* as Edgy Text: Television Police Drama and Australian Multiculturalism' 25(4) *Continuum: Journal of Media & Cultural Studies* 573.

Tom O'Regan (1989) 'Film and Its Nearest Neighbour: the Australian Film and Television Interface', *Culture and Communication Reading Room, Murdoch University*, wwwmcc.murdoch.edu.au/ReadingRoom/film/AFTV.html.

Amy Remeikis (2014) '*Gold Coast Cops* Mocked by Colleagues', *Brisbane Times*, 30 September.
Margaret Rogers (2008) 'Arresting Drama: The Television Police Genre' 5(2) *Studies in Learning, Evaluation Innovation and Development* 78.
Anne Rutherford (2015) 'Walking the Edge: Performance, the Cinematic Body and the Cultural Mediator in Ivan Sen's *Mystery Road*' 9 *Studies in Australasian Cinema* 312.
Anthony Smith (1998) 'Introduction', in Anthony Smith (ed.), *Television: An International History*, Oxford University Press.
Bruce Tranter and Jed Donoghue (2003) 'Convict Ancestry: A Neglected Aspect of Australian Identity' 9 *Nations and Nationalism* 555.
——— (2007) 'Colonial and Post-colonial Aspects of Australian Identity' 58 *The British Journal of Sociology* 165.
Sue Turnbull (2014) *TV Crime Drama*, Edinburgh University Press.
We Are Social (2019) 'Digital 2019: Australia Report', *We Are Social*, https://wearesocial.com/au/blog/2019/02/digital-report-australia.
Daniel Ziffer (2008) '*Underbelly* Wins Ratings War', *The Age*, 14 February.

Primary legal sources

Broadcasting and Television Act 1956 (Cth).
Broadcasting Services Act 1992 (Cth).
Broadcasting Services (Australian Content Standard) 2005 (Cth).
Special Broadcasting Act 1991 (Cth).
Television Act 1953 (Cth).

Television series

Blue Heelers (1993–2005) Southern Star Entertainment (S1–14).
Blue Murder (1995) Southern Star Sullivan (mini-series).
The Bridge (*Broen*; *Bron*) (2011–18) Nimbus Films and Filmlance International (S1–8).
Carla Cametti PD (2009) Buon Giorno Productions (S1).
Carson's Law (1983–84) Crawford Productions (S1–2).
The Circuit (2007–09) Media World Productions (S1–2).
City Homicide (2007–11) Seven Productions (S1–5).
Cop Shop (1977–83) Crawford Productions (S1–8).
Crash Investigation Unit (2008–11) Seven Productions and Greenstone Pictures (S1–2).
Crownies (2011) Screentime Pty Ltd (S1).
Division 4 (1969–75) Crawford Productions (S1–7).
East West 101 (2007–09) East West 101 Season 3 (S1–3).
Gold Coast Cops (2014–15) Eyeworks Australia (S1–2).
Highway Patrol (2009–18) Greenstone TV (S1–10).
Homicide (1964–77) Crawford Productions (S1–14).
Janet King (2014–17) Screentime (S1–3).
The Kettering Incident (2016) Porchlight Films and Sweetpotato Films (S1).
The Killing [Forbrydelsen] (2007–12) Fox Television Studios, Fuse Entertainment and KMF Films (S1–4).
Matlock Police (1971–76) Crawford Productions (S1–6).

Phoenix (1992–93) Australian Broadcasting Corporation (S1–2).
Police State (1989) Southern Star (S1).
Prisoner (1979–86) Reg Grundy Organisation (S1–8).
Rake (2010–18) Essential Media and Entertainment (S1–5).
Rush (2008–11) Southern Star Entertainment (S1–4).
Scales of Justice (1983) Australian Broadcasting Corporation (S1).
SeaChange (1998–2000) Australian Broadcasting Corporation and Artist Services (S1–3).
Secret City (2016–18) Matchbox Productions and Secret City Productions (S1–2).
Stingers (1998–2004) Beyond Simpson Le Mesurier Productions and MBP (S1–8).
Territory Cops (2012) Eyeworks Television (S1).
Underbelly (2007) Screentime (S1).
Underbelly: Badness (2012) Screentime (S5).
Underbelly: The Golden Mile (2010) Screentime (S3).
Underbelly: Razor (2011) Screentime (S4).
Underbelly: Squizzy (2013) Screentime (S6).
Underbelly: A Tale of Two Cities (2009) Screentime (S2).
Water Rats (1996–2001) Hal McElroy and Southern Star Entertainment (S1–7).
Wentworth (2012–17) FremantleMedia (S1–6).
White Collar Blue (2002–03) Knapman Wyld Television (S1–2).
Young Lions (2002) Southern Star International (S1).

Chapter 3

Whose country? Colonialism and the rule of law in *Sweet Country* and *Charlie's Country*

Jack Quirk and Julian R. Murphy

> Repressive law is perhaps less terrible than lawless repression, but it can be terrible all the same.[1]
>
> – Martin Krygier

Introduction

'I wish they'd have just shot us like in the old days', says Faith (Jennifer Budukpuduk Gaykamangu, Yolngu people), one of the Aboriginal characters in *Charlie's Country*, after police officers ransack her makeshift home on the outskirts of Darwin. In the 'old days' to which she refers, many colonial Australians – police and civilians alike – massacred countless Indigenous people.[2] Yet how, the viewer wonders, does Australia's dark history compare with our current era – the era of *Charlie's Country*? Whatever one thinks of the contested status of Australia as a 'post-colonial' state, it is impossible to deny that the country's present legal superstructure, particularly its adherence to a formal conception of the rule of law, is the product of its violent colonial past. This chapter explores how *Charlie's Country* and another recent Australian film, *Sweet Country* (2017), represent the real, material effects of the colonizing impetus that remains embedded in the Australian rule of law and how continued uncritical reverence for the rule of law, despite these deleterious effects, perpetuates the subjugation of Indigenous Australians.

To begin, we briefly set out the prevailing conception of the rule of law in Australia. Turning to the films, we read them to evince a powerful critique of formalistic conceptions of the rule of law, a critique resonating with critical legal philosophers, including Morton Horwitz and Roberto Unger. Our animating purpose is to explore how these two recent Indigenous films force us to think critically about the rule of law, how it operates in Australia and how it prejudices Indigenous Australians in practice. Abstract legal concepts have real-world effects: *Sweet Country* and *Charlie's Country* show that the legal effect of Australia's formalist rule of law is to perpetuate injustice against Aboriginal and Torres Strait Islander people.

The Australian rule of law

Australia remains part of the British Commonwealth, and its legal system emerged from British common law and the Westminster tradition. Like other countries with a similar history, the rule of law is widely considered 'an unqualified human good'.[3] Both of the two major political parties, the Liberal Party and the Australian Labor Party, hold the rule of law as an article of faith, with political party platforms presupposing that just outcomes logically follow from fidelity to the rule of law.[4]

But what do we mean in Australia when we profess a commitment to the rule of law? What even *is* it? Broadly speaking, the rule of law is conceived of as a normative ideal or criteria. Yet the contours of the ideal system, and the exact criteria therein, are controversial. The theoretical literature distinguishes between formal and substantive conceptions of the rule of law.[5] Formal conceptions claim to be ideologically neutral; these are directed to assuring only that law satisfies particular technical requirements, such as clarity, prospectivity, practicability, general applicability, stability, internal consistency and impartiality.[6] Its proponents believe rule of law formalism minimizes the arbitrary exercise of state power and that the stability it affords is a necessary condition for individual liberty and flourishing – a classically liberal, utilitarian naivety that characterizes many colonial democracies. Influenced by the classical liberalism of the Enlightenment, formal approaches neglect to account for circumstances where the law's discharge of formal requirements still leads to unjust outcomes. It is one of our contentions that predicating the efficacy of Australia's judicial system on its ability to adhere to law's formal rules is misguided, since adherence to rules so often results in substantive injustice. Instead, substantive conceptions are concertedly more value orientated – they aim at securing ideological or moral values, like advancing human rights or protecting private property.[7]

Australia's commitment to the rule of law is more formal than substantive. Rule of law formalists consider that any injustice stems from unjust laws and not the rule of law. The rule is split from the law. Laws can be unjust. The rule of law cannot.[8] Where one considers a law to be *substantively* unjust, already always based on one's value orientation or morality, it is not a deficiency in the rule of law, but rather a deficiency in the law itself. The content is the problem, not the form: any substantive injustice occasioned by law is a matter of policy or political preference. Australia's commitment to rule of law formalism is coterminous with its dominant judicial philosophy – legalism or, at its height, 'strict and complete legalism'.[9] Instead, *Charlie's Country* and *Sweet Country* show us the actual effects of law, thereby exposing the shortcomings of Australian formalism.

Sweet Country

Sweet Country, directed by Warwick Thornton, a Kaytej man from Alice Springs, was well received by critics on its release.[10] Thornton is one of the most successful Indigenous directors working in Australia; his debut film, *Samson and*

Delilah (2009), won the Camera d'Or at the Cannes Film Festival, and his films are preoccupied with representing Indigenous life in Australia. *Sweet Country* follows this pattern. Set in a frontier-like outback of post–World War I Australia, an Aboriginal worker accused of murder goes on the run, opening up deep fissures running through colonial Australian society. The opening scene foreshadows the contradictions at the heart of the film – contradictions between image and reality, between form and substance, between law and justice. For the duration of the scene, the camera focuses on water boiling in a teapot on the hot coals of a campfire. After a few seconds, the viewer hears voices in the background. A white man violently beats one of his Indigenous labourers; he yells out the words 'fucking black bastard'. The only other words audible in the background are in an Indigenous language. A hand enters the frame and ceremoniously releases a stream of fine black tea into the waiting water.

The opening scene recalls the moment in 1975 when Prime Minister Gough Whitlam poured a fistful of earth into the cupped hand of Gurindji leader Vincent Lingiari. The celebrated image of Whitlam pouring sand into Lingiari's hand is itself a complex one, as much about optics as about legal effect. The dual legal and symbolic quality of Whitlam's gesture provides the sub-text: 'Vincent Lingiari, I solemnly hand to you these deeds as proof, in Australian law, that these lands belong to the Gurindji people, and I put into your hands this piece of the Earth itself as a sign that we restore them to you and your children forever'.[11] The stylized nature of the interaction is emphasized in the famous photograph – which, unknown to most, documents a staged recreation of the act rather than the original moment.[12] The photograph and the gesture it documented were thought at the time to herald a new governmental commitment to land justice outcomes for Indigenous people, accessible and enforceable at law. Four decades later, the image reminds us of hollow government promises in the area of land rights.[13] *Sweet Country* opens with the interplay of image and reality, form and substance, law and justice. These oppositional forces persist in three sequential movements. First, the film depicts the colonial violence and injustice inflicted upon Indigenous people in early 20th-century Australia. Second, the film promises the rule of law as a check on the forces of violence and injustice. Finally, it shows that the promise of the rule is largely illusory.

A picture of colonial violence and injustice

Sweet Country is based on real events.[14] From its beginning, it offers an unflinching depiction of the plight of Indigenous people in colonial Australia. It opens with disturbing audio of a violent, racialized beating of an Aboriginal labourer. Then the arresting image of a black man shackled at the neck. The almost-still portrait recalls the sepia photographs of Aboriginal prisoners in Australia's frontier wars and the more recent image, which ricocheted around the world in July 2016, of a young Aboriginal boy hooded and restrained in a Northern Territory youth detention centre.[15] The man in the shackles,[16] the viewer later learns, is Sam

Kelly (Hamilton Morris, Walpiri people), an Aboriginal stockman charged with the murder of a white station owner, Harry March (Ewen Leslie). The shooting and Sam's subsequent prosecution for Harry's murder comprise the central narrative thread of the film. Yet, as the film opens, the viewer knows nothing of this; first they hear a black man being assaulted, then they see another in neck irons. These confronting opening scenes show an important aspect of the film's project: to depict the horror experienced by Indigenous people after the European arrival. This project continues throughout the film as it gestures to the apartheid system of bonded labour in early 20th-century Australia, where white station owners paid their Aboriginal cattle workers in rations instead of wages;[17] the widespread rape of Aboriginal women by white men – a practice some scholars have equated to racial terrorism;[18] and the ever-present threat of vigilante violence, which has poignant echoes in the contemporary Aboriginal experience in the Northern Territory.[19]

The promise of the rule of law to check violence and injustice

Against this violence and injustice, the film offers one protection: the rule of law. More precisely, the film represents a legal system governed by a rule of law formalism with a dual emphasis on legal equality and due process.

The film invokes the myth of equality very early, when the (comparatively) benevolent station owner, Fred Smith (Sam Neill), resists the characterization of his Indigenous workers as 'black stock', instead saying, 'We are all equal here, we are all equal in the eyes of the Lord'. Fred's invocation of equality before God is at once also a reference to equality before the law; historically, the two ideas cannot be disentangled.[20] So foundational was the religious-legal idea of equality to colonial Australians that some argue it forms a foundational assumption of the Commonwealth constitution.[21] Apart from Fred's utterance, the principle of legal equality finds repeated expression through the film's depiction of Sam's criminal trial. The law seems to offer Sam rights and protections equal to those of a white defendant – he can testify, call evidence and make submissions. The judge is painstaking in his efforts to preserve all appearances of formal equality and, as we see when he decides in Sam's favour, the commitment to equality seems sound.

Aside from equality, the other formal rule of law quality referred to most by the film's characters is due process. This is not the substantive due process protected in the Constitution of the United States, but an Australian brand of 'procedural' due process.[22] This procedural due process is part of what Raz sees as law's capacity, when operating according to formal criteria, to constrain arbitrary exercises of power.[23] In *Sweet Country*, we see both Indigenous and white characters placing their trust in due process. Sam and his partner Lizzie (Natassia Gorey Furber, Eastern-Arrernte people) hand themselves in to the local police sergeant (Bryan Brown) – we might assume because they trust that the legal process will out the truth that Sam acted in self-defence in shooting Harry. Sam and Lizzie's white ally, Fred, also places his trust in the legal system, observing the duration of the trial and encouraging Lizzie, without success, to take part by giving evidence.

The film's investment in due process and formal rule of law commitments reaches its high-water mark in the characterization of Judge Taylor (Matt Day). He conducts the trial with no appearance of bias, offers equal opportunity to both parties to present their cases and provides his reasoned decision with characteristic deliberation. The judge dismisses the charge and his words – 'I find that this is a case of self-defence. . . . Sam Kelly, you are free to go' – effect Sam's release. As virulent objections are yelled from the crowd, the judge reminds the unhappy onlookers of the verdict's authority: 'This is a court of law'. For the moment, it seems as if rule of law formalism has triumphed over the same trenchant racism that led to Sam's self-defensive killing.

The illusion, revealed

The film's devastating final move is to reverse the redemptive narrative of the trial and to dash the rule of law on the rocks of reality. After Judge Taylor dismisses the charges, Sam and his family are returning to Fred's station when a single shot rings out, killing Sam. As the camera pans the surrounding bushland, there is no one in sight; from the viewer's perspective, the shot literally comes from nowhere. The inference? We are all complicit in the injustice. Thornton shows how worthless the solemn protections of legal equality and due process are in a country where racial violence continues to exceed law's capacity for regulation. Sam and Lizzie's noble act of handing themselves in to the sheriff is their undoing; their faith in the rule is misplaced.

In this aspect, Thornton's film harmonizes with the critique of the rule of law mounted by Roberto Unger, a founder of critical legal studies. He suggests rule of law formalism may legitimate oppressive power structures by operating as a veil on their true, insidious effect, making injustice invisible.[24] Unger argues that rule of law formalism will not constrain the power of the dominant ruling class in any meaningful sense, leading to the entrenchment of the system's prejudices and the outcomes resulting from this.[25] The rule of law in this formulation is an ideological apparatus, sustaining and reifying rather than curtailing hegemonic power structures.[26] Marxist legal historian Morton Horwitz writes along similar lines:

> [The rule of law] undoubtedly restrains power, but it also prevents power's benevolent exercise. It creates formal equality – a not inconsiderable virtue – but it promotes substantive inequality by creating a consciousness that radically separates law from politics, means from ends, processes from outcomes. By promoting procedural justice, it enables the shrewd, the calculating, and the wealthy to manipulate its forms to their own advantage. And it ratifies and legitimates an adversarial, competitive, and atomistic conception of human relations. . . . [The rule of law] inevitably discourages the pursuit of substantive justice.[27]

Sweet Country's greatest strength is its affective power. Thornton acknowledged this to be one of the film's aims: to allow 'audiences to enter the story and . . . so experience the issues faced by an occupied people'.[28] Thornton's affective hooks are many, but the strongest are our allegiance to Sam and Lizzy and our commitment to the positive narrative trajectory that seems assured by the film's final stages.[29] The resulting film is more than a case study aligned with Unger's and Horwitz's critiques; it forces viewers to *feel* rather than *think* the injustice of colonial rule of law. Thornton allows the viewer 106 minutes to become invested in Sam and Lizzie's story and invites us to celebrate Sam's acquittal with relief. Justice and the rule of law buttressing it seem to have won. Thornton's knockout blow comes just a few minutes from the end of the film. Yet, as viewers watch the bloody final scene, we realize we have seen these images before. Thornton prefigures this moment earlier in the film by flashing bloody scenes onto the screen for a split second. The intention is hard to miss: this bloody conclusion, Thornton is telling us, was inevitable from the start; the body politic is rife with racial violence; the rule of law is powerless to prevent it.

Charlie's Country

So far, we have discussed how we can read *Sweet Country* to show the shortcomings of Australia's colonial understanding of the efficacy of the rule of law. The film equivocates with the viewer, convincing them that the rule of law could not exist in the far-flung outback of 1920s Australia. Yet when Thornton hints at Australia's redemption – embodied by the ineffectual Judge Taylor – through proper administration of the rule of law and the rightful acquittal of Sam, it is all too brief. Thornton dashes the audience's optimistic naivety with the shocking display of violence in the film's tragic denouement. The racist vigilantism of the Australian outback supersedes, overrules and supplants the rule of law, showing how adherence to legal process fails to account for substantive injustice.

If *Sweet Country* shows formal protections are small mercies in the face of prevailing racialized animosity and violence, *Charlie's Country* shows another side: how procedurally just laws, supposedly required for order, become insensible and absurd (at best) and unjust (at worst), particularly when based on the liberal proviso that such laws should apply to all individuals equally. The film was cowritten by David Gulpilil, a Yolngu man who also plays the titular character, and the director Rolf de Heer, a Dutch Australian. Gulpilil was in prison when the two men conceived this project, and significant portions of the script are autobiographical.

The resulting film is what Victoria Herche has called a protagonist's journey 'through Australia's institutions',[30] part portrait of an Aboriginal community, part Kafkaesque struggle of humanity against the law. We can also understand Charlie's journey as a resistance against the normative framework of colonial law: the residual, racialized biases of the law cause Charlie to remove himself from it, albeit unsuccessfully. To illustrate, we will look at how the film depicts law in

Charlie's community in its regulatory and peacekeeping functions. Despite wishing to return to an idealized notion of Indigenous pre-colonial life, Charlie cannot do so without contravening the law or endangering his health. Charlie embodies the tense relationship between Australian law and its dominion over Indigenous Australians, particularly those in remote communities. His story makes visible the inequity of the Australian legal system and emphasizes how legal formalism reifies colonial oppression because it denies Indigenous Australians the right to live or to thrive. Caught between the old ways and the new, Charlie exists in a liminal legal space, within the purview of colonial law but prevented from its ability to administer justice, unable to sustain himself under a legal regime without contravening it.[31]

Rule of law or a 'law of rules'?

If the opening of *Sweet Country* foreshadows the physical violence by which white property owners forced their Indigenous stockmen into submission, *Charlie's Country*'s first shot suggests violence of another kind – this time, a symbolic violence occurring when fidelity to rules abrogates law's responsibility to provide justice and fairness. The film opens with an extended shot of a red dirt road at the entrance to an Indigenous community in Australia's Northern Territory. In centre shot, there is a road sign. It reads:

> LIQUOR ACT – RESTRICTED AREA
> The possession or consumption of liquor beyond this point without a permit is a serious offence.

For Australian viewers, the sign calls to mind the Northern Territory National Emergency Response (known as 'the Intervention'), implemented by the Prime Minister John Howard's government in 2007, under which the Australian government legislated to address what it saw as concerns regarding the welfare of children in remote Indigenous communities.[32] In particular, the Intervention implemented a radical raft of changes to regulate welfare, alcohol, indecency and land tenure. To others, however, the sign comes across as a regulatory peculiarity: why is it that alcohol is restricted in this area? While the film does not refer explicitly to the Intervention, this first shot foreshadows the peculiarities – regulatory, legal and discriminatory – following the film's protagonist Charlie (Gulpilil), punctuating life in his rural Australian community with humour, absurdity and violence. As Herche notes, the 'community is presented as a place with few employment opportunities, bad housing, and lots of boredom, all of which present a recurring challenge to living a meaningful existence'.[33] Unlike the rule of law of *Sweet Country*, which shows how the pretensions of the state-sanctioned rule of law are scotched by the racist reality of white Australia's vigilantism, *Charlie's Country* shows a subtler form of systemic violence. Here, Indigenous Australians have their right to self-determination and their right to life subjugated by a legal system that claims to act in the name of formal neutrality.[34] The film makes visible the grave injustice at the core of Australian society, which manifests at the level of a 'law of rules' that forecloses opportunities for subsistence and self-preservation for Charlie.[35] Lynne Henderson notes how an unthinking commitment to rules denigrates into authoritarianism. She writes that 'Obedience to authority itself might best be described as formal authoritarianism – it is solely concerned with identifying authoritative commands or directions and then following them'.[36] We might add to Henderson's account that, given that police make up the most visible site of the law's enforcement, legalistic, authoritarian police are also part of the oppressive structure that considers, practically speaking, that rule formalism and conceptions of justice are coterminous.[37]

Charlie's story is not so much a journey as an attempt to live under the Intervention as an oppressive state apparatus. As Jillian Kramer writes, the Howard government's justification for the measures was purportedly to restore the rule of law in the Northern Territory. According to the prime minister himself, 'Freedom and rights, especially for women and children, are little more than cruel fictions without the rule of law and some semblance of social order imposed by a legitimate authority'.[38] The irony was not lost on many; by attempting to restore the rule of law in the ostensibly lawless Indigenous communities of the Northern Territory, the Howard government's measures enabling the Intervention expressly excluded the application of other laws, including the *Racial Discrimination Act 1975*, deeming them 'special measures'. The Howard government infringed the rule of law in its efforts to implement it – it was a classic example of the hegemonic sovereign declaring the state of exception.[39] Even from the Howard government's perspective, it would seem that rule of law formalism was part of the problem, and it was necessary to depart from the formal requirement of equality in order to pursue substantive justice for the women and children of remote communities.

Further, it seems fitting that Howard – then Liberal Party prime minister – would invoke the rhetoric of early modern English philosopher Thomas Hobbes to justify the Intervention measures.[40] As Hobbes argued, in the state of nature – an imagined state with no superordinate sovereign authority to ensure order – life was 'solitary, poore [sic], nasty, brutish, and short'.[41] For Hobbes, only the near-absolute authority of the sovereign could guarantee the fundamental law of nature: the inalienable right to self-preservation. Hobbes wrote *Leviathan* during the height of the English Civil War, and we should read his work as being directed towards ensuring order at a time of extraordinary political and religious tumult. While historically many have suggested Hobbes's *Leviathan* is an apologia for tyranny and dictatorship – most notably, the Nazi jurist and philosopher Carl Schmitt[42] – more recently, scholars have considered Hobbes a kind of proto-liberal thinker, with the right to individual self-preservation sacrosanct in his vision of the state.[43] The very same rule of law on which the Howard government based its intervention denies Charlie the right to survive.

Policing the right to life

Charlie's life is disrupted by the community police on a regular basis. After the opening scene places us in the aftermath of the Intervention, the film introduces us to its protagonist, a somewhat prickly but affable elderly Aboriginal man living in a makeshift camp on the outskirts of a remote Aboriginal community. He lives alone in his ramshackle accommodation, in turns disgruntled and bored by the reality of his daily existence in the community, which lacks sufficient housing, employment opportunities and affordable access to healthy food. Charlie's first visible encounter with the law occurs as he walks down the main street of the town. Walking past the police station, he pauses, yelling in its direction in his native language, Yolngu Matha, 'You came here from far away, and brought your bastard culture, your alcohol, your food and your *ganja* [marijuana]'. The young police officer, Luke (Luke Ford), hearing the shouting, comes to the door of the police station. Charlie then yells in English to Luke, 'You white bastard!' Luke replies, 'You black bastard!'[44] and they both chuckle. We see the inherent tension embodied by the police officer as the arbiter of the law and keeper of the peace in Charlie's community. Although Luke is unaware of Charlie's dissent, made insensible through language, Charlie blames Luke and other whitefellas for the troubles his community faces – housing shortages, a lack of access to nutritious food and employment and drug and alcohol abuse. Charlie, it seems, will put on a happy face to the law, but in reality, he harbours a deep resentment for Luke's presence in his community and the police station on his land. The performatively amicable relationship characterizes Charlie's interaction with the law, always inside yet trying to escape its purview. The faith in mateship as the bedrock on which we base the myth of Australian egalitarianism and classlessness, the 'fair-go' attitude that underscores the Australian rule of law, does not apply to all Australians.

Despite his distaste for the whitefella on his land, Charlie cooperates as best he can, even assisting the officers in apprehending local *ganja* dealers. Charlie, however, appears dissatisfied. We learn that he is ill; his diet is poor after having eaten too much sugary 'white man junk food' over the years. That such food is generally easier and cheaper to get in remote Aboriginal communities than fruit or vegetables is a regrettable fact.[45] Out of boredom and a desire for something more wholesome, Charlie accompanies his friend Black Pete (Peter Djigirr) on a quest to hunt down a water buffalo. After they hunt down and kill the beast, they are stopped by a local policeman (John Brumpton), who interrogates them about the buffalo. When asked by the police officer for their firearms licences, Charlie replies in jest, 'Licence? We're not gonna drive 'em, we're gonna shoot 'em'. The policeman confiscates their guns and impounds their car – buffalo attached. Flashing to the next shot, we see the beast rotting in the fierce heat, surrounded by flies out in front of the community police station – the giant, rotting beast a potent symbol of the unintended consequences of the officer's strict legalism. Charlie's quest for food and connection to traditional ways of living are deprecated by the officer, more concerned with administering strict regulatory order in the community without reference to the socio-cultural context of the community's needs. Through the lens of Unger's and Horwitz's substantive critique, the beast comes to represent, at the grotesque, material level, the practical consequences of a formalist approach to the law.

The buffalo scene begins Charlie's journey through the Kafkaesque processes of Australian regulatory law. Learning from Luke that ignorance of law is no defence and that he needs a recreational shooting licence, Charlie returns home. In his own mind, however, Charlie is not a recreational shooter but a hunter. Determined to return to the old ways of life, we see Charlie taking time and considerable effort to craft a hunting spear. After he crafts it, however, it, too, is confiscated by police officer Luke as Charlie walks through the community. After admiring the craftsmanship of the weapon, Luke tells Charlie he will confiscate the spear because it is a dangerous weapon and thus prohibited. Charlie, bewildered by the implication he would use the weapon on a person, assures Luke that the spear is a hunting spear, not a fighting spear. Luke replies, 'You know what happened in that other community – one bloke dead and another one in hospital'. Charlie responds, exasperated, 'But you took my gun!' The confiscation of the spear, even more than the confiscation of the firearms, shows some of the difficulties in a strict application of the law of rules. It affords Luke, one of two or three police officers in the community, the discretion to determine at that moment whether Charlie's weapon offends the relevant regulation and whether he will seize the weapon. There is no room for interpretation from Luke's perspective: an Aboriginal man has a spear, a dangerous weapon, and since a dangerous weapon was involved in the death of a man in another Aboriginal community, it follows that an Aboriginal man in a different community may not carry a similar spear, despite Charlie's assertion that he crafted the spear for hunting – his sustenance and ability to live.[46]

What Luke fails to recognize is that his strict, legalistic approach to law, whether exercised by a policeman, lawyer or some other legal agent, is always one of discretion and interpretation. Actions such as the buffalo's impounding and the confiscation of the spear are hermeneutic acts – legal acts of interpretation that subscribe to a strict formalism that declines to afford viability to alternative modes of interpretation. Charlie is bewildered by the officers' interpretations – his normative understanding of the use of weapons relates not to their use against humans, but their use in obtaining sustenance. Yet in Luke's assessment, the tool – the purview of the colonial gunman – is legible only as a risk to the community. In Charlie's formulation, a weapon is a tool, affording him the ability to sustain himself in accordance with the fundamental principles of natural law – the right to self-preservation. The film shows a conflict of laws scenario: the laws of the whitefella against the ancient laws of Charlie's own country. It shows how the application of formal legal rules in administering justice and maintaining order can have unintended consequences, which we might consider unfair or unjust; the everyday realities of such consequences demean, degrade and inhibit Charlie's ability to live.

Law's administration and the upholding of the rule always come down to discretion. Whether a police officer pulls over a speeding driver, writes them a ticket, waives a fee, prosecutes an alleged crime or carries out any other act properly construed as legal, there is always room for interpretation. It is naïve and perhaps even insulting to suggest that the law is always properly construed and administered to the letter. With Charlie, however, it seems that a formal approach to maintaining order, upholding the rule of law (or law of rules, as we have been calling it) trumps all other methods deemed necessary to maintain order in the community. This is particularly jarring for the viewer to watch when what is at stake is not the endorsement of wanton destruction of the fauna of Charlie's country, but a compulsion to live and thrive on the land he still rightly considers his own.

Living outside the law

Charlie resolves to remove himself from the oppressive legal system of the community, which denies him the right to life. In leaving the community, he seeks a traditional life out in the bush – a life away from the strictures of whitefella laws and whitefella junk food.[47] In returning to country, he removes himself from the community, a legal universe imposed on his people through colonial dispossession, and also removes himself from the purview of the settler state's rule of law, returning to the rule of his country. Although initially successful, Charlie's wish to return to country nearly kills him. Caught between an unwillingness to continue to live in a (legal) community that is killing him, made more difficult through legal imposition, and unable to live the idealized old life of his ancestors, Charlie resigns himself to a new life among a group of Indigenous people in a Darwin public park, whom he meets after he checks himself out of hospital. By now, Charlie has lost all desire to live – indeed, he is scarcely living at all. The liminality of Charlie's new existence precipitates the film's violent climactic moment: as Luke and another police officer invade Charlie's new home in the park, Charlie turns violent, smashing the police car with a shovel. After being savagely beaten by his former 'friend' Luke – 'You know, you can't just sit on the grass all day and call it the old ways. These times have changed' – Charlie responds, 'No they haven't'. There is a bitter irony here. Charlie is right that the law's stubborn refusal to allow Aboriginal people to live persists; however, he is wrong that an Indigenous life can exist outside the immanent whitefella law under a rule of law formalism communicated by acts of physical and symbolic violence. It is little wonder that Charlie erupts with violence. His *passage à l'acte* is another form of vigilantism – like Sam's – an illegal act necessary for his right to life and self-preservation.

At his trial, Charlie speaks to the magistrate in his native language, Yolngu Matha, before translating his words into English: 'I was living in my home nice and peacefully, and then the police came and threw me out'. Charlie is no longer the young Aboriginal man who danced for the Queen of England at the commemoration of the Sydney Opera House many years earlier: he now plays the role of convicted man under territory laws, under the ostensibly just and due procedure of '*The Queen v Charlie*'. The perturbed magistrate sentences Charlie to prison. Like the spear, the language of *Charlie's Country* is not intelligible to the law. We see here how a formal and legalistic method of adjudication papers over and legitimates oppressive social forces.[48] As Henderson writes, 'law and legality may be sources of authority that are always at risk of becoming authoritarian in the substantive sense, because law is interconnected with state and private forms of power'.[49] In Henderson's account, this inherent tendency within the law towards preservation of power inequalities is compounded by legalistic judges.[50] Therefore, on Henderson's account, while law and legality purport to remain ideologically neutral, their real effects can be substantively authoritarian or unjust.

Yet, somehow, life in prison is more healthful and replenishing than that outside. Charlie is fed a bland but nourishing diet, restoring him to health. He does not have the agency or the ability to sustain himself outside prison without indulging in food and other activities deleterious to his health, yet in prison, the film shows him regaining his health before he returns to his remote community on release. The law refuses to allow Charlie to live (outside prison), while refusing to let him die (within its confines). Unlike *Sweet Country*, where rule formalism is subordinated by white society's deep superiority over its Aboriginal workers, *Charlie's Country* shows a contemporary Australia where the police officer smiles and pretends to be mates with legal subjects. The law, however, does not apply to Charlie; he exists under a legal system that, on its face, is *formally* just, but proves in turns to be both unsustainable and unfair.

Conclusion

The two films show us two distinct issues with a formalist approach to the rule of law. Rule formalism is a ruse: it cloaks inequity in the shroud of neutrality, and it abrogates our responsibility to address why the law seems to be working better for some Australians than for others. We cannot cleave the two from one another; they are related, and they spring forth from the same ideological underpinning. First, the claimed neutrality of positive laws and their administration means very little when superseded by vigilantism or populist bigotry. Second, the negative obligations of formalist legal approaches fail to consider the relevance and legitimacy of culturally diverse practices and thus discriminate against groups while failing to recognize the fact. Lastly, we think it is important to notice that these films do not show us two different and discrete legal systems; rather, they show the workings of Australian law and the real effects of its flawed logic – the logic of the presumed justice afforded by formal conceptions of the rule of law.

Notes

1 Krygier (1990), pp 633, 641.
2 Reynolds (2001).

3 Thompson (1975), p 266.
4 See, for example, 'The Federal Platform of the Liberal Party of Australia' (2002), https://cdn.liberal.org.au/pdf/FederalPlatform.pdf (listing the 'rule of law' as one of the core beliefs of the Australian Liberal Party); 'Australian Labor Party National Platform' (2018), www.alp.org.au/media/1539/2018_alp_national_platform_constitution.pdf (15 mentions of the 'rule of law').
5 See Craig (1997); Waldron (2002); and, for a third category, Waldron (2011).
6 Raz (1979), p 211.
7 See Bingham (2010), Ch 7 (advancing a human rights–orientated conception of the rule of law); Epstein (2011) (advancing a private property–orientated account of the rule of law).
8 A clear illustration of Australia's commitment to a formal conception of the rule of law can be found in the mission statement of the Attorney-General's Department. That department states its role as ensuring that 'laws are clear, predictable and accessible . . . publicly made . . . [and] publicly [efficiently and independently] adjudicated'. See Australian Government, Attorney-General's Department, 'Rule of Law', www.ag.gov.au/About/Pages/Ruleoflaw.aspx.
9 Dixon (1965), p 247.
10 See Bradshaw (2017).
11 Gough Whitlam, quoted in Ward (2016).
12 It has recently been revealed that one photographer, Rob Wesley-Smith, did capture the original gesture: see Dias (2016).
13 See Vincent (2017). The unfulfilled promises of land rights were perhaps best expressed by Mick Dodson in 2012: 'It is now apparent that many of our aspirations and expectations about the promise of native title were unrealistic and that our hopes have been largely dashed'. Dodson (2012), p xvii.
14 That *Sweet Country* asserts a claim to historical accuracy is itself a political statement in the context of Australia's 'history wars' about the true extent of colonial violence against Indigenous people. Of course, Australian cinema – particularly *Rabbit-Proof Fence* – has been a central site of this historiographical conflict. See Collins and Davis (2004), pp 135–7.
15 We are not the first people to notice the similarities between the colonial images of manacled Indigenous people and modern images of restrained Indigenous children in detention. See Bogle (2016).
16 Another visual reference to the shackled Aboriginal man is David Gulpilil's character in *The Tracker*: de Heer (2002).
17 Anthony (2007).
18 See Jalata (2013), p 8.
19 Editorial, *New Matilda* (2015).
20 For an account of the secular and religious values of equality, see Kukathas (2003), p 61. For a secular account of equality before the law written in 431 BCE, see Thucydides (1914), p 121 ('If we look to the laws, they afford equal justice to all').
21 *Leeth v The Commonwealth* (1992), 487 (Deane and Toohey JJ). The Australian Constitution's protection of equality is, however, doubtful in light of the decision in *Kruger v Commonwealth* (*Stolen Generations Case*) (1997). An equal protection clause modeled on the 14th Amendment to the US Constitution was drafted and proposed in Australia but rejected partially out of a fear that it would prevent the passage of racially discriminatory laws. See La Nauze (1972), pp 230–2.
22 See Wheeler (2018), pp 928–51.
23 Raz famously called this the 'negative value' of the rule of law. See Raz (1979), p 224.
24 Pierre Bourdieu (1987), p 817 calls the invisibility by which the oppressed are unable to recognize that which is precisely anathema to their own interests a 'miscognition'.

He attributes the miscognition to the division of juridical labour, which has the effect of foreclosing visibility to the disadvantaged in society.

25 Unger (1976), pp 176–81, 192–223.
26 See Bourdieu (1987); Althusser (2012).
27 Horwitz (1977), p 566.
28 Thornton (2018).
29 For a discussion of the affective power of character and narrative engagement, see Plantinga (2013), pp 104–7.
30 Herche (2017), p 228.
31 We note that we do not intend to posit a solution to the fraught and complex nature of Indigenous self-determination or invoke an instrumental approach to law as facilitative of such. Instead, we align ourselves with a critique of a formal approach to the rule of law that we think *Charlie's Country* does an exemplary job of showing to the viewer.
32 The *Northern Territory National Emergency Response Act 2007* (Cth) ('NTER Act') was superseded by the Gillard government's 'Stronger Future Policies', which included the *Stronger Futures in the Northern Territory Act 2012* (Cth), retaining many of the measures of the NTER Act.
33 Herche (2017), p 235.
34 The right to self-determination for Indigenous peoples is enshrined in international law via the United Nations Declaration on the Rights of Indigenous Peoples, ratified by the Rudd government on 3 April 2009. For a stimulating interpretation of *Charlie's Country* through the context of Indigenous self-determination, see Herche (2017).
35 It is beyond the scope of this chapter to discuss the Intervention at length; however, we should note that the events continue to be a controversial topic in Australian politics and law. Some, such as Peter Sutton, have argued that the Intervention was a necessary step to ensure the wellbeing of Indigenous Australians, while numerous others, including Larissa Behrendt, have argued that the Intervention was driven by ulterior motives, such as the reclamation of land, and illegal and regrettable backward steps in Aboriginal Australians' journey toward self-determination. The Intervention was not, however, condemned unanimously by the Indigenous community. Shortly after its implementation, Indigenous academics Marcia Langton and Noel Pearson expressed some qualified support: Langton (2008); Pearson (2007). In a 2014 interview, de Heer was asked whether *Charlie's Country* tried to show the Intervention as a good thing. He responded: 'The Intervention is a complex thing. It isn't an unalloyed good thing or bad thing. . . . The Intervention is not entirely bad, there are some good things in it, but overall, it does far more harm than it does good, because its patronizing, it doesn't allow independence, it doesn't allow development'. See O'Connor (2015); Behrendt (2018).
36 Henderson (1991), p 390.
37 See Simon (2002), p 39 ('the identification with the rule of law . . . [is seen by some] as the defining aspect of the police and a way to reconcile their fundamentally authoritarian character with the democratic society they were policing').
38 Quoted in Kramer, p 127.
39 See Agamben (2005), pp 1ff.
40 See Kramer (2015), pp 136–42.
41 Hobbes (1651), p 62.
42 See, for instance, Schmitt's discussion of the cardinal importance of the relation of protection to obedience in Hobbes's philosophy: Schmitt (1996), p 72.
43 Gaus, Courtland and Schmidtz (2018).
44 As noted earlier, the 'black bastard' epithet is used also in *Sweet Country*. Although the naïve Luke seemingly thinks of such pejoratives as anachronistic, the viewer will later see how such performative gestures of mateship belie a residual racial violence lying below the surface.

45 Bortolin (2018); Browne, Laurence and Thorpe (2009).
46 On Australia's colonial project and its relation to Indigenous subsistence, see Wolfe (2016), p 37.
47 In this escape to the bush from the law, the film can be seen to reference another film from the Arnhem Land canon, *Yolngu Boy* (2001), which also illustrates the white legal system's interruption and destruction of traditional Aboriginal ways of life.
48 For a detailed and devastating account of this process in Singapore, see Rajah (2012).
49 Henderson (1991), p 398.
50 Henderson (1991), p 383.

References

Secondary literature

Giorgio Agamben (2005) *State of Exception*, Kevin Attell (trans), University of Chicago Press.

Louise Althusser (2012) 'Ideology and Ideological State Apparatuses (Notes Towards an Investigation)', in Slavoj Žižek (ed.), *Mapping Ideology*, Verso.

Thalia Anthony (2007) 'Unmapped Territory: Wage Compensation for Indigenous Cattle Station Workers' 11 *Australian Indigenous Law Review* 4.

Larissa Behrendt (2018) 'Closing the Gap in Our Knowledge' 97 *Australian Educator* 20.

Tom Bingham (2010) *The Rule of Law*, Allen Lane.

Ariel Bogle (2016) 'How Images Like #DonDaleKids Let Us "Perform" Our Shock and Outrage', *Mashable*, 28 July, http://mashable.com/2016/07/28/don-dale-viral-image.

Natalia Bortolin (2018) 'Food Provision Among Food Relief Agencies in Rural Australia, and Perceived Barriers and Enablers to Provide Healthy Food' 26 *Australian Journal of Rural Health* 86.

Pierre Bourdieu (1987) 'The Force of Law: Toward a Sociology of the Juridical Field' 38 *The Hastings Law Journal* 817.

Peter Bradshaw (2017) 'Brutal Australian Western Soars with Biblical Starkness', *The Guardian*, 16 September, www.theguardian.com/film/2017/sep/15/sweet-country-review-brutal-australian-western-tiff.

Jennifer Browne, Sharon Laurence and Sharon Thorpe (2009) *Acting on Food Insecurity in Urban Aboriginal and Torres Strait Islander Communities*, https://pdfs.semanticscholar.org/88fa/cb39cd108e471de0b76e673af92190d695b0.pdf.

Kukathas Chandran (2003) 'Ethical Pluralism from a Classical Liberal Perspective', in Richard Madsen and Tracy B. Strong (eds), *The Many Pacqiuo and the One: Religious and Secular Perspectives on Ethical Pluralism in the Modern World*, Princeton University Press.

Felicity Collins and Therese Davis (2004) *Australian Cinema After Mabo*, Cambridge University Press.

Paul P. Craig (1997) 'Formal and Substantive Conceptions of the Rule of Law: An Analytical Framework' *Public Law* 467.

Avani Dias (2016) 'Activist Captured "Original" 1975 Photo of Whitlam Pouring Sand into Lingiari's Hand', *ABC News*, 3 September, www.abc.net.au/news/2016-09-03/activist-took-original-gough-whitlam-vincent-lingiari-sand-photo/7805880.

Owen Dixon (1965) *Jesting Pilate and Other Papers and Addresses*, Law Book Co.

Mick Dodson (2012) 'Introduction – The Limits of Change', in T. Bauman and L. Glick (eds), *The Limits of Change: Mabo and Native Title 20 Years On*, AIATSIS.
Richard Epstein (2011) *Design for Liberty: Private Property, Public Administration, and the Rule of Law*, Harvard University Press.
Gerald Gaus, Shane D. Courtland and David Schmidtz (2018) 'Liberalism', in Edward N. Zalta (ed.), *The Stanford Encyclopedia of Philosophy*, https://plato.stanford.edu/archives/spr2018/entries/liberalism.
Lynne Henderson (1991) 'Authoritarianism and the Rule of Law' 66 *Indiana Law Journal* 379.
Victoria Herche (2017) 'Reassessing Indigenous Self-Determination in Rolf de Heer's *Charlie's Country*', in Elisabeth Baehr and Barbara Schmidt-Haberkamp (eds), *'And There'll Be NO Dancing': Perspectives on Policies Impacting Indigenous Australians Since 2007*, Cambridge Scholars.
Thomas Hobbes (1651) *Leviathan; or the Matter, Form, and Power of a Common-Wealth, Ecclesiastical and Civil*, printed for Andrew Crooke.
Morton J. Horwitz (1977) 'The Rule of Law: An Unqualified Human Good?' 86 *Yale Law Journal* 561.
Asafa Jalata (2013) 'The Impact of English Colonial Terrorism and Genocide on Indigenous/Black Australians' *SAGE Open* 1.
Jillian Kramer (2015) '"Legitimating Fictions': The Rule of Law, the Northern Territory Intervention and the War on Terror' 19 *Law, Text, Culture* 127.
Martin Krygier (1990) 'Marxism and the Rule of Law: Reflections After the Collapse of Communism' 15 *Law and Social Inquiry* 633.
John A. La Nauze (1972) *The Making of the Australian Constitution*, Melbourne University Press.
Marcia Langton (2008) 'Trapped in the Aboriginal reality show', *ABC News*, 7 February, http://www.abc.net.au/news/2008-02-08/trapped-in-the-aboriginal-reality-show/1036918.
Clint O'Connor (2015) 'Rolf de Heer Talks About *Charlie's Country*: Director at Capitol Theatre Monday Night', www.cleveland.com/moviebuff/2015/06/rolf_de_heer_talks_about_charl.html.
Noel Pearson (2007) 'Pearson fears for Indigenous Parents' Freedom', June 22, http://www.abc.net.au/news/stories/2007/06/22/1959706.htm?section=Australia.
Carl Plantinga (2013) 'The Affective Power of Movies', in Arthur P. Schimamura (ed.), *Psychocinematics: Exploring Cognition at the Movies*, Oxford University Press.
Jothie Rajah (2012) *Authoritarian Rule of Law: Legislation, Discourse and Legitimacy in Singapore*, Cambridge University Press.
Joseph Raz (1979) *The Authority of Law: Essays on Law and Morality*, Oxford University Press.
Henry Reynolds (2001) *An Indelible Stain? The Question of Genocide in Australia's History*, Penguin.
Carl Schmitt (1996) *The Leviathan in the State Theory of Thomas Hobbes: Meaning and Failure of a Political Symbol*, George Schwab and Erna Hilfstein (trans), Greenwood Press.
Jonathan Simon (2002) 'Speaking Truth and Power' 36 *Law & Society Review* 37.
E.P. Thompson (1975) *Whigs and Hunters: The Origin of the Black Act*, Pantheon Books.
Thucydides (1914) *History of the Peloponnesian War*, Richard Crawley (trans), J.M. Dent.
Roberto Unger (1976) *Law in Modern Society*, Simon and Schuster.

Eve Vincent (2017) *Against Native Title*, Aboriginal Studies Press.
Jeremy Waldron (2002) 'Is the Rule of Law an Essentially Contested Concept (in Florida)?' 21 *Law and Philosophy* 137.
——— (2011) 'The Rule of Law and the Importance of Procedure', in James Fleming (ed.), *Getting to the Rule of Law*, NYU Press.
Charlie Warde (2016) *A Handful of Sand: The Gurindji Struggle, After the Walk-Off*, Monash University Publishing.
Fiona Wheeler (2018) 'Due Process', in Cheryl Saunders and Adrian Stone (eds), *The Oxford Handbook of the Australian Constitution*, Oxford University Press.
Patrick Wolfe (2016) *Traces of History: Elementary Structures of Race*, Verso.

Primary legal sources

Kruger v Commonwealth (Stolen Generations Case) (1997) 190 CLR 1.
Leeth v The Commonwealth (1992) 174 CLR 455.
Northern Territory National Emergency Response Act 2007 (Cth).
Racial Discrimination Act 1975 (Cth).

Films

Rolf de Heer (2002) *The Tracker*, Vertigo Productions.
——— (2013) *Charlie's Country*, Bula'bula Arts and Vertigo Productions.
Warwick Thornton (2009) *Samson and Delilah*, Scarlett Pictures and CAAMA Productions.
——— (2018) *Sweet Country*, Bunya Productions and Sweet Country Films.

Chapter 4

Taking a lens to the chase in Australian settler state colonialism

Thalia Anthony and Kieran Tranter

Introduction

The chase is a staple for the representations of law and justice in film and television. The chase, with its reversible codings of good/bad, chaser/chasee and justice/injustice, intermixed with the visceral excitement of action and suspense, is a compelling frame for storytellers and viewers. There is a nomos to the chase. The story scaffolding either has the audience hoping that the 'good' chasee escapes the 'bad' chaser or that the 'bad' chasee is apprehended or eliminated by the 'good' chaser. Justice is done – or not done – and law and order are maintained or usurped.

Yet there is also a counter-nomos that invokes the experiences of the chased and their escape from the legal shackles imposed on the roads and beyond. This forces us to consider the laws that they are seeking to escape, which for many young First Nations males includes the lived experience of settler colonial policing. Criminologist Mark Halsey, who conducted in-depth interviews with young offenders involved in high-speed police pursuits, states that it is

> necessary to reach past the stereotype [of the high-speed police chase] toward a more nuanced conversation about how and why these events occur. Doing this means paying something more than lip service to the narratives of those arrested and convicted of such crimes.[1]

Policing conducted through the chase is experienced through the formal execution of law and informal legal practices. In settler colonies, it is exhibited through the agency of the police and the settler alike – their roles are blurred and indistinct as they are both complicit in racial violence and the colonial project. Their use of the motor vehicle as a weapon in the chase is both aspirational and functional: it exhibits and asserts power with violent ends. The motion of the chase is a moment in which the First Nations chasee endeavours to escape the law *and* confront it, refusing and resisting its reach while also being subject to its pattern of control. At times, this is enacted on foot, but mostly the chasee is in a vehicle – a place of sociality for First Nations people who have appropriated the white automobile as a means of subverting settler law.[2]

Through the lens of the First Nations chase, the chase acquires a justice frame that speaks to the injustice towards First Nations people. This is most telling in the characters of Gary in *Backroads* and Molly, Daisy and Gracie in *Rabbit-Proof Fence*. Settler colonialism, cultural conflicts and negotiation are narrated through the structure of the chase. Australian chases reflect the imposition of, and resistance to, colonial sovereignty and competing rights of occupation and mobility. The First Nations chasee threatens the legitimacy of the colonial settler state through embodying pre-existing sovereign claims to land. The reality of the chase, as illustrated in a number of recent case studies discussed towards the end of this chapter, is a mechanism for police and settlers to drive down First Nations people – especially young people – and remove them from their land. These cases embody the same violent intent and fatal consequences that have been depicted in Australian film over the past 60 years.

Recorded by Australian lenses, chases of First Nations young people show a white sovereign order needing to perform – to defend its order – a brutal repression of First Nations peoples and cultures. We contend in this chapter that these chases involve a movement across contested country that challenge settler claims to space. These chases are profoundly visual in the traversing of remote and urban First Nations Country, which has the effect of centring Indigenous place and unsettling the settler colonial order. It often juxtaposes First Nations knowledge of Country with settler ignorance. In most representations, colonial settler law and order is violently affirmed yet its justice is suspended.

This chapter examines how justice is particularized in Australian chases of First Nations people. The chase is variously the enactment of sovereignty claiming by occupiers in their attempts to eliminate the 'Other',[3] and resistance and refusal by First Nations people. The chapter begins by establishing the basic logic of the chase involving occupiers and First Nations people as a narrational device for settler colonialism and its resistance. The chasee and chasers are reversible markers for this narrative, which hinges on the power play between occupier and First Nations person.

The second section explores how Australian film and documentary makers have deployed the chase in narratives centring on colonialism and cross-cultural conflict and negotiation. From Charles Chauvel's influential *Jedda* (1955) through to *The Chant of Jimmie Blacksmith* (1978), *Backroads* (1977) and *Rabbit-Proof Fence* (2002), a superficial reading would be that they depict righteous agents of the settler state pursuing disobedient First Nations people. However, they also tell the story of the righteousness of First Nations to be free from colonial constraints and to be themselves by returning to their lands, families, skin relationships and ceremonies – although this is accompanied by degrees of stereotyping on the part of directors. These films reflect the reality of the racialized chase: the incensed and angry agent of the settler state in pursuit of First Nations persons – often children – who are usually caught by the state, through or resulting in violence. Often the chasee is seeking to escape the imposed settler colonial order and its burdens and return to a place of cultural identity – even if that is within the free movement of their car or bicycle.

There is a repeated telos to the Australian chase that ends in the death of the First Nations young person – which is in keeping with projections of a 'doomed' Aboriginal race.[4] First Nations people who succumb to assimilation by surrendering to the chase are usually 'saved', but more often those resisting its shackles and pursuits are simply treated as collateral damage in the colonial project. This chapter identifies the repetition and transmission of these elements of the Australian chase from the big screen to the many screens hosting contemporary media. It examines the representations of three particular chases that ended in the death of First Nations children: TJ Hickey in Redfern, Sydney in 2004; Elijah Doughty in Kalgoorlie-Boulder in 2016; and Chris Drage and Trisjack Simpson in the Swan River in Perth in 2018.

The elements of the Australian chase are enlivened in old and new media content. The lens has the effect of reinforcing the intentions of white chasers in settling the land against the errant (and itinerant) First Nations person who is choosing to be free on Country. While there are subversive messages, the films have the effect of reinforcing the racial narrative – the in-control occupier seeking to tame the 'native'. Their narratives reverberate in the legal texts. Court narratives reinstate the superficial Manichean divide between good (white settler) chaser and bad (First Nations) chasee to impugn white people responsible for killing First Nations children in the process of a chase – or, in our configuration, using their vehicles as weapons.[5]

The nomos of the chase

The chase is a perennial and universal narrational structure for human expression. It features in Greek mythology with the Goddess of the Chase (or Hunt), the tale of Moses' Israelites fleeing Pharaoh's chariots in Exodus from Egypt and the Star Dreaming story of the Seven Sisters from Central Australia. Prosaically, the chase narrative is simple: it involves three elements: a chaser, a chasee and movement across space and time. However, the meaning that can be wrought from a chase narrative is significant. For instance, the Greek Goddess of the Chase, Artemis, was a huntress armed with a golden bow and arrow who chased wild animals in the forest. She rejoiced in the chase. She brought sudden death with her arrow, including in pursuit of justice and purity. Orion was a victim of her chase, having met a violent death when he sought to take the virtue of this virgin goddess.[6]

The Star Dreaming story of the Seven Sisters relates to the star cluster known as Pleiades. In Central Australia it appears to launch from the Earth, then travels low on the horizon before setting quickly; it also appears to be pursued by a singular large star in Orion's belt. For the Warlpiri people, this is the story of the seven Napaljarri sisters who are being pursued by Jukurra-jukurra, a lawbreaker who desires to take one of the sisters as his wife. However, the Napaljarri sisters and Jukurra-jukurra belong to different skin groups, so the sisters flee from Jukurra-jukurra, who wants to break the law that forbids relations between the skin groups. Every night they take to the sky, with their pursuer behind them.[7]

The strength of this simple story – exquisitely represented in the work of Warlpiri artist Alma Nungarrayi Granites[8] – lies in its capacity to convey complex meaning pertaining to Warlpiri laws and relationships. The astrological phenomenon becomes nomos,[9] a telling of the law of human relations and correct conduct. The chase frames a sense of justice and just conduct, of right and wrong, of appropriate and taboo behaviours.

In the filmic culture of the Global North, the chase is intrinsic to the American 'Western' genre – with armed cowboys on horseback conquering the wild desert landscape, the 'Indians' and outlaws.[10] It culminates in a shootout where the righteous prevail. A chase is a frequent feature of the Western,[11] in which the reversibility of the chase as nomos contrasts with the assigned, unalterable roles of ancient stories: the pursuit against the wild and unvirtuous by chaser Artemis or the fleeing from the lawbreaker of the Seven Sisters as chasees. In the Western, either the good sheriff can be in pursuit of the bad outlaw; or the good outlaw can be pursued by the corrupt, degenerative sheriff; or the innocent ranchers are on the run from bad outlaws.[12] On rare occasions, the Western contends with settler colonial morality in the pursuit: a white settler protagonist bravely fleeing vengeful First Nations people[13] or in search of the 'Indian'.[14] Although the coding of the chaser and chasee is reversible, it hinges on the same 'colonial canon asserting white supremacy and Indigenous inferiority'.[15] The 'Indians' are the wild and dangerous 'other'.[16] This whitewashes the experience of colonialism for North American First Nations people, including their legitimate resistance to invasion and displacement.

The narrative structure of the Western is retold in the industrial, action movie guise of the car chase, which gained traction in the 1970s,[17] following the car chase sequence in *Bullitt* (1968).[18] This reduced the chase to its pure structure: the adrenalin of the chase encompassed the entire film. The visceral experience of the chase carries no explicit morality. The audience is driven along by the action: whether the chasee evades, is apprehended by or is eliminated by the chaser. It is usually only in the explosive climax that the nomos of the chase is reasserted and the hero protagonist – whether chasee or chaser – prevails. In retrospect, the chase is a disjunction of the universe, where right or wrong, good or bad is in suspension until it is resolved. This is clearly demonstrated in the immateriality of damage caused to innocent bystanders during the chase by both protagonist and villain. The action movie car chase leaves devastation in its wake – broken and destroyed vehicles and property and, if it were a reality, death and injury to many. Yet this violence can be trivialized, rendered humorous through mean parodies (the overweight man having to run clumsily to avoid being run over by the chasing vehicles). It can also be reversible: the good police officer/Secret Service agent/criminal could be the chasee or the chaser of a bad police officer/Secret Service agent/criminal.

In the Western and in the car-focused action movie, there is a telos to the chase, which conveys a just end: the triumph of right/good over wrong/evil. Unlike the repetition and irresolution of the Star Dreaming story of the Seven Sisters, in modern films the chase ends, and in that ending, the nomos of the narrative is reaffirmed. This reflects a desire in the Global North for individual and total resolution, arguably in contrast to Indigenous notions of resolution based on circular and holistic change.[19] The mission of the chase is to reach this finality at any cost. Accordingly, the chaser and chasee proceed on a path of invincibility and inevitability. Especially in their vehicle, they are undeterred by obstacles. This is no different in Australian films involving First Nations chasees (whether in Western or action car-chase tropes); there is also an unswerving pursuit of the chaser (police officer, settler, 'Aboriginal protector'), irrespective of the human cost of the pursuit. This is a metaphor for the colonizers' drive to settle, leaving First Nations people in their trail of terror. The settler colonial project is intent on completing its occupation yet constantly thwarted by the continued existence and expression of First Nations people and their lawful claims to Country.

The chase through Australian film lenses

The chase in Australian films became particularized to the settler colonial context from the 1950s. Like the chase captured by the lens in the Western or action car-chase movies, Australian films pertaining to the pursuit of First Nations escapees involve the suspension of the law in favour of settler sovereignty. This reflects the colonial truism articulated by pastoralist Gordon Buchanan in relation to occupying the Australian interior in the 1880s: 'Every [white] man was his own police man'.[20] He went on to state that 'the letter of the law was often ignored in favour of summary justice', and the settlers became skilled in 'savage reprisal' due to the impracticality of imprisonment.[21] The chase in Australian film is therefore a microcosm of First Nations people's experience of settler colonialism and their subjection to the 'zone of exception', where they are stripped of legal rights, protection and identity.[22]

These formulaic Australian films have the righteous agents of the settler state chasing after 'wrongful' First Nations people. While they may be characterized as 'subversive' by seeking to highlight settler colonial injustices,[23] they nonetheless reinforce stereotypes of First Nations people as brutal and lawless,[24] thus replicating national myths about the 'other'. Through this, the elements of the Australian chase become clear. The Australian chase is racially coded: it is always the agents of the settler state who are in pursuit, and often the pursued is a First Nations child. The chase involves a movement across contested country and often a juxtaposition of First Nations knowledge of Country with settler state ignorance. Finally, there is an explicit problematizing of justice. The law and order of the settler state is violently affirmed yet its legal protections are suspended. The usual telos to the Australian chase is the death of the First Nations young person. If they survive this settler colonial 'fate', they are otherwise captured and restrained in its nomos.

One of the key films that marked the emergence of the modern Australian film and film industry was Charles Chauvel's *Jedda* (1955).[25] *Jedda* is famous for being Australia's first colour feature film, with the searing red ochre of Northern Territory landscapes – which was a key consideration for choice of site locations[26] that included Coolibah Station, Standley Chasm, Ormiston Gorge and the Mary River – and for casting two First Nations actors, Rosalie Kunoth-Monks (Ngarla Kunoth) as the titular Jedda and Robert Tudawali (Bobby Wilson) as Marbuck in the lead roles. The genre of the film is difficult to characterize. Colin Johnstone has suggested that it is a strange hybrid – with motifs and tropes from Western and jungle adventure films overlaid with what he regards a Chauvel's 'ideological' vision of both First Nations and white settler authenticity.[27] The parochial and 'complex' meanings in *Jedda* transcend the one-dimensional adventurism of Westerns and jungle narratives.[28]

The plot follows Jedda, an Arrernte baby who is held 'captive' into her teenage years by white station owners, especially the Mistress.[29] Despite her pleas, Jedda is forbidden from engaging with her Arrernte people and their cultural practices. She comes into contact with Marbuck,[30] who ultimately kidnaps Jedda and takes her back to his Country. His people condemn him, both for desiring Jedda – who is not of the right skin group – and for his actions in taking her. He then flees with Jedda to taboo land where the couple are disturbed by the condemnation of his people and followed by the station owner, stockmen and Jedda's love interest, Joe (the embodiment of successful assimilation[31] of mixed parentage),[32] a successful head stockman played by English actor Paul Reynall, who is 'blackfaced' to appear Aboriginal. The film ends with a deranged Marbuck dragging Jedda to both their deaths over a cliff.

The chase and law are tightly associated in the film and instantiated at various junctures. In the chase of Marbuck and Jedda, they are chased off country by Marbuck's people for Marbuck's unlawful taking of a young woman contrary to skin and marriage laws. They are also chased for Marbuck taking Jedda in breach of the white 'law' – the unofficial 'settler' law of taking a First Nations woman out of the care of white people (which is primarily pursued by the settler's First Nations protégé Joe) and the official state law when a police officer announces that they are chasing Marbuck for the murder of another First Nations woman. The film's culmination in Jedda's and Marbuck's death has been subject to conflicting readings:[33] as the problematization of assimilation policies of the settler state[34] and also as an affirmation of the 'dying pillow'.[35] Barnett suggests that the death of the two leading figures – 'both of whom have fallen short of Hasluck's assimilationist expectations' – represents the impermanent lives of First Nations deviants. Marbuck is deviating from his law *and* settler law, while Jedda is deviating from white station norms in seeking to engage with her Arrernte law.[36] The chase is a means to put them back into the fold: Marbuck chased by his community to subject him to his customary law and Jedda chased to put her back into the confines of colonial society. Yet the chase, like assimilation, fails horribly. Joe, the exemplar of assimilation and the ultimate chaser, is rendered ineffective and broken. He does not retrieve Jedda, he does not bring Marbuck back to settler state justice and he struggles in pursuit, ignorant of the First Nations law of the Country he is traversing.[37]

The death of the First Nations protagonist is also the resolution in Fred Schepisi's *The Chant of Jimmie Blacksmith* (1978).[38] Based on the 1972 novel by Thomas Keneally,[39] which drew upon the lives and deaths of Jimmie and Joe Governor,[40] the film concerns the murders of four white women and their aftermath. Unlike *Jedda*, which was set in the broadcast contemporary period of the 1950s, *The Chant of Jimmie Blacksmith* is historical, looking back to the turn of the 20th century in New South Wales and the eve of the Australian Federation. Jimmie (Tom E. Lewis), the child of a First Nations mother and white father has – like Jedda – been raised by a white family. He is discriminated against when looking for work and, when he does find work, he is short-changed and refused a reference by his employer, partly because he has been joined by his brother Mort (Freddy Reynolds) and uncle Tabidgi (Steve Dodd).

Eventually, Jimmie and his extended family find employment with the Newbys, who also under-pay him. On the Newbys' property, Jimmie is joined by his very pregnant white girlfriend Gilda Marshall (Angela Punch McGregor). In response to the Newby women trying to separate Jimmie and his now-wife Gilda, Jimmie and his uncle plan to threaten the women with axes. This goes wrong, and the women are axed to death. Up to the point of the murders, the emphasis is on racialized prejudices and violence against Jimmie and his First Nations people.[41] The murders come suddenly, arguably to denote the hot-blooded, innately savage native, who is prone to unleashing violence against feminine colonial women and civility without warning.[42] The second half of the film is the chase, with the agents of the settler state – Newby (Don Crosby) and the hangman – in pursuit of Jimmie, Mort and Tabidgi. More death and violence ensues, and at one point Jimmie, previously a subdued man, declares war – although, without deliberate execution, this bold statement falls flat.

The chase elements of *The Chant of Jimmie Blacksmith* are less cinematic than those of *Jedda*. There is a visual sense of Jimmie's skills as a bushman in outwitting the chasers and in performing 'bush medicine' on his injuries, but he is not shown to be 'at home' in the bush.[43] Indeed, Jimmie 'shows an embarrassed hostility towards . . . his mother's people'.[44] From the chase, the law and legal process of the settler state prevail: Jimmie is wounded, captured and executed by hanging. However, its 'justice' does not extend to First Nations victims, namely the young First Nations man who is raped and murdered in custody by one of Jimmie's early (police) employers, Farrell (Ray Barrett). Farrell's horrific crimes, including his unprovoked beating of First Nations people (with Jimmie's silent complicity) early in the movie, go unpunished. Any sense of justice is utterly absent from the chase. There is just a revolting sense of injustice.[45]

Contrary to a reading of Jimmie's homicidal rampage, and the film more generally, as a racist narrative about First Nations men,[46] First Nations author Tony Birch argues that the violence represents the 'problem' of the assimilated First Nations person. He remarks that 'Jimmie is the spectre that haunts both colonial society and the new Australia, for he is of their own making'.[47] Jimmie has been the witness, victim and perpetrator of grotesque, racialized and, as Eualeyai/Kamillaroi woman and professor Larissa Behrendt emphasizes,[48] gendered violence. Equally compelling for Birch is the violence in the state's response to Jimmie and his relatives, which demonstrates that 'Australia was born (at the time of Federation) with original sin at its core, and the violence of the colonial parent was carried into the twentieth century by the child-nation'.[49] While the legal pursuit proceeds unabated against the First Nations deviants, so does the racial violence of the settler state.

The small-budget film *Backroads* (1977)[50] was directed by Phillip Noyce with considerable input from Gumbainggir activist and actor Gary Foley.[51] This film focuses on the racial dynamic between First Nations and white Australia. This is personified in the dialogue and interactions between Gary, a First Nations outlaw and radical who handles a gun in the car and has been described as a modern version of Marbuck and Jimmie Blacksmith,[52] and Jack (Bill Hunter), a white outlaw and redneck. This road movie depicts a 'classic cops and robbers'[53] car chase and begins when Jack and Gary steal a car. While Gary does not kill anyone, his kinsman 'Uncle' Joe (Zac Martin) kills the owner of the second car they steal in an unexpected fashion. They drive through the 'backroads' of contemporary 1970s New South Wales discussing issues of race and politics. At the outset of the film, Gary is shown as constantly running from 'the cops'. Jack, equally an outlaw, is not in fear of the police, which is evident from his first encounter with police who question him about unlawful parking (Jack blames the parking on 'that bloody Abo' – Gary – who is in the passenger seat, and the police accept this stock story), then later when he waves at a police car to put them off their chase (which it does). The fatal chase is when Gary is hunted down by the police and 'shot like an animal' when attempting another escape.[54] Jack, with Joe, is spared, merely facing arrest. At one point, Essie Coffey sings a famous Aboriginal country music song that speaks to the relentless chase:

> People in town they just runnin' us down and they gave us a big bad name so we drink and we fight but it's quite alright because the others is all the same.[55]

A different yet equally outrageous sense of injustice and racial violence emerges from *Rabbit-Proof Fence* (2002).[56] This is another film directed by Phillip Noyce, which depicts the story of First Nations forced child removal as well as a heroic escape from the mission and back to Country and family. It is based on Doris Pilkington's book *Follow the Rabbit-Proof Fence* (1996),[57] which narrates Pilkington's mother's and aunt's experiences as members of the Stolen Generations. It traces their brutal taking from their mothers by the white settler state, which was part of the racist and genocidal policy of protectionism and assimilation in 1931.[58] The film is pure chase in that the chase *is* the film; it is also pure chase as the codings of chaser and chasee are unambiguous. In *The Chant of Jimmie Blacksmith* and *Backroads*, the codings are blurred, such as in relation to Jimmie's declaration of war and Gary's stealing. There is also an unequivocal fault assignment to the settler state in its taking of Aboriginal children from their families.

In *Rabbit-Proof Fence*, the early chase at Jigalong, where the three children – sisters Molly (Everlyn Sampi) and Daisy (Tianna Sansbury) and their cousin Gracie (Laure Monaghan) – are pursued by Constable Riggs (Jason Clarke) in a motor car[59] and are violently removed from Molly's and Daisy's mother Maude (Ningali Lawford), sets the tone of the film. The scene shows Maude's intense, desperate grief and the struggles of the children as they are dragged and thrown in the car with Riggs clutching the removal order shouting to Maude that she is not the children's legal guardian. It transpires that their legal guardian is the Chief Protector of Aborigines A.O. Neville (Kenneth Branagh), who is intent on a social Darwinist agenda. He illustrates his plan for Australian social engineering – breeding out Aboriginality – via Aboriginal and white people's cohabitation, inter-marriage and procreation. Legally sanctioned stealing of Aboriginal children under settler law was the first stage of his plan, which resonated with policies in place across Canada, Aotearoa/New Zealand, the United States and other colonies.[60]

Following the initial police chase of the families, the film's defining chase begins when Molly, Daisy and Gracie escape the Moore River Native Settlement camp near Perth, 1,800 kilometres away from home. They follow the rabbit-proof fence north, pursued by Riggs and First Nations tracker Moodoo (David Gulpilil), with Branagh's urbane, bureaucratic Neville coordinating and scheming from his well-furnished Perth office. Through the chase, the strengths of the First Nations' knowledge of Country are apparent through Molly's excellent bush skills in finding food and hiding their tracks over the journey. There is a spectacular visual palette – the sandy browns and electric blue sky at Jigalong, the shadow of the fence, the deepest blue-black night sky; these colours parallel the 'chromopolitics' of skin tones[61] that occupied Neville, who is located in an equally monochrome office.[62]

The fence, present in most scenes, is a contested motif. Formally, it is an impressive manifestation of the settler state and its sovereignty; however, it is also ironic. As explained in the film, the fence divides the land. On the coastal side is farmland, and on the other side is land surrendered to another alien invader from the North. It is the settler state's technical solution to its own biological mismanagement. In rough timber and wire, it renders visible the settler state's other biological mismanagement present in the film – the policy of assimilation and outbreeding. Yet it is a co-opted landmark, guiding Molly and Daisy to a twilight reunion with their mother and grandmother.[63] It might be imposed on the land by the settler state, but in the film, it is a line back to kin and Country.

The film seemingly ends with justice for Molly and Daisy in the face of the oppressive settler law. Having apprehended Gracie through spreading the rumour that her mother is waiting for her at a railway station, Neville discontinues the pursuit of Molly and Daisy due to the cost involved. The final visuals are of the reunion of the children with their mother – until the epilogue, which tells that Molly and Daisy did not remain safe; that the law of the settler state did eventually take Molly; that they never saw Gracie again; and that Molly's daughter was also taken from her, never to be returned. This is the revolting injustice at the conclusion of the film: the 'justice' of reunion is transitory, and the settler state's legalized violence towards First Nations people is indefatigable.[64] First Nations people and children are endlessly chased by its apparatus and constantly in a mode of escape.

Through these four films, a particular Australian articulation of the chase can be seen. First, the nomological elements of the chase are emphasized. The chases tell of law and justice, but not in the Western genre of good sheriff chasing base outlaws in a cinematic Wild West. The Australian chase animates a profound disjunction between the laws and legality of the settler state and its imposition on First Nations peoples. Through the films, 'settler law' – its practice and agents – is repeatedly shown as focused on the chasing and apprehending of First Nations young people and children. The chase embodies the settler state's desire to socially engineer First Nations people into compliance. This separate legality for First Nations people requires the suspension of universal settler colonial legality, enabling oppressive strategies in pursuit of First Nations people without any of the protections and safeguards. In *Backroads*, Gary is always the focus of attention and harassment, while white Joe seems invisible to the policing gaze.

The films have an essential intertwining with death: the thanatopolitics of the settler state. The pursued young First Nations people die. In *Rabbit-Proof Fence*, Gracie is taken and never seen again; Jimmie Blacksmith is tortured and hung; Gary is shot; and Jedda and Marbuck fall from the cliff top in the final scene. The endurance of the law of the settler state is not without incident. It is precarious yet exceptionally enduring – devoid of legality and relying on extreme bodily violence and injustice. Bodies are hurt, violated, taken, cut and orientated towards death by actions and agents sanctioned by settler state law. In these ways, the settler state exists in a zone of exception as much as the First Nations people who suffer under it. Authority is only ensured through exceptional acts of might. The chase is the thread that connects the chaser and chasee to this exceptional zone. Ultimately, the Australian chase reveals the uncertain sovereignty of the settler state. It is an uncertainty that drives angry white men to pursue First Nations young people to their deaths.

There could be a tendency to see metaphor alone in these representations – a suggestion that the chase through the lens of Australian cinema animates the jurispathic tendency of the settler state towards First Nations sovereignty.[65] However, the chase in Australian film is not metaphoric: it is demonstrative and performative. This was witnessed clearly in the early 1990s in the documentary *Cop It Sweet* (1991),[66] which followed the everyday practices of Redfern Police in inner-city Sydney. The chase – especially of young Aboriginal men in cars – was the mainstay of police activity, which involved looking out for cars 'that are a bit suss', according to the filmed police officers – including 'any cars' with Aboriginal people in them.[67] After one chase, in which the chasee got away, the police reflect on their frustrated attempt to uphold the law in the face of lawless

Aboriginal boys.[68] But it doesn't end there: in post-millennial Australia, the films represent a template through which to make sense of repeated tragedies, of First Nations children being chased to death, including on the streets of Redfern.

The contemporary Australian chase beyond the big screen

The poignancy of the chase in Australian films is the sense that it is not fiction. Realism is the dominant form in Australian film, and *Jedda*, *The Chant of Jimmie Blacksmith*, *Backroads* and *Rabbit-Proof Fence* can all be seen as strongly 'realist'.[69] They reflect broad lived experiences of First Nations people under siege from the settler colonial state and its legal apparatus, but they also emanate from the real stories of individuals, which is explicit in *The Chant of Jimmie Blacksmith* and *Rabbit-Proof Fence*, and also evident in *Jedda* (where the treatment by Elsa Chauvel of Ngarla/Rosalie Kunoth-Monks mimics the treatment by the white Mistress of Jedda)[70] and the dialogue on racism in *Backroads*, which was often the unscripted expression of the views of the First Nations actors in the car.[71]

The settler colonial chase on the big screen is not simply an historical account of thanatopolitics, but also gives meaning to the post-millennial chase and contemporary settler colonial governance. The fatal chase continues to feature in the lived experience of First Nations children, whether chased by welfare authorities and police in the process of child removal from First Nations families,[72] chased by white settlers while riding motorcycles or chased by the police. It continues to be a violent process, which often results in a violent end in which settler state law triumphs for the white settler but not the First Nations victim. This section examines some recent chases by police and settlers that vividly demonstrate the contemporary chase by the settler colonial state through the lenses of the settler state's own legal texts, the mainstream media and social media. The focus is on three high-profile cases: TJ Hickey in Redfern, Sydney in 2004; Elijah Doughty in Kalgoorlie-Boulder in 2016; and Chris Drage and Trisjack Simpson in Perth in 2018. Like their filmic counterparts, narratives on these chases (whether recorded by the media or legal lens) embrace the righteous agents of the settler state, child victims and a highly contested legality.

TJ Hickey, a 17-year-old Kamillaroi boy, was chased by Redfern police on the morning of 14 February 2004 while he was riding a bicycle.[73] The fatal chase caused him to be impaled upon a white steel fence just outside Redfern, and he subsequently died at Sydney Children's Hospital in the early hours of 15 February 2004. The context of his death is highly contested between the settler state lenses that recorded a tragic accident and First Nations lenses that saw a police killing. This contest was played out in the coronial and parliamentary inquiries in which Aboriginal witness accounts of the police killing and cover-up were consistently denied by police, with the police version upheld by these processes – partly because the Aboriginal witnesses were not viewed as credible.[74] As with all other chases resulting in the death of Australian First Nations people, charges and prosecutions were never pursued by the state against the police.

The primary lens of the settler state's recording of TJ's death was the report of the NSW State Coroner, which was completed in August 2004. The report tells of an 'unfortunate' confluence of events. On the morning of TJ's death, there was a heightened police presence on the streets of Redfern – including two armoured trucks – seeking a First Nations man suspected of a robbery.[75] TJ had reasons to avoid the police – including being under an apprehension order for breach of bail, with a condition of bail being that he was not allowed into the 'Block' neighbourhood of Redfern.[76] Also relevant was the condition of TJ's bike, particularly its defective brakes.[77] As to the chase itself, the report's iris is clouded. The coroner determined that the chase did not fit within formal definitions of a police pursuit.[78] The testimony of the police involved was partial and contradictory.[79] Yet the vision that emerged from the report does not have the police involved in TJ's death. The police in at least one of the trucks 'follow[ed] the boy'[80] – which suggests a casual following without strong intent. This lens sees TJ's death as a self-induced accident due to his losing control as a result of speed and the perceived defects of his bicycle, effectively shifting responsibility to the First Nations child victim.

For Redfern's Aboriginal community, including TJ's family, a different vision of the chase was recorded. Where the settler state saw TJ as accidently caught up in another police operation and as casually followed by a police truck, the First Nations lens saw a much more active, intentional chase that culminated in police involvement in his death.[81] There was evidence by civilian witnesses and an Aboriginal Community Liaison Officer that the police 'rammed' into TJ's bike.[82] This evidence was discounted by the coroner, who preferred the police version of events. However, there were enough significant factors to cast doubt on the police account. Proper procedures were not followed in the aftermath of TJ's death: the boy's body was moved by the pursuing police[83] and police backup rather than the assistance of paramedics being called for in the first instance.[84] The internal police investigation into the operation, which should have begun immediately, commenced a week later.[85] Contrary to protocol, the police involved were allowed to write their statements together,[86] and the Redfern superintendent altered statements.[87] During the coronial inquiry, police witnesses did not answer questions, and the lead senior constable refused to give evidence.[88] There were claims that the bicycle presented to the coroner was not the one that TJ was riding on the morning of 14 February,[89] the site of TJ's death was cleaned by police and the vehicles involved were repaired before the internal investigation commenced.[90] TJ had good reasons to flee from the police, having previously been bashed in police custody.[91] This community lens records a different scene: a large police vehicle bearing down on a terrified First Nations child on a bicycle. The vehicle possibly clipped or hit the bicycle, causing TJ to be flung to his death. Further scenes of police officers colluding to get their story straight and evidence suitably arranged. The deep injustice of the Australian chase is manifested in the disjunction between these two recordings of TJ's death.

For TJ's family and the Redfern Aboriginal community, the sense of injustice from TJ's death was palpable. A gathering of the community on the evening of 15 February 2004, to mourn and express anger at the police involvement, prompted the settler state to further mobilize.[92] What developed became known, problematically, as the 'Redfern Riot'.[93] Through the lenses of the mainstream Australian media, and in subsequent reactions of the settler state, the clash led to injuries to participants on both side[94] and numerous arrests of First Nations people, eclipsing TJ's death.[95]

Media lenses were framed according to moral panic narratives of dangerous and threatening First Nations people, which legitimized the settler state adopting a punitive law and order response.[96] As can be seen in the image published in the *Sydney Morning Herald*, the response was military in its aesthetics and reminiscent of a pursuit.[97] The police had placed the First Nations community under siege in their deployment of the tactical response, military-clad police.[98] They instigated the confrontation before any violence had erupted on the part of the First Nations community. The subsequent 'Strike Force Coburn', like the coronial inquest into TJ's death, saw the fault placed with the First Nations people,[99] in turn leading to a further intensification of police and police resources in Redfern[100] and to the arrest and prosecution of many in the Redfern community,[101] including TJ's relatives.[102]

What can be seen in the chase that led to TJ's death is that the settler state and its enforcement agents endure through the lives and bodies of First Nations people. There was a profound dissymmetry: TJ's fatal vulnerability compared with the armoured invulnerability of the police trucks. The perfunctory comments about a deceased child against the statements of care and respect for police officers. The First Nation community's spontaneous expression of grief and anger against the indefatigable, calculated chasing down of First Nation 'trouble makers' by the settler state. The 'justice' of the settler state's law is seen as being done in a context of disquieting injustice.

These framings of the Australian chase are also manifest in the chase that led to the death of 14-year-old Wangkatja boy Elijah Doughty on the morning of 29 August 2016 on a track at Gribble Creek Reserve, located in Kalgoorlie-Boulder. Elijah Doughty died when he was either knocked off the small motorcycle he was riding or knocked off and then run over by a large off-road utility vehicle driven by the offender, known only as WSM.[103] In the legal lenses of the settler state – two written judgments of the Supreme Court of Western Australia – there was no ambiguity regarding the motive of the chaser. WSM was angry: the evening before Elijah's death, he had returned home to find his motorcycles stolen.[104] The attending police casually suggested that stolen motorcycles were often subsequently spotted in Gribble Creek Reserve.[105] The next morning, while driving his vehicle, WSM spied Elijah Doughty on what seemed to be one of the stolen motorcycles. The chase was brief, with the lens of a home security CCTV system recording Elijah Doughty riding a motorcycle into Gribble Creek Reserve followed by WSM's vehicle.[106] Less than half a minute later, Elijah was dead.[107] WSM was charged with manslaughter but was ultimately convicted of the lesser offence of dangerous driving and served just 18 months of a three-year sentence.[108]

There are distinct parallels with the chase and death of TJ Hickey as well as its aftermath. Expressions of grief and anger by the Kalgoorlie-Boulder First Nations community around the courthouse where WSM was arraigned became, through the lens of the settler state, a 'riot'.[109] The minor damage to police and court property[110] was seen by the settler state as particularly onerous.[111] The Supreme Court variously derided the protestors as 'ill-informed',[112] 'uncontrolled'[113] and an 'unruly group'.[114] This is in contrast to the sympathetic framing given to WSM. Tranter and Anthony have documented how, at each stage, the settler state minimalized WSM's culpability and underscored his good character. That he was driving a large vehicle at speed over unstable terrain in close proximity to a child on a small motorcycle disappears from the sentencing remarks,[115] in which Elijah Doughty, his family and his community haze to insubstantiality as victims. WSM becomes a victim of circumstance, a good white man who was having a very bad day.[116]

Through the lens comprising the settler state's judicial reckoning with Elijah Doughty's death, the rule of law is seen to be done. WSM is brought to a version of justice, and law and order is reimposed around the Kalgoorlie-Boulder courthouse. Yet the injustice – that a First Nations child was killed because an angry white man wanted his property back – is lost in dust tracks. There emanates throughout a vision of settler state–condoned vigilantism. The police initially suggested that WSM search Gribble Creek Reserve, and the settler state seems particularly careful in reducing WSM's culpability and penalty.

There is a further set of lenses involved in framing the chase that ended in Elijah Doughty's death that connect directly to vigilantism. In the months preceding the incident, various social media sites became dedicated to identifying and vilifying young First Nations children and promoting the 'chase'.[117] These sites functioned as panopticons of hate, where the white community circulated images of First Nations youths and urged violent chasing and retaliation. Under the pretext of concerns with crime, these sites – with 18,000 followers[118] – became marked by racial vilification and urgings to violence.[119] An example of the discourse being circulated was the chain of comments in response to a post claiming to have seen two First Nations youths breaking into a vehicle. One response was 'Feel free to run these oxygen thieves off the road if you see them', and 'Everyone talks about hunting down these sub human mutts, but no one ever does'.[120] In May 2016, an image of Elijah Doughty riding his own motorcycle was uploaded.[121] A post underneath urged 'Run the f***kers over'.[122] This social media activity incited the chasing of First Nations children and hideously celebrated Elijah Doughty's death. As the news of WSM's chasing and killing of Elijah became known, one contributor posted, 'Don't think you'll be touching another bike any time soon ahaha About time someone took it into their own hands hope it happens again'[123] and 'That's good that young boy got killed. Aboriginals don't own Australia. Aboriginals live in the bush. They are filthy animals. They all need the death sentence'.[124]

The chase and death of Elijah Doughty show the visuality of the Australian chase transmuted into a participatory culture of surveillance and hate. The filmic chases show that the pursuing agents were not just the authorized officials, but settlers of the wider community. In *Jedda*, the settler pastoralist Doug sanctions his workers' chase of Marbuck and notifies the police officer, who is otherwise pursuing Marbuck for another murder, of his abduction of Jedda. In *The Chant of Jimmie Blacksmith, Backroads* and *Rabbit-Proof Fence,* the police are joined by settlers in the pursuit, and they share information on the chasees. The colonialism of the settler state is shown to be a collective enterprise.

The final chase is still being recorded. It involves the deaths of two First Nations boys, Chris Drage and Trisjack Simpson, both 17 years old,[125] in Perth, Western Australia, on 10 September 2018.[126] The media tell a story of police responding to reports of five First Nations young men 'jumping fences'.[127] This chase had a soundscape, with witnesses reporting hearing multiple sirens rapidly converging on the river.[128] This chase is framed by not only Elijah Doughty's death two years before, but particularly by the inexplicable running down of 18-year-old First Nations man William Farmer by a police vehicle in Perth in May 2018.[129] The reports show Chris Drage and Trisjack Simpson and three other First Nations youths pursued by two officers on foot and by the sounds of sirens. The chase ends with the boys attempting to swim across the Swan River.[130] The movement and cacophony of the chase terminates with the silence of drowning. The full cinematography of this chase is yet to be produced, with a Coroner's Court of Western Australia report pending.[131] However, as Sophie Gillfeather-Spetere observes, the second the chase was sounded:

> The group of teens were more than young bodies moving quickly from one fence to the next; they were young black bodies, trespassing boundaries both figurative and non-figurative. In this moment, they are spoken into being as inherently criminal and as such, children worthy of being chased.[132]

As with Elijah Doughty, there were reports that various social media crime and vigilante sites were hosting racist and hateful content in response to the deaths.[133]

Associated with the report on the ABC Online website are three particularly telling images. The first is a recording from a mobile phone, which shows the police on the edge of the river with the boys farther out. This video captures a sense of horror – of confusion and yelling by the police chasers and determination by the chasees. Also associated with the report are images of police watercraft on the river and of mounted police. The manifestation of the settler state as augmented mobility – strongly present in the car that takes Molly, Daisy and Gracie in *Rabbit-Proof Fence* and in the central images associated with the chasing and deaths of TJ Hickey and Elijah Doughty – is forcefully present in the contrast between these images of machine order and human grief.

The deaths of TJ Hickey, Elijah Doughty, Chris Drage and Trisjack Simpson show that the filmic representation of the Australian chase goes beyond metaphor.

The images of agents of the settler state chasing First Nations children to their deaths are not just an enactment of the jurispathic nature of the settler state against First Nations sovereignty. They are a real and recurring reality in the ongoing occupation of First Nations Country by the settler state. First Nations children are caught in a necrotransport regime where law, machines and optics pursue and take them to their deaths.[134] The etchings of these chases on various lenses show how the nomos of the chase in Australia is tied to sovereignty and ownership. The endurance of First Nations people and law provokes in the settler state a desire to chase, to subdue and to kill. Revealed at its core in the social media vitriol, a colour-coded hate drives a collective enterprise to watch, report and pursue First Nations people. This thanatological desire is legalized in the construction of settler state law – laws of property of land, persons and motorcycles; laws that establish and sustain a militarized police force with a 'law and order' agenda; laws that reduce the culpability of angry men who kill First Nations children; laws that translate First Nations reactions of grief and anger as threatening riots; laws that allow racists' hate and urgings to violence to go unchecked on social media.[135] In short, the Australian chase shows a white sovereign order needed across time and country to perform the brutal repression of First Nations peoples and cultures by killing their children – this is just as true on the screen as it is in the streets, police cells and prisons.

Notes

1 Halsey (2008), p 107 refers to the fact that one-third of deaths in custody involve police chases.
2 Blagg and Anthony (2019).
3 Wolfe (2006).
4 Jeremy Beckett, cited in Haebich (2008); Rekhari (2011).
5 Tranter and Anthony (2019).
6 There are, however, a number of variations to this version: see Fontenrose (1981).
7 Johnson (2014), p 74.
8 Granites (2019).
9 Cover (1983).
10 Tompkins (1993), p 5.
11 See: Teo (2019); Teo (2017).
12 White (2010), p 8.
13 Aleiss (1994).
14 Ford, *The Searchers* (1956).
15 Bird (2004), p 33; see also Jafri (2013).
16 Bird (2004), p 33; see also Jafri (2013).
17 Romao (2004).
18 Yates, *Bullitt* (1968).
19 Walker (2004), p 529.
20 Buchanan (1933), p 117.
21 Buchanan (1933), p 117.
22 Agamben (1998), p 95. In relation to settler colonialism, see Blagg and Anthony (2019), Ch 7; Bignall (2014), p 38.
23 Cunningham (1991), p 147.

24 Gerry Grant, 'Jedda' *Overland*, No. 6, 1956 cited in Cunningham (1991), p 159; Wilson (2007), p 194.
25 Chauvel, *Jedda* (1995).
26 Chauvel (1973), p 127.
27 Johnson (1988), p 55; Miller (2007), p 151.
28 Palmer and Gillard (2002), p 129.
29 On this critical reading of captivity, see Creed (2001).
30 Marbuck is a complex representation of First Nations masculinity. Belittled by a name suggesting a young male cloved herbivore, Robert Tudawali's magnetic performance (Turner 1988, p 137) embodies First Nations masculinity and sovereignty (Johnson 1988, p 53), as well as superstition and brutality. It is Marbuck's knowledge of Country that allows him to take Jedda to his people – he kills the crocodile while another crocodile takes one of Joe's trackers, and he knowingly covers his tracks.
31 Barnett (2019).
32 In the film, Joe is described as having an Aboriginal mother and an Afghan father. Critics have suggested that Joe's position in relation to the McManns, the station owners; the grooming of Jedda to be his partner; and the sexual reality of the Northern frontier during the period suggest that Joe is the son of Douglas McMann (George Simpson-Lyttle). See Johnson (1988), p 53.
33 Palmer and Gillard (2002), pp 129–30.
34 Rekhari (2008), p 126; Palmer and Gillard (2002), p 129.
35 Elkin (1951), p 181.
36 Barnett (2019).
37 Turner (1988), p 137.
38 Schepisi, *The Chant of Jimmie Blacksmith* (1978).
39 Keneally (2004).
40 Henry Reynolds carefully explains the differences between the film (and novel) and the historical lives, bushranging and deaths of the Governor brothers. See Reynolds (2008) and Ryan-Fazilleau (2002).
41 Hickling-Hudson (1990), p 268.
42 Johnson (1988), p 50.
43 Wilson (2007), p 204.
44 Hickling-Hudson (1990), p 268; Ryan-Fazilleau (2002), pp 33–4.
45 Turner (1988), p 141.
46 See, for example, Johnson (1988), p 50; Wilson (2007), p 194.
47 Birch (2015).
48 Behrendt (2000), pp 358–60.
49 Birch (2015).
50 Noyce, *Backroads* (1977).
51 Pike (1977), p 598.
52 Teo (2017), p 210.
53 Probyn-Rapsey (2006), p 106.
54 Goldsmith and Lealand (2010), p 210.
55 Cited in Muecke (2001).
56 Noyce, *Rabbit-Proof Fence* (2002).
57 Brewster (2002); Pilkington (1996).
58 D'aeth (2002).
59 On the motor vehicle as instrumental in making possible the discrete targeting and taking of children, see Tranter (2018), pp 180–2.
60 See Blagg and Anthony (2019), Ch 4.
61 Granata (2017), pp 109–11.
62 Birch (2002), p 126.

63 Dolin (2009), pp 139–40.
64 Birch (2002), p 119.
65 Newton (1994), p 1004.
66 Brockie, *Cop It Sweet* (1992).
67 Probyn-Rapsey (2006), p 106.
68 Brockie, *Cop It Sweet* (1992); Chan (1995), pp 35–9.
69 O'Regan (1988), p 22; Turner (1993).
70 Chauvel (1973), p 155.
71 Muecke (2001).
72 Royal Commission into the Protection and Detention of Children in the Northern Territory (2017), p 91.
73 State Coroner of New South Wales (2004), p 71.
74 Anthony (2018).
75 State Coroner of New South Wales (2004), pp 73–4.
76 State Coroner of New South Wales (2004), pp 72–3. On the 'Block' of Redfern as the centre of the First Australian community, see Spark (2003).
77 State Coroner of New South Wales (2004), pp 79, 84, 88.
78 State Coroner of New South Wales (2004), p 87.
79 State Coroner of New South Wales (2004), pp 85–8.
80 State Coroner of New South Wales (2004), p 87.
81 Jackson (2014).
82 Paul Wilkinson evidence, Parliament of New South Wales (2004), p 22; State Coroner of New South Wales (2004), p 79.
83 Vincent (2006), p 126.
84 Vincent (2006), p 126.
85 State Coroner of New South Wales (2004), p 87.
86 State Coroner of New South Wales (2004), p 87.
87 State Coroner of New South Wales (2004), p 74.
88 State Coroner of New South Wales (2004), p 86.
89 Jackson (2014); Vincent (2006), p. 126.
90 Jackson (2014).
91 Anon (2004b).
92 Birch (2004), p 18; Gargett (2005), p 10.
93 Cunneen (2007).
94 New South Wales Police (2004), pp 52–4.
95 Anthony (2011); Birch (2004), p 20.
96 Budarick (2011); Cunneen (2007); Gargett (2005).
97 See www.smh.com.au/specials/redfern.
98 Anthony (2011), p 405.
99 Anthony (2013), p 166; Funnell (2005).
100 Watkins (2004).
101 Anon (2004a).
102 Corder (2004); Colman (2004).
103 *State of Western Australia v WSM* [2017], [8], [10] (Martin CJ).
104 *State of Western Australia v WSM* [2017], [2] (Martin CJ).
105 *State of Western Australia v WSM* [2017], [3] (Martin CJ).
106 *State of Western Australia v WSM* [2017], [6] (Martin CJ).
107 *State of Western Australia v WSM* [2017], [10] (Martin CJ).
108 *State of Western Australia v WSM* [2017], [11] (Martin CJ); Wahlquist (2018).
109 *MWSD v State of Western Australia* [2017], [53], [55], [58] (Jenkins J).
110 *MWSD v State of Western Australia* [2017], [56] (Jenkins J).
111 *MWSD v State of Western Australia* [2017], [53] (Jenkins J).

112 *State of Western Australia v WSM* [2017], [35] (Martin CJ).
113 *State of Western Australia v WSM* [2017], [36] (Martin CJ).
114 *State of Western Australia v WSM* [2017], [37] (Martin CJ).
115 Tranter and Anthony (2019), pp 120–32.
116 Tranter and Anthony (2019), p 128.
117 Murphy-Oates (2017).
118 This is a remarkable number of followers, considering that the population of Kalgoorlie-Boulder was just over 30,000. See Cunneen and Russell (2017), p 11; see also the chapter by Cunneen and Russell in this volume.
119 Cunneen and Russell (2017), p 11.
120 Purtill (2016).
121 Toohey (2016).
122 Toohey (2016); see also Behrendt (2016).
123 Social media post quoted in Purtill (2016).
124 Social media post quoted in Toohey (2016).
125 Some reports gave Trisjack Simpson's age as 16. See Taylor (2018).
126 Trigger and Carmody (2018).
127 Taylor (2018).
128 Taylor (2018).
129 Lorena (2018b).
130 Hughes (2018); Lorena (2018a).
131 Caccetta (2018). As of 9 September 2019 – a full 12 months since their deaths – neither the inquest nor a report has been announced.
132 Gillfeather-Spetere (2019), p 117.
133 Trigger and Carmody (2018).
134 Perera and Pugliese (2019).
135 See the chapter by Chris Cunneen and Sophie Russell in this volume.

References

Secondary sources

Giorgio Agamben (1998) *Homo Sacer: Sovereign Power and Bare Life*, Daniel Heller-Roazen (trans), Stanford University Press.

Angela Aleiss (1994) 'A Race Divided: The Indian Westerns of John Ford' 18 *American Indian Culture Research Journal* 167.

Lorena Allam (2018a) 'Drownings of Boys in Perth being Treated as "Death in Police Presence"', *The Guardian*, www.theguardian.com/australia-news/2018/sep/12/drownings-of-boys-in-perth-being-treated-as-death-in-police-presence.

——— (2018b) 'Police Car Filmed Veering Across Road and Hitting Aboriginal Man', *The Guardian*, www.theguardian.com/australia-news/2018/may/10/police-car-filmed-veering-across-road-and-hitting-aboriginal-man?CMP=Share_iOSApp_Other.

Anon (2004a) 'Dozens Arrested in Redfern Drug Raid', *ABC News*, 30 June, www.abc.net.au/news/2004-07-30/dozens-arrested-in-redfern-drug-raid/2017726.

——— (2004b) 'Chased or Not, TJ Had Reasons to Run' *Sydney Morning Herald*, 17 February, www.smh.com.au/national/chased-or-not-tj-had-reasons-to-run-20040217-gdidcw.html.

Thalia Anthony (2011) 'Sentencing Indigenous Riot Offenders in a Spatial Fantasy' 20 *Griffith Law Review* 385.

——— (2013) *Indigenous People, Crime and Punishment*, Routledge.

——— (2018) 'Policing in Redfern: Histories and Continuities' 12 *Courts of Conscience* 46.

Chelsea Barnett (2019) *Reel Men: Australian Masculinity in the Movies 1949–1962*, Melbourne University Press.

Larissa Behrendt (2000) 'Consent in a (Neo) Colonial Society: Aboriginal Women as Sexual and Legal "Other"' 15 *Australian Feminist Studies* 353.

——— (2016) 'Debbie Carmody – Kalgoorlie Unrest Following the Death of a 14-Year-Old Boy', *Speaking Out*, 11 September, www.abc.net.au/radio/programs/speakingout/kalgoorlie-unrest-following-death-ofteenager/7832164.

Simone Bignall (2014) 'Postcolonial Redemption: Agamben's Thought as Transformative Chrēsis' 40 *Concentric: Literacy Cultural Studies Review* 29.

Tony Birch (2002) '"This is a True Story": Rabbit-Proof Fence: "Mr Devil" and the Desire to Forget' 8 *Cultural Studies Review* 117.

——— (2004) '"Who Gives a Fuck about White Society Anymore?" A Response to the Redfern Riot' 175 *Overland* 18.

——— (2015) '*The Chant of Jimmie Blacksmith* by Thomas Keneally for Reading Australia', *Australian Book Review*, June–July, www.australianbookreview.com.au/reading-australia/thomas-keneally/the-chant-of-jimmie-blacksmith-by-thomas-keneally.

Harry Blagg and Thalia Anthony (2019) *Decolonizing Criminology*, Palgrave Macmillan.

Anne Brewster (2002) 'Aboriginal Life Writing and Globalisation: Doris Pilkington's *Follow the Rabbit-Proof Fence*' 62 *Southerly* 153.

Gordon Buchanan (1933) *Packhorse and Waterhole: With the First Overlanders to the Kimberleys*, Angus & Robertson.

John Budarick (2011) 'Media Narratives and Social Events: The Story of the Redfern Riot' 35 *Journal of Communication Inquiry* 37.

Wendy Caccetta (2018) 'Police Prioritise Investigation into Tragic Teen Drowning', *National Indigenous Times*, 19 September, https://nit.com.au/police-prioritise-investigation-into-tragic-teen-drowning.

Janet Chan (1995) 'Damage Control: Media Representation and Reponses to Police Deviance' 2 *Law Text Culture* 32.

Elsa Chauvel (1973) *My Life with Charles Chauvel*, Shakespeare Head Press.

E. Colman (2004) 'Magistrate Refuses Bail for Alleged Riot Ringleader', *The Australian*, 25 February.

M. Corder (2004) 'Dead Boy's Aunt in the Dock Over Sydney Riot', *The Independent*, 21 February.

Robert M. Cover (1983) 'Nomos and Narrative' 97 *Harvard Law Review* 4.

Barbara Creed (2001) 'Breeding out the Black: *Jedda* and the Stolen Generations in Australia', in Barbara Creed and Jeanette Hoorn (eds), *Body Trade: Captivity, Cannibalism, and Colonialism in the Pacific*, Pluto Press.

Chris Cunneen (2007) 'Riot, Resistance and Moral Panic: Demonising the Colonial Other', in Scott Poynting and George Morgan (eds), *Outrageous! Moral Panics in Australia*, ACYS Publishing.

Chris Cunneen and Sophie Russell (2017) 'Social Media, Vigilantism and Indigenous People in Australia', in Nicole Rafter and Michelle Brown (eds), *The Oxford Encyclopedia of Crime, Media, and Popular Culture*, Oxford University Press.

Stuart Cunningham (1991) *Featuring Australia: The Cinema of Charles Chauvel*, Allen & Unwin.

Tony Hughes D'aeth (2002) 'Which Rabbit-Proof Fence? Empathy, Assimilation, Hollywood' 27 *Australian Humanities Review* 2.

Kieran Dolin (2009) 'Law and Identity at the Fence' 3 *Studies in Australasian Cinema* 133.

Adolphus Peter Elkin (1951) 'Reaction and Interaction: A Food Gathering People and European Settlement in Australia' 53 *American Anthropologist* 164.

Joseph Eddy Fontenrose (1981) *Orion: The Myth of the Hunter and the Huntress*, University of California Press.

Neal Funnell (2005) 'Non-Lethal Intelligence: Strike Force Coburn and the Police Response to the Redfern Riot' 6 *Indigenous Law Bulletin* 4.

Andy Gargett (2005) 'A Critical Media Analysis of the Redfern Rot' 6 *Indigenous Law Bulletin* 8.

Sophie Gillfeather-Spetere (2019) 'From Pursuit to Progress: Critical Reflections on Concepts of Young People and Crime in Australia' 31 *Current Issues in Criminal Justice* 111.

Ben Goldsmith and Geoffrey Lealand (2010) *Australia and New Zealand Directory of World Cinema*, Intellect.

Yvette Granata (2017) 'False Color/Real Life: Chromo-Politics and François Laruelle's Photo-Fiction' 6 *NECSUS European Journal of Media Studies* 105.

Anna Haebich (2008) *Spinning the Dream: Assimilation in Australia 1950–1970*, Fremantle Arts Centre Press.

Mark Halsey (2008) 'Narrating the Chase: Edgework and Young People's Experiences of Crime', in Thalia Anthony and Chris Cunneen (eds), *The Critical Criminology Companion*, Hawkins Press.

Anne Hickling-Hudson (1990) 'White Construction of Black Identity in Australian Films About Aborigines' 18 *Literature/Film Quarterly* 263.

Carl Hughes (2018) 'Dispatch: The Recent Derbal Yerrigan Drownings and "Aboriginal Deaths-in-Custody"', *Deathscapes: Mapping Race and Violence in Settler States*, www.deathscapes.org/engagements/dispatch-the-recent-derbal-yerrigan-drownings-and-aboriginal-deaths-in-custody.

Ray Jackson (2014) 'TJ Hickey Injustices', http://nationalunitygovernment.org/content/ray-jackson-provides-overview-tj-hickey-injustices.

Beenash Jafri (2013) 'Desire, Settler Colonialism, and the Racialized Cowboy' 37 *American Indian Culture Research Journal* 73.

Colin Johnson (1988) 'Chauvel and the Centring of the Aboriginal Male in Australian Film' 1 *Continuum: Journal of Media and Cultural Studies* 47.

Dianne Johnson (2014) *Night Skies of Aboriginal Australia: A Noctuary*, Sydney University Press.

Thomas Keneally (2004) *The Chant of Jimmie Blacksmith: A Novel*, Perennial.

Ben Miller (2007) 'The Mirror of Whiteness: Blackface in Charles Chauvel's Jedda' Special Issue of the *Journal of the Association for the Study of Australian Literature* 140.

Stephen Muecke (2001) 'Backroads: From Identity to Interval', *Koori Web*, October, www.kooriweb.org/foley/resources/story7.html.

Laura Murphy-Oates (2017) 'Kids of Kalgoorlie: In the Wake of Elijah Doughty, Vigilantism Thrives', *The Feed*, SBS, 11 September, www.sbs.com.au/news/the-feed/kids-of-kalgoorlie-in-the-wake-of-elijah-doughty-vigilantism-thrives.

New South Wales Police (2004) *Strike Force Coburn: Final Report – Part A. Analysis – Redfern Local Area Command Civil Unrest 15–16 February 2004*, New South Wales Police.

Nell Jessup Newton (1994) 'Memory and Misrepresentation: Representing Crazy Horse' 27 *Connecticut Law Review* 1003.

Alma Nungarrayi Granites (2019) 'Yanjirlpirri or Napaljarri – Warnu Jukurrpa (Star or Seven Sisters Dreaming)', https://gallery.aboriginalartdirectory.com/aboriginal-art/alma-nungarrayi-granites/yanjirlpirri-or-napaljarri-warnu-jukurrpa-star-or-1.php.

Tom O'Regan (1988) 'Australian Film in the 1950s' 1 *Continuum: Journal of Media and Cultural Studies* 1.

Dave Palmer and Garry Gillard (2002) 'Aborigines, Ambivalence, and Australian Film', *Metro Magazine: Media Education Magazine* 128.

Parliament of New South Wales (2004) *Report of Proceedings Before Standing Committee on Social Issues Inquiry into Issues Relating to Redfern-Waterloo, Sydney*, Parliament of New South Wales.

Suvendrini Perera and Joseph Pugliese (2019) 'Necrotransport', *Deathscape: Mapping Race and Violence in Settler States*, www.deathscapes.org/galleries/necrotransport.

Andrew Pike (1977) 'Aboriginals in Australian Feature Films' 36 *Meanjin* 592.

Doris Pilkington (1996) *Follow the Rabbit-Proof Fence*, University of Queensland Press.

Fiona Probyn-Rapsey (2006) 'Bitumen Films in Postcolonial Australia' 88 *Journal of Australian Studies* 97.

James Purtill (2016) 'Racist. Violent. Deleted: The Facebook Posts Dividing Kalgoorlie', *Triple J Hack*, ABC Radio, 1 September, www.abc.net.au/triplej/programs/hack/the-facebook-posts-dividing-kalgoorlie/7805346.

Suneeti Rekhari (2008) 'The "Other" in Film: Exclusions of Aboriginal Identity from Australian Cinema' 21 *Visual Anthropology* 125.

——— (2011) 'Jedda', in James Bennett, James E. Bennett and Rebecca Beirne (eds), *Making Film and Television Histories: Australia and New Zealand*, Bloomsbury 5.

Henry Reynolds (2008) *The Chant of Jimmie Blacksmith*, Currency Press.

Tico Romao (2004) 'Guns and Gas: Investigating the 1970s Car Chase Film', in Yvonne Tasker (ed.), *Action and Adventure Cinema*, Routledge 130.

Royal Commission into the Protection and Detention of Children in the Northern Territory (2017) *Final Report*, Royal Commission into the Protection and Detention of Children in the Northern Territory.

Sue Ryan-Fazilleau (2002) 'Thomas Keneally's *The Chant of Jimmie Blacksmith* and the Palimpsest of Jimmy Governor' 25 *Commonwealth: Essays Studies in Australasian Cinema* 27.

Ceridwen Spark (2003) 'Documenting Redfern: Representing Home and Aboriginality on the Block' 17 *Continuum* 33.

State Coroner of New South Wales (2004) 'Inquest into the Death of TJ Hickey, Findings of State Coroner John Abernethy', *Office of the State Coroner of New South Wales*, www.coroners.justice.nsw.gov.au/Documents/dic2004%20final.doc.

Paige Taylor (2018) 'Swan River Deaths a Tragic Tale of Two Truants Trying to Reform', *The Australian*, 13 September, www.theaustralian.com.au/nation/swan-river-deaths-a-tragic-tale-of-two-truants-trying-to-reform/news-story/4bbaf3886ed78a8880adff4576f9a8a8.

Stephen Teo (2017) *Eastern Westerns: Film and Genre Outside and Inside Hollywood*, Routledge.

——— (2019) *Eastern Approaches to Western Film: Asian Reception and Aesthetics in Cinema*, Bloomsbury.

Jane Tompkins (1993) *West of Everything: The Inner Life of Westerns*, Oxford University Press.

Paul Toohey (2016) 'The Seething Streets of Kalgoorlie-Boulder, WA, Where Racism Towards Indigenous Boys Has Hit a Flashpoint', *Perth Now*, 13 November, www.perthnow.com.au/news/wa/the-seething-streets-of-kalgoorlie-boulder-wa-where-racism-towards-indigenous-boys-has-hit-a-flashpoint-ng-d47a67bb37f772da4239e83dbb31ae13.

Kieran Tranter (2018) *Living in Technical Legality: Science Fiction and Law as Technology*, University of Edinburgh Press.

Kieran Tranter and Thalia Anthony (2019) 'Race, Australian Colonialism and Technologies of Mobility in Kalgoorlie' 45 *University of Western Australia Law Review* 99.

Rebecca Trigger and James Carmody (2018) 'Swan River Deaths: Family Left Reeling after Loss of Grandson in Fatal Maylands Police Chase', *ABC News*, 12 September, www.abc.net.au/news/2018-09-12/family-reeling-death-of-boy-in-swan-river-after-police-chase/10236562.

Graeme Turner (1988) 'Breaking the Frame: The Representation of Aborigines in Australian Film' 10 *Kunapipi* 135.

——— (1993) 'The Genres are American: Australian Narrative, Australian Film, and the Problem of Genre' 21 *Literature/Film Quarterly* 102.

Eve Vincent (2006) 'Tour of Beauty' 65 *Meanjin* 121.

Calla Wahlquist (2018) 'Man Who Struck and Killed Aboriginal Teen Elijah Doughty Released from Prison on Parole', *The Guardian*, 27 March, www.theguardian.com/australia-news/2018/mar/27/man-who-killed-indigenous-teenager-elijah-doughty-given-parole.

Polly O. Walker (2004) 'Decolonizing Conflict Resolution: Addressing the Ontological Violence of Westernization' 28 *American Indian Quarterly* 527–49.

John Watkins (2004) 'Redfern Crime Plan: Enhanced Numbers, Training, Response and Relations', *Minister for Police*, www.redwatch.org.au/govt/nsw/police/redfernenhanced2004/REL16%20Redfern%20Plan_1.pdf.

John White (2010) *Westerns*, Routledge.

Janet Wilson (2007) 'Reconsidering Fred Schepisi's *The Chant of Jimmie Blacksmith* (1978): The Screen Adaptation of Thomas Keneally's Novel (1972)' 1 *Studies in Australasian Cinema* 191.

Patrick Wolfe (2006) 'Settler Colonialism and the Elimination of the Native' 8 *Journal of Genocide Research* 387.

Michael Yellow Bird (2004) 'Cowboys and Indians: Toys of Genocide, Icons of American Colonialism' 19 *Wíčazo Ša Review* 33.

Primary legal sources

MWSD v State of Western Australia [2017] WASC 125 (5 May 2017).

State of Western Australia v WSM [2017] WASCSR 128 (21 July 2017).

Films

Jenny Brockie (1992) *Cop it Sweet*, Australian Broadcasting Corporation.

Charles Chauvel (1955) *Jedda*, Columbia Pictures.

John Ford (1956) *The Searchers*, Warner Brothers.

Phillip Noyce (1977) *Backroads*, Backroads Production.

——— (2002) *Rabbit Proof Fence*, Becker Entertainment.

Fred Schepisi (1978) *The Chant of Jimmie Blacksmith*, Hoyts.

Peter Yates (1968) *Bullitt*, Warner Bros.

Chapter 5

Vilification, vigilantism and violence

Troubling social media in Australia

Chris Cunneen and Sophie Russell

Introduction

Drawing primarily on Australian evidence, we argue in this chapter that racism and racist violence have been empowered through the use of social media and increasingly normalized through these technologies of mass communication. The racist violence manifesting on social media draws on a much deeper colonial mentality towards Aboriginal peoples and other racial minorities, and the emboldened racism in social media has been legitimized and supported by various elites and mainstream media outlets. We demonstrate in this chapter that one of the most troubling outcomes of racism on social media has been the rise of vigilantism and conclude by showing the inadequacies of current regulatory regimes in terms of responding to social media hate speech and vigilantism.

Social media have transformed human interaction and are now a key form of communication in our hyperconnected world. While social media are a relatively recent development – Facebook was established in 2004, YouTube in 2005, Twitter in 2006, Instagram in 2010, Snapchat in 2011 and Tinder in 2012 – the explosion of these and other platforms has transformed the way ordinary citizens experience crime and victimization and how they engage with criminal justice processes. The recent mass killing of 51 people at two mosques in Christchurch, New Zealand, and its live streaming on Facebook have ignited debate about the regulation of social media and the responsibility of social media companies for the content that they distribute via their platforms.[1]

Older media platforms such as newspapers connected 'one to many' – that is, they connected the content producer (for example, the newspaper) with a mass audience (the readership). In contrast, new digital and online technology connects 'many to many' through multi-modal (photos, videos, texts, audio recordings) forms of communication.[2] For example, a single Facebook user or group can engage in rapid, interactive and relatively unmonitored communication between many thousands of individuals. These technological developments have fundamentally changed the way individuals can communicate with one another.

The relationship between new technologies and crime has been a growing focus of criminology.[3] Recent research has explored policing and new media,[4] sexting,[5] revenge porn,[6] sexual assault survivors' use of social media,[7] the use of social media to expose police misconduct[8] and the growth of what has been referred to as 'anti-social' media such as fight pages.[9] Indeed, a range of criminal activities have been aided by new media technology, such as identity theft, online fraud, hacking, cyberbullying and the activities of criminal gangs and terrorist networks. Through social media, messages can spread at rapid speed, authors have the option to remain anonymous and cyberspace remains largely unregulated.[10] Yet there has been little research on online hate speech, incitement to violence and vigilantism, despite consistent criticism of social media companies such as Google and Facebook for failing to respond to online hate crime and extremism[11] and the problems this extremism poses for police and prosecutors.[12]

Vigilantism in the digital age

Citizens have often engaged in various forms of community justice, including in recent times Neighbourhood Watch and citizen policing. Arguably, the most volatile form of community justice is vigilantism yet there has been little exploration of how social media has both facilitated and changed the way that vigilantism is coordinated and carried out. Les Johnston's 1996 definition of vigilantism continues to be widely used today. He defines vigilantism as:

> A social movement giving rise to premeditated acts of force – or threatened force – by autonomous citizens. It arises as a reaction to the transgression of institutional norms by individuals or groups – or to their potential or imputed transgression, such acts are focused upon crime control and/or social control and aim to offer assurance (or 'guarantees') of security both to participants and to other members of a given established order.[13]

Such definitions of vigilantism were developed before the rise of social media and fail to capture how social media platforms have transformed the ways in which people interact and engage with crime and criminal justice agencies – and, indeed, how criminal justice agencies interact with various members of the public through social media.

As our social interactions increasingly take place in the cyber realm, unofficial crime control has flourished, and various forms of 'cyber-vigilantism' have emerged.[14] Two areas that have been particularly prominent in hate speech and incitement to violence have been vigilante-style Facebook groups directed against racial, ethnic and religious minorities on the one hand and people accused of sex offences on the other. In the case of people (often allegedly) accused of sex offences, social media platforms (particularly Facebook and Tinder) that name, shame and expose alleged paedophiles have become the most conspicuous examples of community members advocating for citizen action and, in some cases, taking the law into their own hands,[15] with such activities reported widely in Australia[16] and elsewhere.[17] Some vigilante-style Facebook groups may be short-lived and established around a particular incident,[18] while other groups include 'relatively organized civilian groups that rely on the expertise of initiated volunteers to carry out their activities'.[19] Examples focused on targeting alleged paedophiles include the group Perverted Justice in the United States and groups such as Dark Justice and Letzgo Hunting – the latter with over 15,000 Facebook followers – in the United Kingdom.[20]

The physical presence of a more or less cohesive and committed vigilante group is now unnecessary for violence to occur against particular people alleged to have committed sex offences. For example, in all likelihood the majority of members of the Letzgo Hunting Facebook group in the United Kingdom or the 11,000 followers of the Kangaroo Court of Australia Facebook group or the 112,000 followers of the Fighters Against Child Abuse Australia Facebook group will never meet or have common interactions with fellow members of the group other than online through the particular social media site.

While research evidence about the transmission of social media hate speech into real-life behaviour is scarce,[21] social media sites like Facebook have a presence that can legitimatize the beliefs of their members – for example, that violence against a named person is justified because of the alleged failure of the justice system. Further, these sites can provide specific information (the name, photo, residential address, place of employment) of people alleged to have broken the law. In these circumstances, for those members of social media sites who decide that vigilante action is necessary, it is not difficult to locate individuals. In this context, it only takes one or a few of the many thousands of members of these social media groups to decide to engage in violence against identified individuals. As Roose argues, social media can act as an accelerant, 'bringing together disparate, often isolated figures to feed off one another'.[22]

Supporting this view of social media acting as an 'accelerant', Karsten Müller and Carlo Schwarz found links between social media and the frequency of hate crimes aimed at refugee groups in Europe and the United States.[23] Using Facebook data in Germany, they demonstrated that right-wing anti-refugee sentiments on Facebook could predict violent crimes against refugees in locations with higher social media usage.[24] Correlations found between Twitter usage and hate crimes in the United States similarly indicated that social media plays a role in the reproduction of hate crimes and political polarization. The research suggests that while social media itself may not cause crime, it can act as a propagation mechanism between online hate speech and real-life violent acts.[25] It is this problem of racist hate speech and calls for vigilante action on social media, and subsequent communal violence, that we address here in the specific context of Australia.

Racialization and vigilantism: 'anti-crime' Facebook groups in Australia

'Anti-crime' Facebook groups have appeared across all states and territories in Australia. Often, these groups are created by local residents concerned about crime in their neighbourhood and have emerged from frustration with formal criminal justice processes and a perceived need for community policing in order to address (primarily) youth crime. These Facebook groups may have particular positive functions for members: allowing residents to share experiences, alerting others to potential criminal behaviour and providing a discussion platform for local community issues. At the same time, though, these groups largely present a racialized explanation of crime, legitimatize the violent and racist rhetoric of their members and often provide specific details about potential targets for vigilantism.

The overtly racialized content (in particular, referring to Aboriginal and Torres Strait Islander young people) and the racialization of crime through social media are key focuses of our analysis. Posts on these Facebook pages often refer to Aboriginal and Torres Strait Islander people as 'animals', 'scumbags' and 'oxygen thieves'.[26] Overwhelmingly, these posts emphasize the racial or physical appearance of these young people and are highly derogatory. The following are typical of racist comments in posts about alleged offences committed by Aboriginal people in various parts of Australia:

> I'm not trying to be racist but my personal opinion of aboriginals is . . . they are oxygen thieves.
>
> (Kalgoorlie Crimes Group, 24 October 2016)

> Fucking abos getting out of control . . .
>
> (Kalgoorlie Crimes Group, 3 December 2016)

> . . . those kids ain't human, they're animals
>
> (Dubbo Crimes Page, 22 October 2018)

Posts to these pages are made in real time and, as shown by the comments here, often mention the location of young people, potentially allowing vigilantes to find them easily. The following redacted comments were made on a post about an Aboriginal child 'between the ages of 8–10' who was alleged to have committed a theft offence.

> One boys name is ________ lives at ________ Hodges crescent, Vincent.
>
> (Townsville Crime Alerts & Discussion, 25 March 2017)

> They hang around Cambridge Park. There is a group of them, two girl are in high school and the other all go to vincent primary. There go there everyday afterschool to get the free piece of fruit. They live next the park. As that where ive seen them went walking with the family. they laugh at security and police.
>
> (Townsville Crime Alerts & Discussion, 25 March 2017)

> Hi mate try the house 2 doors down Fitzroy street mosque (fitsroy street south) I seen him on the bike as I was driving past. Those shoes give it away.

> There was another fulla with him which I near missed seemed to be off his tree wandering across the road. Hope this helps I don't know the correct number though sorry
>
> Mark, if you could be more accurate with your posting I'd appreciate it. I'm two doors up from the mosque and I don't want anyone thinking I'm involved in this theft. That sort of information would be best private-messaged, and detail in that message which direction from the mosque you are talking about. Regards, John Ryan.
>
> (Dubbo Crimes Page, 1 November 2018)

Often, the very presence of Aboriginal people is considered to be synonymous with crime:

> Here you go [smiley face, followed by an image of four youngsters in hoodies]
>
> Young gangster, soon they will rape, steal and kill. and the end of the day you will see them lying with their blood. poor children.
>
> (Dubbo Crimes Page, 15 October 2018)

These posts often encourage community members to take the law into their own hands and make suggestions as to how alleged offenders should be dealt with:

> I know what 1 looks like and if him or any of his thieving mates come around my place again I dont care what age he might be, he's getting a cricket bat to his head . . . Im over this shit, 3 breakins this year
>
> (Dubbo Crimes Page, 15 October 2018)

> Catch n kill
>
> (Dubbo Crimes Page, 15 October 2018)

> Wrap a bat around his teeth
>
> (Kalgoorlie Crimes Group, 4 October 2017)

> Sharpen your star pickets people
>
> (Kalgoorlie Crimes Group, 4 October 2017)

> This is why people should have guns if it looks like they're going to get away shoot them Just Shoot Em anyway doesn't matter
>
> (Townsville Crime Alerts & Discussion, 16 October 2017)

> Should've run the bastard over! Reversed up and got a run u at him
>
> (Townsville Crime Alerts & Discussion, 25 January 2018)

> Don't ring the cops just beat the fuck out of them with poles and leave them in the gutter and just call the ambos

> Thats it Mick your right. No point at all calling the cops . . . its a pretty bad situation here in Dubbo. They just dont want to face facts.
>
> (Dubbo Crimes Page, 30 October 2018)

> keep the shovel handy and flog the oxygen out of the scum
>
> (Dubbo Crimes Page, 12 November 2018)

> Take the law into your own hands now i reckon. It will work better that way.
>
> (Dubbo Crimes Page, 18 October 2018)

Comments that include clearly racist and violent threats are posted with apparent impunity. Posters rarely make an effort to conceal their identity, which indicates a lack of shame about the nature of their posts. Often those who are commenting will display their full name, date of birth, employer and where they live. There is an assumed social consensus around what is being stated on the pages – that overt racism and calls to vigilante violence are acceptable on sites that ostensibly exist to develop community responses to local crime problems.

Our research suggests that many of these Facebook groups have emerged in regional areas and often have around 4,000 members. Some, though, attract a significantly greater public following.[27] A Facebook group in the regional city of Townsville, Queensland – the Townsville Crime, Alerts & Discussions group – has over 48,000 members, in a city with a residential population of approximately 190,000. The Townsville Crime Alerts & Discussions Facebook page has carried commentary calling for direct vigilante-style action against those alleged to have broken the law. The Townsville group has also had a direct impact on public policy in Queensland. The creators have consistently pushed for more punitive approaches to handling youth crime and organized various petitions, protests and community meetings that have featured prominently in the media. The group advocated for the punitive youth justice legislation that was introduced in Queensland in 2014, and it was referred to specifically during the second reading speech in parliament. While police have issued official warnings against vigilante action in Townsville,[28] vigilante-style attacks have reportedly occurred in recent years.[29] In the Northern Territory, it was reported that over 3,000 residents had joined the online vigilante Facebook group Darwin Community Justice and had been patrolling the streets in response to youth crime.[30] Vigilante groups were also operating in Alice Springs, where a 13-year-old Aboriginal boy was beaten unconscious in what was reported to be a racially motivated attack.[31] Similar issues relating to vigilante action have been raised in the Pilbara and Kimberley in Western Australia.[32]

Perhaps the best-known Australian example of a violent attack following social media calls for violence was the death of 14-year-old Aboriginal boy Elijah Doughty in Kalgoorlie in 2016. Elijah was riding a motorcycle when he was struck and killed by a vehicle driven by a 55-year-old non-Indigenous man pursuing him in response to an alleged theft (see also Chapter 4 in this book). Following

Elijah's death, violent protests took place between community members and the police, when the driver of the vehicle that killed the child was charged with manslaughter (rather than murder), and Aboriginal people were denied entry to the courthouse when the accused first appeared.[33] The driver of the vehicle was subsequently found not guilty of manslaughter by a jury that did not include any Aboriginal people. He was instead found guilty of the lesser charge of dangerous driving occasioning death and was sentenced to three years' imprisonment. (The maximum penalty for the offence is ten years.) The verdict was met with reactions of grief and anger from the local community. It was reported that over 100 people marched in the streets of Kalgoorlie in protest.

Elijah's death occurred against a backdrop of rising racial tensions and longstanding community divisions in Kalgoorlie. The population of Kalgoorlie sits at around 30,000, and, in the months prior to Elijah's death, the two main anti-crime Facebook groups (Name Shame Crimes Kalgoorlie and Kalgoorlie Crimes Whinge and Whine) had approximately 18,000 members.[34] In the days prior to Elijah's death, posts on these Facebook pages had encouraged racist violence and vigilantism. Specifically, posts were encouraging community members to 'run the oxygen thieves off the road if you see them'. Following Elijah's death, posts included 'Good job you thieving bastard. Don't think you'll be touching a bike anytime soon ahaha about time someone took it into their own hands hope it happens again' and 'Aboriginals don't deserve to live. That's good that young boy got killed. Aboriginals don't own Australia. Aboriginals live in the bush. They are filthy animals. They all need the death sentence'.[35] Sentiments reflecting this type of overt racism and the promotion of racist violence were not unusual on these sites at this time – and, indeed, have continued since.

The two Kalgoorlie Facebook groups were both eventually closed down after the death of Elijah. The group's creator was quoted in the media as saying that people running the groups should not be held responsible for the content:

> I maintain all comments or posts made in the group belong to the writer and the writer only . . . you can close this site down, but I guarantee another 10 will pop up.[36]

Indeed, not long after they were closed down, new Facebook groups emerged to take their place, again filled with the same sentiments. The (new) Kalgoorlie Crimes Group, which has over 12,000 members, continues calls for vigilante action.[37]

> Since the death of this Elijah doughty all the Aboriginal people have gone on crime wave coz they know they can get away with it
>
> (Kalgoorlie Crimes Group, 12 March 2018)

> Won't b long until some one else is hurt and we're to blame. They keep asking for trouble. Ud think they would learn . . . But u can't teach the stupid I spose

> They break into my house and i catch them i will take there hands
> (Kalgoorlie Crimes Group, 12 March 2018)

Since Elijah's death, Aboriginal children have been racially taunted, photographed and chased by unknown white men in vehicles in Kalgoorlie,[38] and racial tensions in the town have remained high.[39] In January 2018, the Derby Chamber of Commerce wrote to the Chief Magistrate of Western Australia, arguing that children between the ages of 6 and 17 were being released from the courts without conviction, and

> this has caused the community to take action themselves to protect their property and we can foresee that vigilante groups [are] being formed on social media, who will patrol the streets to apprehend offenders. . . . there's concern that it will eventuate in a Kalgoorlie situation.[40]

The anti-crime Facebook groups discussed in this chapter show clearly overt racist hate speech, calls for vigilante violence and the associated violence and racial tensions within particular communities. These groups also disseminate particular views about the nature of crime. Within the comments can be found constant repetition of the key assumptions of what Russell Hogg and David Brown refer to as a populist 'law and order common sense', including that crime rates are soaring, that the criminal justice system is 'soft on crime' and that there should be more police with greater powers, as well as tougher penalties from the courts.[41]

While the various anti-crime Facebook sites convey a particular narrative that corresponds with the elements of law and order 'common sense', a dominant aspect of this narrative specifically pathologizes Aboriginal and Torres Strait Islander people.[42] In particular, the narrative feeds into a colonialist view that Indigenous cultures are not only primitive, but also intrinsically criminal. Aboriginal and Torres Strait Islander people are repeatedly depicted as 'lazy' alcoholics who are unable to look after their children, rather than crime and offending being linked to long-standing social and economic inequalities within Australia.

> It's blame every one else for their life. Yet the only ones that can fix it is themselves but they to busy blaming others
> The more you hand out the more they will take
> So true roger. They keep saying they hate us yet they keep taking from us
> With one hand and with the other
> (Kalgoorlie Crimes Group, 11 November 2017)

> Teach them how to be a good pillar of society and get of their asses and get a job and stop taking and believing the good hard working people of Australia [Australian flag emoji] owe them something and should pay for all the welfare they receive and government grants and so on and get over the past move on and teach the next generation to be better people

> Obviously have no idea where their kids are, welfare should step in . . . but wait for it . . . stolen generation we cant take these kids away from them
>
> (Kalgoorlie Crimes Group, 13 January 2018)

> I'm downright sick of black people telling me I can't think/act/acknowledge anything because I'm white, its not fair to rally against racism yet have so much hatred for white people and children living today, even teaching their children white people are racist, carrying on the racist antics. Blacks need to stop being so racist towards white people just as much! I'm glad this has Come to attention
>
> (Alice Springs Community Open Forum, 20 November 2018)

In the Facebook groups we observed, there is little thought or care regarding the ongoing effects of colonization, dispossession, oppression, racism and centuries of the systemic and structural violence that continues to be experienced by Aboriginal and Torres Strait Islander communities today. This structural violence is reflected in high rates of child removal, poor health outcomes, higher rates of disability, lack of access to housing, poor economic outcomes and higher rates of incarceration.[43] As we have argued elsewhere, the contemporary structural disadvantage and racism faced by Aboriginal communities was created through laws, policies and practices as a fundamental part of the dispossession of Indigenous peoples in settler colonial states.[44] In contrast, the Facebook pages we analyzed continue the colonialist fantasy that the colonized are the authors of their own misfortune. Next, we argue further that this colonialist fantasy is reinforced in sections of the 'old media' and political discourses more generally.

Racism, politics and mainstream media

In the reporting of crime and criminality, the media are not a monolithic entity, with mainstream media (TV, newspapers, radio) usually considered separate from social media (for example, Facebook, websites, blogs). Yet they do share a number of characteristics, one of the most important of which is that they reinforce cultural fears of 'otherness'.[45] As Phil Scraton notes:

> No group conceives itself as *the One,* the *essential,* the absolute, without conceiving and defining the *Other*. The Other is the *stranger,* the *outsider,* the *alien,* the *suspect community:* Otherness *begets* fear, *begets* hostility, *begets* denial.
>
> (emphasis in original)[46]

The racism and threats of violence that have come to characterize anti-crime Facebook groups are apparent across social media more generally. Research has established that online racial vilification and harassment are common experiences for many Aboriginal and Torres Strait Islander people and other racialized minorities.[47] Furthermore, while social media platforms such as Facebook, Twitter and YouTube may be a source of some of the most unrestrained racial vilification in contemporary discourse, overt and casual racism increasingly emanates from parliament and is echoed through television, on talkback radio and in print and online media.[48] In December 2017, the UN Expert Panel on the Elimination of Racial Discrimination found that racism and racial discrimination in the public sphere, in political debates and in the media are on the rise in Australia, recommending that Australia 'put an end to racist hate speech'.[49] Since then, there have been numerous examples of racist rhetoric from senior politicians and media reporting in Australia.

Perhaps most notably, in October 2018, One Nation's Pauline Hanson introduced a motion that included the white supremacist slogan 'It's okay to be white', which was originally backed by coalition government senators. Following intense media backlash, the government claimed its vote supporting the motion was an 'administrative error' and demanded a second vote to reverse its position.[50] As Jack Latimore argues, 'the fact that coalition senators were given an opportunity for a "do over" the next day must be peak white privilege' and 'is a clear indication of the ideological position of the coalition government'.[51] Weeks later, signs declaring 'It's okay to be white' appeared outside the offices of MPs who were critical of the government's original support of the motion.[52] Hanson's motion came not long after right-wing Australian senator Fraser Anning used his maiden speech to the Senate to call for a return to the White Australia Policy and a 'final solution' to immigration, echoing the infamous Nazi phrase used to describe the genocide of Jews in Europe.[53] Anning was later censured by the Australian Senate for his comments blaming the Christchurch massacre on Muslim immigration. A few months prior to Senator Anning's maiden speech, Home Affairs Minister Peter Dutton stated that white South African farmers who wanted to migrate to Australia 'deserve special attention',[54] describing them as 'the sort of migrants that we want to bring into our country'.[55]

Mainstream media has repeatedly come under fire for the promotion of racist content. In September 2018, an investigation by the Australian Communications and Media Authority (ACMA) found the Seven Network's breakfast television programme *Sunrise* to be in breach of the code of practice after airing an all-white panel discussion on the adoption of Aboriginal children. During the discussion, it was stated that the Stolen Generations policy that removed Aboriginal children from their families was for their own 'wellbeing' and 'perhaps' it should happen again.[56] Just a few months later, *Sunrise* host David Koch made a slavery 'joke' live on air.[57]

Bill Leak's infamous cartoon published in the national broadsheet *The Australian* in 2017 provides another example. The cartoon was printed on Aboriginal and Torres Strait Islander Children's Day and just days following the ABC *Four Corners* documentary *Australia's Shame*, which showed the abuse, tear-gassing and use of mechanical restraints that had occurred against (primarily) Aboriginal young people in youth detention in the Northern Territory, triggering a royal commission.[58] Leak's cartoon depicted an Aboriginal boy being handed by a police officer back to his father, who is shown to be so drunk he is unable to recall his child's name. The implication of the cartoon was that the responsibility for the over-incarceration of Aboriginal children and the abuse they endure in youth prisons lies solely with their parents.[59] As Bronwyn Carlson and colleagues argue, the Leak cartoon and 'the colonial discourse it reproduced, thus worked to contain the political potential of national outrage by redirecting its source back onto Aboriginal people'.[60] These colonial motifs are long-running and are reproduced often on the anti-crime Facebook pages we noted earlier.

Racialized and misleading crime reporting on 'African gangs' in Victoria following the 2016 Moomba 'riot' has been intensified by comments from senior government officials.[61] Perhaps most notably, Home Affairs Minister Peter Dutton appeared on talkback station 2GB to claim that 'people are afraid to go out to restaurants in the night-time because they're followed home by these gangs'.[62] In January 2019, then-Senator Fraser Anning attended a far-right rally against 'African gangs' in Melbourne. It has been argued that these claims have lent legitimacy to far-right groups now planning vigilante action.[63] Indeed, research by Kathryn Benier and colleagues found that as a consequence of racialized media reporting, young South Sudanese Australians have been subject to increasing racial abuse online and in public settings.[64] Their research found that racialized media coverage 'served to embolden people with pre-existing racist and xenophobic beliefs while simultaneously exacerbating the institutionalised racism that young South Sudanese Australians experience on a daily basis'.[65]

The ABC's Triple J *Hack* programme, the Seven Network and most recently Sky News have all aired interviews with neo-Nazi and chairman of far-right organization United Patriots Front (UPF) Blair Cottrell,[66] who has a criminal history of racial vilification and has previously argued that a portrait of Adolf Hitler be in 'every (Australian) classroom and every school'.[67] The UPF was one of a number of far-right organizations that vowed to take vigilante action against the so-called 'African gang crisis' in Victoria.[68] The person charged with the Christchurch shootings, Brenton Tarrant, has been a public supporter on social media of Cottrell and the UPF.[69]

As Andre Oboler points out, the acceptance or, indeed, promotion of racism and racist language by those in trusted positions of authority – such as senior politicians and police officers – works to normalize racist discourse and marginalizes victims within society.[70] Carlson and Ryan Frazer note that 'social media can facilitate the reproduction of power hierarchies in which Indigenous people are subjected to racial violence, subjugation and discrimination'.[71] We argue that this applies equally to other racialized minorities. Indeed, it is the racism and hate speech that are increasingly found in mainstream political and media discourses that support the ubiquitous nature of racism and violence permeating online social media.

Witnessing and experiencing the kinds of racism discussed in this chapter have real and significant effects on social, emotional, mental and physical health and wellbeing.[72] Latimore argues that racist discourse emanating from parliament works to sustain systemic racism:

> Psychological distress stemming from exposure to racism is often a key contributor to substance abuse. Elite racism – the kinds of racism filtering down from parliament, for example, to fuel racist attitudes amongst the general public – also leads to unequal access to societal resources requires for good health and well-being, such as education, employment and housing.[73]

Carlson and colleagues use the concept of 'shared recognition' to describe 'the collective sense of anger and frustration experienced by Indigenous people when traumatic events in the public domain act as reminders of the enduring-ness of colonial violence'.[74] They argue that:

> The collective experience of trauma emanates from a 'shared recognition' of the continuity of colonial practices. This manifests often from the deep seated internalizing of inferiority that comes with the repeated onslaught of racism; Indigenous people, whether politically motivated or not in the 'white' sense of that term, have a deep and abiding knowledge of how we have been, and continue to be perceived.[75]

While it might be reasoned that, in some cases, social media platforms provide the opportunity to disseminate 'counter-hegemonic discourses' in relation to crime,[76] we argue that the anti-crime Facebook pages that we have examined are quite the opposite. They feed into well-worn populist views of law and order. More deeply, they reproduce a mostly racialized explanation of crime – in fact, on many anti-crime Facebook sites, the very presence of Aboriginal youth in public is presented as synonymous with crime. Such a view reproduces a long-running motif of colonial ideology within Australia – namely that Aboriginal people constitute a racially inferior, crime-prone group who deserve either incarceration or permanent removal.

We also recognize, however, that under particular conditions 'the internet can be a powerful source for social good'.[77] The rise of 'hashtag activism' – from Black Lives Matter to #MeToo – has seen social media as a driving force behind social movements throughout the world.[78] While it is not the focus of this chapter, it is important to acknowledge that platforms such as Facebook and Twitter have developed as important political tools for strengthening and amplifying the voices of Aboriginal and Torres Strait Islander people, who use social media to connect, advocate and speak on their own terms about issues that are affecting them.[79] As Carlson and colleagues highlight, social media sites can be powerful vehicles for opposition for Indigenous politics and can form a basis for discursive shifts and potential change.[80] Social media sites have created new opportunities for counter-hegemonic discourse and counter-racist mobilization by Aboriginal and Torres Strait Islander people into spaces that historically have been devoid of Indigenous voices, such as mainstream media. The crucial #SOSBLAKAUSTRALIA campaign against the closure of remote Aboriginal communities provides an example of this.[81]

The online response to Bill Leak's cartoon discussed previously provides another example of a creative strategy for 'resisting, subverting and challenging the political status quo'.[82] Following the publication of Leak's cartoon, Aboriginal and Torres Strait Islander people took to social media to post photographs with their families under the hashtag #IndigenousDads. As Carlson and colleagues highlight, the images and stories 'stood in direct contrast to the colonial stereotype of the neglectful Indigenous parent while also promoting culturally specific parenting practices that involve wider familial networks'.[83] The viral Twitter reaction countering the narrative of 'African gangs' in Victoria was similarly powerful. Under the hashtag #AfricanGangs, members of the Australian Sudanese community shared photographs of weddings, graduation ceremonies, birthday parties and family celebrations.[84]

The regulation of online hate speech and cyber-racism

The expansion of social media platforms alongside the development of new technologies presents a wide range of regulatory challenges with regard to preventing cyber-racism, abuse and racial vilification. In this section, we explore the various mechanisms available to address this in Australia. They include civil and criminal racial vilification laws, criminal law, cyberbullying legislation, the *Broadcasting Services Act 1992* (Cth) (the BSA), intermediary terms of service and codes of conduct and international protocols and standards.[85] However, as Gail Mason and Natalie Czapski concluded from their analysis of the regulation of cyber-racism in Australia, 'there is no comprehensive system for expressly denouncing and remedying the harm of cyber-racism by offering an efficient and accountable process for removing harmful material, backed by a mechanism of enforcement'.[86] Other Australian scholars have similarly highlighted the difficulties of enforcing online racism and racial vilification.[87]

At the federal level, section 18C of the *Racial Discrimination Act 1975* (Cth) (the RDA) makes it unlawful for a person to carry out an act that is reasonably likely to 'offend, insult, humiliate, or intimidate' another person or a group of people if that act is done on the basis of 'race, colour, or national or ethnic origin'. There are limitations to the protection under the RDA. Section 18D excludes from section 18C anything said or done 'reasonably and in good faith'.[88] Further, while section 18C potentially provides a powerful protection against hate speech, racism and racial vilification, there have reportedly been few successful prosecutions under this section.[89] Data from the Australian Human Rights Commission indicates that while complaints made in relation to racial hatred under section 18C of the RDA more than doubled, from 77 in 2015–16 to 159 in 2016–17, just 5 per cent of complaints in the latter period related to material that was published on the internet (including email, social media, websites and chat rooms).[90] While these figures indicate that complaints of racial hatred under the RDA are increasing, it remains an under-utilized avenue for the remedy of online cyber-racism. An explanation for this may be that under Australian civil hate speech legislation, the locus of enforcement responsibility lies with the victims.[91] As Gelber and McNamara argue:

> Australia's primary model of hate speech regulation places a heavy burden on the targets of hate speech. The legislation can only be invoked in relation to a given incident if a member of the vilified group is willing to step up and take on the arduous, stressful, time-consuming, and possibly expensive task of pursuing a remedy on behalf of the wider community. In a sense, the regulatory model *assumes* the existence of such a person in each of the targeted communities.[92]

The fact that proceedings under civil racial vilification legislation must be victim initiated is made even more difficult in the context of anti-crime Facebook groups. These pages are generally closed to the outside public, meaning that one must first request to join the page and be approved by a group administrator. From our analysis of these groups, the vast majority of the members of these pages are not themselves the targets of the racial vilification.

The *Racial Discrimination Act 1975* is complemented by section 474.17(1) of the *Criminal Code Act 1995* (Cth), which makes it an offence to use a carriage service to 'menace, harass, or cause offence'.[93] Mason and Czapski report that this section has been employed more extensively to deal with harmful conduct online, with 308 successful prosecutions between its introduction in 2005 and 2014.[94] Although we do not know how many of the 308 prosecutions involved racial vilification, the section of the legislation was used to address racial vilification on Facebook in 2016 when an NSW man was convicted under section 474.17(1) after posting racist and abusive comments on Facebook towards former Northern Territory Senator Nova Peris.[95] In addition to federal racial vilification laws, each state and territory (with the exception of the Northern Territory) has enacted legislation intended to operate alongside the Commonwealth laws. However, research has questioned the ability of state and territory vilification laws to effectively address online racial vilification, which is not bound by geographical lines.[96]

At the federal level, cyberbullying legislation has been introduced; this is administered by the Office of the eSafety Commissioner. Under the *Enhancing Online Safety for Children Act 2015* (Cth), the Commissioner has the power to investigate complaints about serious cyberbullying material targeting Australian minors. The legislation has the potential to encompass racial vilification but can only deal with such content if it is directed at a specific Australian child, not a particular racial group.[97]

Hosts and intermediaries that control websites and social media platforms typically have a set of terms that govern the behaviour of the users who subscribe to their service, with mechanisms for reporting or dealing with harmful content. On Facebook, these include the Statement of Rights and Responsibilities, which requires users not to use the service to bully, intimidate, harass, post content that is hate speech or threaten to use or actually use Facebook to do anything unlawful, malicious or discriminatory. Additionally, Facebook's Community Standards state that Facebook will remove hate speech, including attacks on people based on their race, ethnicity, national origin or religious affiliation. It is important to note, though, that the anti-crime Facebook groups to which we refer in this chapter are regulated by administrators (who are members of the groups being monitored) and who are themselves tasked with deleting inappropriate and offensive content. It is a reasonable assumption that the comments to which we refer, calling for vigilante racist violence, have been deemed by administrators to be acceptable content for public discussion and in compliance with Facebook's Statement of Rights and Responsibilities.[98]

In cases in which Facebook *is* alerted to breaches of its community standards and rights and responsibilities, there is evidence that Facebook itself is often slow to regulate the racist conduct of its users or may even fail to do so.[99] Oboler has detailed the significant shortcomings and failures of Facebook in its willingness to address hate speech on its platform.[100] In 2012, a number of racist images (memes) targeting Aboriginal people began circulating on social media.[101] Facebook's response to the 'Aboriginal Memes' page was that it did not breach its terms of service. Facebook originally removed the pages and then restored them on the condition that the creator label the page as 'controversial content'.[102] It was only when ACMA became involved that Facebook blocked the pages, and then it only did so in Australia.[103] As Oboler argues, Facebook's failure to appropriately address online hate creates an attitude in which people feel that racism is acceptable.[104]

Ariadna Matamoros-Fernandez uses the concept of 'platformed racism' to describe how new forms of racism are articulated via social media and the ways the platforms operate to amplify and manufacture racist discourse in society – specifically through their design, algorithms and policies.[105] Platforms like Facebook, Twitter and YouTube are not neutral players in the promotion of particular content.[106] It has been argued that self-regulation has failed in Australia and that governments need to explore the possibility of stronger regulatory regimes for major social media platforms:

> Such platforms [Facebook and Twitter] sell significant advertising into the Australian market and should be held accountable under Australian law or be held subject to trade sanctions for failing to voluntarily comply with a reasonable human rights regime based on international treaties of which Australia is a signatory.[107]

Although Facebook and Twitter have recently taken steps to remove white nationalist and other hate groups from their platforms,[108] it remains to be seen whether this will be able to stymie the flow of racist rhetoric online. In response to the unwillingness of social media platforms to address online hate crime, Germany passed anti-online hate speech legislation in mid-2017, which threatens to fine providers of online platforms up to €50 million if they fail to delete criminal and unlawful hate speech content.[109] The tightening of anti-online hate speech mechanisms has reportedly led to an exodus of neo-Nazi and other alt-right groups, with many moving their online activities to unregulated spaces.[110] The legislation introduced in Australia after the Christchurch massacre – the *Criminal Code Amendment (Unlawful Showing of Abhorrent Violent Material) Act 2019* (Cth) – requires tech platforms to 'expeditiously' remove 'abhorrent violent material', including acts of terrorism, murder, torture, rape and kidnapping. The legislation does not cover hate speech or calls for vigilante action. As a result, the current regulatory regime has thus far proven incapable of stemming the rise of racist hate speech and promotion of racist violence on social media.

Conclusion

As we have argued previously, social media provides a real-time way of publicizing a vision of moral unity – a unity that is achieved through the exclusion and sometimes violent control of racialized 'others'.[111] The anti-crime Facebook groups we have examined foster a culture of vitriolic racism and vigilante violence, acting as echo chambers that reinforce racialized explanations of crime. These groups do little to question the broader ideological and political frameworks that present crime and disorder as being disconnected from structural and historical contexts and, even more problematically, advocate for the direct use of violence against various individuals and groups.

The regulation of cyber-racism, abuse and racial vilification appears to be profoundly inadequate for addressing the concerns outlined in this chapter. As Imran Awan – writing in the context of online Islamophobia – argues, the response to online hate speech requires a multifaceted and international approach from different agencies, including the police, social networking sites and government, that tackle online hate speech as a rising phenomenon.[112] We would add to that list the importance of civil society in directly challenging the racist content on social media. However, while such an approach may address some of the issues we have raised here, we also recognize the need for broader political interventions: the views expressed throughout these groups mirror white nationalist sentiments that are found in sections of mainstream media and, increasingly, in Australian political discourse.[113]

Notes

1 Grattan (2019).
2 Salter (2013), p 228.
3 See McGovern (2015); Milivojevic (2011); Milivojevic and McGovern (2014).
4 McGovern (2014).

5 Crofts et al. (2015); Karaian (2014).
6 Henry and Powell (2014, 2016).
7 Salter (2013).
8 Goldsmith (2010).
9 Wood (2017).
10 Awan (2016), p. 2.
11 For example, House of Commons Home Affairs Committee (2017).
12 Awan (2016).
13 Johnston (1996), p. 232.
14 De Silva (2018); Smallridge, Wagner and Crowl (2016).
15 Hill and Wall (2015).
16 Mills (2015); Olding (2016b).
17 BBC News (2018); Milne (2018); Perraudin (2017).
18 See, for example, Trenwith (2010).
19 Smallridge, Wagner and Crowl (2016), p 62.
20 In 2013, Gary Cleary committed suicide after being publicly confronted by members of Letzgo Hunting and accused of being a paedophile (see BBC News 2013).
21 Müller and Schwarz (2018a).
22 Roose (2018).
23 Müller and Schwarz (2018a, 2018b).
24 Müller and Schwarz (2018a).
25 Müller and Schwarz (2018a).
26 The quotes from the Facebook pages that are referenced throughout this chapter are verbatim as they appeared on Facebook.
27 For example, the now-defunct Moreton Crime Watch public Facebook group in Brisbane was one of the larger groups, with over 75,000 members. The group shared the names and photographs of 18 young people who had allegedly been involved in property offences and their associates, in contravention of laws prohibiting the publication of identifying information of children (White 2017).
28 Atkin (2016).
29 McMahon (2016).
30 Smee (2014).
31 Campbell (2017).
32 Parke (2018a, 2018b).
33 Wahlquist (2016).
34 Tomlin (2016).
35 Cunneen and Russell (2017).
36 Tomlin (2016).
37 McKinnon (2018).
38 Toohey (2016).
39 Tomlin (2018).
40 Parke (2018a).
41 Hogg and Brown (1996).
42 As well as other racialized minorities, as we discuss further later in this chapter.
43 Australian Institute of Health and Welfare (2017, 2018).
44 Cunneen and Tauri (2016).
45 Greer and Jewkes (2005), p. 20.
46 Scraton (2005), p 3 in Cunneen and Tauri (2016), pp 23–4.
47 Carlson et al. (2017); Carlson and Frazer (2018).
48 Ho (2017).
49 Committee on the Elimination of Racial Discrimination (2017), p 3.
50 *SBS News (2018)*.

51 Latimore (2018).
52 Boisvert (2018).
53 Masters (2018).
54 Burke (2018).
55 Koziol (2018).
56 Meade (2018).
57 Morgan (2018).
58 Meldrum-Hanna and Worthington (2016).
59 Carlson et al. (2017), p 13.
60 Carlson et al. (2017), p 13.
61 For example, former Prime Minister Malcolm Turnbull said he was 'very concerned at the growing gang violence and lawlessness in Victoria', and Federal Health Minister Greg Hunt claimed that 'African gang violence in some areas . . . is clearly out of control' (Wahlquist 2018, see also Benier et al. 2018).
62 Hunter and Preiss (2018).
63 Mannix and Bucci (2018).
64 Benier et al. (2018).
65 Benier et al. (2018), p 4.
66 Davey (2018).
67 Bachelard and McMahon (2015).
68 Kourbaridis (2018); Mannix (2018); Mannix and Bucci (2018).
69 Mann, Nguyen and Gregory (2019).
70 Oboler (2012), p. 61.
71 Carlson and Frazer (2018), p 12.
72 Carlson et al. (2017); Latimore (2018).
73 Latimore (2018).
74 Carlson et al. (2017), p 1.
75 Carlson et al. (2017), p 7.
76 Salter (2013), p 226.
77 White, Maunder and Verrelli et al. (2018).
78 Bonilla and Rosa (2015); Sandoval-Almazan and Gil-Garcia (2014).
79 Latimore and Galbraith (2013); Rice et al. (2016).
80 Carlson et al. (2017), p 14.
81 Carlson (2016).
82 Carlson and Frazer (2018).
83 Carlson et al. (2017), p 13.
84 Bowen (2018); Dunstan (2018).
85 Mason and Czapski (2017).
86 Mason and Czapski (2017), p 4.
87 Herborn (2013); Hunyor (2008); Montgomery (2014).
88 *Racial Discrimination Act 1975* (Cth), s 18D.
89 Herborn (2013).
90 Australian Human Rights Commission (2016, 2017).
91 Gelber and McNamara (2015).
92 Gelber and McNamara (2015), p 649.
93 *Criminal Code Act 1995* (Cth), s 474.17(1).
94 Trenwith (2010), p 20.
95 Olding (2016a).
96 Mason and Czapski (2017).
97 Mason and Czapski (2017), p 28.
98 McGovern (2014), p 12.
99 Herbon (2013); Maier (2016); Montgomery (2014); Oboler (2012).

100 Oboler (2012).
101 Oboler (2012).
102 Oboler (2012), p 10.
103 Matamoros-Fernandez (2017).
104 Oboler (2012), p 56.
105 Matamoros-Fernandez (2017); see also Roose (2019).
106 Oboler (2012), p 56; see also Wood (2017) on 'algorithmic deviancy amplification'.
107 Oboler (2012), p 11.
108 Yarvin (2017).
109 Müller and Schwarz (2018a), p 6.
110 Such as the Russian-hosted social media platform VK: see Ross (2018).
111 Cunneen and Russell (2017).
112 Awan (2014), p 138.
113 Wilson (2018).

References

Secondary sources

Michael Atkin (2016) 'Townsville Police Issue Vigilante Warning as Youth Crime Rates Soar', *ABC News*, 13 December, www.abc.net.au/news/2016-12-13/townsville-police-vigilante-warning-youth-crime-rates-soar/8115002.

Australian Human Rights Commission (2016) *2015–2016 Complaint Statistics*, www.humanrights.gov.au/sites/default/files/AHRC%202015%20-%202016%20Complaint%20Statistics.pdf.

Australian Human Rights Commission (2017) *2016–2017 Complaint Statistics*, https://www.humanrights.gov.au/sites/default/files/AHRC_Complaints_AR_Stats_Tables%202016-2017.pdf.

Australian Institute of Health and Welfare (2017) *Youth Detention Population in Australia 2017*, AIHW.

——— (2018) *Aboriginal and Torres Strait Islander Stolen Generations Aged 50 and Over*, AIHW.

Imran Awan (2014) 'Islamophobia and Twitter: A Typology of Online Hate Against Muslims on Social Media' 6 *Policy and Internet* 133.

——— (2016) 'Islamophobia on Social Media: A Qualitative Analysis of the Facebook's Walls of Hate' 10 *International Journal of Cyber Criminology* 1.

Michael Bachelard and Luke McMahon (2015) 'Blair Cottrell, Rising Anti-Islam Movement Leader, Wanted Hitler in the Classroom', *Sydney Morning Herald*, 16 October, www.smh.com.au/national/blair-cottrell-leader-of-aussie-patriots-upf-wanted-hitler-in-the-classroom-20151016-gkbbvz.html.

BBC News (2013) 'Letzgo Hunting Denies Blame for Man's Suicide', *BBC News*, 18 September, www.bbc.com/news/uk-england-leicestershire-24145142.

——— (2018) 'Birmingham Teacher Snared by "Paedophile Hunters"', *BBC News*, 29 March, www.bbc.com/news/uk-wales-south-east-wales-43585266.

Kathryn Benier, Jarrett Blaustein, Diana Johns and Sara Maher (2018) *'Don't Drag Me into This': Growing Up South Sudanese in Victoria After the 2016 Moomba 'Riot'*, Centre for Multicultural Youth.

Eugene Boisvert (2018) '"White Supremacist" Signs Declaring "It's Okay to Be White" Appear Outside MPs' Offices', *ABC News*, 1 November, www.abc.net.au/news/2018-11-01/its-okay-to-be-white-signs-appear-outside-mps-offices/10457140.

Yarimar Bonilla and Jonathan Rosa (2015) '#Ferguson: Digital Protest, Hashtag Ethnography, and the Racial Politics of Social Media in the United States' 42 *American Ethnologist* 4.

Ebony Bowden (2018) 'Melbourne's Sudanese Community Reclaims "African Gangs" Slight in Powerful Campaign', *The Age*, 11 January, www.theage.com.au/national/victoria/african-gangs-slight-reclaimed-in-powerful-campaign-for-sudanese-community-20180110-h0g2ao.html.

Jason Burke (2018) 'Murders of Farmers in South Africa at 20-year Low, Research Shows', *The Guardian*, 27 June, www.theguardian.com/world/2018/jun/27/murders-of-farmers-in-south-africa-at-20-year-low-research-shows.

Claire Campbell (2017) 'Indigenous Boys Beaten Unconscious in Alice Springs, Family Believe Attack "Racially Motivated"', *ABC News*, 26 October, www.abc.net.au/news/2017-10-26/nt-police-aware-of-vigilante-violence-on-alice-springs-streets/9090588.

Bronwyn Carlson (2016) '12 Deadly Indigenous Australian Social Media Users to Follow', *The Conversation*, 17 October, https://theconversation.com/12-deadly-Indigenous-australian-social-media-users-to-follow-66479.

Bronwyn Carlson and Ryan Frazer (2018) *Social Media Mob: Being Indigenous Online*, Macquarie University.

Brownyn Carlson, Lani Jones, Michelle Harris, Nelia Quezada and Ryan Frazer (2017) 'Trauma, Shared Recognition and Indigenous Resistance on Social Media' 21 *Australasian Journal of Information Systems* 1.

Committee on the Elimination of Racial Discrimination (2017) *Concluding Observations on the Eighteenth to Twentieth Periodic Reports of Australia*, United Nations.

Thomas Crofts and Murray Lee, Alyce McGovern and Sanja Milivojevic (2015) *Sexting and Young People*, Palgrave Macmillan.

Chris Cunneen and Juan Tauri (2016) *Indigenous Criminology*, Policy Press.

Chris Cunneen and Sophie Russell (2017) 'Social Media, Vigilantism and Indigenous People in Australia', in Nicole Rafter and Michelle Brown (eds), *The Oxford Encyclopedia of Crime, Media and Popular Culture*, Oxford University Press.

Melissa Davey (2018) 'Channel Seven Under Fire Over Interview with Far-Right Activist', *The Guardian*, 15 January, www.theguardian.com/australia-news/2018/jan/15/channel-seven-under-fire-interview-far-right-activist-blair-cottrell.

K.K. de Silva (2018) 'Vigilantism and Cooperative Criminal Justice: Is there a Place for Cybersecurity Vigilantes in Cybercrime Fighting?' 32 *International Review of Law, Computers & Technology* 21.

Kevin Dunn and Rosalie Atie (2015) 'Regulating Online Racism in the Online Age', paper presented at the Perspectives on the Racial Discrimination Act: Papers from the 40 Years of the Racial Discrimination Act 1975 (Cth) Conference, 19–20 February, Australian Human Rights Commission.

Joseph Dunstan (2018) 'Melbourne African Community Comes Together After Vigilante Facebook Posts', *ABC Online*, 25 August, www.abc.net.au/news/2018-08-26/melbourne-youth-crime-vigilante-posts-spark-community-meeting/10161862.

Facebook (2015) 'Statement of Rights and Responsibilities', 30 June, www.facebook.com/legal/terms.

Karen Gelber and Luke McNamara (2015) 'The Effects of Civil Hate Speech Laws: Lessons from Australia' 49 *Law & Society Review* 631.

Andrew Goldsmith (2010) 'Policing's New Visibility' 50 *Theoretical Criminology* 914.

——— (2019) 'Morrison Flags New Laws to Stop Social Media Platforms Being "Weaponized"', *The Conversation*, 26 March, https://theconversation.com/morrison-flags-new-laws-to-stop-social-media-platforms-being-weaponised-114237.

Chris Greer and Yvonne Jewkes (2005) 'Extremes of Otherness: Media Images of Social Exclusion' 32 *Social Justice* 20.

Nicola Henry and Anastasia Powell (2014) 'Beyond the "Sext": Technology-facilitated Sexual Violence and Harassment Against Adult Women' 48 *Australian and New Zealand Journal of Criminology* 104.

——— (2016) 'Sexual Violence in the Digital Age: The Scope and Limits of Criminal Law' 25 *Social and Legal Studies* 397.

Daniel Herborn (2013) 'Racial Vilification and Social Media' 8 *Indigenous Law Bulletin* 16.

Graham Hill and David Wall (2015) 'How Online Vigilantes Make Paedophile Policing More Difficult', *The Conversation*, 4 June, https://theconversation.com/how-online-vigilantes-make-paedophile-policing-more-difficult-42562.

Christina Ho (2017) 'Racist Reporting Still Rife in Australian Media', *The Conversation*, 15 December, https://theconversation.com/racist-reporting-still-rife-in-australian-media-88957.

Russell Hogg and David Brown (1996) 'Law and Order Common Sense' 8 *Current Issues in Criminal Justice* 175.

House of Commons Home Affairs Committee (2017) *Hate Crime: Abuse, Hate and Extremism Online*, House of Commons (UK).

Fergus Hunter and Benjamin Preiss (2018) 'Victorians Scared to Go to Restaurants at Night Because of Street Gang Violence: Peter Dutton', *Sydney Morning Herald*, 3 January, www.smh.com.au/politics/federal/victorians-scared-to-go-to-restaurants-at-night-because-of-street-gang-violence-peter-dutton-20180103-h0cvu4.html.

Jonathan Hunyor (2008) 'Cyber-racism: Can the RDA Prevent It?' 35 *Brief* 30.

Les Johnston (1996) 'What is Vigilantism?' 36 *British Journal of Criminology* 220.

Lara Karaian (2014) 'Policing "Sexting": Responsibilisation, Respectability and Sexual Subjectivity in Child Protection/Crime Prevention Responses to Teenagers' Digital Sexual Expression' 18 *Theoretical Criminology* 282.

Andrew Kourbaridis (2018) 'Scared Melbourne Residents Want New "Vigilante" Group', *news.com.au*, 15 February, www.news.com.au/national/victoria/scared-melbourne-residents-want-new-vigilante-group/news-story/d034c8c4595a3ef3a5110ab2d067abab.

Michael Koziol (2018) 'Peter Dutton Wants a Refugee Intake of White South African Farmers', *Sydney Morning Herald*, 15 March, www.smh.com.au/politics/federal/peter-dutton-wants-a-refugee-intake-of-white-south-african-farmers-20180315-p4z4gr.html.

Jack Latimore (2018) 'When it Comes to Racism, Australia is Clueless – And I'm Exhausted', *The Guardian*, 20 October, www.theguardian.com/commentisfree/2018/oct/20/when-it-comes-to-racism-australia-is-clueless-and-im-exhausted.

Jack Latimore and Georgina Galbraith (2013) 'Social Media Giving Voice to Indigenous Communities', *The Citizen*, 30 August, www.thecitizen.org.au/articles/social-media-giving-voice-Indigenous-communities.

Lilly Maier (2016) 'Germany Investigates Mark Zuckerberg and Facebook Over Slow Removal of Hate Speech', *Forward*, 7 November, http://forward.com/news/world/353625/germany-investigates-mark-zuckerberg-and-facebook-over-slow-removal-of-hate/.

Alex Mann, Kevin Nguyen and Katherine Gregory (2019) 'Christchurch Shooting Accused Brenton Tarrant Supports Australian Far-Right Figure Blair Cottrell', *ABC News*, 23 March, www.abc.net.au/news/2019-03-23/christchurch-shooting-accused-praised-blair-cottrell/10930632.

Liam Mannix (2018) 'Far Right Group Threatens to Take a Stand Over "African Gangs"', *The Age*, 12 January, www.theage.com.au/national/victoria/far-right-group-threatens-to-take-a-stand-over-african-gangs-20180112-h0hcha.html.

Liam Mannix and Nino Bucci (2018) 'Dutton, Turnbull Legitimizing Anti-Immigrant Vigilantes, Say Experts', *The Age*, 15 January, www.theage.com.au/national/victoria/dutton-turnbull-legitimising-antiimmigrant-vigilantes-say-experts-20180115-h0ikfc.html.

Gail Mason and Natalie Czapski (2017) 'Regulating Cyber-Racism' 41 *Melbourne University Law Review* 284.

Adam Masters (2018) 'Fraser Anning's "Final Solution" Speech Points to a More Dangerous Threat to Australia', *ABC News*, 15 August, www.abc.net.au/news/2018-08-15/fraser-anning-final-solution-more-dangerous-threat/10123350.

Ariadna Matamoros Fernandez (2017) 'Platformed Racism: The Mediation and Circulation of an Australian Race-based Controversy on Twitter, Facebook and YouTube' 20 *Information, Communication & Society* 930.

Alyce McGovern (2014) 'Police–Citizen Interaction on Social Media', in Bruce A. Arrigo (ed.), *Encyclopedia of Criminal Justice Ethics*, Sage.

——— (2015) 'Special Issue: Crime Media and New Technologies' 27 *Current Issues in Criminal Justice* 137.

Alex McKinnon (2018) 'Racism Flares in Kalgoorlie', *Saturday Paper*, 27 March, www.thesaturdaypaper.com.au/thebriefing/2018/03/27.

Chris McMahon (2016) 'Man Claims Serious Injuries Behind Racial Attack from Masked Men', *Townsville Bulletin*, 2 June, www.townsvillebulletin.com.au/news/man-claims-serious-injuries-behind-racial-attack-from-masked-men/newsstory/afeda78c89ce975430fe332e6ec617a1.

Amanda Meade (2018) '*Sunrise* Breached Racial Contempt Rules with Indigenous Children Discussion – Watchdog', *The Guardian*, 4 September, www.theguardian.com/media/2018/sep/04/sunrise-breached-racial-contempt-rules-discussion-indigenous-children-watchdog.

Caro Meldrum-Hanna and Elise Worthington (2016) 'Australia's Shame', *Four Corners*, ABC TV, 25 July.

Sanja Milivojevic (2011) 'Social Networking Sites and Crime: Is Facebook More Than Just a Place to Procrastinate?', in Murray Lee, Gail Mason and Sanja Milivojevic (eds), *Proceedings of the 4th Australia and New Zealand Critical Criminology Conference*, Sydney University and University of Western Sydney.

Sanja Milivojevic and Alyce McGovern (2014) 'The Death of Jill Meagher: Crime and Punishment on Social Media' 3 *International Journal for Crime, Justice and Social Democracy* 22.

Tammy Mills (2015) 'Melbourne Vigilantes Claim to Expose Paedophiles in Tinder Experiment', *The Age*, 6 January, www.theage.com.au/technology/melbourne-vigilantes-claim-to-expose-paedophiles-in-tinder-experiment-20150106-12iwxk.html.

Oliver Milne (2018) 'Police Ordered to Hunt the Paedophile Hunters in Crackdown on Vigilante Groups Snaring Abusers', *Mirror*, 16 January, www.mirror.co.uk/news/uk-news/police-ordered-hunt-paedophile-hunters-11858909.

Hugh Montgomery (2014) 'The Internet: The Benefits, Problems and Legal Difficulties for Indigenous Australians' 8 *Indigenous Law Bulletin* 19.

Riley Morgan (2018) '*Sunrise* Host Kochie Landed Himself in Hot Water After a Bizarre Slavery "Joke"', *SBS News*, 16 October, www.sbs.com.au/news/sunrise-s-david-koch-stuns-panel-with-usain-bolt-slavery-joke.

Karsten Müller and Carlo Schwarz (2018a) *Fanning the Flames of Hate: Social Media and Hate Crime*, CAGE Online Working Paper Series 373, Competitive Advantage in the Global Economy (CAGE), https://papers.ssrn.com/sol3/papers.cfm?abstract_id=3149103.

——— (2018b) 'Making America Hate Again? Twitter and Hate Crime Under Trump', https://papers.ssrn.com/sol3/papers.cfm?abstract_id=3082972.

——— (2012) *Aboriginal Memes and Online Hate*, Hate Prevention Institute.

Rachel Olding (2016a) 'Chiropractor Chris Nelson Sentenced for Racist Posts on Nova Peris' Facebook', *Sydney Morning Herald*, 5 July, www.smh.com.au/nsw/chiropractor-chris-nelson-sentenced-for-racist-posts-on-nova-peris-facebook-20160705-gpys9d.html.

——— (2016b) '"Coffs Coast Pedo Hunter"' Poses as Girl on Dating Sites to Confront Paedophiles', *Sydney Morning Herald*, 8 December, www.smh.com.au/national/nsw/coffs-coast-pedo-hunter-poses-as-girl-on-dating-sites-to-confront-paedophiles-20161207-gt5o98.html.

Erin Parke (2018a) 'Vigilante Threats on the Rise as Break-ins, Car Thefts, Vandalism Point to Juvenile Justice Failings', *ABC News Online*, 24 March, www.abc.net.au/news/2018-03-25/threats-of-vigilante-violence-amid-juvenile-justice-failings/9583744.

——— (2018b) 'Kimberley Town of Kununurra Just One of Several Hit by Wave of Youth Crime, Rising Racial Tensions', *ABC News*, 15 August, www.abc.net.au/news/2018-08-15/youth-crime-sees-racial-tensions-boil-over-in-kimberley/10051406.

Frances Perraudin (2017) 'Judge Rules "Paedophile Hunters" Can Continue Posing as Children Online', *The Guardian*, 8 April, www.theguardian.com/society/2017/apr/08/judge-rules-paedophile-hunters-can-continue-posing-as-children-online.

Emma Rice, Emma Haynes, Paul Royce and Sandra Thompson (2016) 'Social Media and Digital Technology Use Among Indigenous Young People in Australia: A Literature Review' 15 *International Journal for Equity in Health* 1.

Joshua Roose (2018) 'Are Men's Movements a New Form of Terrorism?', *ABC News*, 24 November, www.abc.net.au/news/2018-11-25/incel-alt-right-mens-movement-masculanism-proudboys-milo/10482032.

Kevin Roose (2019) 'The Making of a YouTube Radical', *New York Times*, 8 June, www.nytimes.com/interactive/2019/06/08/technology/youtube-radical.html.

Kaz Ross (2018) 'The New Nazis: How the Meme-rich World of the Internet is a Threat to Australia', *ABC News*, 13 October, www.abc.net.au/news/2018-10-14/the-new-nazis:-how-the-world-of-the-internet-is-a-threat/10370928.

Michael Salter (2013) 'Justice and Revenge in Online Counter-Publics: Emerging Responses to Sexual Violence in the Age of Social Media' 9 *Crime Media Culture* 225.

Rodrigo Sandoval-Almazan and J. Ramon Gil-Garcia (2014) 'Towards cyberactivism 2.0? Understanding the use of social media and other information technologies for political activism and social movements' 31 *Government Information Quarterly* 365.

SBS News (2018) 'New Race Commissioner Chin Tan Grilled Over "It's OK to Be White" Vote', *SBS News*, 23 October, www.sbs.com.au/news/new-race-commissioner-chin-tan-grilled-over-it-s-ok-to-be-white-vote.

Phil Scraton (2005) 'The Authoritarian Within: Reflections on Power, Knowledge and Resistance', Inaugural Professorial Lecture, Queens University Belfast, 9 June.

Joshua Smallridge, Philip Wagner and Justin Crowl (2016) 'Understanding Cyber-Vigilantism: A Conceptual Framework' 8 *Journal of Theoretical and Philosophical Criminology* 57.

Ben Smee (2014) 'Darwin and Palmerston Vigilantes Take up War on Suburban Crime Epidemic', *NT News*, 27 December, www.ntnews.com.au/news/northern-territory/darwin-and-palmerston-vigilantes-take-up-war-on-suburban-crime-epidemic/news-story/f44bccea89ea3fbb86a553c756aba50a.

Sam Tomlin (2016) 'Facebook Pages Shut Down After Violence in Kalgoorlie', *ABC News*, 2 September, www.abc.net.au/news/2016-09-02/toxic-social-media-culture-in-the-spotlight-kalgoorlie-riot/7805050.

——— (2018) 'Nazi Flags Flown on Australia Day "Hurts Everybody", Kalgoorlie Police Say', *ABC News*, 5 February, www.abc.net.au/news/2018-02-05/nazi-flags-flown-on-australia-day-a-symptom-of-a-deeper-problem/9391298.

Paul Toohey (2016) 'The Seething Streets of Kalgoorlie-Boulder, WA, Where Racism Towards Indigenous Boys Has Hit a Flashpoint', *Perth Now*, 13 November, www.perthnow.com.au/news/wa/the-seething-streets-of-kalgoorlie-boulder-wa-where-racism-towards-indigenous-boys-has-hit-a-flashpoint-ng-d47a67bb37f772da4239e83dbb31ae13.

Courtney Trenwith (2010) 'Police Monitor Online Vigilante Group', *Sydney Morning Herald*, 24 February, www.smh.com.au/technology/police-monitor-online-vigilante-group-20100224-p221.html.

Calla Wahlquist (2016) 'Violent Protest Outside Kalgoorlie Court Where Man Charged Over Death of Boy', *The Guardian*, 30 August, www.theguardian.com/australia-news/2016/aug/30/violent-protest-outside-kalgoorlie-court-where-man-charged-over-death-of-boy.

——— (2018) '"We're Not a Gang: The Unfair Stereotyping of African-Australians', *The Guardian*, 6 January, www.theguardian.com/australia-news/2018/jan/06/were-not-a-gang-the-pain-of-being-african-australian.

Fiona White, Rachel Maunder and Stefano Verrelli (2018) 'How Research is Helping to Reduce Prejudice Between People Online', *The Conversation*, 13 November, https://theconversation.com/how-research-is-helping-to-reduce-prejudice-between-people-online-1061755.

Nic White (2017) '"Your Car is Next": Woman Taunted by Teenage Gang Who Stalked Her and Took Pictures of Her Vehicle Then Bragged About Stealing It', *Daily Mail Australia*, 15 February, www.dailymail.co.uk/news/article-4223894/Brisbane-teenage-car-thieves-posts-photos-conquests.html.

Jason Wilson (2018) 'Why is the Australian Media Promoting White Nationalist Ideas?', *The Guardian*, 8 August, www.theguardian.com/australia-news/commentisfree/2018/aug/08/why-is-the-australian-media-promoting-white-nationalist-ideas.

Mark Wood (2017) 'Ant-Social Media and Algorithmic Deviancy Amplification: Analysing the ID of Facebook's Technological Unconscious' 21 *Theoretical Criminology* 168.

Jessica Yarvin (2017) 'These Tech Companies are Purging White Supremacist Groups from Their Platforms', *PBS News Hour*, 18 August, www.pbs.org/newshour/nation/tech-companies-purging-white-supremacist-groups-platforms.

Chapter 6

Picnic at Hanging Rock

Coming of age as a girl in the Gothic colonial institution

Penny Crofts and Honni van Rijswijk

Introduction

The novel *Picnic at Hanging Rock* was written by Joan Lindsay and published in 1967. It depicts Australia's natural, 'wild' bush environment, contrasting it with the Victorian population of the newly established British colony, whose members try to maintain a semblance of colonial 'civilization'. Peter Weir's 1975 film of the same name continues to be regarded as an Australian classic; moody, unsettling and enigmatic, critics regard it as 'a masterpiece of Australian cinema',[1] with a Rotten Tomatoes rating of 95 per cent. Roger Ebert called it a 'film of haunting mystery and buried sexual hysteria'.[2] More recently, *Picnic at Hanging Rock* was adapted again for a six-episode television series (2018 FremantleMedia and Foxtel). The series received fair reviews and was regarded as 'a stylish retelling of an Australian classic', with a rating of 79 per cent on Rotten Tomatoes, a highly influential review-aggregation website for film and television. The focus of this chapter is on the 2018 series, which has a different aesthetic to both the 1975 film and the novel.

The iconic Peter Weir film *Picnic at Hanging Rock* (1975) is emblematic of Australian cinema, signifying among other things continuing cultural unease at ongoing colonial violence. The film is remembered primarily for the unexplained disappearance of girls on a school excursion, encapsulated by the haunting loss of the most beautiful victim, Miranda, whose recurring face and figure stand in for multiple harms and losses. This figure of the missing child in the Australian landscape is key to the Australian Gothic, and the twist of Weir's interpretation lies in the way the Australian bush figures in the film are both an incitement to the girls' freedom and a threat to white girls' sexuality. Our reading of Foxtel's 2018 remake of the film in this chapter extends previous interpretations of *Picnic* by viewing it not through the lens of the child, but rather through the contemporary cultural-legal lens of systemic institutional failure, exemplified by revelations of abuse uncovered by the Royal Commission into Institutional Responses to Child Sexual Abuse (2013–17).[3] We provide an interpretation of the 2018 version of *Picnic* as exploring the contemporary, colonial, Gothic institution, rather than reflecting on the drama of the missing children.

Weir's film portrays the harsh imposition of arbitrary law at the girls' school, which is classed as privileged yet is also somehow unsavoury – filled with 'natural' children and orphans and facing financial ruin. In order to explore the nature of institutional responsibility raised in the story, we consider Appleyard College through the prism of dominant legal accounts of corporate culpability – nominalism and realism. Nominalist theories regard corporations as nothing more than a collective of individuals – they view corporations as acting only through individuals.[4] This is epitomized in the sadistic and violent headmistress Mrs Appleyard, her minion Miss Lumley and their maltreatment of the orphan Sara Waybourne. The Foxtel remake thematizes the institutional irresponsibility of the school to a larger extent than either the film or the book, explicitly giving Mrs Appleyard a fraudulent background and providing the school itself with a Gothic character – not only the building, but its leaders, finances and policies. We argue that this portrayal is consistent with a *realist* approach to corporate liability: the idea that a corporation is, at least to some extent, an entity independent of its members.[5] The significance of this approach to conceptualizing collective responsibility is that the institution is found to have its own discrete responsibility beyond the aggregation of the responsibilities of individual members.

The first section of this chapter provides a background and synopsis of *Picnic*. The next section applies a nominalist perspective of corporate liability, with Mrs Appleyard as the directing mind of the organization, and thereby vicariously liable for the violence and excesses of Miss Lumley. The third analyzes Appleyard College as an implicated Gothic institution from the realist perspective of corporate liability. We then explore the ways in which the series presents Appleyard College's complicity and confinement within patriarchal structures and how this gender analysis connects to our insights about corporate responsibility. The chapter concludes that, despite the series's innovative contribution of the figure of 'Gothic corporation' to the contemporary imaginary, it ultimately fails to contend with Australia's violent colonial history.

Background and synopsis

In all its iterations, *Picnic* is an historical fiction set in 1900, a story that focuses on a group of students at an Australian girls' boarding school who vanish at an isolated bush area, 'Hanging Rock', while on a Valentine's Day holiday picnic. During the picnic, Miranda climbs the monolith with classmates Edith, Irma and Marion. The girls' teacher, Greta McCraw, follows behind them. As they ascend the rock in a dreamlike state, Miranda, Marion and Irma vanish into the rock while Edith watches them from below. Edith returns to the picnic in hysterics, stating that she has no memory of what occurred. Miss McCraw is also nowhere to be found. The rock is scoured by the teachers and then later by the police and the wider community, but the missing girls and their teacher are not found. The disappearances provoke much local and international attention, with rape, abduction and murder posited as probable explanations. Days later, Irma is found alone at the Rock and also says she remembers nothing. The film focuses on the aftermath of the disappearances and the effects on the school and community.

The film and novel focus primarily on the girls as aesthetic beings, lacking interiority and agency.[6] The girls are largely unknown (and unknowable) except as desired objects, representatives of specific virtues of beauty or knowledge, and for their mysterious departure. In the film, wedding veils were put over the camera to create scenes in which the girls seemed to glow; the bridal veils symbolized the girls on the precipice of adulthood, but also had the effect of creating a layer between the viewer and the scene. The viewer becomes a voyeur, watching the girls in their private moments but having no understanding of what they are thinking or feeling.[7] This absence of development of character is particularly epitomized in Miranda, described as a 'love object par excellence'.[8] She is generally understood to be the heroine, and yet she has no agency or interiority. Miranda is a metonym for a story of loss (from the colonizer's point of view, as we will address later). In the film's most memorable and haunting image, Miranda waves and turns from the camera in slow motion with an irresolute, parting gesture. This is followed by a still image of her turned head, after she has told Mademoiselle de Portiers not to worry, that they 'shall only be gone a little while'. Miranda represents youth, beauty and ephemerality, and the story of her disappearance is not focalized through her, but rather through other characters' longing for her. With her disappearance, she encapsulates a truly unattainable love object entering the realm of the sublime.

In contrast to the film, the television series, serialized at more than six hours in length, explores the story from the girls' point of view. The writers and producers had the space and time to pick up hints from the novel and film to explore and develop, and they chose to emphasize different aspects of the original story than Weir's interpretation. Alongside the key question of what happened to the girls is the question of who they were in the first place. Part of this exposition of character includes the school and the society in which the girls lived. Some of the 'mysteries' of the novel and film versions are revealed to have socio-political explanations, including structural sexism and institutional culpability. The series explores the characters and how they chafe at the restrictions and repression of their Victorian education.[9] In the series, the audience gets to know some of the interiority of the characters and becomes aware not only of the structural limits on their choices, but also of their capacity for agency. The question is less *how* the girls disappeared than *why*. While neither the novel nor the film offers reasons for the girls' disappearance from the girls' point of view, the television series does: 'their vanishing feels deliberate – a way to reject their prescribed futures for a different, freer path'.[10] The *Picnic* television series provides no sense that the girls have anything to go back to or to which they might wish to return. The series suggests that they were caught between a rock and a hard place.

Competing narratives and multiple viewpoints

The story in the film is told primarily from viewpoints external to the girls, with an absence of interiority, satisfied primarily by the beauty and mystery of the girls. The girls are unknown and unknowable, objects of the quintessential male gaze. In contrast, in the television series, there are multiple, intersecting and at times competing narratives, many from the girls' own points of view. The story is not only about Miranda, who emerges as a fully fleshed character, but also about other students, the teachers, the headmistress Mrs Appleyard and the school itself. This broadening of the narrative can be seen in promotional material for the series, which includes Mrs Appleyard (played by Natalie Dormer) and Irma (played by Samara Weaving).[11] The reimagining of *Picnic* is consistent with feminist rewritings of classics – fleshing out peripheral characters, picking up hints, developing the context in which characters were constituted.[12]

The novel and film both gesture towards institutional abuse. In contrast, the television series develops both the narrative and the imagery of Appleyard College as an institution of abuse, making this abuse a key part of the story. The recent Australian Royal Commission into Institutional Responses to Child Sexual Abuse demonstrated the scale of institutional failures that have recurred across time and place.[13] Shurley Swain's analysis of past Australian inquiries into institutions providing care for children highlights an historic tendency to ignore abuse and, where it could not be ignored, a willingness to individualize the problem – whether by blaming the victim or the acts of individual 'perverts' or 'sex fiends'.[14] The film and the novel versions of *Picnic* mirror this tendency: the abuse at and by the school is represented fleetingly but is largely ignored. It is clear to the audience that there is something awry at Appleyard College, but this is not a major plot theme, nor is it particularly remembered by the audience. This mirrors the dominant cultural story, picked up by Swain and others, that there is often tacit community recognition of abuse within and by institutions, alongside a cultural acceptance that nothing can or will be done. According to Swain, there was a lack of almost any criminal legal response to abuse within institutions until the 1990s. For example, before the 1990s, although many children died in 'care' in Australia, Swain asserts that there were only three instances in which a coronial inquiry led to criminal charges being laid. Only one of these deaths led to imprisonment while, in the other two cases, it was asserted that 'although the behaviour that led to the deaths was lamentable, it was understandable given the difficulties posed by the types of children who were being "cared" for'.[15] As we explore next, in the film and novel, it is arguable that, in accordance with this cultural narrative, the orphan Sara is portrayed as a difficult child who is responsible for her own demise.

The television series mirrors shifts not only in the cultural domain, but also in the politico-legal recognition of abuse, which has been exemplified by the change in the type of evidence admitted to inquiries into institutional abuse. Prior to the late 20th century, most inquiries relied solely upon the evidence of 'experts' – including the perpetrators of abuse.[16] However, more recently, survivor testimony has been relied upon as evidence.[17] In the Royal Commission into Institutional Responses to Child Sexual Abuse, this significant change provided for more than 8,000 victims testifying about their experiences in private hearings, in addition to victims providing evidence in public hearings. The emerging pattern of survivor testimony disrupted the notion that sexual abuse was an individual problem and showed that the problem was endemic to institutional settings. In the television series of *Picnic*, the development of the point of view of the schoolgirl characters is consistent with the emerging cultural-legal significance of survivor testimony. Rather than being perceived as objects, with their story being told *for* them, the girls' perspectives and interiority are explored, highlighting the context in which they disappeared. This results in the television series devoting more time to the abuse at the school, in contrast to the earlier film and novel versions, and ultimately revealing the school to be a Gothic, colonial, implicated institution. This mirrors important developments in the contemporary juridico-political imagination, which has introduced, alongside the figures of exceptional predators and difficult children, the figure of the culpable institution.

Through processes such as the recent Royal Commission into Institutional Responses to Child Abuse, as well as the recent Royal Commission into Banking, the 'irresponsible institution' is a crucial emergent figure in the contemporary imaginary and is increasingly significant to growing cultural and legal understandings of collective culpability. Far from being neutral structures that may happen to host corrupt or monstrous 'exceptional' individuals, the Royal Commission into Institutional Responses to Child Sexual Abuse has highlighted the failure of a large number of secular and religious institutions dedicated to the care of children to protect children from, and respond adequately to, child sexual abuse in institutions. The Royal Commission showed that systemic failures of institutions to protect against, and respond adequately to, child sexual abuse in institutions are egregious failures in their own right. It was not a matter of chance that sex offenders were able to perpetrate crimes many times over many years in specific institutions. They were enabled – or at least not prevented – by the systems, policies and reactions of those specific institutions.[18] Accordingly, the findings of the Royal Commission extended models of responsibility beyond those of victim and perpetrator to consider the responsibility of the institution itself in inflicting and sustaining harm.

It should be noted that these findings have so far not resulted in criminal legal reforms ascribing criminal legal responsibility for institutional failure. This is due in part to the difficulty of conceptualizing corporations through the lens of the dominant mode of responsibility in criminal law – that of individual culpability[19] – based on the enlightenment ideal of the autonomous individual, which is itself part of a long historical process.[20] Dominant accounts of corporate liability, such as vicarious principles and identification theory, attempt to fit corporations into this individualist model. Labelled a nominalist theory of corporations, this account views corporations as nothing more than a collective of individuals – that is, the idea that corporations can only act through individuals. These accounts regard corporate responsibility as derivative: it must be located through the responsibility of an individual actor. In contrast, realist theories assert that corporations have an existence that, to some extent, is independent of the existence of their members. Corporations can act and be at fault in ways that are different from the ways in which their members can act and be at fault.[21] We draw out these historical understandings of the corporation as they continue to influence how criminal legal responsibility is ascribed. Here, we explore the idea of Appleyard College as a Gothic institution in terms of both the nominalist and realist perspectives as a means of contributing to ideas of institutional responsibility and how the cultural domain makes sense of different kinds of corporate responsibility.

The film and television series cross a number of genres – drama, romance, period costume drama, tragedy, detective novel and horror. Theorists have highlighted connections to the pastoral,[22] but it is predominantly critically considered to be part of the Gothic genre.[23] For example:

> If Weir's film was a romantic, surreal, shimmering mystery – *Twin Peaks* by way of John Keats – the new *Hanging Rock* is a more Gothic work of horror, revealing the rot that permeates the blooms of the Victorian bouquet.[24]

The classic Gothic genre is heavily gendered and based on the victimhood of the female, dependent on a male hero to rescue her and return her to safety via patriarchal protection.[25] The TV reinterpretation of *Picnic* is harmonious with the novel and film, but the rewriting is also consistent with contemporary feminist reinterpretations of Gothic fiction.[26] The television series rewrites and reworks the Gothic genre and explores female victimhood and agency within patriarchal structures. This rewriting recognizes the destructive forces of the past and present but also the agency of female protagonists to counteract these destructive forces and to escape from or rebuild the confining Gothic home.[27] Instead of relying on a male hero to rescue them, damsels in distress are portrayed as the only people capable of saving themselves. Far from providing protection, the patriarchal system is portrayed as oppressive and abusive. The series self-consciously rewrites gender; however, as we argue next, the issues of race and colonialism are more deeply buried. We seek here to bring them out through understanding the figure of the Gothic institution – which stands in for a range of post-colonial failures – and to draw upon corporate theories of (ir)responsibility in understanding this institution.

Individual responsibility at Appleyard College

Picnic at Hanging Rock arguably portrays Appleyard College in terms that are consistent with the dominant nominalist approach – particularly identification theory and vicarious liability. We will consider nominalist and realist theories in turn.

Mrs Appleyard: the directing mind

According to the nominalist account, the corporation exists as an aggregation of the natural persons who constitute the corporate enterprise.[28] Criminal action derives from the actions of individuals; liability for the corporation is attributed through identification doctrine and vicarious liability. The principle of identification is that those persons who control or manage the affairs of a company are deemed to embody the company itself. This principle permits criminal liability to be imposed on a corporation for an offence that requires *mens rea*. As Denning LJ noted in the civil context, the 'state of mind' of 'directors and managers who represent the directing mind and will of the company, and control what it does' is the 'state of mind of the company and is treated by the law as such'. The leading authority is *Tesco Supermarkets Ltd v Nattrass* (*Tesco*).[29]

A great difficulty with the identification principle is determining who the directing mind is and whether that mind controls what the organization does.[30] As a small organization, Appleyard College is deeply associated with its flawed founder – after whom it is named. Unlike *Tesco*, there is no difficulty in identifying the directing mind of Appleyard College. The directing mind of Appleyard College is clearly Mrs Appleyard, overcoming practical difficulties that corporate law has had in identifying the corporate mind. The very foundations of the college are imbricated with Mrs Appleyard's fraudulent constructions. In the novel, Mrs Appleyard is described as a 'mysterious widow', 'newly arrived from England with a considerable nest-egg' with which to establish the college, a girls' boarding school, in the final decade of the 19th century.[31] The television series develops Mrs Appleyard's character as a mysterious widow. In the opening scenes of the series, she is not only veiled but filmed primarily from behind, in the dark. Not only is she not a widow, but she is hiding her past and/or from someone. It is apparent from the opening scenes that the college is established on fraudulent and violent foundations. In contrast to her posh speaking voice, Mrs Appleyard's voiceovers and flashbacks are in a cockney accent, highlighting her fraudulent construction of herself as upper class. Early on, she states in voiceover that she is seeking a 'new beginning', saying, 'You'll never find us out here'. Like many a Gothic heroine, Mrs Appleyard sought to escape her past by recreating herself. She chose her name, and the name for the college, from a tin of Appleyard soap. In Episode 4, it transpires that Mrs Appleyard used the soap to clean her hands after pushing a bullet further into the chest of her 'husband' Alfred after he was shot, leaving him for dead.[32]

Mrs Appleyard is strongly influenced by Alfred in the way she presents and constructs herself and the college. In the opening scenes, Mrs Appleyard quotes Alfred fondly: 'people always believe what they see. Dressed like a tart you are a tart, dressed like a widow . . .'[33] The audience realizes much later that Alfred was Mrs Appleyard's abuser. She was selected by Alfred as a child from an orphanage and trained to commit crime. Her training to focus on appearances and distractions was consistent with Victorian conventions and informed the ethos of

Appleyard College, where Victorian conventions are actively and positively (and ironically) imposed. At the college, the veneer of purity is preserved: the bare breasts of sculptures are covered with signs of 'purity', and the college provides 'firm discipline and ladylike behaviour', which are 'offered as a substitute for learning'.[34] This is in accordance with what Mrs Appleyard learned as a child: a veneer of ladylike behaviour is sufficient – although it should be noted that Iris easily sees through the veneer: 'She's a fraud – clearly didn't come from real society. She was a climber'.

Mrs Appleyard and her minion Miss Lumley inflict casual and systemic violence, with the novel and film both gesturing towards cruelty at the school. In the film, Sara is arbitrarily prevented from going to the picnic. No reason is offered, and the only explanation is that the headmistress is a monster. When Sara's guardian falls behind in the payment of fees, Mrs Appleyard threatens to send her back to the orphanage. In the film, Mrs Appleyard is the primary tormentor of Sara. There are suggestions of institutional cruelty and a consequent awareness by the audience that this sort of thing happens, but no response is proffered, and it is not developed as a major plot element.

Unlike the film, in the series Mrs Appleyard has a complex relationship with Sara Waybourne. The TV series explains Mrs Appleyard's prohibition of Sara's attendance at the picnic as a nefarious form of punishment for Miranda's truancy. There are suggestions that she is a figure of punishment because she is perhaps most similar to Mrs Appleyard. For example, after the others go to the picnic without her, Mrs Appleyard brushes out all Sara's hair and talks about how her own head had been shaved at the orphanage, and she had looked like a squirrel (Episode 1). This makes Mrs Appleyard's threat to send Sara back to the orphanage particularly cruel as Mrs Appleyard already knows how cruel orphanages can be. Mrs Appleyard inflicts the violence of her own foundations upon the character with origins most like her own. Another explanation for Mrs Appleyard's cruelty towards Sara is her snooping and discovery of Mrs Appleyard's secret – that is, that Mrs Appleyard named herself from a soap tin. Whatever the reason, as the directing mind of Appleyard College, Mrs Appleyard inflicts imaginative torture and violence upon Sara.

The story 'reflects colonial unease as the Victorian era draws to its close and utilizes the already well-established literary trope of white vanishing to convey these anxieties'.[35] But the colonial violence rendered invisible within the dominant discourse is figured through the headmistress, Mrs Appleyard, whose compromised character and history lie at the centre of the story. *Picnic at Hanging Rock* is set in 1900, a liminal year in the history of Australia and for the empire. On 1 January 1901, the Commonwealth of Australia was established – without Aboriginal Australians being granted citizenship or voting rights, which would not be bestowed until 1967. In January 1901, Queen Victoria died after a 63-year reign. This year, then, marked the end of an era, bringing the anxiety and unsettlement of change.

Vicarious liability

Miss Dora Lumley, the deportment mistress and religious studies teacher, inflicts much of the violence in the television series. The courts have handled the question of corporate responsibility for the actions of an employee through the concept of vicarious liability. Under this principle, a corporation can be liable for actions or omissions committed in the course of or during the scope of employment. In the recent civil case of *Prince Alfred College Incorporated v ADC* (*Prince Alfred College*),[36] the majority of the High Court of Australia (French CJ, Kiefel, Bell, Keane and Nettle JJ) noted that common law courts had struggled to identify a coherent basis for identifying the circumstances in which an employer should be held vicariously liable for the negligent acts of an employee, let alone for intentional, criminal acts.[37] The courts have grappled with the objective rationale for vicarious liability and its parameters. In some cases, they have expressed concerns about undue burdens on employers who are not at fault and on their business enterprises, while in other cases, judges have exclaimed that it would be shocking if the employer were not held liable for act of the employee.[38] Many of these cases, including *Prince Alfred College Incorporated v ADC*,[39] involved sexual abuse of children in educational, residential or care facilities by persons who were placed in special positions with respect to children. In *Prince Alfred College*, ADC was sexually abused by Dean Bain, a boarding housemaster employed by the college. Immediately after the abuse was reported, Bain was dismissed. One issue was whether or not the college was vicariously liable for Bain's wrongful acts. The High Court of Australia held that

> in cases of this kind, the relevant approach is to consider any special role that the employer has assigned to the employee and the position in which the employee is thereby placed vis-à-vis the victim. In determining whether apparent performance of such a role may be said to have provided not only an opportunity but also the occasion for the commission of the wrongful act, particular features may be taken into account, including authority, power, trust, control and the ability to achieve intimacy with the victim.[40]

Whether an employee took advantage of their position with respect to the victim may go towards determining that the wrongful act should be regarded as committed in the course or scope of employment in such a way that would render the employer vicariously liable. The High Court of Australia held that inquiries would need to be made as to whether Bain's role as housemaster placed him in a position of power and intimacy and whether his apparent performance of his role as housemaster gave the occasion for the wrongful acts.[41]

Unlike *Prince Alfred College*, Miss Lumley was either acting under the supervision and/or orders of Mrs Appleby. Many actions by Miss Lumley were under the direction of Mrs Appleyard – for example, Miss Lumley viciously and sadistically whipped Miranda for truancy under the supervision of Mrs Appleyard.

Other actions were not taken under the supervision of Mrs Appleyard but were a part of her employment. In particular, Miss Lumley made frequent use of the 'posture board' as a form of torture. It was clear that she knew it was painful, explicitly using it as a form of punishment after Sara knocks another student over in the gymnasium. In Episode 4, Sara is left strapped to the posture board against the wall, separate from her classmates and hidden from view, forgotten. Upon her discovery, Miss Lumley shrieks, 'It's for her own good! To cure her terrible stooping'.[42] There are no punishments or criticisms of Miss Lumley for inflicting the torture board on Sara, suggesting that this instrument is part of the educational regime of the college and that cruel treatment of students is tacitly permitted. Miss Lumley only loses her job because Mrs Appleyard is feeling personally threatened, not because of anything she has done wrong in the course of her employment. Miss Lumley clearly feels wronged: 'I am the good girl. I do everything you say. It's not fair'. This shows that she perceives that she has acted under the direction of Mrs Appleyard. Accordingly, it is clear that Appleyard College would be vicariously liable for the actions of Miss Lumley.

Both the film and television series ostensibly portray a nominalist view of the college, whereby any organizational culpability can be attributed through Mrs Appleyard as the directing mind and via vicarious liability for the acts of Miss Lumley. The nominalist approach is ostensibly shown with the deaths of Mrs Appleyard and Miss Lumley at the culmination of the novel, film and series. Mrs Appleyard disappears, and her body is found two days later. In the novel it is suggested that she is distraught over events that have occurred and kills herself by jumping from a peak on Hanging Rock. Similarly, Miss Lumley also dies. In the novel, both she and her brother are killed in a hotel fire. In the series, she has returned (unhappily) to her brother's house. They fight, and his shirt catches fire; they are both killed. However, both Mrs Appleyard's and Miss Lumley's deaths are understated and anticlimactic, depicted only fleetingly. Despite the irrevocable downfall of both villains, neither provides a satisfying denouement. In addition, these deaths are consistent with the theme that there is no good place for any of these women to be.[43] This suggests that Mrs Appleyard and Miss Lumley are victims as much as victimizers, which undermines a purely nominalist approach to corporate liability.

The implicated Gothic institution: a realist approach

The series can also be analyzed in terms of the realist perspective of corporate liability. This perspective asserts that corporations are more than just the sum of their parts[44] and is informed by studies in organizational behaviour, which show that organizations often develop an identity that is independent of and transcends the specific individuals who control or work within the organization.[45] Thus, rather than focusing solely on Mrs Appleyard and Miss Lumley, this would focus on the institution itself – Appleyard College. In this section, we explore the ways in which the fraud and violence extends beyond Mrs Appleyard and Miss Lumley as individuals to permeate the entire school, which is meaningfully represented as a distinct entity – capable in its own right of producing harm and of being brought to account for that harm.

A classic Gothic trope is the naivety or outright falsehood of foundational tenets of society.[46] This includes the pointlessness, fraudulence and potential harmfulness of the education of the girls, with the idea that they will become 'ladies', which is verging on the ridiculous with a dark underside of violence. Mrs Appleyard expresses that the ideal of the school is one of teaching purity and refinement. Another character comments, 'I didn't know purity could be taught'. Both the film and the book couple a nostalgic aesthetic with implicit criticism of the characteristic strictures of the Victorian era – particularly as they regulated the lives of young women. In contrast, the television series is more explicit. The girls are schooled to appeal to men and to submit to the patriarchy. They spend hours perfecting their posture, sewing, Christianity and submissiveness. The end results of their education are boredom, mischief, idle gossip and hysteria.[47] In response to the disappearance of the girls, the remaining students are told to read or sew. No 'idle gossip' is permitted about the school's 'morbid affair'. Any response is silenced. The girls are not permitted to write home to their parents.[48]

The clothing of all the females epitomizes the restrictions of education and society. The girls and their teachers are all dressed in Victorian clothing that emphasizes modesty and inconvenience.[49] The girls are dressed in long, white Victorian dresses, which are unsuitable for the Australian terrain but 'code the missing girls as angelic, ethereal and spirit-like; the dresses restrict yet visually enable them to float, as more practical clothes would not'.[50] Both the film and television series enjoy the aesthetics of the clothes while simultaneously offering a critique that the clothes were ridiculous and confining.

Although Appleyard College is constructed as a sanctuary for girls to become young ladies, the series explores the dark side of abuse. Fraudulence permeates the college. Not only is Mrs Appleyard not who she says she is, but the fraudulent foundations of the boarding school extend to the employment of teaching staff. Her staff are at the 'arse end of the world' because they can't be employed elsewhere. Just like Mrs Appleyard, the teachers are seeking to escape their own past. As police investigate the school after the disappearances, it becomes apparent that there is an 'epidemic of forged references'.[51] Mrs Appleyard responds that there is 'no need for deception here – this is a college for young ladies'. She employs inexperienced women who are grateful for their jobs and women who are seeking to escape scandal and, like her, start afresh. As a consequence of their lack of experience and awareness of their lack of employability elsewhere, the teachers do not recognize, intervene in or criticize the abuse at the college. The college's inadequate structures enable teachers to perform their jobs negligently, thereby allowing harm. It is only after the girls have disappeared and Appleyard College is falling apart that the teachers begin to criticize the culture of the school. The art teacher asserts that Miss Lumley is Mrs Appleyard's 'attack dog', noting the mindless violence, and warns Mrs Appleyard to 'be careful she doesn't bite you'.

The college accepts and practices casual classism and racism. Irma Leopold is a beautiful heiress, and upon her arrival, she receives a special introduction and welcome. In contrast, orphan Sara receives no welcome and no introduction. Despite her beauty and wealth, Irma is the subject of racism, communicated from the moment we first meet her, with Miss Lumley saying that it is a 'pity she's a Hebrew'.[52] In Episode 3, Irma has been talked into saying goodbye to the other schoolgirls, who are in a pointless lifesaving class in the school hall.[53] They surround her in a threatening way, demanding to know where the missing girls are. Miss Lumley is the teacher in 'charge' and exacerbates what is already a scary scene with an anti-Semitic rant. The attack on Irma only ends with the French teacher slapping Edith, the girl who ran hysterically from Hanging Rock.

The teaching staff are aware of the casual violence imposed at the college by Miss Lumley and Mrs Appleyard. The violation of the female body and the psychological toll of physical and sexual abuse are Gothic tropes.[54] There is an almost farcical emphasis on dress, deportment and speech at the college, and any deviation is vindictively punished by Mrs Appleyard and her minion Miss Lumley. In Episode 4, as the college is gradually falling apart, the art teacher tells Mrs Appleyard, 'You run this establishment abominably. The only thing they learn here is fear'.[55] This shows awareness and complicity by the staff of the practices of violence and fear at the college.

The treatment of Sara epitomizes the violence of Appleyard College. Miss Lumley regularly uses the posture board as an implement of torture on Sara while Mrs Appleyard uses Sara as a pawn to punish Miranda for her truancy. Sara is frequently 'forgotten' and left to her punishment – whether on the posture board or in the attic. The French teacher, Mademoiselle Sara de Poitiers, knows that Sara is punished frequently and kept in the tower, like Rapunzel. There is genuine suspense in the series as to whether Sara's brother, Albert, will find her in time to prevent her fate – even though the audience knows that he will not. Irma comments that 'Sara reminds me of a little deer Papa brought home once. I looked after it, but it died. Mama said it was doomed'. The abuse culminates in Sara's death. In the film there is a deliberate suggestion that Mrs Appleyard was responsible for Sara's suicide – that she pushed Sara beyond the limit of her life. The series goes further, suggesting that Mrs Appleyard killed Sara.

It is only after Sara has disappeared that the teaching staff openly challenge Mrs Appleyard. The French teacher is suspicious of Mrs Appleyard's claim that Sara's guardian had come to pick Sara up that morning.[56] In Episode 6, the French teacher pushes the police to find Sara, but it is only after Sara's guardian Cosgrove has turned up that it becomes apparent that Mrs Appleyard has lied, that the investigation is taken seriously.[57] In the final episodes, there is a frenzy of assertions of responsibility by various characters for failing to protect Sara. The French teacher comments more generally, 'I am a bad teacher. I have been a friend to the girls, but they did not need a friend, they needed a protector. I have been blind and weak'.[58] In Episode 6, the police officer says, 'I should have listened', and Cosgrove demurs, saying, 'She was my responsibility'.[59] Sadly, these assertions of responsibility fail to save Sara's life. There is systemic failure not only within Appleyard College, but also outside the school, by family structures, her guardian and the police.

Although Appleyard College is a small organization and Mrs Appleyard is clearly the directing mind, culpability for fraud, violence and abuse extends beyond her to the culture of the institution. The abusive culture could not have been sustained for so long in the absence of the complicity of desperate, inexperienced employees, either untrained or unable to challenge the violence and abuse. Although promising sanctuary, Appleyard College is a Gothic institution, restricting, endangering and imposing abuse on female heroines.

Complicity with and confinement by patriarchal structures

The school is imbricated within broader structures.[60] A classic Gothic trope is that of confinement, 'the imprisonment and vulnerability of women within structures purportedly designed for or devoted to their safety, especially the family home'.[61] The television series powerfully portrays that there is no safe place for the girls to be. The patriarchal system, the community and the families that have sent the girls to the school to 'protect' them are all threatening. Society is a network of overlapping institutions from which the girls cannot escape.

The threat of the 'outside' is established in Episode 1 when Miranda plays truant. She escapes from a boring school social event to the stables. As she nuzzles a horse, a soldier tries to rape Miranda, speaking to her as though she were a horse he needed to tame and ride: 'Easy now!' Miranda escapes by driving a pitchfork into his foot – demonstrating purity, but also a definite lack of refinement. Mrs Appleyard reprimands Miranda in ways that show an awareness of how the patriarchy works, saying she is a 'ruinously spoiled child. You abandoned restraint. Imagine if you had to marry that brute as a result? You lack refinement'.[62] The consequence of 'lack of restraint' could have been a forced marriage to her rapist.

In the series, family provides no protection and is actually complicit in the patriarchal structures. Sara tells Miranda to show her family the scars from the vicious caning by Miss Lumley, saying, 'Show her your hands, she won't make you go back to school'. However, her mother is simply part of the structure, saying to Miranda while tightening her corset, 'You need an education so you can marry up'. Similarly, Irma tells the police sergeant that her stepfather has abused her, and her mother did not believe her. He portrays no reaction – concerned only with solving the mystery of the missing girls.

The college is portrayed as a safe place for the girls to become young ladies; however, the series mocks the fragility of the Victorian order upon which the college depends. Mrs Appleyard comments that the school is protected by a wall, 'fortified by standards, values, one brick holds up the next, so it is with the edicts of society'.

But the doctor responds that the wall is 'like a parasol in a blizzard'. Irma also ridicules the school and its tenets: 'You think your spelling could have saved me from what happened? This is absurd. Everything I have learned here I've learned from Marian and Miranda'.[63] The series highlights the pointlessness of what they are taught in providing any protection from the outside world. Not only does the college fail to provide protection from the outside world, it is a place of violence, enforcing the tenets of patriarchy. As she becomes increasingly suspicious and critical of Mrs Appleyard, the French teacher proposes returning to the college, despite being 'a woman alone'. The clockmaker, her lover, says to her, 'I believe you should not go back [to the school]'. She replies, 'I am safe – she will not harm me. The remaining girls will leave for Easter. I must stay and protect them'.

The television series provides a contemporary critique of the school and patriarchal structures as sites of violence. In the novel and film, no reasons are offered for the disappearance of the girls, although there are vague intimations of nature and some kind of unknown Aboriginal myth. In contrast, the series suggests that the girls have exercised agency. The Gothic heroine has limited agency within confining structures – feminist rewrites recognize the confining structures but allow more agency to the female heroine. The sergeant expresses awareness of the problems at the school: 'Something's not right about that college. What about if these girls got lost on purpose?'[64] He later asks Irma, 'Was there a plan to run away?' and she replies, 'There was no plan'.[65] When Marion seduces her teacher, Miss McCrew, by reading *The Turn of the Screw* (Christmas 1899), Miss McCrew says 'everything ends unless you stay in between'. A later episode shows the girls sealing a promise to each other by tearing their hands on rose thorns so that their blood commingles with the petals, earthy and ethereal.[66] The audience does not know what the promise is, but there is a suggestion that they chose to disappear at Hanging Rock – the in-between – rather than being forced to fit the confining strictures of school and society.

The series presents the fraudulence and violence as exceeding the acts of individuals – meditating on structural limitations. Mrs Appleyard initially regards the disappearance of the girls as 'retribution' from Arthur; however, towards the end of the series, she is informed that she had left Arthur to die. She responds: 'If Arthur's dead then where are they? Where are my girls?' Despite the centrality of her character as a directing mind, the series demonstrates that her actions, too, are circumscribed by society and patriarchal structures. She is threatened by a past acquaintance and is proposed to by the doctor as a means of escaping scandal. She is not fully in control and is unable to provide an additional story of origins to create another college.

The post-colonial Gothic

The 2018 serialization of *Picnic* prompts viewers to engage actively with formal strategies of representing abuse and institutional responsibility. The series exceeds realism at a number of key moments, undermining the viewer's faith in social 'reality', which tends to be shored up in televisual realism. Thematically, the TV series of *Picnic at Hanging Rock* has been reframed through the prism of contemporary values. In addition to being critical of Victorian values, the central trio of girls ticks contemporary feminist, anti-racist and pro-queer boxes – with Irma a Jewish girl and Marion an Aboriginal lesbian. The anti-Semitism of Miss Lumley is not applauded and is represented as problematic. The character of Marion appears to address criticisms of the film and novel that the sole Aboriginal character – the silent black tracker – was an example of the displaced Indigenous presence. As Kathleen Steele points out, the dehumanization of the Indigenous 'other' in *Picnic* is taken a step further in the movement from novel to film with the replacement of the 'black tracker' by a bloodhound. When his search proves unsuccessful, the Indigenous 'other' is presented as 'a domesticated animal of limited use'.[67] In contrast, in the television series, Marion is Aboriginal, the illegitimate daughter of a judge, and is played by an Aboriginal actress (Madeleine Madden).[68] In comparison with Miranda, Marion is not really provided with much of a back-story. The offer by Mrs Appleyard to Marion of a job as a teacher is in recognition that her future is circumscribed due to her (mixed) race, and the school is (arguably) a place of sanctuary from the outside world. This provides some awareness of the racist structures permeating society. However, aside from this offer, Marion is not subject to racism – unlike Irma. The series is not clear whether she is protected because she is the daughter of a judge or because the series fails to engage with the racism of the era. It is, however, questionable whether this nod to Aboriginal history is too superficial – including a character who is indexed as Aboriginal without contending with the colonial violence, either of the contemporary moment or at the turn of the 20th century. The early years of the 20th century saw the inception of state laws that removed Aboriginal children from their families and communities, a systemic legal violence that was subsequently documented by the *Bringing Them Home* report.[69] Including Marion as an institutionalized Aboriginal child without referencing child removals seems incredible – even irresponsible.

As discussed earlier, the series focuses on the aftermath of the disappearances and the effect on the school and community. Much of the 'mystery' of the earlier versions is revealed to be the socio-political facts of sexual violence, sexism and, to a lesser extent, racism. The colonial context of the story is referenced but not adequately challenged or revised. Despite its modern interpretation, the television series contributes to the 'great Australian' narrative of vanishing white girls. A central theme of the Australian Gothic is the confrontation between settler colonial society and the ancient and unfamiliar enormity of the Australian landscape. For example, in his analysis of the film, the critic Roger Ebert notes that Weir 'employs two of the hallmarks of modern Australian films: beautiful cinematography and stories about the chasm between settlers from Europe and the mysteries of their new home'.[70] The film and series both portray a highly aestheticized bush landscape, with a nod to Australian impressionists such as Streeton, but the pastoral idyll gives way to Gothic nightmare.

It is worth asking whether a story of a lost white child in the Australian bush could ever be told responsibly, without also marking the experiences of the Stolen Generations and the frontier massacres that caused ongoing genocide to the First Nations people. This is especially the case as the story of the missing girls raises the spectre of the colonizer's grand narrative of raped white femininity, which pits sex against race.[71] In the novel, Mrs Appleyard reflects on the maths instructor's disappearance with regret as 'It was inconceivable that this woman of masculine intellect . . . should have allowed herself to be spirited away, lost, raped, murdered in cold blood like an innocent schoolgirl'.[72] Australia's colonial legacy provides a particular and important historico-political context to our understanding of Gothic tropes and, therefore, of the anxiety, hauntings, spatial evocations and repressions that are produced through the Gothic genre in the Australian imaginary. Stuart Hall observes that 'we always knew that the dismantling of the colonial paradigm would release strange demons from the deep, and that these monsters might come trailing all sorts of subterranean material'.[73] Alison Rudd argues that issues of (colonial) guilt and innocence were inchoate for early Australian writers, but these questions have become key for more recent cultural works such as Peter Weir's *Picnic at Hanging Rock* (1975).[74] The story relies on established Australian tropes of 'the lost child' and 'the bush'. Gelder and Weaver argue that the bush figures as 'a kind of Gothic vacuum' – a site of disorientation and death.[75]

Representations of the colonial child combine the hope and confidence imbued in the white child who is read metonymically for the nation; at the same time, though, this child figures (white) vulnerability, with the bush luring white children from civilization into a savage death.[76] The 'lost white child' figure has historically, and paradoxically, supported the colonial logic of the vanishing Aboriginal, or 'the inevitability of a white future against a fading black past'.[77] This trope was in popular use in children's literature from the 19th century onwards – from short stories by Francis Adams and Hume Nisbet and Marcus Clarke's story 'Pretty Dick' (1869) to Frederick McCubbin's famous paintings *Lost* (1886) (formerly known as *The Lost Child*) and *Lost* (1907) and Clarke's 'convict Gothic' work, *For the Term of His Natural Life* (1870–72).[78] This trope framed the ways in which urban Australians came to understand the meaning of the Australian bush.[79] The trope of the lost child also overlaps with other Gothic Australian 'white vanishing' stories. This sub-genre includes Patrick White's novel *Voss* (1957), which focuses on a group of adult explorers who get lost while trying to 'explore' Australia's interior.[80] The historical truth of this era, however, was not the mass vanishing of white children, but rather the experience of the Stolen Generations: the state-sponsored removals of Aboriginal children that occurred between 1909 and 1969, eventually documented in the *Bringing Them Home* report.[81]

Ken Gelder argues that the colonial Australian Gothic can best be understood as a way of representing the violence that settlers inflicted on Indigenous people at the frontier.[82] Here, 'frontier' refers to the physical site of violence – which, although posited as remote from 'civilization', was often very close to the centre – and also the temporal period of violence, the traumatic effects of which extend to the present. The novel, film and television series all retain the pretence that they are based on a true story.[83] Indeed, Hanging Rock is an actual place near Mount Macedon,[84] and the local tourist industry capitalizes on Hanging Rock's association with *Picnic at Hanging Rock*, with the Discovery Centre at Hanging Rock dedicating considerable display space to the myth. Every year on 14 February, Peter Weir's film adaptation is screened outdoors at the Hanging Rock Reserve. Countless tourists climb the rock, calling out for the 'main character' Miranda.

The novel, film and series contribute to the repression of colonial history. In 2017, in conjunction with the 50th anniversary of the novel's publication, Australian doctoral student Amy Spiers gained attention by starting a 'Miranda must go' campaign, criticizing what she perceived to be the novel's propagation as a true story, while disparaging local tourism at Hanging Rock. Spiers asserted that 'Hanging Rock is haunted by a convenient fiction rather than an uncomfortable truth'.[85] A great deal of information is made available to tourists about the fictional schoolgirls' disappearance at Hanging Rock, but there is a lack of material about the real Aboriginal losses and traumas that occurred in the area. The history of violence, abuse, dispossession, invasion and theft of Aboriginal land is mentioned only cursorily or ignored in tourist presentations at the site.

Spiers asks:

> Why do we obsessively retell a myth of white vanishing? Why don't we cast as much attention to the actual losses and traumas that took place at the Rock? Whose absences matter?[86]

On her website, Decolonizing Solidarity, Clare Land asserts that for non-Aboriginal allies, 'the most basic way to show respect to Aboriginal people is to find out what happened here'.[87] The rightful name of Hanging Rock is Ngannelong. The novel, film and series reinforce the silence surrounding Aboriginal people, the denial of their history both historically and in the present. This portrayal of an unpeopled land before European settlement/invasion creates a void or absence that haunts *Picnic*.[88] It is not just the disappearance of the girls that is haunting, but the erasure and absence of Aboriginal people, reflecting the imperial ideology underpinning *terra nullius*.[89] The construction of blankness, the legitimized occupation and the uncanny absence of Aboriginal history created 'a space that appeared to reside outside both God and man',[90] a problematic construction of Australia as empty and blank.

Conclusion

Halberstam argues that the Gothic genre is based on fear of the 'other', maintaining that Gothic monsters were designed for the purposes of multiple interpretations – whether race, sexuality, class or genre.[91] The colonial Gothic is racialized – it is premised on the foundational and continuing fact of historical invasion, signifying that which is denied explicitly by the national narrative. For Halberstam, the monster in Gothic fiction provides the audience with an ability to describe, codify and define the 'other', whom they fear. However, there is no monster in *Picnic at Hanging Rock*. As a consequence, white fears of the untamed Australian bush and Aboriginal people remain nebulous and undefined, undermining a contemporary rewriting of post-colonial national narratives. The series *Picnic* is a contemporary portrayal of an Australian classic, an example of a feminist re-engagement with the Gothic. Unlike the novel and film, the series ruminates on female agency and character development beyond externalities of beauty while simultaneously representing the patriarchal structures confining all the female characters. The series also meditates on Appleyard College as a Gothic institution – an entity with violent and fraudulent foundations. The series goes beyond fleeting portrayals of abuse and violence to explore the ways in which individuals and the institution itself are culpable. The college exists and is complicit with violent social structures. The series provides a contemporary critique of the limits of the patriarchy, hinting at the girls exercising agency and choosing the 'in-between' by escaping to the Rock, a stark portrayal of the limited options available to females. However, the series fails to engage with post-colonial national narratives, retaining the central colonial Gothic narrative of the white vanishing. Alison Whittaker's brilliant poem, 'Many Girls White Linen', takes up the story of Hanging Rock. Whittaker asserts there is 'no mystery' (line 1)[92] and, between lines 3 and 5, makes the turn between 'white linen' and 'white women', placing between them 'harsher things' (line 5). Whittaker points to the complicity of white women with colonialism, as well as the fact that the trope of the raped white woman disguises the significance of the role of colonialism in the ongoing higher rates of sexual violence inflicted against Aboriginal women – all these histories are obscured in the story of *Picnic*.

Acknowledgement

Penny Crofts's research on corporations is funded by an Australian Research Council Grant, Rethinking Institutional Culpability: Criminal Law, Horror and Philosophy (DE18010057).

Notes

1 Anon (2018).
2 Erebert (1998).
3 The television series was written by Beatrix Christian and Alice Addison and directed by Larysa Kondracki, Michael Rymer and Amanda Brotchie.
4 Colvin (1995). This approach regards corporations as being essentially 'mere clusters or aggregates of individuals': Dan-Cohen (1986).
5 Colvin and Argent (2016); Field and Jorg (1991); Woolf (1997).
6 Gilbert (2018).
7 Gilbert (2018).
8 Wild (2014), pp 127–30.
9 Gilbert (2018).
10 Gilbert (2018).

11 The trailer for the series, voiced by the headmistress, slips from the picnic to the school. See 'Official Trailer from Picnic at Hanging Rock' (2018) IMDb, www.imdb.com/title/tt6038954/videoplayer/vi2457843737?ref_=tt_pv_vi_aiv_1.
12 Tilley (2012), p 7. Feminist reimagining of classics include *Wide Sargasso Sea* by Jean Rhys, a response and prequel to Charlotte Bronte's *Jane Eyre*.
13 For example, see Daly (2014).
14 Swain (2014).
15 Swain (2014), p 9.
16 The shift to hearing survivor testimony is powerful but not as yet fully accomplished. For example, the Royal Commission into the Protection and Detention of Children in the Northern Territory drew evidence primarily from 'experts', some of whom were allegedly perpetrators, rather than from the children. See Anthony (2018a, 2018b).
17 Swain asserts that the practice changed with the HREOC *Bringing Them Home* report (1997), p 162. Although sexual abuse was not specified in the terms of reference, it was singled out for special treatment in the subsequent reports. Australian Senate Community Affairs References Committee (2001), p 75; Senate Community Affairs References Committee (2004), p 103; Forde (1999), p 87. The recent Royal Commission also relied upon victim testimony and released an interim report with hundreds of pages devoted to summarizing survivor testimony, Commonwealth Royal Commission into Institutional Responses to Child Sexual Abuse (2014).
18 For example, Patrick Parkinson (2014) has analyzed ways in which the Catholic Church failed to adequately protect against and respond to child sexual abuse and, as a consequence, argues that sex offenders were attracted to the church. See also Sullivan and Beech (2004), who argue that 15 per cent of professional perpetrators chose their profession so that they could abuse children. Another 41.5 per cent admitted that this was a motivation.
19 Crofts (2016); Veitch (2007).
20 Lacey (2001).
21 Campbell (2018).
22 Bladen (2012). 'Pastoral embodies an encounter with the mystery of life because it situates the human at the liminal periphery or urban space and culture and at the frontier of that which humanity has emerged from and to which it is tied, albeit estranged in many ways: nature'.
23 Steele (2010).
24 Gilbert (2018).
25 For example, Bram Stoker's *Dracula*.
26 Meyers (2001), p 19.
27 Paruolo (2011).
28 Kim (2000).
29 [1971] 2 All ER 127. Although recognized as an authority, there was different reasoning by the Law Lords as to the principle's precise content. This lack of clarity has exacerbated practical problems of prosecution. The directing mind test has since been tempered somewhat by the Privy Council in *Meridian Global Funds Management Asia Ltd v Securities Commission* and reaffirmed in *AG's Reference (No 2 of 1999)* [1995] 3 All ER 918.
30 Campbell (2018).
31 Lindsay, *Picnic at Hanging Rock* (1967), 8. In the film, Mrs Appleyard is widowed in England before coming to Australia to establish the college – adhering in her dress to the Victorian conventions of 'half mourning', which allowed for the additional wearing of grey and lilac in the final six months of the expected two-year mourning period. She regresses to full mourning later in the film, complete with the cameo of her late husband, Arthur, at her neck. Her mourning is also described in Lindsay's novel. Mrs

Appleyard is described as wearing 'a cameo portrait of her late husband flat on her respectable chest' in *Picnic at Hanging Rock*, 9.

32 *Picnic at Hanging Rock* (2018) S1 Ep 4.
33 *Picnic at Hanging Rock* (2018) S1 Ep 1.
34 Ebert (1998).
35 Miller (2017), p 154.
36 [2016] HCA 37.
37 *Prince Alfred College Incorporated v ADC* [2016] HCA 37, [39].
38 *Prince Alfred College Incorporated v ADC* [2016] HCA 37, [39].
39 [2016] HCA 37, [148].
40 *Prince Alfred College Incorporated v ADC* [2016] HCA 37, [81].
41 *Prince Alfred College Incorporated v ADC* [2016] HCA 37, [84].
42 Rymer, Kondracki and Brotchie (6 May 2018) *Picnic at Hanging Rock* S1 Ep 4.
43 'A segment of the pattern begun at Hanging Rock literally burning itself out, five weeks later, in a city hotel': Lindsay (1967), p 171.
44 Campbell (2018); Dan-Cohen (1986); Kim (2000).
45 Robbins (2016); Whetten and Godfrey (1998).
46 Bailey (2010), p 271.
47 In Episode 1, a teacher comments that 'The girls will stuff themselves at the picnic'. Mrs Appleyard responds, 'It's the boredom'. See *Picnic at Hanging Rock* (2018) S1 Ep 1.
48 A similar response was adopted in *Prince Alfred v ADC* [2016]. After Bain was dismissed from employment, students were instructed not to talk of it outside the school [143].
49 Ebert (1998).
50 Bladen (2012), p 166.
51 The importance of checking references prior to employment was apparent in the *Royal Commission into Institutional Responses to Child Sexual Abuse*. See the Report into YMCA. See also *Prince Alfred College*, where the High Court noted the failure to follow up on rumours concerning Bain's conduct at a previous school. There was no practice of schools undertaking criminal record checks at the time [145].
52 *Picnic at Hanging Rock* (2018) S1 Ep 1.
53 *Picnic at Hanging Rock* (2018) S1 Ep 3.
54 Bailey (2010).
55 *Picnic at Hanging Rock* (2018) S1 Ep 4.
56 *Picnic at Hanging Rock* (2018) S1 Ep 5.
57 *Picnic at Hanging Rock* (2018) S1 Ep 6.
58 *Picnic at Hanging Rock* (2018) S1 Ep 5.
59 *Picnic at Hanging Rock* (2018) S1 Ep 6.
60 Woodiwiss and Hobbs (2009).
61 Bailey (2010), p 273.
62 *Picnic at Hanging Rock* (2018) S1 Ep 1.
63 *Picnic at Hanging Rock* (2018) S1 Ep 3.
64 *Picnic at Hanging Rock* (2018) S1 Ep 4.
65 *Picnic at Hanging Rock* (2018) S1 Ep 5.
66 Gilbert (29 May 2018).
67 Steele (2010).
68 Gilbert (2018).
69 HREOC (1997).
70 Ebert (1998).
71 For feminist analysis of the instrumentalization of these figures in post-colonial contexts, see, for example, McClintock (1991), p 104.
72 Lindsay (1967), p 121.

73 Hall (1996), p 259.
74 The Australian Gothic is covered in detail in Rudd (2010), p 233.
75 Gelder and Weaver (2007), p 5.
76 McGennisken (2012), p 142.
77 McGennisken (2012), p 142.
78 Gelder (2016).
79 Pierce (1999), p 55.
80 Miller (2017), p 156.
81 HREOC (1997).
82 Gelder (2016), p 2.
83 In the foreword to the novel, Lindsay (1967) states, 'Whether *Picnic at Hanging Rock* is fact or fiction, my readers must decide for themselves. As the fateful picnic took place in the year nineteen hundred, and all the characters who appear in this book are long since dead, it hardly seems important'.
84 Crawley (2018).
85 Available at www.mirandamustgo.info/aims.
86 Available at www.mirandamustgo.info/why.
87 Available at https://decolonizingsolidarity.org/what-can-i-do.
88 Bladen (2012), p 172.
89 Steele (2010).
90 Steele (2010).
91 Halberstam (1995).
92 Whittaker (2017).

References

Secondary sources

Anon (2018) '*Picnic at Hanging Rock*', *Rotten Tomatoes*, www.rottentomatoes.com/m/picnic_at_hanging_rock.

Thalia Anthony (2018a) 'Growing Up Surplus to Humanity: Aboriginal Children in the Northern Territory' 51 *Arena Journal* 71.

——— (2018b) '"They were Treating Me Like a Dog": The Colonial Continuum of State Harms Against Indigenous Children in Detention in the Northern Territory, Australia' 7 *State Crime* 251.

Australian Senate Community Affairs References Committee (2001) *Lost Innocents: Righting the Record Report on Child Migration*, Senate Printing Unit.

Peggy Dunn Bailey (2010) 'Female Gothic Fiction, Grotesque Realities and Bastard Out of Carolina: Dorothy Allison Revisits the Southern Gothic' 63 *Mississippi Quarterly* 269.

Victoria Bladen (2012) 'The Rock and the Void: Pastoral Loss in Joan Lindsay's *Picnic at Hanging Rock* and Peter Weir's Adaptation' 23 *Colloquy: Text Theory Critique* 159.

Liz Campbell (2018) 'Corporate Liability and the Criminalisation of Failure' 12 *Law and Financial Markets Review* 57.

Eric Colvin (1995) 'Corporate Personality and Criminal Liability' 6 *Criminal Law Forum* 1.

John H.C. Colvin and James Argent (2016) 'Corporate and Personal Liability for "Culture" in Corporations?' 34 *Company and Securities Law Journal* 30.

Commonwealth Royal Commission into Institutional Responses to Child Sexual Abuse (2014) *Interim Report*, Vol 2, Australian Government.

Peter Crawley (2018) 'Picnic at Hanging Rock Gets a Gutsy 21st Century Makeover', *The Irish Times*, 11 June, www.irishtimes.com/culture/tv-radio-web/picnic-at-hanging-rock-gets-a-gutsy-21st-century-makeover-1.3561951.

Penny Crofts (2016) 'Legal Irresponsibility and Institutional Responses to Child Sex Abuse' 34 *Law in Context* 79.

Kathleen Daly (2014) 'Conceptualising Responses to Institutional Abuse of Children' 26 *Current Issues in Criminal Justice* 5.

Meir Dan-Cohen (1986) *Rights, Persons, and Organizations*, Oxford University Press.

Roger Ebert (1998) 'Picnic at Hanging Rock', *RogerEbert.com*, www.rogerebert.com/reviews/great-movie-picnic-at-hanging-rock-1975.

Stewart Field and Nico Jorg (1991) 'Corporate Manslaughter and Liability: Should We be Going Dutch?' *Criminal Law Review* 156.

Leneen Forde (1999) *Report of the Commission of Inquiry into Abuse of Children in Queensland Institutions*, Queensland Government.

Ken Gelder (2016) 'Colonial Australian Gothic Literature', *Oxford Research Encyclopedia of Literature*, Oxford University Press.

Ken Gelder and R. Weaver (eds) (2007) *The Anthology of Colonial Australian Gothic Fiction*, Melbourne University Press.

Sarah Gilbert (2018) 'The Mysterious Girls of *Picnic at Hanging Rock*', *The Atlantic*, 19 May, www.theatlantic.com/entertainment/archive/2018/05/picnic-at-hanging-rock-review-amazon/561263/?utm_source=feed.

Jack (Judith) Halberstam (1995) *Skin Shows: Gothic Horror and the Technology of Monsters*, Duke University Press.

Stuart Hall (1996) 'When Was "the Post-colonial"? Thinking at the Limit', in Iain Chambers and Lidia Curti (eds), *The Post-colonial Question*, Routledge.

Human Rights and Equal Opportunity Commission (HREOC) (1997) *Bringing Them Home: Report of the National Inquiry into the Separation of Aboriginal and Torres Strait Islander Children from Their Families*, HREOC.

Susanna M. Kim (2000) 'Characteristics of Soulless Persons: The Applicability of the Character Evidence Rule to Corporations' *Illinois Law Review* 763.

Nicola Lacey (2001) 'Responsibility and Modernity in Criminal Law' 9 *Journal of Political Philosophy* 249.

Anne McClintock (1991) 'No Longer in a Future Heaven: Women and Nationalism in South Africa' 51 *Transition* 104.

Jane McGennisken (2012) 'Growing Up Australian: The National Imaginary in School Readers' 22(1) *Papers* 142.

Helene Meyers (2001) *Femicidal Fears: Narratives of the Female Gothic Experience*, State University of New York.

Rosemarie Miller (2017) 'Return to Hanging Rock: Lost Children in a Gothic Landscape' 21 *Green Letters* 152.

Patrick Parkinson (2014) 'Child Sexual Abuse and The Churches: A Story of Moral Failure?' 26 *Current Issues in Criminal Justice* 119, www.austlii.edu.au/au/journals/CICrimJust/2014/16.pdf.

Melissa Paruolo (2011) *Anything Dead Coming Back to Life Hurts: Beloved, Bastard Out of Carolina, and Gods in Alabama as Contemporary Female Gothic*, University of Central Oklahoma.

Peter Pierce (1999) *The Country of Lost Children: An Australian Anxiety*, Cambridge University Press.

Stephen Robbins (2016) *Essentials of Organizational Behaviour*, Pearson.
Alison Rudd (2010) *Postcolonial Gothic Fictions from the Caribbean, Canada, Australia, and New Zealand*, University of Wales Press.
Senate Community Affairs References Committee (2004) *Forgotten Australians: A Report on Australians Who Experienced Institutional or Out-of-Home Care as Children*, Senate Printing Unit.
Kathleen Steele (2010) 'Fear and Loathing in the Australian Bush: Gothic Landscapes in Bush Studies and *Picnic at Hanging Rock*' 20 *Colloquy: Text Theory Critique* 33.
Joe Sullivan and Anthony Beech (2004) 'A Comparative Study of Demographic Data Relating to Intra- and Extra- Familial Child Sexual Abusers and Professional Perpetrators' 10 *Journal of Sexual Aggression* 39.
Shurlee Swain (2014) *History of Australian Inquiries Reviewing Institutions Providing Care for Children*, Royal Commission into Institutional Responses to Child Sexual Abuse.
Elspeth Tilley (2012) *White Vanishing: Rethinking Australia's Lost in the Bush Myth*, Rodopi.
Scott Veitch (2007) *Law and Irresponsibility: On the Legitimation of Human Suffering*, Routledge.
David Whetten and Paul Godfrey (1998) *Identity in Organizations*, Sage.
Alison Whittaker (2017) 'Many Girls White Linen' 226 *Overland*, https://overland.org.au/previous-issues/issue-226/poetry-prize-alison-whittaker.
Harriet Wild (2014) 'Darling Miranda: Courtly Love in *Picnic at Hanging Rock*' 8 *Studies in Australasian Cinema* 127.
Michael Woodiwiss and Dick Hobbs (2009) 'Organized Evil and the Atlantic Alliance: Moral Panics and the Rhetoric of Organized Crime Policing in America and Britain' 49 *British Journal of Criminology* 106 https://academic.oup.com/bjc/article/49/1/106/374864.
Tahnee Woolf (1997) 'The *Criminal Code Act 1995* (Cth): Towards a Realist Vision of Corporate Criminal Liability' 21 *Criminal Law Journal* 257.

Primary legal sources

Meridian Global Funds Management Asia Ltd v Securities Commission [1995] 3 All ER 918.
Prince Alfred College Incorporated v ADC [2016] HCA 37.
Tesco Supermarkets Ltd v Nattrass [1971] 2 All ER 127.

Film, televison and novel

Joan Lindsay (1967) *Picnic at Hanging Rock*, Penguin.
Picnic at Hanging Rock (2018–) FremantleMedia Australia (S1–) (TV series).
Peter Weir (1975) *Picnic at Hanging Rock*, McElroy & McElroy Picnic Productions.

Chapter 7

Haunted colonialism

Space, place and colonialism in *The Babadook*

Pauline Klippmark

Introduction

Jennifer Kent's film *The Babadook*[1] received international critical acclaim upon its release in 2014. At the time, Kent described *The Babadook* as a film that 'doesn't feel particularly Australian'.[2] Set largely in interiors, the film avoids the iconic Australian bush that sets the scene of *Picnic at Hanging Rock*[3] and the desolate deserts we see in *Mad Max*.[4] The protagonist, Amelia Vanek (Esther Davis), is haunted in the comforts of her home in an anonymous Australian suburbia. In relation to this, Kent states that she wanted to distance herself from the Australian landscape and 'create a myth in a domestic setting'.[5] Beyond its placelessness, the film is also difficult to contextualize in a specific time period due to the way Amelia's femininity is framed. She does not invoke 21st century notions of femininity; instead, her hair and clothing are reminiscent of a fragile and delicate whiteness, becoming a 'trace of colonial anxieties'.[6]

In showcasing the public and private struggles of Amelia, a widowed mother raising her six-year-old son with 'behavioural issues', *The Babadook* tells a story about whiteness, femininity and its intersection with class, while invoking the complex themes of trauma, mourning and repression. *The Babadook* uses haunting to explore psychological themes. At the outset of the film, Amelia is haunted by the trauma of her husband's death; her son's birthday coincides with the violent death of her husband, rendering his life and their relationship deeply intertwined with this violent loss and consequent absence. A spectral haunting ensues when the book *Mister Babadook* appears in Amelia's home. Consequently, Amelia navigates and performs the roles ancillary to her womanhood (carer, mother, widow) in the public domain while haunted by the Babadook in her private space. As the film unfolds, Amelia grows increasingly paranoid under the watchful eyes of the institutions that demand her love and compliance while being driven mad in her haunted home. Ultimately, she is seemingly possessed by the Babadook – until it is expelled from her body to the confines of the basement of her home, remaining under her care as the film ends. Although the haunting of the Babadook that ensues throughout the movie is often conceived as representative of the trauma Amelia experienced in association with her husband's death, this chapter takes up the idea that Amelia's personal trauma should be contextualized and read against her position as a traumatized settler subject, considering the film's concern with personhood, space and place.

This chapter first sets the scene of the Australian cultural context against which the film is read. It then draws upon Sigmund Freud's uncanny and theories of the ghost to explore what haunts the Australian legal subject, which is simultaneously at home but unsettled. Here, psychoanalysis allows the conceiving of white settler subjectivity as grounded in the original crime of proclaiming the Australia continent to be *terra nullius*, which seeks not only to possess, but also to reconstruct, eliminate and repress its First Nations sovereignty and subjectivity.

Setting the scene of uncanny Australia

As a settler colonial country with a First Nations population that inhabited the land long before the settlers reimagined it as something else, the presence of First Nations people in Australia causes anxiety to settler colonial logic and rule. In cultural texts belonging to settler colonial countries, the hauntings that plague white protagonists have at times been connected to historical injustices committed against First Nations people.[7] This trope of hauntings connected to wrongs committed by settlers against First Nations people has been termed the 'Indian' or 'Indigenous' uncanny (a play on Freud's 'uncanny') by North American scholars.[8] In this literature, the uncanny is used to describe and understand cultural texts that employ the First Nations ghost to 'express the moral anxieties and uncertainties provoked by the dispossession of a place's Indigenous inhabitants',[9] where the settler subject 'is obsessed with an originary sin against native people that both engenders the subject and irrevocably stains it'.[10] This chapter locates *The Babadook* within a body of texts that invokes Freud's 'uncanny' and utilizes the figure of the ghost/spectre to manage the anxiety that is part and parcel of settler law and sovereignty.

The figure that haunts Amelia throughout *The Babadook* – 'Mister Babadook' – has been read as representing 'the Aboriginal . . . the shadowy figure that haunts the white Australian consciousness as a result of collective cultural trauma, a legacy of colonialism'.[11] This chapter seeks to conceptualize the Babadook's haunting of Amelia's person and place as telling of the trauma that informs her existence and thus telling of the thing that haunts the Australian legal subject. In doing so, there is no intention to construe the Babadook as a ghost from the past that is haunting the present and no attempt to employ the ghost to reproduce the colonial fantasy of First Nations presence as part of the past, playing into the hands of the self-serving colonial discourse that imagined First Nations people as unable to survive modernity.[12] Instead, this chapter advances the idea that *The Babadook*'s explicit absence of race, careful blurring of time and place and simultaneous haunting of person and place are telling of the trauma that informs the existence of the Australian legal subject and their continued navigation of public life in the Australian landscape.

Critical theory and analysis allow the understanding that the Australian justice system remains instrumental in the colonial dispossession of land and is complicit in First Nations people's removal from the public eye and disqualification from civil life. The creation of the Australian justice system necessitated the colonial dispossession of land and displacement of First Nations people as settler sovereignty was premised on territorial jurisdiction.[13] This means that settler sovereignty and law exist solely by virtue of a colonial dispossession made possible by proclaiming Australian land to be *terra nullius* – a legal fiction construing the continent as empty;[14] through this, First Nations land and law were effectively declared to be nothing and thus free for the taking.[15] This entailed employing law as an instrument of domination over First Nations people, having them displaced from their country to missions 'to erase indigeneity through spatial, social and legal domination'.[16] Acting according to a logic of elimination, settler societies continue to subject First Nations people to forms of elimination through various policies and laws[17] in an endeavour to perfect a fundamentally imperfect sovereignty.[18] *Terra nullius* thus necessarily means that the disappearing First Nations person is foundational to Australian sovereignty.

Australian sovereignty is a structure that has to be reproduced,[19] requiring First Nations people's continual disappearance. It follows that in modernity, the settler colonial project remains invested in framing First Nations subjectivity so as to support the settler project of disappearance.[20] Quandamooka Elder and scholar Aileen Moreton-Robinson refers to the settler's need to possess as 'the possessive logic of patriarchal white sovereignty'[21] and describes its methodology as one that 'operates at the level of beliefs, and discursively at the level of epistemology to naturalize the nation as a white possession'.[22] Contemporaneously, this disappearance is effected by a visual and discursive framing that informs and affects the physical exclusion of indigeneity from the social body. This colonial project of ensuring invisibility excludes First Nation people from urban and suburban spaces and disqualifies them from public and civic life by means of over-incarceration, poverty and inadequate housing. Despite these projects of occlusion and repression, the reality of ongoing socio-political existence in Australia is that of ongoing First Nations sovereignty. The persistence of First Nations sovereignty unsettles the settler at the level of the subject and the institution.[23] Moreton-Robinson offers that 'Indigenous sovereignty invokes different sets of relations, belonging and ownership that are grounded in a different epistemology'[24] from that which informs the white settler possessive logic.[25] It also follows that First Nations people's presence in Australia is an ongoing reminder of Australia's violent origins, in which settlers need to repress First Nations sovereignty as its disavowal is a precondition to the existence of settler sovereignty.

The ongoing dispossession of land and contestation of space are crucial in terms of the way they inform ongoing settler relations in Australia. Attesting to this, courts in modernity have proven unable to adequately reckon with the land claims of First Nations people as doing so would unsettle their own jurisdiction. The case of *Mabo*[26] illustrates the complexity of the settler colonial anxiety that haunts the

Australian legal system. Although *Mabo* rejected *terra nullius*, the court held that it would be 'impossible for the common law to recognize such rights and interests if the basic doctrines of the common law are inconsistent with their recognition'.[27] Thus, despite acknowledging *terra nullius* as inaccurate and as fiction, the court continues to endorse ongoing dispossession, leaving First Nations people in the fictional landscape *terra nullius*.[28] It has thus been reasoned that 'the High Court of Australia cannot nullify the colonial condition which gives it the jurisdictional capacity to determine the questions which flow from the acquisition of sovereignty'.[29] Following this rationale, settler sovereignty continues to repress the sovereignty of First Nation people, upholding the mystical origins of its own authority.

Subjectivity and its traumatic origins

Mabo and its acknowledgement of *terra nullius* being a fiction can be conceived as symptomatic of Australia's originary violence.[30] Here, psychoanalyzing Australian law and sovereignty reveals its original crime committed against First Nations people.[31] In Freud's myth of the primal horde, the primal father owned and decided everything until his sons banded together and killed him – creating a guilt that resulted in an internalization of the father's law and subsequent organization around this guilt.[32] As such, psychoanalytical thought conceptualizes the origin of law as a crime 'so radical it redefines the existing standards of legality and illegality',[33] where the subject's guilt and denial of the same provide the precondition for their legal subjectivity.[34] This implies that the individual subject is bound to law by internalized limitations.[35] In this sense, subjects are bound to the law through 'their own construction in a myth of law's authority'.[36]

Psychoanalytical theory offers the analysis that the ongoing repression of persisting First Nations sovereignty marks the traumatized nature of Australian settler existence. In presenting the origin of law 'as a crime story',[37] in which law finds its beginning in trauma,[38] psychoanalysis offers the colonial context that the 'foundation of subjectivity' occurs 'through an originary repression'.[39] Here, the subject emerges because of a loss that has to be disavowed.[40] There is therefore 'no subject without loss'[41] and no subjectivity without repression.[42] By tracing the Australian state's existence to this founding violence, it is revealed that the rights and subjectivity of Australian legal subjects are forever intertwined with and historically premised on this crime and its subsequent repression. It follows that Australian law and sovereignty repress that which informs its origins and unsettle its continued authority.

It is in the context of this contested existence that *The Babadook* deals with a new-found order and its inception from a horrific event, thus saying something about the founding violence in Australia and the trauma this event turned structure has instilled on the legal subject. Amelia and Samuel's familial constellation is in a constant 'lack' since her husband was violently taken away from them, marking the beginning of Samuel's life with trauma and death and leaving Amelia unable to move past her loss. Amelia represses, keeping the memory of her husband and his possessions in the basement of their home and never celebrating Samuel's birthday on the day of his birth, which coincides with her husband's death. Their trauma is not reckoned with but suspended in the basement of their home – the physical manifestation of their unconscious.

The Babadook has been reviewed as a 'Freudian thriller'[43] due to its clear codings of repression. According to Kent, the 'terror of not being able to face something' was always at the core of the film.[44] In interviews, Kent has offered that she wanted to 'take a woman who'd really run away from a terrible situation for many years and make her face it'[45] with the horror just being a 'byproduct'.[46] The film follows Amelia, a widowed mother raising her troubled six-year-old son Samuel (Noah Wiseman) somewhere in suburban Australia. Only minutes into the film, it is revealed that it is the sudden and violent loss of Amelia's husband that haunts her and her family. The loss of her husband is linked to the birth of her son, Samuel; Amelia's husband was killed in a car accident while taking her to the hospital to give birth to Samuel. Her son is a peculiar child, frightened of ghosts lurking in the empty spaces of his home and frequently spending the night in his mother's bed. Amelia's relationship with Samuel is seemingly 'infected' by the trauma that is inextricably linked with his birth and her motherhood. She feels conflicted about their relationship and cannot stand his affection – retracting from his embrace, saying 'don't do that' when he tries to squeeze her too hard and removing his hands from her body to quietly move away from him when he is asleep with her in bed. Beyond displaying Amelia's complex feeling towards motherhood, the film taps into white femininity and women's double burden, with Amelia being a carer for the elderly at work and for her son at home. Kent has offered that she 'wanted to show a real woman who was drowning in that environment',[47] and, in commenting on Amelia's feminine altruism, she suggests that although terrible things have happened to Amelia, when people want to help, Amelia cannot accept but instead says, 'I'm fine, I'm fine. I'll do something for you'.[48]

The introduction of the character of the Babadook can then be read as a ghost concerned with trauma, grief and repression. Reviews of the film read Amelia as 'a woman unable to move beyond the grief of losing her husband . . . also struggling with her relationship with her only child'[49] and suggest that the film is about 'the demons that lurk in the mother's psyche and that she must confront',[50] with a general consensus that the Babadook that haunts and possesses Amelia is a metaphor for grief[51] or depression.[52] This seems to connect with Kent's claim that the film is about how 'terrible things happen to people, and they have to find a way to live with that';[53] and with the film, she wanted to 'talk about the need to face the darkness in ourselves and in our lives'.[54] The haunting that Amelia endures throughout the film can thus be read as representative of the trauma that follows her and informs her existence. Interestingly, Kent made the Babadook appear in and depart from a storybook in order to create a mythical creature – tying into the mystical origins of settler sovereignty.

Amelia's life is constituted by a traumatic loss that informs and defines every part of her existence and that of her son. Scholars engaged with theorizing the spectral have considered the language of trauma as similar to the language surrounding the ghost.[55] Ghosts have been theorized as 'part of a symptomatology of trauma, as they become both the objects of and metaphors for a wounded historical experience'.[56] In this context, trauma theorist Cathy Caruth suggests that to be traumatized is to be 'possessed by an image or event',[57] with the notion of being haunted representing the past haunting the present, where the notion of being haunted represents the past haunting the present. Traumatized subjects then carry 'an impossible history within them or . . . become themselves the symptom of a history they cannot entirely possess'.[58] Reading the figure of the Babadook as embodying the trauma which follows Amelia following the untimely death of her husband, taps into the way this loss informs her continued existence despite her repression. The Babadook is that which returns despite being hidden as Amelia is continuously possessed by history.

The way in which Amelia's relationship to her son is intertwined with the loss of her husband haunts their relationship at the outset of the film. Signifying the way in which their relationship, continued existence and navigation of the social body are informed by this loss, the film opens with a dream sequence depicting Amelia and her husband on their way to the hospital for Samuel's birth, only moments before Amelia's husband dies violently in a car accident. Here, Amelia is woken up from her nightmare at the moment of impact by Samuel screaming 'Mummy!'. Compounding this is the abjection that follows her widowhood and single motherhood and the way the loss and grief experienced by Amelia and Samuel position them within society.[59] Both are shown as painfully out of place in the context of their places of education, employment and social life. As a single, widowed mother, Amelia operates from a site of exclusion. In this space, she does not appear to connect with anyone beyond her elderly neighbour. This alienation is superimposed on us by just how out of place she appears among her sister's female friends and then further exacerbated by the helplessness that accompanies her interactions with various public institutions. Similarly, Samuel cannot connect with other students at school, is removed from his place of education and is despised even by his own family. Amelia's and Samuel's loss follows them everywhere; it is ongoing and impacts all social relations. The trauma they have suffered is intertwined with their everyday life and dictates their encounters with and treatment of public institutions. Amelia's encounters with the Departments of Education, Public Health and Child Safety and the criminal justice system exacerbate her alienation and out of place-ness to the point that she is consumed by madness.

Haunted sovereignty in uncanny Australia

Amelia's fraught relationship with Samuel is already established in the film when the mysterious *Mister Babadook* book appears. The book contains pop-up illustrations to accompany its narrative – 'If it's in a word or if it's in a look – you can't get rid of the Babadook'[60] – and warns that 'once you see what is underneath you're going to wish you were dead'.[61] Samuel is horrified by the contents of the book, which prompts Amelia to hide it, hoping its subject matter will not linger with Samuel. Nevertheless, the Babadook lingers in Samuel's mind, and a disturbing series of events causes Amelia to tear the book to shreds, leaving the remains in the garden. Yet Amelia finds *Mister Babadook* reconstructed on her doorstep the next day. This time, the book features additional narrative and illustrative pop-ups depicting her killing her dog, her son and at last herself – along with the words 'I'll make you a bet – the more you deny – the stronger I get',[62] commanding 'let me in' and that 'the Babadook [is] growing underneath your skin'.[63] The Babadook's influence over Amelia increases until her haunting culminates in its seeming possession of her and subsequent expulsion. At the conclusion of the movie, although terrified, Amelia cares for the Babadook, which now lives in the basement of her home. Commenting on how Amelia is afraid even after interrogating her ghost and being in charge of its care, director Kent states, 'Yeah, that's not going away anytime soon!'[64]

It is regularly suggested that the ghost is the direct figure of the 'uncanny'.[65] The uncanny provides for a way to theorize around the unsettling experience that is Amelia's haunting in *The Babadook*. Freud's 'uncanny' – meaning 'the familiar that has become strange' – has been instrumental in theorizing 'alienation as an economic, political, psychological and existential condition'.[66] Here, the uncanny 'is the feeling of unease that arises when something familiar suddenly becomes strange and unfamiliar'.[67] It refers to the *heimlich* (the familiar place) meeting the *unheimlich* (the unfamiliar) and the experience of 'being in place and out of place simultaneously'.[68] The unfamiliar (or unhomely) refers to that which was secret but has been revealed, or the return of the repressed.[69] In the familiar place of one's home, the uncanny is something that should have been hidden but emerges within familiar domesticity, rendering the homely unhomely.

Amelia's experience in the film is precisely uncanny, her home rendered strange by the Babadook. Attesting to this, the film has been described as a movie that 'takes a familiar domestic scene and nudging it, quietly, into something dark and unsettling',[70] with Kent describing the work as an interior film that plays with shadow and empty space.[71] Ripe with all the hallmarks of the haunted house, the hallways of Amelia's home are dark, the colours dreary with a bluish tinge that projects a particular feeling of uneasiness. Amelia's home, which appears to have been full of promise at some point, now seems empty. Already desolate, the house grows increasingly strange to Amelia during the film as she is increasingly influenced by the Babadook. Kent plays with the darkness and emptiness throughout the film (as the movie was filmed in a studio, space could be altered on an ad hoc basis – for example, walls could be moved to make spaces appear bigger or smaller), exacerbating the vastness and darkness of the empty spaces as the film progresses. Attesting to this, she has Amelia drifting to the side of the frame to 'create further negative space . . . which would make the audience – whether they are aware of it or not – start to feel uneasy'.[72] This invokes Anthony Vidler's 'architectural uncanny',[73] which finds its location in architecture, foremost in the haunted house 'that pretends to afford the utmost security while opening itself to the secret intrusion of terror'.[74] Amelia's house is framed so as to remove the feeling of security and homeliness, rendering those empty spaces in her house places of terror instead of familiarity.

Throughout the film, the Babadook's haunting is one of person and place, in which its ability to move seamlessly between text, person and place is derived from its spectral nature. Hauntings have been analyzed by sociologist Avery Gordon as making visible those power relations that underpin contemporary society,[75] where the ghost presses on the presence of an absence to reveal what lies beneath.[76] The concept of the spectral, or the ghost, and its presence in academic scholarship are largely inspired by Freud's uncanny[77] and Jacques Derrida's 'hauntology', proposed in *Spectres of Marx*.[78] In the context of the uncanny, ghosts are the return of the repressed, coded by a terrifying familiarity 'which leads us back to something long known to us'.[79] They reintroduce the past into the present with the promise of threatening existing social structures and are intolerable due to the way they obliterate what separates past from future and life and death.[80] With respect to Derrida's hauntology, the spectral enters the present through the failure of processing loss[81] and is always 'invoking what was' and 'announcing what will come' – operating on a number of temporal planes, 'most crucially the future and its possible interactions with the present and the past'.[82] Here, Derrida's spectre 'not only signals the unbidden imposition of parts of the past on the present, and the way in which the future is always already populated with certain possibilities derived from the past',[83] but also the rearticulation of these possibilities.

In the context of *The Babadook*, the figure of the Babadook should not be conceived as merely a figure of the past, haunting the present. Beyond being read as representative of collective or individual trauma,[84] the ghost has, due to its habit of traversing metaphysical boundaries, been conceived as representative of liminality and border crossing.[85] Able to move beyond the boundaries of worlds and from person to place – the Babadook seeks to contest space and unsettle the ordinary nature of things. In demanding both entrance and hospitality, the Babadook transgresses the boundaries of time and space, moving between text and person and place, rendering historical power relations transparent and 'playing ambiguously between opposites like life and death, or visibility and invisibility',[86] thus interrupting and problematizing the past, present and future. In this, the spectral Babadook resonates with post-colonial concerns in being connected to and moving between pasts and presents, interrupting both simultaneously.[87]

As the Babadook's haunting intensifies, so does Amelia's repression of its presence – fulfilling its promise 'the more you deny me, the stronger I get'. The further Amelia disavows the Babadook's presence, the further her haunting intensifies – and so does her dispossession. Mister Babadook's haunting increasingly unsettles Amelia until she is (dis)possessed. In this process, Amelia unravels before various institutions that project surveillance and governance (reflecting what First Nations people may encounter in their navigation of the public sphere). This continues until Amelia effectively 'lets him in', to then expel him to the confines of her basement. In the moment at which Amelia stops disavowing her haunting so as to enable her to face that which has returned to haunt and terrorize, she screams, 'This is my house. . . . you are trespassing in my house!'[88] In demanding the Babadook's expulsion from her home and framing her rights within terms of trespass, Amelia speaks of possession and place. Juliet Rogers, in theorizing and critiquing the language of protest, writes that

> mirroring the gestures and language of the sovereign . . . ensures that the object in question is precisely the object that the sovereign has to give, as such it can be returned. This isn't mourning the loss.[89]

Here, in adopting the settler sovereign language and logic of possession, Amelia is refusing to accept that the place and object that she is speaking of have always been lost and may never be returned.

Departing from the traditional ghost story, the Babadook is not 'killed' or expelled from the site of its haunting after Amelia claims possession of the site and psyche of its haunting. Instead of disappearing following its expulsion from Amelia's body, although commanded to leave, the Babadook remains in the basement of her home. In interviews, Kent has explained that she had to defend the ending of the movie and that if she had needed to kill the Babadook, she would not have made the film as 'you can't kill the monster, you can only integrate it'.[90] As the Babadook remains, Amelia is compelled to care for it. Yet, although reckoning with its presence and entertaining the possibility of a new relationship, Amelia remains afraid and filled with terror when she faces the revenant (the returned). The way in which the Babadook remains in the basement of Amelia's home – in the same space where she has suspended her grief – opens up a shared space of negotiation. Here, Amelia's *revenant* becomes an *arrivant,* in claiming a right rather than being expelled with the promise of possessing that which Amelia desires. This could be theorized as hospitality 'out of a concern for justice',[91] in which the Babadook remains without any expectation of anything being given in return.

Amelia's uncanny experience resonates with the settler colonial experience in Australia where the uncanny, on a larger scale, concerns itself with every aspect of Australian settler existence. Ken Gelder and Jane Jacobs have considered the uncanny in the Australian context, stating that beyond the psyche, the uncanny also speaks to the 'question of one's place in the world',[92] which occurs when the past returns to haunt the present, making you aware that you have unfinished business with the past.[93] Gelder and Jacobs conceive the *Mabo* decision as being unfinished business, in which the anxieties that followed invoked the uncanny. The persistence of First Nations sovereignty unsettles settler sovereignty due to the possibility that 'what is ours, is also potentially, or been always already, "theirs"'.[94] Thus, contextualizing the uncanniness of Amelia's home within Australian history and place invokes the experience of the Australian legal subject who finds that they are both home and out of place simultaneously.

First Nations sovereignty and the ability to dream and exist beyond white possession and framing haunt the Australian landscape in the same way that the

Babadook haunts Amelia and her suburban existence. It follows that the settler subject questions her own history and place in the Australian landscape. This is precisely the uncanny experience. It occurs when existence is revealed as having departed from this interruption and dislocation of history, language, knowledge and geographies. The haunting endured by Amelia in the private confines of her home occurs alongside her public decline. The constant lack that defines Amelia's familial constellation grounds her subjectivity and informs the way in which she is seen and accepted in the wider society. Indeed, as she is unsettled at home, so is her ability to function in civic life. This 'collapse' between the public and private and interconnectedness of Amelia's unsettlement at home and her ability to function in civic life speak to the importance of place (of home) – and appropriate the deep feeling of unease the legal subject feels about ongoing social and spatial relations in settler Australia.

Conclusion

The trauma that follows Amelia in conjunction with the location of the Babadook's haunting, its contestation of space, its representations of colonial anxiety and the film's occlusion of First Nations people in its visual framing speaks of the way First Nation sovereignty haunts the Australian landscape and the settler's mind and space. What followed *terra nullius* was settler violence of physical, epistemic and ontological proportions, invested in obliterating the presence of First Nations people to justify the settler's existence and their claim to the land. First Nations sovereignty interrupts settler discourse, history, law and jurisdiction by its very existence – revealing its crimes across time and place. The settler subject 'part-takes' in the nation's practices – which at best consist of the liberal promise of 'closing the gap' or providing an official apology for historical wrongs – but never accepts First Nations people as persistent and sovereign independent legal subjects. As such, Indigenous subjectivity that exists above, beyond, before, during and after settler sovereignty is deeply unsettling and becomes in and of itself an undoing of settler sovereignty and law. It follows that the Australian settler subject finds the Australian landscape uncanny and remains haunted by ongoing First Nations sovereignty.

The Babadook and its haunting of Amelia provide a tool that can help us to negotiate some justice in settler colonial Australia. Here, the Babadook's ability to move between worlds, haunting both person and place, speaks to the way in which harm to and possession of land and subjectivity are intertwined. It also speaks to the way in which this trauma haunts across time and space, and thus everywhere and everything. In the Babadook, the repressed that returns renders the homely spaces increasingly uncanny and dispossessed. Yet here the terror of that which returns opens the possibility for a negotiated space. The Babadook takes up a place of contestation of space, destabilizing the structure of things, by settling into the basement of Amelia's home. Here, the hospitable relationship that emerges between Amelia and the Babadook speaks to the terror of trauma and its permanence in the settler subject's psyche, connecting it to both place and space.

Notes

1 Kent (2014), *The Babadook.*
2 Lambie (2014).
3 Weir (1975) *Picnic at Hanging Rock.*
4 George Miller (1979) *Mad Max.*
5 Lambie (2014).
6 Balanzategui (2017), p 28.
7 Dickey (2016); Douglas (2015), *Amityville Horror*; Kubrick (1980) *The Shining*; Hooper (1982) *Poltergeist.*
8 Boyd and Thrush (2011).
9 Boyd and Thrush (2011), p 10.
10 Boyd and Thrush (2011), p ix; Bergland (2000), p 22.
11 Dempsey (2015), pp 131–2.
12 Behrendt, Cunneen and Libesman (2009), p 24; HREOC (1997).
13 Ford (2010), p 13.
14 *Mabo v Queensland (No. 2)* (1992) 175 CLR 1.
15 Fitzpatrick (2002), p 243.
16 Ford (2010), p 206.
17 Dalsheim (2004), p 153; Wolfe (2006).
18 Ford (2010), p 210.
19 Wolfe (2006), p 388.
20 Dalsheim (2004), p 152.
21 Moreton-Robinson (2015), p 82.
22 Moreton-Robinson (2015), p 82.
23 Moreton-Robinson (2015), p 92.
24 Moreton-Robinson (2015), p 92.
25 Moreton-Robinson (2015), p 92.
26 *Mabo v Queensland (No. 2)* (1992) 175 CLR 1.
27 Motha (1987), p 83; *Mabo v Queensland (No. 2)* (1992) 175 CLR 1, 49.
28 Kerruish and Purdy (1998); Motha (1987).
29 Motha (1987), pp 92–4.
30 Rogers (2017), p 693.
31 Veracini (2008), p 365.
32 Freud (1950), pp 141–2; Rogers (2017), pp 688–92.
33 Aristodemou (2014), p 66.
34 Aristodemou (2014), p 66.
35 Goodrich (1997), p 1038.
36 Fitzpatrick (1992), p 11.
37 Douzinas and Gearey (2005), p 306.
38 Dean (2004), p 4.
39 Goodrich (1997), p 1036.
40 Aristodemou (2014), pp 17–19.
41 Aristodemou (2014), p 18.
42 Bergland (2000), p 10.
43 Bradshaw (2014).
44 Lambie (2014).
45 MacInnes (2014).
46 MacInnes (2014).
47 MacInnes (2014).
48 Ehrlich (2014).
49 MacInnes (2014).
50 Murphy (2014).

51 Mattson (2016); Teeman (2017)
52 Bradshaw (2014).
53 Lickona (2014).
54 MacInnes (2014).
55 Blanco and Peeren (2013), p 11.
56 Blanco and Peeren (2013), p 13.
57 Caruth (1995), p 5.
58 Weinstock (2013), pp 61–8.
59 Howell (2017), p 131.
60 Kent (2014), *The Babadook.*
61 Kent (2014), *The Babadook.*
62 Kent (2014), *The Babadook.*
63 Kent (2014), *The Babadook.*
64 Ehrlich (2014).
65 Freud et al. (1976), p 542; Palmer (2012), p 66.
66 Derrida (2012); Kristeva (1988); Masschelein (2011), p 136; Mehlman (1977).
67 Masschelein (2011), p 1.
68 Gelder and Jacobs (1998), p 111.
69 Murphy (2018), p 7.
70 MacInnes (2014).
71 Kent (2019).
72 Kent (2019).
73 Kent (2019).
74 Vidler (1992), p 11.
75 Gordon (2008), p 3.
76 Gordon (2008), p 7; Villano (2012), p 2.
77 Freud (2004), pp 74–101.
78 Derrida (2012), p 10.
79 Freud et al. (1976), p 542; Gelder (2000).
80 Freud et al. (1976), p 542; Gelder (2000).
81 Derrida (2012).
82 Blanco and Peeren (2013), p 13.
83 Blanco and Peeren (2013), p 13.
84 Murphy (2018), p 6.
85 Palmer (2012), p 66.
86 Del Villano (2012), p 2.
87 Del Villano (2012), p 11.
88 Rogers (2009), pp 271–2.
89 Rogers (2009), p 270.
90 Ehrlich (2014).
91 Derrida (2012), p 220.
92 Gelder and Jacobs (1999), p 111.
93 Gelder and Jacobs (1999), p 111.
94 Gelder and Jacobs (1999), p 111.

References

Primary source

Mabo v Queensland (No. 2) (1992) 175 CLR.

Secondary sources

Maria Aristodemou (2014) *Law, Psychoanalysis, Society: Taking the Unconscious Seriously*, Routledge.
Jessica Balanzategui (2017) '*The Babadook* and the Haunted Space between High and Low Genres in the Australian Horror Tradition' 11 *Studies in Australasian Cinema* 18.
Larissa Behrendt, Chris Cunneen and Terry Libesman (2009) *Indigenous Legal Relations in Australia*, Oxford University Press.
Renee Bergland (2000) *The National Uncanny: Indian Ghosts and American Subjects*, University Press of New England.
Colleen E. Boyd and Coll-Peter Thrush (eds) (2011) *Phantom Past, Indigenous Presence: Native Ghosts in North American Culture and History*, University of Nebraska Press.
Peter Bradshaw (2014) '*The Babadook* Review – A Superbly Acted, Chilling Freudian Thriller', *The Guardian*, www.theguardian.com/film/2014/oct/23/the-babadook-review-chilling-freudian-thriller.
Cathy Caruth (1995) *Trauma: Exploration in Memory*, Johns Hopkins University Press.
Joyce Dalsheim (2004) 'Settler Nationalism, Collective Memories of Violence and the "Uncanny Other"' 10 *Social Identities* 151.
Jodi Dean (2004) 'Zizek on Law' 15 *Law and Critique* 1.
Maria del Pilar Blanco and Esther Peeren (2013) 'Introduction: Conceptualising Spectralities', in Maria del Pilar Blanco and Esther Peeren (eds), *The Spectralities Reader: Ghosts and Haunting in Contemporary Cultural Theory*.
Bianca Del Villano (2012) *Ghostly Alterities. Spectrality and Contemporary Literatures in English*, Ibidem Press.
Aoife M. Dempsey (2015) '*The Babadook*' 14 *The Irish Journal of Gothic and Horror Studies* 130.
Jacques Derrida (2012) *Specters of Marx: The State of the Debt, the Work of Mourning and the New International*, Routledge.
Colin Dickey (2016) 'The Suburban Horror of the Indian Burial Ground', *New Republic*, 19 October, https://newrepublic.com/article/137856/suburban-horror-indian-burial-ground.
Costas Douzinas and Adam Gearey (eds) (2005) *Critical Jurisprudence: The Political Philosophy of Justice*, Hart.
David Ehrlich (2014) '*The Babadook* Director Jennifer Kent Talks About Drawing Horror from Life', *The Dissolve*, https://thedissolve.com/features/emerging/834-the-babadook-director-jennifer-kent-talks-about-dr.
Peter Fitzpatrick (1992) *The Mythology of Modern Law*, Routledge.
——— (2002) '"No Higher Duty": Mabo and the Failure of Legal Foundation' 13 *Law and Critique* 233.
Lisa Ford (2010) *Settler Sovereignty: Jurisdiction and Indigenous People in America and Australia, 1788–1836*, Harvard University Press.
Sigmund Freud (1950) *Totem and Taboo*, Routledge.
——— (2004) 'The Uncanny', in D. Sandner (ed.), *Fantastic Literature: A Critical Reader*, Praeger.
Sigmund Freud, James Strachey, Helene Cixous and Robert Dennome (1976) 'Fiction and Its Phantoms: A Reading of Freud's Das Unheimliche (The "Uncanny")' 7 *New Literary History* 525.
Ken Gelder (2000) *The Horror Reader*, Psychology Press.

Ken Gelder and Jane Jacobs (1998) *Uncanny Australia: Sacredness and Identity in a Postcolonial Nation*, Melbourne University Publishing.

——— (1999) 'The Postcolonial Ghost Story', in Peter Buse and Andrew Scott (eds), *Ghosts: Deconstruction, Psychoanalysis, History*, Palgrave Macmillan.

Peter Goodrich (1997) 'Maladies of the Legal Soul: Psychoanalysis and Interpretation in Law' (1997) 54 *Washington and Lee Law Review* 1035.

Avery Gordon (2008) *Ghostly Matters: Haunting and the Sociological Imagination*, University of Minnesota Press.

Amanda Howell (2017) 'Haunted Art House: *The Babadook* and International Art Cinema Horror', in Ryan M. Goldsmith (ed.), *Australian Screen in the 2000s*, Palgrave Macmillan.

——— (2018) 'The Terrible Terrace: Australian Gothic Reimagined and the (Inner) Suburban Horror of *The Babadook*', in Adrian Danks, Stephen Gaunson and Peter Kunze (eds), *American-Australian Cinema*, Palgrave Macmillan.

Human Rights and Equal Opportunity Commission (HREOC) (1997) *Bringing Them Home: Report of the National Inquiry into the Separation of Aboriginal and Torres Strait Islander Children from their Families*, HREOC.

Jennifer Kent (2019) 'Director Explains How She Made *The Babadook* and *The Nightingale*', *Vanity Fair Video*, https://video.vanityfair.com/watch/director-explains-her-creative-process-for-the-babadook-and-the-nightingale/?_ga=2.19296497.89927160.1569768733-431706584.1569768733.

Valerie Kerruish and Jeannine Purdy (1998) 'He Look Honest – Big White Thief' 4 *Law Text Culture* 146.

Julia Kristeva (1988) *Strangers to Ourselves*, Harvester Wheatsheaf.

Ryan Lambie (2014) 'Jennifer Kent Interview: Directing *The Babadook*', *Den of Geek!*, www.denofgeek.com/movies/the-babadook/32451/jennifer-kent-interview-directing-the-babadook.

Matthew Lickona (2014) 'Interview with The Babadook Writer-director Jennifer Kent', *San Diego Reader*, www.sandiegoreader.com/news/2014/dec/17/screen-interview-babadook-jennifer-kent.

Paul MacInnes (2014) '*The Babadook*: "I Wanted to Talk About the Need to Face Darkness in Ourselves"', *The Guardian*, 18 October, www.theguardian.com/film/2014/oct/18/the-babadook-jennifer-kent.

Anneleen Masschelein (2011) *The Unconcept: The Freudian Uncanny in Late Twentieth-century Theory*, SUNY Press.

Kelcie Mattson (2014) 'Through a Mother's Eyes: *The Babadook* and Examining Trauma', *A Medium Corporation*, https://medium.com/@wewillbethestars/through-a-mothers-eyes-the-babadook-and-examining-trauma-women-in-horror-series-e1f25804dca9.

Jeffrey Mehlman (1977) *Revolution and Repetition: Marx/Hugo/Balzac*, University of California Press.

Aileen Moreton-Robinson (2015) *The White Possessive: Property, Power and Indigenous Sovereignty*, University of Minnesota Press.

Stewart Motha (1987) '*Mabo*: Encountering the Epistemic Limit of the Recognition of Difference' 7 *Griffith Law Review* 79.

Fiona Murphy (2018) 'The Whispering of Ghosts: Loss, Longing, and the Return in Stolen Generations Stories' 29 *The Australian Journal of Anthropology* 332.

Mekado Murphy (2014) 'That Book! It's . . . It's . . . Aaaaaaahhhh!', *New York Times*, 23 November, www.nytimes.com/2014/11/23/movies/inside-the-horror-pop-up-book-in-the-babadook.html.

Pauline Palmer (2012) *The Queer Uncanny: New Perspectives on the Gothic*, University of Wales Press.
Juliet Rogers (2009) 'Beyond the Script of Law: Dildos, Tranny Cops and Protesting Anti-terrorism' 18 *Griffith Law Review* 269.
——— (2017) 'Is Psychoanalysis Universal? Politics, Desire, and Law in Colonial Contexts' 38 *Political Psychology* 685.
Tim Teeman (2017) 'Scene by Scene, This Is What Makes the Babadook Such an LGBT Icon', *The Daily Beast*, www.thedailybeast.com/scene-by-scene-this-is-what-makes-the-babadook-such-an-lgbt-icon.
Lorenzo Veracini (2008) 'Settler Collective, Founding Violence and Disavowal: The Settler Colonial Situation' 29 *Journal of Intercultural Studies* 363.
Anthony Vidler (1992) *The Architectural Uncanny: Essays in the Modern Unhomely*, MIT Press.
Jeffrey Andrew Weinstock (2013) 'Introduction: The Spectral Turn', in Maria del Pilar Blanco and Esther Peeren (eds), *The Spectralities Reader: Ghosts and Haunting in Contemporary Cultural Theory*, Bloomsbury.
Patrick Wolfe (2006) 'Settler Colonialism and the Elimination of the Native' 8 *Journal of Genocide Research* 387.

Films

Andrew Douglas (2015) *Amityville Horror*, MGM Distribution.
Tobe Hooper (1982) *Poltergeist*, MGM Entertainment.
Jennifer Kent (2014), *The Babadook*, Screen Australia.
Stanley Kubrick (1980) *The Shining*, Warner Bros.
George Miller (1979) *Mad Max*, Roadshow Film Distributors.
Peter Weir (1975) *Picnic at Hanging Rock*, Australian Film Commission.

Chapter 8

Being engaged in colonial critique by Mojo Juju's 'Native Tongue'

Kirsty Duncanson

Prologue

It starts with the soft crackle of a needle in the groove of an old 45. The black screen fades into the image of a person against a classic Australian landscape of bleached yellow grass and distant trees. The person is looking down, walking towards the receding camera. She wears a heavy fur coat with the turned-up collar almost encompassing her head. Solid necklaces rest against a black top. This is Mojo Juju.

A rhythmic humming begins like undulating waves. Juju's eyes flash up to directly address the viewer. The pace of the camera's retreat increases, granting a fuller image of Juju staring into its lens, and reveals two men walking in time on either side. They pop against the pale horizon in vivid orange overalls. Their socks and shoes are brilliant white. Their skin is dark. They are Aboriginal Australian. The men begin to sway as the lyrics cut through the lower tenor of the hum.

Acknowledgement of country

This chapter was written on the land of the Wurundjeri people and developed at a symposium held on the land of the Yugambeh people. I acknowledge the traditional owners of these lands. I pay my respects to Elders past, present and emerging. Aboriginal and Torres Strait Islanders remain strong in their enduring connection to land and culture. Aboriginal sovereignty was never ceded.

Introduction

> I don't speak my father's native tongue;
> I was born under a Southern sun.
> I don't know where I belong
> I don't know where I belong[1]

As a music video, 'Native Tongue' lasts just over four minutes, but it is a powerful four minutes during which the members of its audience are enticed to lose themselves in the pleasures of its sound. They might even sing the lyrics with Mojo Juju as they watch through the movement of the camera and unconsciously imagine their own bodies dancing with the men. In this chapter, I argue that the experience of consuming or engaging with 'Native Tongue' is laden with legal philosophy. On one level, it offers to grant empathic access to an experience of the criminalizing and carceral marginalization of Western colonial law, which fragments the legal subjecthood of those whose bodies do not conform. At the same time, the video directly challenges parts of its audience and threatens to shatter the internal coherence of legal subjecthood, while also performing a continuation of culture and Indigenous sovereignty never ceded.

To demonstrate this argument, I rely on a rich heritage of critical and cultural legal scholarship that continues to expose the depths and breadths to which law is entangled with popular culture and the bodies that consume it. Bringing legal theory and analysis together with music and visual culture methodologies, I analyze 'Native Tongue' as a specifically audio-visual product.

To do this I first set out my methodology that incorporates legal theory, cinema studies and music analysis. Implementing these methods, I explore the expression of marginalization and the assertion of resistance before identifying the jurisprudence of sovereignty as it permeates the experience of consuming the music video text. Before I begin, however, let me tell you a bit about 'Native Tongue'.

About 'Native Tongue'

The marketing of 'Native Tongue' was explicitly political. Interviews with Mojo Juju foreground identity politics as a central motivation for both the song and the album as a whole, also called *Native Tongue*.[2] Despite my adherence to Barthes's assertion that the author is dead, and thus there is no inherent meaning in a text derived from the author's intent, my analysis in this chapter is shaped by Juju's politics in two ways.[3] First, in Juju's interviews I find validation for some of my interpretation and admonishment to think more deeply and carefully about some of my other initial readings. This is especially important to me as a straight white woman writing about the work of a queer woman of colour. Second, knowledge of Juju's politics as present in the popular (online) press contributes to the way audiences interpret the components of the video. In presenting the details and contexts of the video, I seek to emphasize the politics manifest throughout them.

Juju explains that she had avoided politicizing her music until a journalist commented on her 'surprising' success in the industry as a 'queer woman of colour', stating, 'That's really confronting'.[4] These words consolidated feedback she had received throughout her career that she 'didn't look right, sound right or act right', that she was 'too queer or too brown or just not attractive enough to sell records'.[5] *Native Tongue* marks Juju's decision to take control of the politics generated around her identity by addressing them directly. Consequently, the album is an expression of Mojo Juju's identity politics. During the album tour, Juju talked between songs about her family and her sense of who she is as the daughter of a

Filipino migrant and the great-granddaughter of a secret relationship between an Indigenous man and a white woman. Juju also identifies as queer and explicitly plays with gender stereotypes in her dress. Prior to 'Native Tongue', she often wore tailored suits with waistcoats and fedoras, a sexy gender-bending play on blues and swing attire. While the songs present experiences of marginalization and discrimination while growing up in rural Australia and working in the Australian music industry, they also speak of cultural loss, displacement, racism, homophobia, sexism and colonialism.

The single 'Native Tongue' was released on 24 July 2018 through ABC and Universal music, and the video was made available on YouTube.[6] As the title track and forerunning single, 'Native Tongue' had the role of setting the tone for an album that at that point was yet to be released. In this role, the song and video clip potently encapsulate themes promised to characterize the album. Both the song and the video continue to receive critical acclaim, with politics at the forefront of each review. While Wang at the ABC states that the single 'has been praised by critics and embraced by audiences', she also writes that it 'wraps themes of colonialism, cultural loss, racism and displacement in personal and political terms'.[7] In *The Guardian*, Nicol describes the clip as 'powerful' and as fighting back with 'gloves off'.[8] Jack from Stasheverything describes it as 'a song [that] is both personal and painful, yet simultaneously empowering and anthemic' and quotes Juju's hope that it reaches 'anyone who has ever felt stuck between two worlds'.[9] In the year of its release, Juju won the Dreamtime Award for Female Artist of the Year. The video won Triple J's Best Video of the Year Award and Best Music Video Award at the inaugural First Nations Media Awards.[10] In 2019, it won Best Independent Single at the AIR Independent Music Awards and Song of the Year at the National Indigenous Music Awards. Juju won the same awards for Best Album for *Native Tongue*.

The politics of the video are bolstered by a creative team with experience and critical awareness of identity politics. They are Juju's friends, but further than this, Juju says she 'wanted to include other people of colour . . . wanted to include other queer people of colour' in the creation process.[11] The sound was produced by Chinese-Malaysian-Australian hip hop artist Joelistics. He has said of his former rap outfit TZU that they were 'not the white, middle-class experience of Australia and we [commented] from where we come from'.[12] His solo work is animated by a similar critical observation of contemporary mainstream Australian culture, with lyrics criticizing right-wing politics and shaming refugee-related xenophobia. As a music producer, festival organizer and social media personality, Joelistics talks about promoting ethnic and gender diversity and inclusivity.

The team also includes dancers from Djuki Mala, an Indigenous company originally from Elcho Island, off the coast of the Northern Territory. Their work combines traditional Yolngu choreography, a range of pop culture styles and techniques, and a great deal of humour. They formed the company after their informal 'Zorba the Greek' video 'went viral' on YouTube.[13] The humming rhythm is provided by Pasefika Vitoria Choir, a Melbourne-based group who sing (and speak)

Samoan, Tongan, Rarotongan, Maori and Tokelauan, among other languages.[14] Claudia Sangiorgi Dalimore directed the 'Native Tongue' video. She met Juju while making a documentary about women's experiences of discrimination and success in the Australian music industry.[15] Like Joelistics, Dalimore is candid about the politics of her work.

The success of 'Native Tongue' on Triple J, Australia's national youth radio station, is indicative of the presence of the song and video in Australian popular culture. While Triple J was established to target an alternative music audience, its 2015 ratings survey found it attracting equal numbers of the lucrative 25-to-39-year-old radio market to those of the commercial stations in some regions and even greater numbers in others.[16] The video's accomplishment in this context and as an overtly political video makes it a significant text to explore for the reverberations it might carry for Australian music consumers. I am particularly interested in the way it engages alternative white audiences.

The race politics of writing this chapter

> It's easy enough for you to say
> It ain't no thing
> But I'm the one; you ain't the one
> Been living in this skin.[17]

I want to digress before launching into my analysis to recognize that this chapter, which grants me the points I require to maintain and further my career, takes as its source text a product created by people of colour and of non-heteronormative sexuality. I do this from a position of privilege as a straight, white, middle-class, academic Australian woman. As such, I potentially practise further colonial, imperial violence. I am hoping to avoid this and to act as an 'ally', making a contribution to 'shift feminist whiteness' and Australian culture.[18] A central purpose of my academic work is the deconstruction of current systems of privilege to help create better social justice. To do this, I wish to walk the path Haggis and Schech have marked out, trying to resist the seductive pull to Good White Womanhood towards the White Queen and taking the risk of being BAD in the hope of offering something useful rather than damaging.[19]

In reading *Native Tongue* for the legal stories it tells, I do not profess to speak for Mojo Juju or suggest that I hold the truth of what she and her creative team assert. I read the text for what I perceive it to offer an 'alternative' white Australian culture, much of which is generated and consumed through a normative lens of white heteronormativity and what Goenpul scholar Aileen Moreton-Robinson calls the 'possessive logic of patriarchal white sovereignty', even when the creators and consumers are not white, male, heteronormative or ostensibly patriarchal.[20] This is a framework for interpreting audio-visual media that people in Australia learn from the practices of media consumption established through a monopolized history of art, popular culture, Eurocentric education and so much more.[21]

Juju describes writing *Native Tongue* in the hope of speaking to and with 'other people of colour' and particularly 'queer people of colour'.[22] The video is consumed by a broader audience as well. For the purposes of this chapter, I predominantly presume the hegemonic lens as consumer in order to explore how mainstream audiences have been trained to read the video and how the video uses that lens to challenge the ideologies with which that lens is entangled. I pay particular attention to the category positions of 'good white womanhood' described by Haggis and Schech because I walk dangerously along the edges of these identities and because these are also significant, potentially powerful subject positions through which the music video is enthusiastically consumed in its location within the alternative Australian music scene. I do so because I believe the music video speaks powerfully to this audience with a generosity that confronts without alienating. This fascinates me as it awes me, and I proceed with gratitude to Juju and her team.

Reading a music video

My analysis owes considerably to cultural legal scholarship, feminist and queer legal theory, Australian law and society and the law and the humanities communities, both in the research that precedes me and the collegiality that nurtures me. As the work in this collection demonstrates, law is now recognized as manifest in cinema, television and art. Manderson states that children's books and literature are sources of law.[23] We learn law and experience legal concepts while consuming these texts. Moran and colleagues argue that film is not just a site of passive consumption of law, but a place where it is questioned, critiqued and negotiated.[24] MacNeil demonstrates that law is theorized across a full gamut of textual forms that make up popular culture.[25] He calls this *lex populi*, or popular jurisprudence. Buchanan and Johnson, separately and together, illustrate how cinematic texts engage our bodies in their legal arguments.[26] As Young writes, representations of crime and justice get under our skin.[27] They are part of our visceral pleasures and pleasurable discomforts in the entertainment of our leisure time.

In this chapter, I apply methodologies drawn from this scholarship to a powerful fragment of Australian alternative popular culture, to explore how it coaches the straight, white, privileged part of its audience to recalibrate their embodied knowledge of Australian law. Following my peers, I use cinematic analysis with my legal scholarship, but I also delve into music analysis. This is an area new to me and not common in cultural legal studies, so I will take some time to describe my methods.

As a music video, 'Native Tongue' lends itself to an ocular-centric reading, allowing the analyst (me) to remain within the enlightenment knowledge traditions that 'privilege the eye' to focus on the surface layer of what can be seen.[28] I do examine the images of the video for what it represents and how. However, as music, 'Native Tongue' engages its audience sonically, affecting the body and drawing the listening viewer in to become part of the text: identifying with, being confronted by, getting lost within and embodying the sound, even performing (singing, dancing) the rhythms.

To explore the jurisprudential possibilities this text might generate with its audience, I use semiotic analysis as it has been developed and implemented through the traditions of cinema studies, informed as these traditions are by psychoanalysis. I extend the semiotic field to incorporate the 'acculturated sensorium' that is the whole of our consuming body, trained through our exposure to the cultural specificities and coding of our milieu, to interpret and make meaning from an audio-visual text.[29]

Sound and music have the reputation of eluding analysis. Berland explains that music is thought to disdain 'all boundaries of language and location',[30] while Attali asserts that 'no theorising accomplished through language or mathematics can suffice any longer; it is incapable of accounting for . . . the qualitative and the fluid, threats and violence'.[31] Music is imagined as reaching beyond legible interpretation.

Barthes theorizes that music's resistance to analysis offers a loss of self or subjectivity for the listener.[32] Using Kristeva's work on poetry, Barthes calls this *signifiance.* Signifiance 'places the subject . . . in the text . . . as a "loss", a disappearance'.[33] For music, this means the listener is able to lose their sense of self in the experience of listening. To me, this echoes those contemporary lyrics celebrating sonically induced loss of self, from Sister Sledge's description of being 'Lost in Music'[34] through Eminem's suggestion to 'lose yourself in the music'[35] and Daft Punk's celebratory inducement to 'lose yourself to dance'.[36] I identify this loss of subjectivity in the moments when my son and I sing, with delicious passion, with Mojo Juju on our car journeys to and from childcare, when we dance with his sister in the kitchen or when I run to the rhythm in my headphones. Although for Attali the experience of music holds violence, for Barthes it is erotic as he imagines the listener penetrated by the music and merging with the performers or sound in their listening imagination. This is 'the erotic thrill enabled by signifiance'.[37]

For Kristeva, signifiance enables access to a feminine *jouissance* that can bring the feminine subject closer to what she calls 'the semiotic'. This is similar to Lacan's 'real' – that which defies the symbolic order and cannot easily be expressed through the 'phallic trappings of language'.[38] Heath explains that signifiance is the inverse or the contrary of significance (the way in which an object, image or word gains meaning through culturally generated codes of language and discourse).[39] This is because signifiance 'cannot be reduced to . . . communication, representation, expression'.[40] Rather, I understand signifiance as that which sits on the edge of vision or tangibility, like the fleeting movement of a zombie across the screen in *28 Days Later*[41] that the viewer registers at one level, but is denied fully comprehensive recognition, leaving them uttering 'Was that a . . .?' Signifiance is that which cannot be translated easily into the dominant codes of language and meaning available, in that more-challenging-to-map field of affect and the senses.

However, music and sound are far from a vacuum of meaning, as is the experience of loss. Meaning pervades Barthes's loss of self and erotic merging with sound. Further than this, that meaning is granted power through its interweave with the associated embodied experience. Situated in the body, and thereby ostensibly in nature, this meaning is rendered beyond language and thus also beyond critique. Attali absolutely reads sound as bearing meaning. He writes that, running parallel to human society, music 'is a mirror'[42] caught up in the movements of human history, while everywhere 'codes analyse, mark, restrain, train, repress, and channel the primitive sounds of language, of the body, of tools, of objects, of the relations to self and others'.[43] Its ethereal nature is integral to the meaning it holds, such that Attali describes music to be

> an immaterial recording surface for human works . . . a shred of Utopia to decipher, information in negative, a collective memory allowing those who hear it to record their own personalised, specified, modelled meanings . . . a collective memory of order and genealogies, the repository of the word.[44]

The meaning music holds is attached to the moments in which it was produced and initially consumed. This is a meaning gained through the culturally shared moment of its circulation through radio stations; on personal stereos; and at parties, bars and nightclubs. In this manner, a popular song used in cinema calls on its original context, as well as its snowballed accrued meaning across social history since that time. Simultaneously, each listener has their own relationship to a piece of music, which invokes memories of a holiday, a drug-related adventure or other fleeting moments of life. These meanings are held in difficult-to-apprehend affective experiences of hearing a bar, melody or rhythm of a song. This is discernible in the practice of sampling, through which artists capture a scrap of an earlier song that usually contrasts the style of the new piece but powerfully evokes significance from the older song. There is often a deepened feeling of nostalgia in the play of old and new.[45]

Barthes theorizes that the loss of self is in part made possible by the 'grain of the voice', through which the listener builds from their perception of voice textures, musical style and so on an imaginary embodiment of the performer.[46] Young explains that 'the listener will unwittingly use timbral clues to create a visual imagining of the physical entity they hear'.[47] Ostensibly inscribed through the texture of a singer's voice is evidence of their physical and sociological manifestation: their gender, race, ethnicity, age and health. As Kheshti demonstrates in her deconstruction of world music, 'gender and ethnicity – like place . . . temporality . . . and religion . . . are sonically and texturally/textually signified'.[48] The performers' signified identities are also constructed through contextual information provided via marketing, press coverage, live performances and music videos. As listeners, though, 'we can only ever *imagine* the artist we hear in a recording. And our imagining is based on clues provided by *the grain* of the voice'.[49] The margin of error is extensive in the audio identification of these conditions of being, with listeners regularly 'misrecognizing' sex, race, age and so on. However, even in its very lack of accuracy, the grain of the voice is rich with significance. This grain facilitates the erotic merging of the listener with their imaginary visual configuration as the listener experiences losing themselves within the aural manifestation of something or someone who is not themselves.

For Young, this fantastical merging creates an opening for empathy.[50] The voice invites the listener to experience physical empathy as the listener's ear and body wrestle with the physicality we hear in the other's voice, thereby producing a kinaesthetic relation. In listening to speech or song, we are invited to hear another's voice with our own body, in relation to our own. This is a powerful affect that works beyond linguistic or visual semiotics, potentially enabling a degree of understanding or connection with the experience or feelings of another person who might possibly be significantly different from the listener.

I want to explore how such empathy functions in 'Native Tongue', offering access to the experience of fragmented subjecthood in the face of carceral colonialism. Yet the song and music video do more than this. The way in which the empathy generated is not an easy invitation to sympathy. This is due to a resistance to the politics of music production and Western practices of intercultural listening. Let me explain how I understand these politics before I return to 'Native Tongue'. Politics are discernible in the grain and signifiance of sound. Sterne argues that throughout the production and consumption of music relations of power can be traced, explaining that 'structures of listening, whether interpersonal, institutional or mediatized are also configurations of power'.[51] Kheshti carefully and affectively demonstrates how gender and race are mobilized sonically in the ostensibly 'intercultural' genre of World Music, such that it reaffirms white privilege. Marketing establishes the ideal listener of World Music as white, middle class and female. She is 'transported' by World Music to an exotic world in which she is encouraged to lose herself. Through the sense of lost self, Kheshti explains how 'the magic of signifiance allows listeners . . . to *feel* something that they are otherwise removed from'.[52] Signifiance is created through the genre's explicit blend of sounds associated with its Western producers and ethereal sounds of other, non-Western places. On a technical and material level, the voice of the 'other', a woman singing in Arabic in Kheshti's example, becomes another sound captured and dropped into the soundscape of crickets, tropical birds and wild dogs as another signifier of exotic, foreign climes. The singer, Kheshti notes, is not credited on the album cover. A conflation of the singer with the other sounds of the exotic is thus encouraged. In this way, she is rendered less culturally sophisticated than the credited Western producers. The singer's subjecthood is obfuscated.

On another level, white privilege is reified as it is serviced by the uncredited female singer. The ethereal voice provides the white woman's *jouissance*, enabling her to pleasurably lose herself and merge with her fantasy of the singer. An ostensible empathy is offered, allowing the white woman a sense of connection, which is strengthened by the apparent cultural difference and augmented by the juxtaposition of Western listener/Western producers and foreign singer. The listener can enjoy a sense of 'good white womanhood' in her feeling of connection with the exotic singer. But because the *jouissance* relies on the ethereal and thus the unidentifiability of the singer, the connection is inevitably built on the denial of the singer's subjecthood. She is reduced to the function of providing pleasure for the white woman – again.

I use Young[53] and Khesti's[54] signifiance to explore the possibilities within the loss of self that is enabled by 'Native Tongue', rich as it is in raced, sexed and colonial signification. Rather than exploiting the accessed alterity to enrich white privilege, however, 'Native Tongue' offers the white women who make up just part of its audience a journey within its signifiance that shifts from empathic merging with the performers through a confrontational jolt. The listening white woman finds herself merged with the grain, articulating a challenge towards herself as part of the 'you' who make the singer feel 'ill at ease', who are challenged to confront their homophobia, sexism and racism. An order is restored at the end of the song as it executes a gentle delivery to the listener's self on Juju's lamenting refrain. But this is a self potentially altered by the journey of being lost in and comforted by the music.

When this sonically enabled journey is paired with the video, it includes an engagement with a jurisprudence of continuing Indigenous sovereignty. Although I use a theory of signifiance developed for the analysis of music, in this chapter I seek to apply it to dance as well. Dance is another form that defies established semiotics. Although it does not appear to 'transport' the viewer to a lost self in the immersive manner that music does, it functions with music to do something very similar. MacDougall writes of cinema triggering bodily memories of movement.[55] This line of argument has resonated for me in my experience of watching dance, such that I experience a ghostly aching of muscle as I see choreography performed that I have only ever dreamt of copying. My ears are haunted by the memory of turning and swaying, bending and leaping. I will attempt to extend my analysis of signifiance to the dance through which the viewer is drawn to lose themselves and access an alterity that might enable a kind of 'empathy' experienced through the embodiment of the 'other'. In an empathic experience with another, the audience is granted brief access to the cosmology of Indigenous sovereignty never ceded. This is a quiet jurisprudential moment of learning about Indigenous culture as long lived, dynamic and continuing.

Lost

> My great granddaddy was Wiradjuri
> My father came here from the Philippines
> It's where I live, its where I wanna be
> But you make me feel so ill at ease.[56]

My three-year-old tells me that this song he loves so much is sad because the singer 'sounds lost'. The repeated refrain, the lyrics over which Juju's voice stretches and lingers, where it sweetens and breaks, tells us she doesn't know where she belongs. Juju describes it as 'a song about longing . . . for anyone who has ever felt like they are stuck between two worlds, struggling to find a place in either'.[57] I begin my analysis with 'Native Tongue's' outermost layer of loss and longing as it is expressed and experienced through word, image and sound. While the music video tells a political story of fractured citizenship and legal subjecthood issuing from loss of culture, it also conjures sensations of criminalized subjecthood through its layering of music and cinematic technique.

The lyrics present Juju's mixed heritage as Aboriginal and Filipino. The words speak of lost cultural heritage, with culture signified by her father's languages, or 'native tongue', and extended through gender-patterned referencing to her Wiradjuri great-grandfather. Since Kevin Rudd's Apology to Australia's Indigenous Peoples, Indigenous dispossession and cultural loss through colonization have become part of mainstream Australian popular consciousness.[58] In reviews and interviews about the album, this politics sits at the forefront with discussions of Juju's experiences of discrimination as a queer woman of colour in the music industry and in Australia more broadly. Juju nostalgically describes hearing her father speak 'a "mash up" of Tagalog, llonggo, Spanish and English' with family overseas and expresses her regret that she did not learn them. The album tour incorporated further stories that lie behind each song, including her great-grandmother's secret relationship with a Wiradjuri man.

Juju's lyrics evoke both multiculturalist and Indigenous discourses. Moran observes the way that 'the discourse of multiculturalism in Australia . . . has largely proceeded along parallel lines to discourse about Aboriginal rights and self-determination'[59] He describes the two as bearing qualitatively different claims,[60] responding to many considerably different instruments and tactics of that possessive logic of patriarchal white sovereignty.[61] Curthoys argues that attempting to bring these discourses together creates an 'uneasy conversation'.[62] One specific danger, according to Moran, is that the colonial violence of dispossession, child removal and other genocidal practices is diminished by a multicultural framework focused mainly on culture and tradition.[63] Mojo Juju embodies this uneasy conversation as she foregrounds her Wiradjuri and Pilipino heritage through the words of her song. She embodies an intersectionality, not only of heritage but also of sexuality, in which exists myriad tensions between aligning and divergent politics of marginalization.

The conjunction of being born in Australia, 'under the Southern Sun', and not knowing where she belongs echoes Hage's theory of two-tiered 'belonging'.[64] Active belonging, or feeling that 'the nation belongs to you', embodies managerial citizenship: the subject has rights to the nation's infrastructure, including education, welfare and health care. But this subject also feels the right to take up space physically and politically. Like Žižek's Nation-Thing, there is a sense that this subject's values align with those of the nation – that they are *national* values.[65] Additionally, the actively belonging subject feels they have the right to manage the space of the nation: mandating who is permitted to enter its borders, who may build places of worship and where, who should live in *this* street . . . and so on.

In contrast, while 'passive belonging' or the feeling of belonging *to* the nation allows a separate subject access to citizenship rights, this subject does not feel their opinions are *national* values. Further, they do not feel they have the right to dictate spatial politics; they do not feel they have the right to take up space in and of themselves. Instead, this subject is one of those elements being managed by the actively belonging citizens. Juju's words appear to speak directly to this second sense of belonging. Her lyrics identify her as a citizen, 'born [and living] under the Southern Sun'. But they also describe Juju being made to feel 'ill at ease', being discriminated against and feeling as if she does not belong. This is an experience echoed by Aboriginal writer, director and actor Leah Purcell, who describes feeling not at home in your home country.[66] In an asserted refusal to 'apologise for taking up this space', Juju's words evidence a pressure she feels to actually do so. Her lyrics indicate that she does not enjoy the right to occupy or manage the national space. She does not enjoy active belonging.

The play of belonging intersects with law's marginalizing practices. While law asserts its universality, so many of its subjects appear fragmented by their sheer multiplicity of divergent signifying identities (queer, female, migrant, Indigenous etc.) in the face of law's requirement that they are each internally unitary and self-adherent in line with the ideal bodily form of the liberal legal subject. As Nedelsky writes, the central concepts of Western political thought rest 'on a unity among people', which is achieved by excluding 'from the public realm those people identified with the excluded characteristics [of] desire, affectivity and bodies'.[67] Law has functioned effectively and persistently to exclude from legally recognized subjecthood bodies that look, experience, perform or desire differently. It has functioned to deny their capacity to access legal subjecthood, such as practising suffrage,[68] negotiating consent and contract[69] or enjoying rights.[70] Rather, as Stychin explains, the constitution of the legal subject as universally applicable 'has been achieved by the relegation of some to the status of other'.[71] The key concepts of equality, universality and impartiality entail a denial of embodied difference.[72] More specifically, the model legal subject has been formed and maintained as universal through the very acts of identifying divergent bodies as deviant or abnormal. In this manner, these embodied legal subjects are prevented from experiencing the full range of privileges and capacities of that elusive ideal that is white, able-bodied, heterosexual masculinity.

The juxtaposition of belonging, taking up space, cultural loss and mixed-race heritage created by the lyrics, combined with the extra-textual knowledge for those who know Juju's queer identity, expresses an experience of political citizenship and legal subjecthood as fragmented and consequently not fully accepted, protected or embraced by the dominant politico-legal sovereign order. Juju's intersectional identity becomes discernible as fragmentation in the visual component of 'Native Tongue'. This is primarily done through pixilation, but it is also in the choreography that weaves the dancers in and out of Juju's shadow. The choreography juxtaposes jolting angular shapes with smoother flows as the music is interrupted by 'glitchy' sounds. In separate split-second flashes, the dancers, Juju and the landscape are pixelated. A relationship to law as deviant, while marked by the lyrics, is extended by the pixilation and confirmed by the dancers' orange jumpsuits. Against the choir's undulating hum, the sound production is 'glitchy', with intermittent explosions, crackling, fizzing, clashing symbols, taut drumbeats, clapping and a sonar pulse. These irregular sounds sync momentarily with the visual glitches. Together, they enrich the song's lamentation of fragmented legal subjecthood with textures of carceral colonialism and the criminalizing gaze.

Pixilation is used to disguise identifying visual information, often to protect the 'innocent', the survivor or the informant.[73] However, as pixilation intersects with the grainy aesthetic of CCTV footage, it also denotes criminality: the criminal act caught on camera. The association between criminality and the pixelated image has been strengthened by the narrative function of CCTV footage in so many TV crime dramas as well as true crime and news programmes. Repeatedly, the 'truth of crime' appears before us in pixelated representations of alleged offences or presumed offenders. At the same time, the momentary transfiguration of human forms into microelements foregrounds visual technology. It makes the viewer aware of the image-making process: that they are watching something created using a camera. The history of photography and cinema interweaves with the histories of criminology, psychology and sexology as these new sciences implemented cutting-edge technology to extend the ocular-centric observation techniques of enlightenment knowledge production at the turn of the previous century.

Under the ostensibly objective guise of science, these disciplines chose and isolated subjects as deviant. These subjects became 'objects of the clinical gaze . . . abstracted from their social environment and subjected to a specialized gaze on their bodies'.[74] Women's bodies, as well as criminal, queer, non-binary, raced and colonized bodies, all apparently offered proof of their necessary subjugation in their visible, measurable limbs; foreheads; fingers; toes; genitals and so on. Cameras were used to record these observations, photographs were used to ascertain essential truths about categories of person and video footage and still images continue to be used to prove the truth of offending.[75] The visual technologies of cinema are tethered to 'the creation of knowledge through visibility [and] the production of the body as a visible and measurable entity'.[76] Consequently, the conventions of cinematic representation continue the objectifying and othering structures of the scientific gaze, echoing the 'colonial structure of seeing'[77] and the heteronormative 'male gaze'.[78]

Mulvey's account of the male gaze demonstrates how power works in Western screen culture. The cinematic apparatus (that combination of camera, direction, editing, filters, sound production, screen and so on) controls what can be seen and how it can be seen because it cuts out other possibilities. As traditional cinema viewers, we watch in a darkened room, denied distraction, caught between the 'darkness of the auditorium [and the] brilliant patterns of light and shade on the screen'.[79] We are thus at the mercy (to some degree) of the film's production team. White heteromasculinity is the imaginary condition of the viewing body in the classic cinematic scenario. The gaze of the apparatus is aligned through point-of-view shots with the male hero and drinks in female bodies, assessing, enjoying, consuming them as objects for the benefit of the audience's pleasure.[80]

This scopophilic drive in cinema replicates patriarchal power dynamics by treating certain people as 'objects and subjecting them to a controlling and curious gaze'.[81] Even though our view is being powerfully controlled, the alignment of camera, hero and viewer grants us as the viewer the sense of control that is wielded by the camera. The control is also over the objects being viewed. Mulvey explains that because we live in a world 'ordered by sexual imbalance', this carries through to the power dynamic of the gaze.[82] The configuration of the look is masculine; the object is feminine. Power is not merely sexed, and the cinematic gaze is thus also infused with the complex weave of power that concerns race, sexuality, class, criminality, culture and so on. In its intimacy with colonialism, sexology and criminology, the cinematic gaze manifests the politics of these sciences. A pixel is the microelement out of which the cinematic image is created. As such, a pixel has 'implicit resonances with . . . the production and framing of madness, hysteria and criminality'.[83] However, as a microelement, its conventional condition is invisible in order that the viewer can lose themselves in the imaginary reality of the image. Visibility of the pixel draws attention to the apparatus: that the image was produced and is a representation. By foregrounding the pixel, 'Native Tongue' remembers the surveillance of pixilated CCTV footage while also referencing the gaze that continues to subjugate, colonize, marginalize and criminalize.

Reference to the criminalizing gaze is underscored visually by the orange jumpsuits and accentuated sonically by the undulating hum. High-visibility clothing was introduced across the United States and the United Kingdom to shame convicted persons in prison or on community service in order to make the punishment of criminal justice processes vividly evident.[84] The controversy over images of detainees in Guantanamo Bay then rendered orange jumpsuits 'critically symbolic' of US detention policy and the legitimacy of punishment regimes more broadly.[85] Orange jumpsuits now figure prominently in critical fictions representing punishment, such as *Orange Is the New Black* and *Misfits*.[86] In the 'Native Tongue' video, because the orange and the dancers' dark skin contrast so strikingly and 'pop' against the landscape, the jumpsuits signify racialized criminalization. Further, because the dancers are Aboriginal, the criminalization is colonial.

Concurrently, the rhythmic humming of the Pasifika Vitoria Choir resonates through the abdomen of the listener, creating a foundation for the song like a slow heartbeat. It has the feel of chain-gang blues. This is evocative of what Middlebrook calls 'prison sound' or the 'sound of incarceration'.[87] In tracing African-American music from field hollers during colonial slavery through chain gangs, blues, rock, funk and hip hop, Middlebrook argues that throughout African-American music history there persist interweaving textures connected to incarceration. He describes this music as a 'sonic documentation' of punitive white supremacist and colonial violence.[88] Contending that imprisonment has been a 'necessary function of white supremacist patriarchal capitalism' in the United States, Middlebrook argues that the spectre of incarceration exists beyond the prison to inform the cultural experience of being African-American.[89] The chain-gang beat is an affective manifestation of this phenomenon.

Juju has explicitly refuted suggestions that 'Native Tongue' is 'about' African-American politics.[90] She states that to assert this is a simplification. Rather than rendering the song about race politics in the United States, these audio-visual signifiers draw on cultural knowledge of raced criminalization and white supremacist punitive practices to articulate concerns about race politics in the Australian context. Criminalization and punishment of Indigenous people have been central to the expansion and maintenance of colonization in Australia, as well as the regulation of bodies considered 'other' by the intersecting gazes of Western knowledge and law. Anthony explains that the 'criminalization of Indigenous people has been a means of control and containment since British colonization'.[91] As part of a regime of punishment, imprisonment has been integral to the management of Indigenous people and the annexing of their land. In Australia, Smith names 'incarceration in the community' as an experience shared by Indigenous people, which echoes Middlebrook's argument that the ever-present spectre of imprisonment informs the cultural consciousness of being black.[92] Smith's evocative term references the policing and surveillance of, and discrimination against, Indigenous people throughout their everyday lives as always already criminalized by a panoptic, criminalizing colonial gaze.

The criminalizing colonial gaze has been an essential tool in the expansion and maintenance of empire by effecting deeply experienced dispossession and fragmented subjecthood. It is one of many instruments of the possessive logic of patriarchal white sovereignty that, as Moreton-Robinson explains, is an ideology, 'a mode of rationalization . . . that produces more or less one inevitable answer reaffirming white occupation and the nation-state's ownership, control and domination'.[93] Anthony writes that punishing 'Indigenous people for colonial transgressions or simply because of their "race" . . . forced [Indigenous people] to become outsiders and experience their home space as an imperial space'.[94] Such displacement is reiterated in Australian's constitutional history, which situated Aboriginal and Torres Strait Islander peoples within the realm of flora and fauna while explicitly excluding them from the population by not including them in the census. Regularly conflated with the conditions of citizenship, this history reflects a texture of legal subjecthood for Indigenous people in white Australian law. As Moreton-Robinson writes, for 'over two hundred years, the possessive logic of patriarchal white sovereignty has served to define attributes of personhood and property through law'.[95] These attributes have functioned to exclude Aboriginal and Torres Strait Islander people from legal subjecthood and to deny Indigenous sovereignty. Such an approach resonates with the fantasy of *terra nullius*, that 'deliberate legal fiction created and deployed to deny Indigenous sovereignty and justify dispossession through the structure of law'.[96] The subsequent acknowledgement of Aboriginal and Torres Strait Islander custodianship in *Mabo*[97] and the official inclusion of Indigenous people in the census have reinstated some level of legal subjecthood; however, as Juju's lyrics suggest, the feeling of belonging is not strongly supported.

At the same time, the lack of belonging articulated in the song also coalesces around the regulation of other bodies considered to deviate from the ideal legal subjecthood. The audio-visual signification of carceral punishment extends out from its colonial manifestations to also signify the experience of the criminalizing marginalization of queer, female and migrant bodies.

By identifying a repertoire of sound in music history as 'prison sound', Middlebrook captures what Kheshti calls a 'sonic marker of Otherness'.[98] Both Young and Kheshti submit that such sonic markers enable listeners to feel that which they might otherwise not be able to access.[99] In the context of this analysis, a straight, white female listener is given some degree of access to the lament that crackles through Juju's voice as she sings about not knowing where she belongs. Simultaneously, the undulating rhythm of the choir resonates not just through the ears, but throughout the body of the listener as a soothing backdrop for the glitchy production and Juju's expressive articulation, working the beat of punishment practices into the muscle and tissue as the listener might imagine or might actually dance in time. An effect of empathic potential is generated by the combination of Juju's sweetest lament and the undulating waves, audio-visual glitches and orange jumpsuits. This empathic merging, or loss of self, in the grain of Mojo Juju's voice is enriched when the listener sings along, articulating the words and simulating her lament or dance in movements mirroring those on screen.

When I contemplate this experience, caution must be exercised not to oversimplify or romanticize the relationship between listener and sound. Kheshti demonstrates the dangers of white privilege reassuring itself of its own goodness when feeling this cross-cultural empathy because feeling sorrow on hearing another's pain does not automatically equate to ever fully knowing the experience of another, nor does it absolve one of the sins of one's privileged society.[100] Carvalho observed how white audiences used their engagement with Billie Holiday's affective performances of 'Strange Fruit' to distinguish themselves from the Southern lynch mobs referenced in the song.[101] Feeling moved by Holiday's expressive suffering allowed these white Americans to feel like better people without requiring them to challenge themselves or the system that was maintaining their own privilege. Ravenscroft echoes this concern in the context of academic practices as she outlines the dangers of repeating or extending colonial violence.[102]

The loss of self that is enabled by the convergence of sound, lyrics and image in 'Native Tongue' offers to its audience a possibility of empathic merging with the grain of Mojo Juju. The affect, the embodied response to experiencing the music video, is granted a legal significance through its use of legal and criminological signifiers. At the level of lamentation, these signifiers texture the affect as a relationship to the state as multiple, criminalized, fragmented subjecthood, a secondary state of belonging, a fractured citizenship. The threat of white privileging's co-option of this empathy into a self-satisfying narrative of good white womanhood is potentially resisted by the manner in which 'Native Tongue' simultaneously affects an internalizing challenge for listeners from the hegemonic order. I turn now to demonstrate the resistance, subversion and challenge that runs concurrently with the empathic engagement.

Resistance

> Every time you cut me down
> I'm gonna come back fierce
> The time is up for being nice,
> Let's call it what it is.[103]

The rhythm of the Pasifika Vitoria's hum is constant and heavy, intermittently joined by the sharper blow of clapping hands. It is an integral component enabling the listener to 'lose themselves by inversion into a space of subjective loss', to feel themselves merging with the music.[104] As a foundational sound, the hum provides signifiance, a resonance that facilitates sonic immersion. The hum thus opens up a space for the listener to access alterity or an experience of difference to themselves. Although signifiance appears to be beyond the symbolic order, the way in which it offers this access is through the political significance its sonic markers bear. And while the hum in 'Native Tongue' replicates the sound of forced labour, referencing carceral colonialism, it also signifies subversion of and resistance to that colonialism. In this section, I explore the resistances and subversions of 'Native Tongue' as well as the ways in which the music video confronts the privileged parts of its audience and the very coherence of the ideal legal subject.

Pasifika Vitoria's undulating hum echoes the beat of the chain gang that keeps the time of rock breaking, mirroring the monotony of hard labour while sustaining prisoners in their unrelenting task, at a steady speed. It remembers the chant of field hollers that connected slaves in the American South supporting each other to maintain their working pace. In Middlebrook's work, this sound of incarceration is not only a 'sonic documentation' of punitive colonial violence;[105] the beat is the sound of survival and resilience. In the contemporary context, Middlebrook writes that 'Listening to, and perhaps playing, prison music is our attempt to hear people survive, and potentially escape and transform' the dehumanizing carceral practices of colonial violence.[106] Despite its replication of the sounds of racist violence, chain-gang music provides corporeal evidence of survival and of existence beyond incarceration.

The persistence of the sound as music also disturbs the logic and legitimacy of the violence. Middlebrook writes that within African-American music, the logics of slavery, genocide and colonialism 'simultaneously coalesce *and* are rendered illogical, problematic, and questionable; simply (or not so simply) by their audibility'.[107] So, although the music ostensibly converges with the rhythms imposed through colonial violence, it makes apparent the mechanisms of that systemic exploitation. At the same time, as something that is created by the whole of human bodies and consumed through the whole of human bodies, music draws attention to the bodies of those making the music. By this means, the music renders discernible the humanity of those potentially being dehumanized by the violence.

Transforming the sound of forced labour into music also subverts the logic that drives its beat. Innovative subversion transfigures modes of control and exploitation into something meaningful and pleasurable to the performer/slave/prisoner, resituating some degree of power to the performer. On a different level, the creation of African-American music historically defied white supremacy because it was used as a means of resistant communication hidden in plain sight from plantation management.[108] As such, it out-maneouvred the devastating determination of slavery. Smith writes of similar subversion in Motown music, which appeared to white folk as love songs and party music while also articulating political concerns, interpolating knowing listeners to action (such as 'Dancing in the Streets') and capturing the shared atmosphere as 'civil rights anthems'.[109] On one level the music defies supremacist power by documenting survival and proving that those making music have not been crushed, extinguished or fully controlled, while on another the music defies the logic by resisting its dehumanizing practices. On a third level, the logic is subverted when the music is harnessed as a means of empowerment.

A similar disruption to white supremacist logic is denoted by the video's dance composition. The dancers combine contemporary dance with traditional Aboriginal choreography. Traditional choreography is evidence of the continuation of culture recognized by Australian law as permissible in the assessment of claims by Indigenous groups to the custodianship of land in native title trials.[110] Concurrently, the contemporary moves demonstrate that Indigenous culture is not static, located in the pre-history of European occupation. Ultimately, the very presence of these dancers performing their composite choreography on the familiarly 'blank' Australian landscape proves the lie of *terra nullius*, that pervasive legal fallacy that the land was not appropriately 'owned' prior to colonization. Their performance defies the very foundational argument and logic of colonial acquisition.

The rhythm of 'Native Tongue' draws on the parallels between the carceral practices of white supremacy in the United States and Australia, but also the resilience and survival of those subject to its violence. However, the sonic documentation is not an overt history lesson. Capacity to discern and interpret 'prison sounds' is developed through pop cultural training, listening to blues, R&B or hip hop. The lyrics and visual stories the listener has previously consumed have built an implicit glossary of audio-visual significance, to which each person has more or less access. That is, some listeners 'get it' while others don't. Comprehension of prison sounds is predominantly not an explicit curriculum, but a learned set of associations built through exposure to popular culture. Much of this knowledge is created at the edges of the symbolic order in the space of signifiance, of enjoying the bodily pleasures of losing yourself to sound.

Sensual enjoyment of the lulling undulation juxtaposes the glitches and Juju's vocal play of lament and confrontation. As such, the hum is an important contributor to the signifiance of the music video, seducing the listener to lose themselves in the sound. This loss of self does not escape significance, but rather is textured by its historical resonance with the politics of criminalizing marginalization and diminished legal subjecthood.

The empathy that Young identifies in merging with the grain of the voice is tangible in Middlebrook's description of listening to prison sound as hearing not only suffering but also survival, resistance and transformation.[111] The pleasure for white people is such that they want to play that music, too, and dance, following the moves and beats of the 'other's' resilience. Kheshti observes how this experience of empathy can ultimately function to sustain white privilege.[112] Although there is a surface sense of connection with something outside their own experience, Haggis and Schech[113] and Ravenscroft[114] draw attention to the dangers of not critically reflecting on white engagement with this empathy, which is used to reassure the white listener or academic that they are a 'good' white person. Through this practice, the 'other' is once again used to service white privilege and the generous offer of access to alterity is missed.

This tendency is not so easy to realize when consuming 'Native Tongue'. Instead, the immersed white viewer is confronted by the lyrics at a mid-point in the journey of signifiance. Lulled by the undulating hum, and perhaps singing Juju's lyrics while feeling her lament, the listener suddenly finds that they are articulating more than resilience in a direct confrontation of privilege and discrimination. The accusation is personal: *you* make the singer feel ill at ease; *you* say prejudice ain't no thing; it is *you* who should say the vilification to Juju's face; it is *you* who cuts her down every time. Ultimately, this means that the privileged listener might find herself articulating a confrontation against herself, her own easy privilege and her prejudicial practices. The challenge is more affective because it threatens to disrupt the comfort of the signifiance.

This challenge is bolstered by the way the gaze functions in the video. While the pixilation draws attention to the production of the image, the apparatus of *Native Tongue* reconfigures the power dynamic of the cinematic gaze. It begins when Juju looks directly into the camera. At first there is a tentativeness in the tuck of her chin, but as the lyrics become a challenge, her gaze becomes more direct. This is reinforced by her forward motion, walking towards a retreating camera. Juju's returning gaze is repeated by the third dancer. Similarly, initially he does not look as he steps forward to take his turn in a sequence of solos. Then he pauses: his pose is recognizably 'Aboriginal', and his gaze is directed off left. But then he turns, and his eyes penetrate the lens as he moves towards the camera and the viewer. The power of this gaze is potentially augmented by the cultural 'knowledge' in Australia that Aboriginal people 'do not make eye contact'. This knowledge is taught as a suite of key principles across health-care and legal studies concerning intercultural communication.[115] Yet in this moment there is an emphatically Aboriginal man in an orange jumpsuit staring at us – returning our gaze.

In Western cinematic traditions, the object of the gaze only looks back within strict parameters: a direct return of the gaze is confronting. 'Native Tongue' does more than return the gaze, though: it reverses the gaze. According to Wiradjuri scholar Sandy O'Sullivan, this repositions Indigenous identity 'as a central author' of the text.[116] Knopf argues that when those usually subject to the gaze control the means of production in cinema, the 'lens of power' and its imaginary are interrogated.[117] Through creative control, the traditional object intercepts the 'politics of representing, stereotyping and objectifying "the other"'.[118] Yugambeh writer and curator Maddee Clark writes with Keluda of a strong emerging tradition of Indigenous women reversing the gaze in Australian cinema, 'using screens as a means of recuperating histories'.[119] By controlling the camera and the means of production, Aboriginal and Torres Strait Islander women do not simply look back at those who have traditionally gazed upon them; they are exerting the agency of telling their own history and turning the gaze to look critically upon colonization and white privilege.

The direct look of Juju and the third dancer exemplify this decolonization emphatically. Their looks assert the creative control of a music video that resides with a team from outside the mainstream, beyond the possessive logic, from the perspective of marginalized identities. In this manner, their looks foreground 'agency and resistance'.[120] Echoing the lyrics that challenge the viewer in their moment of delicious signifiance, in these moments in which eyes meet through the camera and screen, 'the observer becomes the observed'.[121] The challenge within the lyrics is here matched by Juju's look and that of the third dancer.

When the gaze is then read in conjunction with the use of pixilation as fragmentation, it threatens to shatter the assumed coherence of the ideal liberal subject and universal legal subjectivity. Although I have argued that the intermittent pixilation of various parts of the video image conspires with the orange jumpsuits to critique carceral colonial violence while also representing multiplicity as a fragmentary experience for the divergent subject, here I propose a third connotation. This does not supersede the first two but exists simultaneously in a dissonance mirroring law's relationship with non-conforming bodies. This is to read the divergent 'other's' self-represented 'multiplicity' as a threat to law's logic.

Let me illustrate using Bhabha's 'mimicry', in which the colonized is compelled to perform ideal components of subjecthood according to the wishes of the colonizing culture.[122] Inevitably, this performance is never complete. Bhabha references Fanon's mask to indicate its surface quality because the ideal subjecthood of the colonized is like a shifting fantasy that is never fully actualized in any given site or form. Writing in the early 20th century as a black male scholar and activist from Martinique living in French colonial Algiers, Fanon provided compelling socio-psychological insight into the condition of being colonized.[123] Although his work was developed in a distinct temporal colonial context, it continues to provide tools for theorizing other sites of European colonization. In *Black Skin, White Mask*, Fanon argues that the colonized are induced to lose a sense of themselves through the imposition of a colonial structure that refuses to acknowledge them.[124] In order to gain recognition within the colonial order, the colonized are required to assimilate, to assume a mask of whiteness. However, the white mask is never enough: the colonized are never acknowledged. The consequence is a splitting of the colonized subject, who becomes convinced of their own culture's worthlessness.

Bhabha argues that the impossibility of recognition through adorning the white mask is because whiteness is relentlessly constructed in its differentiation from the colonized subject. It is the criminalizing, colonizing sciences that generate and reify the marks of difference. Bhabha demonstrates that thus the 'other', who has been disciplined through these gazes to assimilate, mimics the colonizing culture. As a mimic, there is always that tangible gap between the colonized and colonizer. When the colonized then returns or reverses the gaze, when they look back through some form of representation, the gap is rendered discernible, and the performative nature of the colonizing culture is exposed. Bhabha writes that this mimicry 'shatters the unity of man's being'.[125] Thus, when Juju and the third dancer stare into the camera and through the screen at the listener-viewer, the pixilation and fragmentation exemplifies the 'hidden threat of the partial gaze'.[126]

To then read the returned and reversed gazes through Nedelsky is to understand their threat to the structures of law.[127] Nedelsky explains that 'universal rules [such that law asserts] only make sense if there is something universally identical about the rules'.[128] Thus the visual representation of subjectivities that do not conform to the legal fantasy destabilizes that fantasy. For Nedelsky, this is particularly so when attention is drawn to the embodiment and affective quality of difference. She explains that 'we are immediately confronted with the vast multiplicity of humanity . . . and it becomes difficult to presume universality'.[129] Rather, the 'unitary rights-bearing subject threatens to shatter into unmanageable specificity' when faced with the vast multiplicity of embodied, affective human diversity.[130] The ideal legal subject explodes into fragmentary pieces, like the visual effect of pixilation.

In 'Native Tongue', the sheer multiplicity represented by Juju threatens any easy assumption of essence. She exposes the processes that criminalize her and refuse her full legal subjecthood with her direct address. As she looks into the camera and extends her arms to unapologetically take up space, her subjecthood is asserted in its multiplicity, and it threatens to shatter the liberal legal fantasy of a unitary, coherent, autonomous individual. She confronts that which denies her full legal subjecthood and belonging as she confronts the privileged white audience.

This disrupted journey through signifiance offers the privileged viewer an opportunity to experience both empathy and a sense of responsibility. This is a moment of possible self-reflection. The song does this through a discourse that exists in part beyond the symbolic order of ordinary language, working as it does sensuously through our ears, feet, hearts, bellies and mouths (even our tear ducts if we feel that kind of affective prick of empathy and remorse) as it also engages conscious thought. In this manner, 'Native Tongue' allows the viewer to simultaneously experience the difference of Juju's multiple, subjected, resilient subjecthood and discrete self-reflection for their responsibility, the debt they owe for their privilege built through colonization and marginalization, their possible role in minimizing the problem of prejudice or participating in the discriminatory practices identified by Juju.

One of the many powers of 'Native Tongue' is that this confrontation does not necessarily destroy the pleasure of the text. The viewer is not wholly woken from their reverie; they can remain with Juju as the hum continues and the lyrics return to lament, as though delivering the viewer to a comfortable place to lose themselves once again in the 'other's' less confronting alterity. The possible effect is a nudge rather than an explicit and potentially alienating lesson towards recognition of privilege and responsibility, subtly moving a white audience to safe self-reflection rather than guilty panic.

Sovereignty never ceded

> If you wanna call me something
> Call it to my face
> I will not apologize
> For taking up this space.[131]

Previously, I proposed that the choreography of 'Native Tongue' defies the logic of *terra nullius*. It disrupts the possessive logic of patriarchal white sovereignty. In this section, I suggest that suffusing the lament and resistance of the video is an enduring Indigenous sovereignty. Upon this foundation is a configuration of Mojo Juju as sovereign. In this third layer of my chapter, I argue that, as a music video, 'Native Tongue' presents Indigenous sovereignty as not only never ceded in Australia but as continuing, legitimate and appropriate. This is discernible predominantly in the moving images. However, as these coalesce with the resonance of words and music, their implications are experienced through the body of the viewer.

The landscape is an iconic screen representation of Australia: dry and yellow, vast and ostensibly empty. It is apparently not subject to the agrarian productivity that determines property ownership according to a prominent contract theorist informing colonial expansion since John Locke in the 18th century.[132] It is the material manifestation of Moreton-Robinson's possessive logic of patriarchal white sovereignty.[133] This landscape has provided not merely a pervasive backdrop to an abundance of white Australian literature and cinema. It also resonates as an affect, causing anxiety and discomfort for viewers as it reiterates Australia's foundational untruth of *terra nullius:* that the land was not occupied prior to European arrival. Its affect issues from a cultural knowledge that the land was not empty, and in so many fictions (and non-fictions), there is a Gothic spectre of the original custodians threatening to expose the wrongs of colonial occupation.[134]

Juju, striding through the centre of this landscape surrounded by three Yolgnu men, very simply proves the lie of *terra nullius*. They are Aboriginal presence on the land, foregrounded, vivid and moving ever onwards. Their presence parallels Bunurong historian Bruce Pascoe's detailed documentation of Aboriginal and Torres Strait Islander agriculture, infrastructure, economic management, law and culture at European arrival.[135] The dancers embody this custodianship, this sovereignty.

Coincidental with this sovereignty is a fourth implication of the pixilation, which references the 'disrupted viewing' of television news in so many disaster movies. These popular fictions use glitchy pixilation to simultaneously signify a crisis of technology in the face of natural or alien threat to human society and an interruption to ordinary viewing by breaking news of disaster. In these terms, the 'Native Tongue' pixilation of the landscape suggests a disruption to the ordinary screen representation of it with the breaking news of Indigenous sovereignty.

At the same time, Indigenous custodianship is demonstrated by the choreography, which blends tradition with contemporary dance. As integral aspects of ceremony, performing creation stories and the pattern of relationships between people and land, dance often articulates and embodies part of the cosmologies of Indigenous cultures, baring the 'principles, ideals and philosophies . . . which inform the legal regime'.[136] Kombumerri/Munaljahlai legal theorist Christine Black writes that a 'prerequisite for any legal engagement' with another cultural group is understanding their cosmology, their 'theory of how things came to be and . . . how humans [are] patterned into a certain tract of land'.[137] Dance is a medium through which cosmologies are practised, performing the sovereignty of specific Indigenous nations over certain tracts of land.

For the white viewer, knowledge of such jurisprudence has come into mainstream consciousness through the coverage of native title cases since the 1990s, in which dance is presented as evidence along with painting, stories and music. Like painting, dance is 'a way to communicate knowledge to non-Aboriginal people and to the courts',[138] reminding the High Court of the depth of each claim. More than this, though, ceremony is not just 'a fact about law, it is law'.[139] Anker contends that such evidence is 'supplementary to the facts proper' because they surpass what is measurable in Western law while also appealing to 'the senses through colour and rhythm, a sense of space and a smell of dust'.[140] In this manner, Anker suggests that Indigenous cultural artefacts, including dance, are changing the nature of mainstream law. One aspect of that change is the recognition of Indigenous dance as law and as a practice of a custodian and sovereign relationship with land.

Indigenous sovereignty is demonstrated as continuing because it is still being performed by these young male dancers, and thus the law is being practised. Further than that, the interweave of contemporary and traditional choreography demonstrates the contemporaneousness of Indigenous law. Its multiple jurisdictions are not static and isolated, but rather dynamic, current and interactive with other sovereign nations and cultures.

The steady progression of Juju and the dancers towards the receding camera emphasizes the persistence of Indigenous sovereignty. Then, as the song finishes and the music subsides, Juju turns to walk away. The dancers stand erect, looking into the camera before sweeping ceremonial white across their foreheads and dropping into a shake-a-leg manoeuvre that takes them into Juju's wake. This folding back into the landscape underscores connection to land.

At the centre of these sovereign bodies walks Mojo Juju, looking like a king. Juju's bearing, swathed in a striated fur coat, heavy silver jewellery and blunt haircut call on many portraits of English kings – particularly the Tudors and, most specifically, the Henries. Her countenance, moving endlessly forward through the centre of the landscape, bespeaks sovereign transcending all time. Even as she turns away, she remains splendid, never ceding ground but folding back into the time-space continuum that is the transcendence of majestic authority.

In this moment, she is also recognizable as Hobbes's Leviathan looming over the territory, the great and formidable sovereign power.[141] When she fills the screen, stretching out her arms, refusing to apologize for taking up space, she echoes the proprietorial strength of Leviathan, whose authority derives from its relationship to the land, from the human bodies making up its torso and from the force of the sword in its hand. Hobbes theorized the ideal structure of government through the details of the human body, with a monarch at its head and the executive and judiciary functioning as limbs. This is a body politic of the kind Kantorowicz revealed, charging the physical manifestation of sovereign leadership through a political theology as a *corpus mysticum* that transcends each singular manifestation into each following sovereign.[142] The dancers are Juju's royal entourage, extensions of her body politic, travelling beside her, weaving in and out of her sphere. Their spirit-like character reinforces the mysticism and further naturalizes Juju's legitimate sovereignty, as does their collective folding back into the landscape.

The dancers' relationship with Juju is reinforced by a Kali configuration created at a mid-point in the video. The dancers slip behind Juju and splay out rhythmically, arching and waving their arms. In some images, Kali is given up to ten sets of arms and legs. As a Hindu deity, Kali performs many roles, from destroyer of evil to mother of the whole universe, goddess of time, creation, destruction and power. Significantly, she is female and often black. She is regularly represented as intoxicated with absolute rage, even though she is also the great protector. In the video's passing configuration, Juju is rendered divine while the dancers are incorporated into her mystical being as part of her power.

At the same time, the weave of the dancers and their solo sequences sustains the impression of multiplicity. The dancers potentially remember the many facets of Juju's intersectional identity. The unitary category of the liberal legal subject is once again challenged by this black (both Aboriginal and migrant), queer, matriarchal sovereign whose transcendent body politic is not simply subordinate extensions, but manifestations of diversity. The sovereignty never ceded is not a homogenizing, prehistorical Indigenous law, but vibrant, contemporary and multiple.

This primarily image-based configuration of sovereign authority buttresses the fleeting lyric in which Juju articulates resistance and empowerment: 'I will not apologize for taking up this space'. The audience, carried through this music video on the sound cloud of glitches, undulating rhythm and Juju's voice, is supported to enjoy the visual presentation of continuing Indigenous sovereignty as part of the signifiance enabling their loss of self in the text. So immersed, so affected by the physiological pleasure of enjoying good music, dance and visual representation, the audience is encouraged to understand the audio-visual representation as harmonious, as correct, as natural (as natural as the body that is experiencing the pleasure). In this manner, the visual jurisprudence of Indigenous sovereignty in this video is woven into the experiential and remembering body of its audience.

Conclusion

> I will not apologise for taking up this space.[143]

A contrast pulls between Juju's lament of secondary belonging and her proprietorial reach across the landscape. She is at once not at home in her home country and embodying the most legitimate and natural sovereignty over its terrain.[144] Juju elicits empathy while she also confronts parts of her audience with their responsibility for marginalization. Ultimately, the video generates a soothing loss of self while also drawing privileged white listeners singing along to utter a challenge against their role in generating Juju's experience of secondary belonging. 'Native Tongue' is a potent four minutes of popular culture.

In comparison, this chapter has been lengthy, exploring three layers of politico-legal articulation in the music video; of marginalized and fragmented legal subjecthood; of resistance to and shattering of that legal subjecthood; and of continuing, legitimate and natural Indigenous sovereignty. I have traced these as they weave through the lyrics, music and sound of 'Native Tongue'. My driving purpose was to interrogate my own experience of consuming the video clip, getting lost, singing along, finding myself at once spellbound and self-reflective, challenged. I wanted to understand the innerworkings of it, explore these implications and perhaps to check or prove to myself that I was not just once again reaffirming my Good White Womanhood. Although such a drive is no doubt a very colonial impulse to control that which destabilizes my privilege, I hope I am using it to do something useful.

What I have sought to illustrate are the ways in which the creative team produced an incredible text that speaks to a target audience of 'other queer people of colour', but that also offers an opportunity for privileged white empathic access to the experience of fragmented citizenship. This empathy is extended through the signifiance and the grain of the voice, which invites listeners to lose themselves in the sound. Immersed in the convergence of meaningful sound, lyric and image, the privileged white consumer is also made aware of the machinery of marginalization, of criminalizing colonial violence and of the power of the gaze.

Still immersed, and perhaps singing along, the consumer finds themselves articulating a confrontation. For the privileged white consumer, this challenge is for us – and perhaps especially those of us who feel ourselves to be Good White

Folk. In this moment, we are positioned with Juju looking at ourselves and the small acts of colonial, sexist and homophobic violence that we lapse into because our privilege protects us from seeing the damage we do. I feel that this creates a very powerful moment of realization, as we imagine ourselves merged with Juju singing that actually we aren't the ones living in her skin. This moment has the potential to stop us from falling into the pattern Khesti sees in World Music of reifying Good White Womanhood through the enjoyment of exotic sound. Instead, this moment prompts us to check ourselves.

At the same time, there is another set of challenges for this viewer when coherent legal subjecthood is threatened by the return of the gaze and the resistance of unapologetic multiplicity represented by Juju and the three dancers. It challenges the logic underpinning the system that sustains white privilege: Western law and its ideal subject. It disrupts the possessive logic of patriarchal white sovereignty.

However, the possible alienation triggered by such resistance and confrontation is potentially avoided by the reassuring undulation of the choir's hum. The loss of self is maintained while the privileged white viewer experiences a doubled identification of merging with the singers and being the target of the confrontation. I feel that this is a nudge rather than a lecture, in which the viewer can take up the challenge to correct themselves, to learn. But I have also argued that through this signifiance, as the viewer loses themselves in the pleasures of affective music, the deliberate legal fiction of *terra nullius* and its pervasive imaginary is shattered. Indigenous sovereignty is affirmed. The experience of pleasure concurrent with the visual representation of Indigenous sovereignty potentially authenticates it by associating it with that sensation.

Acknowledgements

This was a tricky but immensely pleasurable chapter to write. There are so many layers to the incredible song and video and the politics it embodies. The critique, advice and direction of my anonymous reviewer were generous and specific. They were essential to the final iteration of this piece. Thank you. Thank you also to the editors of this collection for including and nurturing my work. I particularly want to thank Kieran for so much energy, support and knowledge and Karen for being so smart and compassionate. I feel you have all helped me become a better academic . . . and a better human.

Notes

1 Juju (2018).
2 Juju (2018).
3 Barthes (1977), pp 142–8.
4 Quoted in Wang (2018).
5 Quoted in D'Souza (2018).
6 Juju (2018).
7 Wang (2018).

8 Nicol (2018).
9 Jack (2018).
10 Anon (2018); Eliexer (2018).
11 Quoted in Wang (2018).
12 Quoted in *Sydney Morning Herald* (2006).
13 *Djukimala*, www.djukimala.com.
14 *Pacific Island Creative Arts Australia*, https://picaa.com.au/pasefika-vitoria-choir/pasefika-vitoria-choir.
15 *Her Story Her Sound*, www.hersoundherstory.com; Newstead (2018).
16 McMahon (2015).
17 Juju (2018).
18 Haggis and Schech (2000), p 397.
19 Haggis and Schech (2000).
20 Moreton-Robinson (2015).
21 Turner (2006).
22 Wang (2018).
23 Manderson (2003, 2012).
24 Moran et al. (2012).
25 MacNeil (2007).
26 Buchanan (2011); Buchanan and Johnson (2008, 2001); Johnson (2009).
27 Young (2010).
28 Sterne (2012), p 7.
29 Sobchack (2004); see also Ott (2010).
30 Berland (2012), p 40.
31 Attali (2012), p 30.
32 Barthes (1976, 1977).
33 Heath in Kheshti (2015), p 70.
34 Rodgers and Bernard (1979).
35 Eminem (2002).
36 Bangalter et al. (2013).
37 Kheshti (2008), p 71.
38 Kheshti (2015), p 71.
39 Quoted in Kheshti (2015), p 70.
40 Barthes (1977).
41 Boyle (2002).
42 Attali (2012), p 35.
43 Attali (2012), p 32.
44 Attali (2012), p 35.
45 Take, for example, the work of the Australian group the Avalanches, whose stock in trade is sampling. See one of their particularly nostalgic tracks, available at www.youtube.com/watch?v=wpqm-05R2Jk.
46 Barthes (1977).
47 Young (2016), p 32.
48 Kheshti (2008), p 75.
49 Young (2016), p 32 (emphasis in original).
50 Young (2016), p 32.
51 Sterne (2012), p 19.
52 Kheshti (2008), p 75.
53 Young (2016).
54 Kheshti (2008, 2015).
55 MacDougall (2006).
56 Mojo Juju (2018).

57 Juju quoted in Jack (2018).
58 Rudd (2008).
59 Moran (2017), p 207.
60 Moran (2017), p 208.
61 Moreton-Robinson (2015).
62 Curthoys (2000).
63 Moran (2017), p 209.
64 Hage (1998).
65 Žižek (1993).
66 Purcell in Do (2019).
67 Nedelsky (1997), p 93.
68 Free (2016); Fletcher (2012).
69 du Toit (2009); Hunter and Cowan (2007); Pateman (1988).
70 Douzinas (2007); MacNeil (1998); Stychin (1995).
71 Stychin (1995), p 21.
72 Nedelsky (1997), p 94.
73 Fuggle (2015).
74 Becker (2006), p 108.
75 See, for example, Biber (2007) or Finn (2017).
76 Flynn (2018), p 78.
77 Amad (2013), p 50.
78 Mulvey (2006).
79 Mulvey (2006), p 345.
80 Mulvey (2006).
81 Mulvey (2006), p 344.
82 Mulvey (2006), p 346.
83 Fuggle (2015), p 224.
84 Lister (2010), p 132.
85 Shepherd (2008), p 217.
86 *Orange is the New Black* (2013–19); *The Misfits* (2009–13).
87 Middlebrook (2016), p 820.
88 Middlebrook (2016), p 820.
89 Middlebrook (2016), p 820.
90 Wang (2018).
91 Anthony (2013), p 30.
92 Smith (2018), p 205.
93 Moreton-Robinson (2015), p 82.
94 Anthony (2013), p 31.
95 Moreton-Robinson (2015), p 77.
96 I quote my anonymous reviewer directly here because their words are so powerful that my attempts to rephrase felt inadequate.
97 *Mabo v Queensland (No. 2)* (1992) 175 CLR 1.
98 Kheshti (2015).
99 Kheshti (2015); Young (2016).
100 Kheshti (2015).
101 Carvalho (2013).
102 Ravenscroft (2012).
103 Juju (2018).
104 Kheshti (2015), p 80.
105 Middlebrook (2016).
106 Middlebrook (2016), p 820.
107 Middlebrook (2016), p 820.

108 Middlebrook (2016).
109 Smith (2009).
110 Anker (2005).
111 Young (2016).
112 Kheshti (2015).
113 Haggis and Schech (2000).
114 Ravenscroft (2012).
115 See, for example, http://edcan.org.au/edcan-learning-resources/supporting-resources/aboriginal-and-torres-strait-island-peoples/cultural-saftey/cultural-safety-and-communication.
116 O'Sullivan (2013), p 141.
117 Knopf (2013), p 191.
118 Knopf (2013), p 19.
119 Keluda and Clark (2019), p 118.
120 Keluda and Clark (2019), p 118.
121 Bhabha (2012), p 127.
122 Bhabha (2012), p 127.
123 Nayar (2012).
124 Fanon (1970).
125 Bhabha (2012), pp 126–7.
126 Bhabha (2012), p 127.
127 Nedelsky (1997), p 94.
128 Nedelsky (1997), p 94.
129 Nedelsky (1997), p 94.
130 Nedelsky (1997), p 94.
131 Juju (2018).
132 Locke (1921), pp 218–19.
133 Moreton-Robinson (2015).
134 See, for example, Haynes (1998); Hodge and Mishra (1990); Morris (2002).
135 Pascoe (2014).
136 Black (2010), p 15.
137 Black (2010), p 15.
138 Anker (2005), p 92.
139 Anker (2005), p 92.
140 Anker (2005), p 105.
141 Hobbes (1981).
142 Kantorowicz (1957).
143 Juju (2018).
144 Purcell quoted in Do (2019).

References

Secondary sources

Paula Amad (2013) 'Visual Riposte: Looking Back at the Return of the Gaze as Postcolonial's Gift to Film Studies' 52 *Cinema Journal* 52.

Kirsten Anker (2005) 'The Truth in Painting: Cultural Artefacts as Proof of Native Title' 9 *Law, Text, Culture* 91.

Anon (2018) 'First Nations Media Awards 2018', *First Nations Media Australia*, https://firstnationsmedia.org.au/events/converge/converge-sydney/first-nations-media-awards-2018.

Thalia Anthony (2013) *Indigenous People, Crime and Punishment*, Routledge.
Jacques Attali (2012) 'Noise: The Political Economy of Music', in Jonathan Sterne (ed.), *Sound Studies Reader*, Routledge.
Roland Barthes (1976) *The Pleasure of the Text*, Jonathan Cape.
——— (1977) *Image, Music, Text*, Stephen Heath (trans), Fontana.
Peter Becker (2006) 'The Criminologists' Gaze at the Underworld: Towards an Archaeology of Criminological Writing', in Peter Becker and Richard Wetzell, *Criminals and their Scientists: The History of Criminology in International*, Cambridge University Press.
Jody Berland (2012) 'Contradicting Media: Toward a Political Phenomenology of Listening', in Jonathan Sterne (ed.), *Sound Studies Reader*, Routledge.
Homi K. Bhabha (2012) *The Location of Culture*, Taylor & Francis.
Katherine Biber (2007) *Captive Images: Race, Crime, Photography*, Routledge.
C.F. Black (2010) *The Land is the Source of the Law: A Dialogic Encounter with Indigenous Jurisprudence*, Taylor & Francis.
Ruth Buchanan (2011) '"Passing through the Mirror": *Dead Man*, Legal Pluralism and the De-Territorialisation of the West' 7(2) *Law, Culture and the Humanities* 289.
Ruth Buchanan and Rebecca Johnson (2008) 'Strange Encounters: Exploring Law and Film in the Affective Register', in Austin Sarat (ed.), *Studies in Law, Politics and Society*, Emerald Group.
John M. Carvalho (2013) '"Strange Fruit": Music Between Silence and Death' 71(1) *The Journal of Aesthetics and Art Criticism* 111, https://onlinelibrary.wiley.com/doi/abs/10.1111/j.1540-6245.2012.01547.x.
Ann Curthoys (2000) 'An Uneasy Conversation: The Multicultural and the Indigenous', in J. Docker and G. Fischer (eds), *Race, Colour and Identity in Australia and New Zealand*, UNSW Press.
Djukimala, www.djukimala.com.
Costas Douzinas (2007) *Human Rights and Empire: The Political Philosophy of Cosmopolitanism*, GlassHouse.
Saad D'Souza, (2018) 'Mojo Juju Grapples with Past and Present on Her Soulful New Single', *Noisey Vice*, 5 July, http://noisey.vice.com.
Louise Du Toit (2009) *A Philosophical Investigation of Rape: The Making and Unmaking of the Feminine Self*, Routledge.
Christie Eliexer (2018) 'Middle Kids, Gurrumul, Kwame and Mojo Juju win at J Awards', *The Music Network*, https://themusicnetwork.com/middle-kids-gurrumul-kwame-and-mojo-juju-win-at-j-awards.
Frantz Fanon (1970) *Black Skin, White Masks*, Paladin.
Jonathan Finn (2017) 'Making the Criminal Visible: Photography and Criminality', in Michelle Browne and Eamonn Carrabine (eds), *Routledge International Handbook of Visual Criminology*, Routledge.
Ian Fletcher (2012) *Women's Suffrage in the British Empire: Citizenship, Nation and Race*, Taylor & Francis.
Susan Flynn (2018) 'Medical Gazing and the Oprah Effect in *The Immortal Life of Henrietta Lacks*', in Susan Flynn and Antonia Mackay (eds), *Surveillance, Race, Culture*, Springer.
Laura E. Free (2016) *Suffrage Reconstructed: Gender, Race and Voting Rights in the Civil War Era*, Cornell University Press.
Sophie Fuggle (2015) 'Pixilated Flesh' 11(2) *Cultural Politics* 222.

Ghassan Hage (1998) *White Nation: Fantasies of White Supremacy in a Multicultural Society*, Pluto Press.

Jane Haggis and Susanne Schech (2000) 'Meaning Well and Global Good Manners: Reflections on White Western Feminist Cross-cultural Praxis' 15 *Australian Feminist Studies* 387.

Roslyn Haynes (1998) *Seeking the Centre: The Australian Desert in Literature*, Art and Film Cambridge University Press.

Thomas Hobbes (1981) *Leviathan*, Penguin.

Jackie Hodge and Vijay Mishra (1990) *Dark Side of the Dream: Australian Literature and the Postcolonial Mind*, Allen & Unwin.

Rosemary Hunter and Sharon Cowan (eds) (2007) *Choice and Consent: Feminist Engagements with Law and Subjectivity*, Routledge-Cavendish.

Jack (2018) 'Mojo Juju Releases New Album *Native Tongue*', *stasheverything*, www.stasheverything.com/news/mojo-juju-new-album-native-tongue.

Rebecca Johnson (2009) 'Living *Deadwood*: Imagination, Affect, and the Persistence of the Past' 42 *Suffolk University Law Review* 809.

Rebecca Johnson and Ruth Buchanan (2001) 'Getting the Insider's Story Out: What Popular Film Can Tell Us About Legal Method's Dirty Secrets' 20 *Windsor Yearbook of Access to Justice* 87.

Ernst Kantorowicz (1957) *The King's Two Bodies: A Study in Mediaeval Political Theory*, Princeton University Press.

Odette Kelada and Maddee Clark (2019) 'Beyond the Wonderland of Whiteness: The Blak Wave of Indigenous Women Shaping Race on Screen', in Felicity Collins, Jane Landman and Susan Bye (eds), *A Companion to Australian Cinema*, John Wiley and Sons.

Roshanak Kheshti (2008) 'Inversion, Significance and the Loss of the Self in Sound' 14 *Parallax* 68.

——— (2015) *Modernity's Ear: Listening to Race and Gender in World Music*, New York University Press.

Kerstin Knopf (2013) 'Kangaroos, Petrol, Joints and Sacred Rocks: Australian Cinema Decolonised' 7 *Studies in Australasian Cinema* 189.

Ruth Lister (2010) *Understanding Theories and Concepts in Social Policy*, Policy Press.

John Locke (1921) *Two Treatises on Government*, R. Butler.

David MacDougall (2006) *The Corporeal Image: Film, Ethnography and the Senses*, Princeton University Press.

William MacNeil (1998) 'Law's *Corpus Delecti*: The Fantasmatic Body of Rights Discourse' 9 *Law and Critique* 37.

——— (2007) *Lex Populi: The Jurisprudence of Popular Culture*, Stanford University Press.

Desmond Manderson (2003) 'From Hunger to Love: Myths of the Source, Interpretation and Constitution of Law in Children's Literature' 15 *Law and Literature* 87.

——— (2012) *Kangaroo Courts and the Rule of Law: The Legacy of Modernism*, Routledge.

Neil McMahon (2015) 'Triple J Beats Fox and MMM to Win Ratings for 25–39 Age Bracket', *Sydney Morning Herald*, 15 July.

Jeb Aram Middlebrook (2016) 'Songs in the Key of Incarceration: Prison Music as Sound, Theory and Method' 22 *Qualitative Inquiry* 818.

Anthony Moran (2017) *The Public Life of Australian Multiculturalism*, Palgrave Macmillan.

Les Moran, Elena Loizidou, Ian Christie and Emma Sandon (2012) *Law's Moving Image*, Routledge-Cavendish.
Aileen Moreton-Robinson (2015) *The White Possessive: Property, Power and Indigenous Sovereignty*, University of Minnesota Press.
Meaghan Morris (1998) 'White Panic or, *Mad Max* and the Sublime', in Kuan-Hsing Chen (ed.), *Trajectories: Inter-Asia Cultural Studies*.
Laura Mulvey (2006) 'Visual Pleasure and Narrative Cinema', in Mandy Merck (ed.), *The Sexual Subject: Screen Reader in Sexuality*, Routledge.
Pramod K. Nayar, (2012) *Frantz Fanon*, Routledge.
Jennifer Nedelsky (1997) 'Embodied Diversity and the Challenges to Law' 42 *McGill Law Journal* 91.
Al Newstead (2018) 'Her Sound Her Story is Essential Viewing for Anyone into Australian Music', *Music News*, Triple J, 23 May, www.abc.net.au/triplej/news/musicnews/her-sound-her-story-doco-essential-for-anyone-australian-music/9782568.
Emily Nicol (2018) 'Mojo Juju Fights Back: "I Was Too Queer, Too Brown or Not Attractive Enough to Sell Records', *The Guardian*, 21 July, www.theguardian.com/music/2018/aug/21/mojo-juju-fights-back-i-was-too-queer-too-brown-or-not-attractive-enough-to-sell-records.
Sandy O'Sullivan (2013) 'Reversing the Gaze: Considering Indigenous Perspectives on Museums, Cultural Representation and the Equivocal Digital Remnant', in *Information Technology and Indigenous Communities*, Aboriginal Studies Press.
Brian Ott (2010) 'The Visceral Politics of *V for Vendetta*: On Political Affect in Cinema' 27 *Critical Studies in Media Communication* 39.
Pacific Island Creative Arts Australia, https://picaa.com.au/pasefika-vitoria-choir/pasefika-vitoria-choir.
Bruce Pascoe (2014) *Dark Emu: Black Seeds Agriculture or Accident?*, Magabala Books.
Carol Pateman (1988) *The Sexual Contract*, Polity Press.
Alison Ravenscroft (2012) *The Postcolonial Eye: White Australian Desire and the Visual Field of Race*, Routledge.
Kevin Rudd (2008) 'Motion of Apology to Australia's Indigenous Peoples' 12 *Australian Indigenous Law Review* 1.
Laura J. Shepherd (2008) 'Visualising Violence: Legitimacy and Authority in the "War on Terror"' 1 *Critical Studies on Terrorism* 213.
Kylie Smith (2018) 'Reflections on Design, Country and Community Justice at the Neighbourhood Justice Centre' 27 *Griffith Law Review* 202.
Suzanne Smith (2009) *Dancing in the Street: Motown and the Cultural Politics of Detroit*, Harvard University Press.
Vivian Sobchack (2004) *Carnal Thoughts: Embodiment and Moving Image Culture*, University of California Press.
Jonathan Sterne (2012) 'Sonic Imaginations', in Jonathan Sterne (ed.), *The Sound Studies Reader*, Routledge.
Carl F. Stychin (1995) *Law's Desire: Sexuality and the Limits of Justice*, Routledge.
Sydney Morning Herald (2006) 'Hip-Hop Without the Usual Bling Bling', 27 March, www.smh.com.au/entertainment/music/hip-hop-without-the-usual-bling-bling-20060327-gdn8uc.html.
Graeme Turner (2006) *Film as Social Practice*, Routledge.
Beverley Wang (2018) 'Mojo Juju Talks Race, Family and Representation in her Third Album, *Native Tongue*', *ABC News*, 18 August, www.abc.net.au/news/2018-08-18/mojo-

juju-dissects-race-identity-representation-native-tongue/10114956abc.net.au/news/mojo-juju-disects-race-identity.

Alison Young (2010) *The Scene of Violence: Crime, Cinema, Affect*, Routledge.

Miriam Young (2016) *Singing the Body Electric: The Human Voice and Sound Technology*, Routledge.

Slavoj Žižek (1993) *Tarrying with the Negative*, Duke University Press.

Music and television series

Thomas Bangalter and Guy Mauel de Homem-Christo, Pharrell Williams and Nile Rogers (2013) *Lose Yourself to Dance*, *Random Access Memories*, Columbia.

Danny Boyle (2002) *28 Days Later*, DNA Films and UK Film Council.

Ahn Do (2019) *Anh's Brush with Fame* (S4 Ep 4).

Eminem (2002) 'Lose Yourself' *8 Mile: Music from and Inspired by the Motion Picture*, Aftermath, Shady, Interscope.

Mojo Juju (2018) 'Native Tongue', www.youtube.com/watch?v=JLQ4by3lUJo.

The Misfits (2009–13) Clerkenwell Films UK (S1–5).

Orange is the New Black (2013–19) Netflix with Lionsgate Television (S1–7).

Nile Rodgers and Bernard Edwards (1979) 'Lost in Music: We are Family', performed by Sister Sledge, Nile Rodgers and Bernard Edwards.

Part II

Australian gendered identities and law

Chapter 9

Rake and Rumpole – mavericks for justice

Purity and impurity in legal professionalism

John Flood

Introduction

My thesis is that lawyers regularly fall into two opposing categories in various media: saints or sinners, heroes or villains, conventional or maverick, representing the pure and impure.[1] The classic saint is Perry Mason, who was rather dull but a dependably good lawyer. Over the last 20 years or so, television has emphasized the sinner and the maverick. TV shows such as *LA Law*,[2] *Ally McBeal*,[3] *Boston Legal*[4] and *The Good Fight*[5] have played up the quirky aspects of lawyering – edgy, serendipitous, even whacky. And while US shows identify individual lawyers, they mostly operate in the context of a law firm with partners who can function as a brake when needed.

In the Anglo-Australian context, the barrister tradition thrives. Here the individual lawyer is pitted against bigger opponents, such as business or the state. There is considerably more space for *outré* personality traits and idiosyncrasies to flourish. The British series *Rumpole of the Bailey*[6] and the Australian series *Rake*[7] illustrate two variants of a similar theme: the maverick against the powerful.[8] The Bar as a profession represents a clubbable environment where class, status and education signify one's position in the hierarchy. Horace Rumpole and Cleaver Greene, even though well educated,[9] are portrayed as archetypes of Groucho Marx's maxim: 'I don't want to belong to any club that will have me as a member'. They are barristers in spite of themselves, fiercely independent, clever and ethically fluid. They seek a form of ethics bound to justice rather than ideas of discipline and governmentality.

These two television series are not contemporaneous: *Rumpole* was filmed in the late 20th century and *Rake* in the early 21st century. Nevertheless, they speak to each other over the years in small but detectable ways. Both protagonists are Australian. Leo McKern (*Rumpole*) and Richard Roxburgh (*Rake*) are acclaimed actors of their generations with a range of roles, but both have been captured by these particular characters. Rumpole appears in both television and book form, with the result that McKern's physical representation became that of Rumpole. And although *Rumpole* has been performed on radio by other actors, no visual depiction has yet replaced the original.[10] There is one connection that occurs in an early episode of *Rake*. Cleaver Greene is a witness to a bungled robbery, and his former lover, Scarlet, a crown prosecutor, decides to cross-examine him instead of letting her junior do it. This breaches ethical conduct. As her questions cause Cleaver to squirm, he bursts with frustration and shouts at his somnolent counsel, 'Oi, Rumpole!' in order to get him to object.[11] It is the only time when the two shows acknowledge each other.

There are stark differences between the two shows despite the time differences. English lawyer shows tend to concentrate on the courtroom, with the outside world only barely registering.[12] *Rumpole* is an exemplar of this. We see him at home with Hilda, and we see him in chambers and at Pommeroy's Wine Bar drinking Chateau Thames Embankment, reciting Keats,[13] but the majority of each episode takes place in court. *Rumpole* is also more genteel; on the whole, people are decent to each other – as befitting stereotypes of British society at this time.[14] Rake, however, possibly spends more time outside the court than in and is far less genteel: many bad things happen to Cleaver – as befitting the narratives of a more rough and tumble society in Australia.[15] This is certainly so as the series progresses. Much of *Rake* revolves around Cleaver's relationships – dysfunctional and functional.[16] One other distinguishing aspect is how much of *Rake* is taken up with Cleaver's own legal problems. The first few episodes show him in a tax tribunal because of his own non-payment of taxes. Cleaver is desperate to delay the proceedings as long as possible using all sorts of wiles – including dodgy witnesses and half-destroyed evidence – and he eventually succeeds when, as the judge is about to find against him, the judge conveniently has a heart attack and dies.[17] As this chapter is taken up with comparisons, I dip in and out of the characters; for a sustained analysis of *Rake* as a larrikin, see Chapter 10 of this volume.

The differences I outline here are redolent of the political and social cultures of Britain and Australia. Rumpole's world is essentially Whiggish.[18] It is ordered, tolerant and even liberal. Yet it has some conservative ideals, which the Whigs demonstrated by their support for the aristocracy although this was combined with a commitment to parliamentary supremacy. Even when the hippies appear to challenge the illegitimacy of drug laws, order is soon restored and the hippies are marginalized.[19] There is a natural order to Rumpole's world, and he is nicely situated in it.[20]

The same cannot be said of Cleaver Greene's sphere. In many ways, Australia was a reaction to Whiggish sentiment, abhorring aristocracy and privilege.[21] According to Hugh Collins, Australia is a Benthamite society – utilitarian, legalistic and positivistic. He neatly summarizes these traits:

> It should not be surprising that the Benthamite ideology is compatible with Australians' conventional sense of identity – that myth of national character that depicts them as practical, sporting, fair-minded, and egalitarian. For these are a people proud in their pragmatism, skeptical of speculative and abstract schemes, wedded to 'common sense'. They are passionate about

sport, yet legalistic limits are imposed on competitive zeal: above all else, their sporting ethic demands adherence to the umpire's decision.[22]

Despite the rationality of Australian Benthamite culture, political corruption has been and remains rife.[23] *Rake* articulates this corruption clearly as Greene is manipulated by the political and legal classes. It gives an impression that everything is up for grabs and inherently unfair. Greene talks much about fairness (or rather, how unfairly he is treated) to his ex-wife, to his bookie and to his lovers. He detests irrationality, as demonstrated when, having pushed the traffic light button to cross the road, someone else comes along and pushes it. Greene is so outraged he punches the other person for not properly observing that he had pushed the button himself. He can also be hyper-legalistic. When cross-examining the same individual as a witness in a case, the witness can't be sure of his recollections because he was recently beaten up. Greene plays on this ambivalent Australian identity throughout the series, both as lawyer and as politician.

Partial autobiography

To explain why I am writing about these characters, I need to explain something of my background and how my interests developed over the years during which I have been an academic. To begin, I am British, although I have lived and worked in several countries, including Australia, where I have lived for three years. I'm new here, and there is still much about Australian culture that I find puzzling, so forgive me for my errors.

As much as Horace Rumpole and Cleaver Greene are accidental characters, fate always has a trick or two to play on them. My interests and career are largely also accidental. Therefore, I am not merely interested in them as tropes in legal fiction, but more as ways of understanding myself through them. I don't think of myself as a 'real' person but rather as someone who is made up of perceptions – my own and those of others – and I seem to bounce off these rather like a ball in a pinball machine. When I read and watch *Rake* and *Rumpole*, it is with sympathy and questions and reflection about how well I might have lived my life.

I like Horace and Cleaver in the way I like Sherlock Holmes and other detectives who puzzle their way through problems. These characters inhabit the social world and interact daily with it, but they have chosen professions that commit them to living mostly solitary lives inside their heads. Much to my surprise, this is what I have done throughout my career and life. Lawyers – and detectives too – live reactive lives: problems appear in front of them, and they solve them. They may look for clients, but it isn't feasible to persuade people to commit murder or fraud in order to get cases. That form of proactive marketing won't suffice. The essential point I am making here is quite simply that stuff happens to these characters – as it does to me – and it is how they respond that shapes their characters. One way of viewing these responses is to see them as situating the characters within the ideas of Aristotle's *Rhetoric*. I will return to this later when I discuss the concepts of purity and taboo.

I am not a lawyer; nevertheless, I have been interested in them as a tribe for a long time. I had Michael Zander as one of my teachers; some of his critics would say he was a zealot.[24] He was, and is, highly critical of the legal profession and has no hesitation in calling out its failings and restrictive practices. This led to him being called a 'failed lawyer', which I believe is how many practitioners would frame academic lawyers.[25] Up to this point in my life, lawyers were mysterious, Dickensian figures – rather dull and ponderous. But I soon realized that the legal system was not providing access to justice for people who couldn't afford law and lawyers. Then I encountered phenomena like neighbourhood law centres and other groups advocating for change in law. Thus, lawyers could be activists too.

My fascination with lawyers was strengthened further after taking a course on anthropology of law with Simon Roberts.[26] This took me away from the study of substantive law to those who made and interpreted it. I followed this up by doing an ethnographic study of barristers' clerks,[27] which brought me into intimate contact with the Bar. Spending several months hanging around the Temple and other Inns of Court was appealing to a young and naïve graduate student. This initial involvement with the legal profession shaped my relationships with and perceptions of lawyers.[28]

I use the term 'tribe' as a term of art in how I perceive lawyers but not in an ironic way. I consider them to be occupants of economically and culturally shaped fields of activity that have particularly important consequences for society. For me, it is not so much the discipline of law that is of interest – remember, I am not a lawyer – but those whose task it is to be immersed in law. Law, then, can't be detached from its rituals, history, social structure, culture and economics. It is driven both by external forces – for example, economic imperatives – and by its own internal logics. Neither can exist without the other. It is distinctly tribal.

While I was based in the United States during the 1980s, doing a sociology PhD at Northwestern University in Chicago (on the ethnography of corporate law firms), shows about lawyers and law firms started to appear on television. Of course, there had been others before, but the crucial one was *LA Law*. This show portrayed a modern law firm as populated by whites, blacks, Latinos, gays and lesbians, as well as male and female partners. It was highly unrealistic yet it boosted law school admission figures and had high viewing ratings. *LA Law* helped stimulate the publication of the first issue of the *Yale Law Journal* on law and popular culture in 1989, which included two articles and one commentary on the show.[29] I fully agree with Stephen Gillers in this issue when he distinguishes *LA Law* from shows like *Perry Mason* because *LA Law* is not merely about solving some legal or criminal problems; it is about the lawyers and their lives (and, by extension, academic lawyers).[30]

Since *LA Law*, I have religiously watched television shows (and films) about lawyers.[31] And when people ask me – or criticize me for – what I'm doing, I share Stewart Macaulay's sentiments when he was queried about watching sports on

TV: '[I'm] not wasting time. It's research'.[32] There are, and have been, many TV shows about lawyers, and, in this respect, I defer to the writings of Peter Robson and Michael Asimow, who both write extensively on lawyers in film and TV.[33]

The dramatis personae

For me, Cleaver Greene and Horace Rumpole are interesting because they present different ideal types of professionalism in the Bar. Why does this matter? It matters because professionalism has been one of the most important and enduring forms of occupational control and organization over the centuries.[34] The Bar exemplifies this more than most other professions, with 800 years of history behind it.[35] This is why barristers exalt themselves and lord it over solicitors, whose history is effectively a few hundred years shorter.

The law is one of the traditional professions, along with medicine and the church. It borrowed freely from the other two in that barristers see themselves as a kind of secular priesthood (or, in De Tocqueville's terms, an aristocracy) and because their compact with clients can entail their life or death. Law assured one's daily and future material successes; medicine ensured one lived to enjoy them; and the church secured one's eternal status in the divine realm afterwards. Law has also succeeded in promoting the charismatic status of its members to the wider public, most significantly through the Bar. For example, George Carman was renowned as a libel barrister representing many celebrities, becoming as famous as they were.[36] Geoffrey Robertson is a well-known Anglo-Australian human rights barrister who has represented journalists and newspapers throughout the world.[37] It is, however, difficult to point to any solicitors with the same kind of profile as these barristers. These elements of tribalism also take us into the territory of purity and taboo.[38]

Mary Douglas's portrayal of purity, cleanliness and uncleanliness provides a lens for understanding inter- and intra-professional distinctions.[39] Indeed, Andrew Abbott argues that is the core of status distinctions in professions, which the legal profession exemplifies.[40] Douglas uses the distinctions between cleanliness and uncleanliness as a way of thinking about order and disorder, as well as what is central to our thinking and what is marginal, and all this permeates our culture. These distinctions are not hard-wired into our culture – in fact, they can be fluid and show us how our symbolic lives change over time.[41]

The rules around uncleanliness urge us to pay attention to our material circumstances because they will also impact our symbolic lives. This can be seen in religious invocations to avoid certain foods. As Douglas says:

> It is true that there can be a marvellous correspondence between the avoidance of contagious disease and ritual avoidance. The washings and separations which serve the one practical purpose may be apt to express religious themes at the same time. So it has been argued that their rule of washing before eating may have given the Jews immunity in plagues.[42]

The Bar has many such rituals, from the eating of dinners to being gowned in court to not shaking hands with other barristers and more. One of the most distinctive of these types of rituals is the adoption and use of the cab rank rule.[43] The rule states that barristers are like taxi cabs patiently waiting for the next client, whom they will take regardless of case, crime or demeanour. The principle is that no client – no matter how obnoxious or repellent they may be – will go without representation. As simple as the rule is, it is wrapped up in so many exceptions and exemptions that it has little value in reality. What it does have is enormous symbolic value, since it indicates to the wider public that barristers are different from all other lawyers and professionals.

While conceptions of purity and taboo can assist in demarcating professional groups from the laity, they are especially useful in the categorization of intra-professional distinctions. Andrew Abbott, John Heinz and Edward Laumann show how these distinctions operate in practice. Law practice essentially functions with two conceptual categories: facts and doctrine. One's closeness or proximity to either determines the state of purity. According to Abbott, a lawyer's closeness to legal doctrine situates them in a quasi-priestly role because they are constructing legal arguments around legal disquisition or discourse based on interpretations of the rules. These arguments are no longer based on evidence or factual inquiry; they exist within the refined realm of the pure law as found in the appeal courts.[44] Heinz and Laumann argue on the basis of their extensive surveys that lawyer status depends on client type within the context of legal work.[45]

Lawyers fall into two hemispheres: the corporate and the individual. Corporate work includes such fields as securities and banking while individual includes criminal defence and divorce.[46] Higher status and esteem are accorded to the corporate-sphere lawyers than to those in the individual hemisphere. Securities lawyers deal with documents, financing and investment banks, not with people's problems; rather, they are constructing ways of advancing their clients' interests. Their world is pristine, clean and inhabited by like-minded lawyers, all of whom understand the customs of the securities world.[47] it is about the construction of legal orders. Criminal defence lawyers, however, fundamentally deal with the dirt of society's offenders.[48] Legal norms might be involved, but much of the lawyer's work is sifting truth from lies and then negotiating plea bargains with the prosecution or sowing sufficient doubt about their clients' culpability. Their world is not pristine – it is murky and disturbing.

Interestingly, there are fields of legal work that seem to transgress these boundaries. For example, immigration law largely involves completing bulky forms for administrators or arguing before low-level tribunals.[49] Yet the same field will find itself dealing with the higher echelons of the law in judicial reviews, which can end up in the highest appeal courts. Of course, the lawyers doing these different types of immigration work are themselves distinct from each other. The former have as their clients the migrants themselves, whereas the appellate lawyers are arguing the finer points of judicial review and administrative law; their primary concern is with improving the sanctity of the law, and they are only secondarily concerned with the client.

There are connected distinctions within the legal profession that augment the argument made here. Income distributions among lawyers reflect these, with corporate lawyers remunerated more highly than individual lawyers practising family or criminal law. Although judges are superior to lawyers,[50] they have their own hierarchies, which are based on conceptions of purity and taboo. Those serving on Supreme Courts, High Courts and Courts of Appeal focus on the development and refinement of the law and adjudicate over a purer law.

We also see the distinctions resonate through the tools of lawyers: the words they use to persuade others. Aristotle's *Rhetoric* is salient for the discussion of purity and taboo in which he analyzes three forms of persuasion:[51] pathos, ethos and logos. Lawyers – especially advocates – use all of them.[52] Logos, the most elevated, is reasoning and logic and stands with law as pure law. Ethos is also important as it speaks to character and ethics. But pathos is the emotional content of persuasion and, within this structure, could be interpreted as at the unclean end of the spectrum. Both Rumpole and Greene make enormous use of pathos, since they are often making emotional appeals to juries and judges on behalf of their clients. Appellate cases rarely require recourse to pathos. The most vivid exception is when Darryl Kerrigan's counsel in *The Castle* asks the High Court to decide whether the decision that Darryl should lose his house – 'It's not a house, it's a home'[53] – next to Melbourne Airport was made 'on just terms'.[54] The entire scene is replete with pathos (almost tearful), but the QC clearly uses his ethos as the platform on which to mount his appeal.[55] Pathos and ethos are combined to produce an effective and winning argument for the court.

Presenting professionalism

So here we have our two characters, *Rake*'s Greene and Rumpole, loitering with intent at the low end of their professions. Neither is likely to rise within their profession: Rumpole refuses, and Greene is rejected. They are very different from the likes of Jonathan Sumption QC, a retired UK Supreme Court judge and former Queen's Counsel whose last case before ascending to the Bench was defending the Russian oligarch Roman Abramovich for a brief fee reputed to be 'probably north of £5 million'.[56] When Queen's Counsel are represented on television, like *Kavanagh QC*[57] or Martha Costello in *Silk*,[58] they are mainly criminal defence barristers, not civil lawyers. Does this mean that it is impossible to show professionalism in film because it always deals with the detritus? Not really: we are shown that both Greene and Rumpole ultimately respect the law and strive to uphold its integrity.

Our characters' versions of professional life are revealed to us in dramatically different ways in the shows. At the start of *Rake*, a car careens to a halt in an industrial hinterland. In it are Greene and his bookie's runner, whose task it is to teach Cleaver a debtor's lesson by beating him up and throwing him out of the car. Cleaver eventually wanders into town dishevelled and dirty but sarcastically chipper. Rumpole, in his 60s, muses to himself about the state of his work – will there or won't there be any briefs in the clerks' room? – as he strolls up to 3 Equity Court. His life is sedate and dull.

Both Greene and Rumpole tend to succeed in their cases, but their success doesn't bring them financial or professional rewards and esteem: quite the contrary, every success they register reinforces attitudes against them. They both constantly bemoan their poverty. For Cleaver Greene, his spending seems to be mainly on cocaine, gambling and 'Club Jules', the brothel where Missy works and where she provides him with solace.[59] Now divorced, he skimps his child maintenance frequently to the annoyance of his ex-wife, Wendy. The poverty motif is reinforced by showing Wendy living in the opulent former marital home while Cleaver dosses down in a shabby studio flat above a coffee bar in Kings Cross. The fall from grace appears complete and irreversible for Cleaver. Horace Rumpole, however, lives in a mansion flat in west London with Hilda, 'she who must be obeyed'.[60] Their flat has a run-down appearance that Horace is loath to change, even though his flat came close to starring in a television makeover show that would have given him a sunken 'talk pit' and a 'relationship area' in the living room.[61]

Both Rumpole and Greene lead equivocal lives with women. The roles of women in these shows share some common features: they are largely secondary to the men, and any success they achieve appears to be at the expense of men. In *Rumpole*, the relationship between Claude Erskine-Brown and Phyllida Trant is fraught as he attempts to compete with her brilliance but is convinced her advancement is largely owing to her gender rather than her intellect. When Phyllida applies for and is successful in becoming Queen's Counsel, Claude is consumed with envy, and his feelings are mollified only when Rumpole agrees that women applicants were given a special dispensation by the Lord Chancellor that year. In *Rake*, Scarlet, a crown prosecutor married to solicitor Barney, puts her career on hold while having a family and then finds her return to work difficult. Barney tries to be a more involved father, but it doesn't really work; both seem incapable of adapting to their changed ways. Scarlet is not in the same mould as Janet King, the most successful crown prosecutor on Australian television, who also returns from maternity leave and continues to succeed.[62]

To digress, the place and role of women in the legal profession are difficult. The greediness of legal institutions in the claims they make on people's time militates against the combination of legal practice and family. The three editions of Cynthia Fuchs Epstein's *Women in Law* moved from grim despair to cautious optimism, but not equality.[63] It is one of the reasons women have found corporate law inhospitable and continually move into in-house or government roles. More recent research reinforces this view.[64] More women are entering the profession – although this has occurred only recently – but their progress through the profession is hampered by gender stereotyping, leading to a growing exodus from private practice. On television, however, we are beginning to see more strong women presented. Martha Costello in *Silk* is a strong QC, yet she is hampered by the prejudice against her northern roots in her London chambers.[65] The women in *The Good Wife*[66] and *The Good Fight*[67] are both strong and resilient, as Diane shows in *The Good Fight* when she decides to retire from her firm and is prevented from rejoining after she discovers her life savings have been embezzled. Finding her way blocked in other big Chicago law firms – she is deemed too old and 'past it' – she radically departs from the normal, expected course and joins a medium-sized black firm, where she is in the minority as a white person but not quite so sequestered as a woman lawyer. Her former colleagues ceaselessly denigrate her as if she has lost her mind. As she starts to win cases and get clients for her new firm, she rebuilds some – although not all – respect and esteem. More importantly, Diane finds she *likes* her new colleagues; they are human and not merely money-making automata.[68]

It is interesting that the most successful women in *Rake* are not lawyers: Wendy is a psychotherapist, and Kirsty is a gangster. Missy – sex worker, author, erstwhile law student – is too enveloped in drugs to count as successful, although she won plaudits for her novel in which, only thinly disguised, the legal and commercial elites of Sydney appear to their shame. Greene never remains with his women long: his relationships are passionate but brief, although he is fond of all of them. Wendy divorces him, and Missy leaves him, and both marry others to Cleaver's distress. He needs women to satisfy his appetites and apparently little more; the companions with whom he talks most tend to be men.

Rumpole never has affairs; his subjugation to Hilda's regnal authority in the home is absolute, and we are left unsure of the intimacy of their relationship yet it is evident that neither can live without the other. In chambers, however, Horace is seen as a champion of women. He secured the entry of Phyllida Trant, Fiona Allways and Liz Probert into chambers – previously an all-male environment. Of the two characters, Greene is definitely the more misogynistic, and we can see that he is destined to end up on his own while Horace will never be without Hilda. In general, the women in *Rake* are not portrayed well, not strong, not fully independent – unlike *Rumpole*, where there are strong women. Certainly, sexism and misogyny are rife in both societies, and we might think a Benthamite society more fulfilling for women than its Whiggish alternative. Why this is so remains a puzzle.

Both characters share deep rivers of despair, forcing them to seek solace in cheap red plonk or cocaine and gambling. Despite their moral ambiguity, though, they embody a sense of virtue that justice is worth fighting for. Of the two, Horace Rumpole is more attuned to the context of the Bar and never pushes too hard against its limits. He is older and more resigned to his fate as an 'Old Bailey hack'. Although fiercely protective of his clients, he is committed to behaving ethically and using the tools of his trade to win his clients' cases. His constant reiteration of the *Penge Bungalow Murder Case*, displaying his forensic skills when it comes to blood stains, is a key signifier. Cleaver Greene is a wilder figure, hanging out with prostitutes, taking drugs, gambling, being beaten up. His capacity to be a lawyer is tentative at best. He is always on the verge of being disbarred, but despite that, he is aware of the value of his profession and knows that without it he would be diminished.

There are, of course, differences in age and context. Cleaver Greene is a more modern, younger figure than Horace Rumpole, who constantly quotes the Bard in support of his position, situating him in bygone eras. The English chambers model provides more support and gatekeeping with figures like Henry, the barrister's clerk[69] – it is almost familial. Australian chambers don't insulate the barrister as much from the external world as in England, so Greene is far more exposed to the world and less protected than Rumpole.[70] At least Rumpole has 3 Equity Court as his workplace and respite from home. He belongs to and is part of the community. He struggles against his upright and Christian head of chambers, Ballard; he connives to ensure that pupil barristers he likes are taken in and given a tenancy and those he dislikes are kept at bay. Rumpole understands the balance of his chambers and strives to maintain it. Even when Equity Court's senior clerk is found pilfering small amounts of petty cash, Rumpole tries to protect him, knowing that it is how things have been done for years.[71]

Greene is a character adrift in his chambers. He isn't a full tenant – he can't afford to be – so he squats in rooms left empty while the true tenant is away on holiday or sabbatical. Everything is uncertain and tentative. Greene is completely alienated from other members of chambers. When discovered to have been taking a third of Greene's earnings over the years, his assistant, Nicole, defends her actions by claiming her need to fund a house overcame Greene's right to the money. Cleaver, in resignation, forgives her and continues to employ her on a higher salary to compensate for her loss of the spoils of pilfering.[72] At times like this, Greene is a pitiable character.

Their attitude to money is of interest. Both Greene and Rumpole need it to live and worry about it, but neither is too concerned about accumulating it. However, Hilda is horrified when she finds their bank account overdrawn. 'I have to face the butcher!' she cries. Horace is reasonably sanguine that something will come along to remedy the situation.[73] Cleaver is constantly in debt to his bookies, and even his dalliance with Kirsty, gangster and bookie Mick Corella's wife, can't get him excused from his debts.[74] Horace and Cleaver each get one opportunity to overcome their poverty without success. In 'Rumpole's Last Case', Horace wins a chambers sweepstake on the Derby for £100. Dennis Timson, his client, gives Horace a tip on a four-horse accumulator which would bring him £300,000 for a £100 stake. A prison guard places the bets for him, and after each horse wins its race, Horace is deprived of his winnings when the guard absconds overseas with the money. He is, nevertheless, philosophical about his loss.[75] Cleaver gets his golden opportunity when, high on drugs, he wins enough money at a casino to buy a share in a restaurant. The restaurant never seems busy, and Cleaver is eventually forced out for a pittance by Kirsty for the gambling debts he owes her. Cleaver, too, is resigned to his fate.[76]

Their clothes and body types also distinguish them. Greene is slim and wears a modern black or blue suit with a slim tie – in fact, he is hardly ever seen without it, even when off duty – and carries his wig and gown in a blue bag.[77] In either his suit (the tie is always loose) or his gown, Greene always appears unkempt and untidy. Given the number of times he is beaten up by his bookies, it is understandable that he always seems grubby, too, despite being portrayed as a metrosexual urbanite. Rumpole is corpulent, and his clothes are a matter of dispute with his wife, his chambers and the judiciary. He wears a traditional outfit of striped trousers with black waistcoat and jacket, but they have seen better years. He frequently has egg on his shirt or waistcoat. Rumpole is genteelly shabby, and this state is best signified by the state of his hat. It is a battered Homburg that draws the disdain of all those around him, including Hilda. Various attempts to adopt a new bowler always collapse in despair. He is even chastised in court by the judge for letting his bands slip and putting his hands in his pockets when cross-examining witnesses.

It is with regard to the wider social and cultural environment that greater differences appear. While Rumpole hints at skulduggery by the establishment and the police, it never seems too disruptive, and order is soon restored in a Durkheimian way. In *Rake*, the entire political and legal system appears corrupt and deeply self-serving.[78] Rumpole would not survive in the Australian milieu. Greene fights in a similar manner to his Australian establishment – dirty. And it is the only means by which he can attain self-preservation and justice. The context impels them both to behave in the ways they do, and it is only in their respective contexts that they can thrive. Rumpole's England represents Whiggish order and predictability while the *mise en scène* of *Rake* is more attuned to a splintered and fragmented world where chaos is ever present. In this manner, Australian depictions of law and justice could be seen as more aligned with the neoliberal order of the world as it is now.

Despite the differences, I would argue both are creatures of the establishment. They both inhabit small, hermetic, closed worlds. Rumpole attends dinners at judges' lodgings and gala events, and occasionally visits Keith in the Lord Chancellor's Department.[79] In 'Rumpole and the Genuine Article', Guthrie Featherstone presides over his first case as a Red judge. This is after he feared his wife's gossiping may have cost him his elevation to the Bench. At the end of the case, he says to Rumpole:

> 'That bit of a tizz I was in, about the great secret getting out. No need to mention that to anyone, eh?'
>
> 'Oh, I rang the Lord Chancellor's office about that', Rumpole replied.
>
> 'You what?' Featherstone looked at me in a wild surmise.
>
> 'I assured them you hadn't said a word to anyone and it was just a sort of silly joke. . . . I mean, no one in the Temple ever dreamed that they'd make you a Judge'.[80]

Rumpole traverses these worlds with ease because he doesn't care whether he ever becomes a member. He doesn't expect to be asked. At one stage, there is a rumour that Rumpole will be appointed as a circuit judge, and he is genuinely anxious that this could be true.[81] When his chambers colleague, George Frobisher, applies for a circuit judgeship, he admits to Rumpole that being a judge is a lonely life, and he misses the camaraderie of the Bar.[82] But Rumpole ponders his fate, knowing Judge Frobisher will have a secure pension while he will have a woeful one.

Cleaver Greene, by contrast, uses the same brothel as many other lawyers and members of parliament, which exemplifies his milieu. When he is in danger of being disbarred for some offence, he arranges for one of the 'girls' from the club to visit the two leading members of the disciplinary committee to remind them of their own corrupt infidelities. He is not disbarred.[83] He appears on the news often because of his cases, so he becomes a public figure through his work. Like Rumpole, Greene spurns the political alliances formed by many of his colleagues and foes. David 'Harry' Potter, for example, Greene's nemesis, moves from prosecution work to becoming head of the Labor Party while Cleaver eventually languishes as a fluke independent senator with zero influence or interest.[84]

The working worlds of the courts

It is in their work that we see the characters' true selves and personalities emerge. Both Greene and Rumpole believe in the law and justice. They also recognize that law and justice are not isomorphic, and therefore justice must be seen to trump law. In 'Rumpole and the Last Resort', Horace fails to win an adjournment from Judge Bullingham ('the Bull', his constant antagonist) to summons a vital witness that will vindicate his case.[85] He collapses in court, and rumours abound that Rumpole is dead. The necessary adjournment granted on his collapse provides the breathing space to track down the witness. When the trial is resumed, Rumpole appears in court just as the Bull is giving a eulogy for him:

> 'We're not superior beings as judges; we don't put on "side". We are the barristers' friends. And one of my oldest friends, over the years, was Horace Rumpole'. Both Ward-Webster for the prosecution and [Fiona Allways] looked piously up to the ceiling. We carefully hid our feelings of amazement.[86]

Rumpole goes on to win the case, proving that his (unethical) trick achieved a just outcome.

Achieving justice and the right verdict means that both lawyers must trample over the conventions of the Bar. As junior barristers, they will often be 'led' by Queen's Counsel (QC or silk) in serious cases. The QC takes the lead and sets the strategy for the case. Neither Cleaver nor Horace likes being led, especially by silks who are less competent or less motivated to prove the innocence of their clients. In the first episode of *Rake*, Cleaver is led by a silk who believes their client both mad and guilty. Professor Murray, cannibal, advertised for someone to be eaten by him. Following his consenting victim's suicide, he cooks and eats the corpse and also serves it to his unknowing wife. He is charged with murder – except it isn't. The QC is determined to have him go down for murder, but he has a heart attack and dies.[87] Greene is left to defend the economist professor alone. Now his true brilliance as an advocate is displayed, and his client is cleared of murder, although he is confined indefinitely to a psychiatric hospital. His defence only succeeds when Cleaver undermines the confidence and authority of his client by exposing his inability to predict the Great Recession.[88] Rumpole is in a similar situation when he is defending an actress in a murder case in a small provincial town. The local Bar is tight and doesn't like having a London barrister in their midst. Rumpole's QC also believes the client is guilty, much to Rumpole's disgust – every defendant must be presumed innocent.[89] The QC falls ill, and, instead of abandoning the case as is the local culture, Rumpole continues on – against stiff odds – to secure his client's acquittal. At the local Bar Mess dinner, he is forced to acknowledge his faux pas and pay a forfeit of a dozen bottles of wine.[90] Although Horace cares little for the conventions, he follows them to avoid fuss when necessary.

Both Greene and Rumpole are hacks, outliers in their profession. And this is vividly illustrated by their networks and the status of their clients.[91] Rumpole is fortunate to have a committed set of criminal clients, the Timson family from south London, whose succeeding generations keep Rumpole in Pommeroy's plonk. Greene does not have clients in the same way as Rumpole, but he is frequently used and exploited by them. He is forced to defend those to whom he is in hock or gangsters who will harm him while corrupting the police and government. He sleeps with the Premier of New South Wales and earns the enmity of her husband, Attorney-General Cal McGregor.[92] Greene even ends up in prison for a while on manslaughter charges, framed by McGregor for the killing of a fraudster's neighbour. Greene proves he is a good advocate, but he is not necessarily a good lawyer.[93]

As neither slants to the purity end of the continuum – indeed, Greene is visibly at the danger-taboo end – their desire to do the best for their clients doesn't diminish. At times, both realize they have been *too* successful, and in each case, it is a woman who gulled them.[94] In Rumpole's case, the actress in 'Rumpole and the Show Folk' raises such doubts in Horace's mind when he visits her before the jury returns its verdict that he cannot be rid of her quickly enough. Her performance had overwhelmed and seduced him.[95] Cleaver successfully defends a Muslim woman charged with conspiracy to commit a terrorist act after her stupid husband blew himself up instead of destroying the parliament building. After the verdict, he, too, comes to realize that the widow was looking for an escape from her sorry marriage and had planned the explosion.[96] He was duped.

While they are at heart criminal barristers, they accept that there are financial benefits to doing civil work even if they pretend to disdain it. Greene gets caught up in a 'human rights case' representing Missy's husband, Joshua. He even rents his own chambers, but it all eventually collapses, and his world returns to its shambolic normalcy. Rumpole brushes up against civil work in more indirect ways. When C.H. Wystan, Hilda's father and the head of 3 Equity Court, decides to retire, Hilda pushes Rumpole to claim the headship as the senior barrister. He is defeated by the elevation of younger Guthrie Featherstone QC MP, aided by Wystan's yearning for the chambers to do more civil work.[97] Featherstone, Erskine-Brown and later Ballard – the new head of chambers – continuously promote 'purer' civil work at the expense of 'dirty' criminal defence. For Rumpole, though, the simplicity and directness of bloodstains outweigh the grubbiness of money-based civil work.

Conclusion

The two advocates typify two different generations and two different environments, but within a single profession. Cleaver Greene is wild and unruly. He espouses a concept of law that he thinks doesn't apply to him. His ethical and professional boundaries don't so much blur as get blown away entirely. Horace Rumpole understands the nature of the rules of the game he is playing and gently bends them from time to time. He is too conservative to flout convention completely in Greene's manner.

The taboo, dangerous aspects of Greene's life permeate everywhere. He sleeps with clients (including under-age ones) and wives of friends, he is complicit in corruption and careless of others' feelings and security. Greene is a liability to all those around him. As likeable as he appears, Greene is not good. He is dissolute without integrity. His commitment to clients is laudable, but that varies according to his whims. Ultimately, Cleaver is a loser. We know that whatever opportunities he is given, he will obliterate them. He epitomizes the concept of dirt as matter out of place.

Rumpole is harmless in comparison: a gentle person who tries to help those who deserve to be helped. There is some ethical fading with Rumpole, but it is always to a well-intended end. Ultimately, Rumpole is good, honest and professional in his own way. He has integrity and understands his profession's rules and how to bend them. He is conservative and won't rend society's fabric. Horace enjoys life, but at the same time is mildly disappointed that he didn't exploit it to the full. His dreams of the young hippie woman in 'Rumpole and the Alternative Society' indicate how he might have liked to have lived.[98]

There is a larger question: why are shows and programmes about lawyers and law so popular? And *Rumpole* and *Rake* are certainly popular.[99] One reason is that this is the only way people receive information about the legal system.[100] According to Richard Sherwin:

> For many, perhaps most, the mass media today are in fact the primary if not the exclusive source of the public's knowledge about law, lawyers, and the legal system as a whole. . . . Put simply, [popular culture, especially visual mass media] is a source of both meaning and the meaning-making tools people use to think and speak with.[101]

If this is so, then we come to rely on the media for our knowledge and interpretations of law. The 'cultivation effect' moves us to acquit defendants unless there is forensic DNA evidence to back up the prosecutor's claims.[102] During the trial of O.J. Simpson, it became difficult to distinguish between the media representations of the trial and the grim reality of the murders committed.[103] The issue is that we tend to see only one kind of legalism presented: the adversarial system, where two sides battle it out in court. It is heroic and replete with grand gestures. In his closing address in the O.J. Simpson trial, defence counsel Johnnie Cochran says of the prosecution's argument that Simpson was the murderer in disguise:

> And I said to myself, maybe I can demonstrate this graphically. Let me show you something. This is a knit cap. Let me put this knit cap on (Indicating). You have seen me for a year. If I put this knit cap on, who am I? I'm still Johnnie Cochran with a knit cap. And if you looked at O.J. Simpson over there – and he has a rather large head – O.J. Simpson in a knit cap from two blocks away is still O.J. Simpson. It's no disguise. It's no disguise. It makes no sense. It doesn't fit. If it doesn't fit, you must acquit.[104]

The physicality of putting the knit cap on his head intensifies the drama of the courtroom, forcing each side to more extreme moments. The adversarial system becomes its own theatre.

With the advent of 'Nordic Noir' television, in *policiers* represented by *The Killing*[105] and *The Bridge*,[106] viewers see something different from the adversarial system. They are exposed to the inquisitorial system, which is more judge led than lawyer controlled in the adversarial system. One show that brings this to the fore, in a manner analogous to *Law & Order,* is the French *policier Spiral (Engrenages)*.[107] Lawyers, prosecutors and *juges d'instruction* play significant roles in this series. At times it is difficult to distinguish the judges and prosecutors from the police. This is quite unlike the passive Anglo style of judging, where the lawyers present the evidence. For most viewers of adversarial shows, the civil code system is very alien and disturbing, hence the transformations into different contexts and systems.

We want our legal systems and lawyers and judges to be fair and just. The rule of law is a bulwark against despotism and anarchy. But we know our institutions can be and are corrupted, and we need something to protect ourselves from the injustices of corruption. The law and its application help us remedy those injustices. From consumer complaints in the newspapers to cases in the Supreme Courts, we delight in seeing iniquity overturned and the torn fabric of society repaired.[108] The cultural representation of lawyers is often the closest we come to experiencing a sense of justice – however indirect. Whatever form of repression society throws at us, we know there is a defence of some kind.[109] We rebel against the alienation and emptiness of Kafka's *Before the Law*,[110] where repressive institutions are designed to crush our spirits. For this reason, we owe a debt of gratitude to Horace Rumpole and Cleaver Greene because, despite their cynicism, their cavalier ways with people, their dismissal of order and bureaucratic nicety and their ethical fading, ultimately they demonstrate a fundamental integrity, which almost overrides the taboo nature of their activities, a professionalism that enables us to remain invested in an ideal of justice – however illusory.

Notes

1 As I thought about this chapter dealing with Australian and English lawyers, I did an experiment comparing Vegemite with Marmite by spreading half a slice of toast with each. I think this is a perfect metaphor for *Rake* and *Rumpole of the Bailey*. The results of the experiment, however, do not influence my liking of these two shows – I'm Pareto optimal!

2 *LA Law* (1986–92).

3 *Ally McBeal* (1997–2002).

4 *Boston Legal* (2004–08).

5 *The Good Fight* (2017–).

6 *Rumpole of the Bailey* (1979–92). Rumpole has the advantage of a book series by John Mortimer (e.g. Mortimer 2012), which provides a considerable amount of backstory detail about Horace. There will be a necessary elision in this essay between these two distinct sources.

7 *Rake* (2010–18). Although *Rake* is an Australian TV series, it is also broadcast on Netflix globally.

8 The series are structured differently. *Rake* has some episodes that are numbered but not named, whereas *Rumpole*'s episodes are named after their short story equivalents.

9 Rumpole's education has a precarious air about it as he only gained a third-class degree at Oxford. In modern-day Britain, he would be barred from the Bar for such a poor degree, sometimes referred to as a 'gentleman's degree'. We don't know the status of Cleaver's degree: presumably a good one from the University of Sydney. The Sydney barrister on whom Cleaver Greene is supposed to be based, Charles Waterstreet, attended the University of Sydney; however, see Maddox (2017).

10 According to Leo McKern's Wikipedia page, 'Although he enjoyed the role, McKern expressed doubts about its popularity and the extent to which his life was becoming intertwined with Rumpole's'. McKern was often unhappy, decrying his television fame as an 'insatiable monster'. He stressed that his *Peer Gynt* was a greater performance and lamented, 'If I get an obit in any paper, they will say, "Of course, known to millions as Rumpole"'. See www.wikiwand.com/en/Leo_McKern. Richard Roxburgh, on the other hand, enjoys playing Greene and has lamented that the fifth season is the last one: 'It's really hard to let go' (Wang 2018).

11 *Rake* (2010), S1 Ep 7.

12 Robson (2017).

13 Rumpole quotes poetry, Keats and Shakespeare in the majority of episodes, too numerous to reference each one. The attitude to poetry displays the difference between British and Australian archetypes. Rumpole lives by the Quiller-Couch edition of the *Oxford Book of English Verse* and quotes endlessly and passionately. Greene apparently has no such feelings. In Episode 3 we hear this exchange between Cleaver and his son, Fuzz: '*Cleaver Greene:* [after reading out Byron's "She walks in beauty, like the night"] "Bugger me, he was good". *Fuzz Greene:* "Yeah, but what use is it?" *Cleaver Greene:* "What do you mean 'What use is it?' It's poetry, you knucklehead. It has only one use, and that's pulling chicks"'. *Rake* (2010), S1 Ep 1.

14 The genesis of Rumpole occurred thus: 'Mortimer's 2009 obituary in *The Daily Telegraph* confirmed that Rumpole was, in part, based on a chance meeting in court with James Burge QC: In the early 1970s Mortimer was appearing for some football hooligans when James Burge, with whom he was sharing the defence, told him:

"I'm really an anarchist at heart, but I don't think even my darling old Prince Peter Kropotkin would have approved of this lot". "And there", Mortimer realised, "I had Rumpole"'. See www.wikiwand.com/en/Rumpole_of_the_Bailey; Obituary (2009) 'Sir John Mortimer', *The Daily Telegraph*, 16 January.
15 *Rake* (2010), S1 Ep 1–8.
16 Beasley (2010).
17 *Rake* (2010), S1 Ep 8.
18 Sykes (2014).
19 *Rumpole of the Bailey* (1979), S1 Ep 2.
20 *Rumpole* started before the era of Margaret Thatcher, when British welfarism was eroded as public institutions were privatized on the altar of neoliberalism: Steger and Roy (2010).
21 Of course, that didn't include Aboriginal and Torres Strait Islander people in Australia, who were massacred because Australia was supposedly *terra nullius*: Tatz (1999).
22 Collins (1985), p 157.
23 Perry (2011).
24 See Zander (n.d.).
25 Snow (1950); Twining (1994, 2002).
26 See Abel (2014); Murphy (2014).
27 Flood (1983).
28 Flood (2005).
29 See *Yale Law Journal*, https://digitalcommons.law.yale.edu/ylj/vol98/iss8.
30 Gillers (1989), p 1611.
31 I have to include the genre of *policiers* in this category as they too involve much law. For example, the series *Line of Duty* is full of law, from actual legislation to tiresome administrative requirements. In Episode 1, an armed police squad is about to enter a suspect's house but is held up because the required health and safety assessment hasn't been submitted. See *Line of Duty* (2012).
32 Macaulay (1989), p 1558.
33 For example, see the *Journal of the Oxford Centre for Socio-Legal Studies*, 2017 Special issue on Law and Popular Culture, https://joxcsls.com/archive-4/2017-special-issue-law-and-popular-culture.
34 Sciulli (2008).
35 Brand (1987).
36 George Carman, www.wikiwand.com/en/George_Carman. See also the TV film, *Get Carman: The Trials of George Carman QC*, *IMDb*, www.imdb.com/title/tt0810874.
37 Geoffrey Robertson, www.wikiwand.com/en/Geoffrey_Robertson; https://geoffreyrobertson.com.
38 Cf. Dawes (2016).
39 Douglas (1966).
40 Abbott (1981).
41 Cf. Campkin (2013), p 56, for how the city that Rumpole and Greene occupy leaves more room for the ideas that 'filth, under certain circumstances, might surprisingly be a good or enjoyable thing', which applies to the ways its inhabitants live – thus creating ambiguity around dirt.
42 Douglas (1966), p 30.
43 Flood and Hviid (2013).
44 Abbott (1981).
45 Heinz and Laumann (1982), pp 84–134.
46 Heinz and Laumann (1982), pp 84–134.
47 Heinz and Laumann (1982), pp 84–134.
48 Carlin (1962/2011).

49 Boon and Flood (1999).
50 This is not always so. In our article on lawyers and construction arbitration, Caiger and I found that the lawyers' views of the Official Referees' Court (precursor to the Technology and Construction Court) were entirely negative, and the judges were not held in high esteem; hence, there was much use of arbitration instead of the courts. See Flood and Caiger (1993).
51 Aristotle, Book 1 (2012), p 6.
52 There are obvious resonances with Erving Goffman's *Presentation of Self in Everyday Life* (1959), in which social life is explored through a dramaturgical lens, with the front stage and backstage each claiming their own sets of roles. Robert Post (1987), p 389, uses Goffman to show why we mistrust lawyers: 'The lawyer is the public and unavoidable embodiment of the tension we all experience between the desire for an embracing and common community and the urge toward individual independence and self-assertion; between the need for a stable, coherent, and sincerely presented self and the fragmented and disassociated roles we are forced to play in the theatre of modern life'.
53 See '100+ The Castle Quotes About the 1997 Australian Comedy-Drama Film', https://comicbookandbeyond.com/the-castle-quotes/.
54 *The Castle* (1997).
55 This is quite distinct from when Dennis Denuto is asked by the judge which part of the Constitution he is relying on, and he answers, 'It's the vibe of the thing, your Honour'. This is pathos in the extreme. *The Castle*, 'Quotes', *IMDb*, www.imdb.com/title/tt0118826/quotes/?tab=qt&ref_=tt_trv_qu.
56 Steavenson (2015).
57 *Kavanagh QC* (1995–2000).
58 *Silk* (2011, 2012, 2014).
59 Cleaver is besotted with Missy and is naively convinced that they are in love with each other. He finds out the true commercial nature of their relationship after she leaves the brothel and, on seeing him in the street, cuts him dead: *Rake* (2010), S1 Ep 1. Club Jules also connotes an undercurrent in *Rake* that, despite his low character, Cleaver is well connected to the legal and political elites of New South Wales. His economic capital may be precarious, but his social and cultural capital are strongly established (Redmond 2014).
60 For non-London readers, the term 'mansion flat' could be puzzling, but for someone of Rumpole's standing, it would have been a good purchase when starting out on married life, and its convenience and relative proximity to shops, the Tube and his place of work would have then hindered him from moving on to a bigger house. The following description I have cited comes from an estate agent, Foxtons, but it is the best I could find. *Foxtons*, www.foxtons.co.uk/discover/2019/02/londons-mansion-blocks-victorian-grandeur-from-A465k.html.
61 See Mortimer (2001).
62 *Janet King* (2013–17).
63 Epstein (1993).
64 See, for example, Kay and Gorman (2008).
65 *Silk* (2011, 2012, 2014).
66 *The Good Wife* (2009–16).
67 See *The Good Fight* (2017–).
68 There are issues, however, when Lucca, a black associate, finds herself pregnant by her white prosecutor boyfriend. She has to persuade the partners that it won't affect her work. *The Good Fight* (2018), S2 Ep 6.
69 Flood (1983).
70 Chan, Poynton and Bruce (2014).

71 *Rumpole of the Bailey* (1978), S1 Ep 3.
72 *Rake* (2010), S1 Ep 8.
73 *Rumpole of the Bailey* (1983), S3 Ep 6.
74 *Rake* (2012), S 2 Ep 5.
75 *Rumpole of the Bailey* (1987), S 4 Ep 6.
76 *Rake* (2014), S 3 Ep 8.
77 For the history of barristers' clothing in Australia, see Victoria Law Foundation (2010). Also see, for England and Wales, Ede and Ravenscroft (2003). The colour of the bags barristers use to carry their gowns and wigs has great significance. Junior barristers – those who are not Queen's Counsel or silk – use blue ones. QCs use red bags. If juniors have distinguished themselves in a case with a leader (QC), they can be given a red bag by the leader as a signifier of respect and esteem. Rumpole has a red bag, although he is a junior. See *Brief (law)*, www.wikiwand.com/en/Brief_(law)#/Brief_bag.
78 Perry (2011).
79 The Lord Chancellor's Department is an earlier incarnation of the Ministry of Justice in the United Kingdom. Keith is a senior civil servant, probably a deputy under-secretary or even a permanent under-secretary, and holds the fate of judges' appointments in his hands. When Guthrie Featherstone QC MP, head of Equity Court chambers, is tapped for a High Court judgeship, he lives in fear that it will become widely known, because his wife gossips, and the offer will be withdrawn. It all depends what and how Keith hears.
80 Mortimer, 'Rumpole and the Genuine Article' (2012), p 235.
81 *Rumpole of the Bailey* (1979), S2 Ep 5.
82 *Rumpole of the Bailey* (1979), S2 Ep 5.
83 *Rake* (2010), S1 Ep 3.
84 In Series 5, Cleaver becomes a senator in the Australian parliament, elected on a slate of having no policies. This brings him into contact with government ministers and the like. Even here, his reputation is low as he only wants the regular pay without doing any work. He gets his driver to falsify his attendance and meeting records and diaries, which ultimately puts him under the power of the driver and the government drivers' mafia. Of interest also is the change of colour of his suit. As barrister he wears black; as senator he wears blue. It is never explained.
85 *Rumpole of the Bailey* (1983), S 3 Ep 6.
86 *Rumpole of the Bailey* (1983), S 3 Ep 6.
87 *Rake* (2010), S1 Ep 1.
88 *Rake* (2010), S1 Ep 1.
89 *Rumpole of the Bailey* (1979), S2 Ep 3.
90 *Rumpole of the Bailey* (1979), S2 Ep 3.
91 Heinz and Laumann (1982).
92 *Rake* (2012), S2 Ep 1.
93 In this fraud case, Cleaver thinks he has trapped the fraudster only to find he relied on the wrong statute, as the judge acidly points out to him.
94 There is a tradition of women traducing men in these kinds of stories. Sherlock Holmes, for example, in 'Scandal in Bohemia', has a reverence for Irene Adler who bested him. See Krumm (1996).
95 *Rumpole of the Bailey* (1979), S2 Ep 3.
96 *Rumpole of the Bailey* (1979), S2 Ep 3.
97 *Rumpole of the Bailey* (1978), S1 Ep 2.
98 See Sykes (2014).
99 At its peak, according to Moran (2008), p 298, *Rumpole* was watched by over ten million UK viewers and was distributed to Australia and the United States. *Rake* is

popular but not to the same extent as *Rumpole*. In 2018, *Rake* had Australian viewer numbers of 573,000. See https://mumbrella.com.au/the-block-achieves-biggest-audience-for-series-to-date-with-1-293m-tuning-in-537472.

100 Asimow (2007).

101 Sherwin (2000), p 18.

102 Tyler (2006).

103 Hunt (1999).

104 Johnnie Cochrane: 'If it doesn't fit, you must acquit'. O.J. Simpson trial closing argument, 1994, *Speakola: All Speeches Great and Small,* https://speakola.com/ideas/johnnie-cochrane-oj-simpson-trial-closing-1994.

105 *The Killing (Forbrydelsen),* Danmarks Radio (2007–12). For full credits, see IMDb, www.imdb.com/title/tt0826760/fullcredits?ref_=ttco_ql_1). See also *The Killing,* KMF Films (2011–14). For full credits see IMDb, www.imdb.com/title/tt1637727/fullcredits?ref_=ttco_ql_1). The Nordic Noir oeuvre has led to the development of a programme format with shows being adapted to different legal cultures. *The Bridge,* which began as a joint Swedish and Danish production, has spawned Anglo-French, Austro-German, and US-Mexican productions, among others.

106 *The Bridge (Bron/Broen)* (2011–18).

107 *Spiral (Engrenages)* (2005–).

108 Durkheim (1960).

109 This was brought dramatically to the fore in the UK when private citizens brought cases against the prime minister over his extended prorogation of parliament. The Supreme Court held against the prime minister that the prorogation was unlawful compelling Parliament to resit immediately. See *Cherry and others* (Respondents) *v Advocate General for Scotland* (Appellant) (Scotland) [2019] UKSC 41 and *R* (on the application of Miller) (Appellant) *v The Prime Minister* (Respondent) UKSC 41.

110 Kafka (2007–19).

References

Secondary sources

'100+ The Castle Quotes About The 1997 Australian Comedy-Drama Film', https://comicbookandbeyond.com/the-castle-quotes/.

Andrew Abbott (1981) 'Status and Strain in the Professions' 86(4) *American Journal of Sociology* 819.

Richard Abel (2014) 'In Memoriam – Simon Roberts (1941–2014)' 46(3) *The Journal of Legal Pluralism and Unofficial Law* 87.

Aristotle (2012) *Art of Rhetoric*, HarperCollins.

Michael Asimow (2007) 'Popular Culture and the Adversary System' 40 *Loyola of Los Angeles Law Review* 653.

Richard Beasley (2010) 'Muse: *Rake* – ABC Television 2010', *Bar News*, Winter 116.

Andrew Boon and John Flood (1999) 'Trials of Strength: The Reconfiguration of Litigation as a Contested Terrain' 33 *Law and Society Review* 595.

Paul Brand (1987) 'The Origins of the English Legal Profession' 5 *Law and History Review* 31.

Ben Campkin (2013) '"Matter Out of Place": *Purity and Danger* as Evidence for Architecture and Urbanism' 18 *Architectural Theory Review* 46.

Jerome Carlin (1962/2011) *Lawyers on Their Own: The Solo Practitioner in an Urban Setting*, Quid Pro Books.

George Carman (n.d.) www.wikiwand.com/en/George_Carman.
Janet Chan, Suzanne Poynton and Jasmine Bruce (2014) 'Lawyering Stress and Work Culture: An Australian Study' 37 *University of New South Wales Law Journal* 1062.
Hugh Collins (1985) 'Political Ideology in Australian Society: The Distinctiveness of a Benthamite Society' 114 *Daedalus* 147.
Simon Dawes (2016) 'Introduction to Michel Maffesoli's "From Society to Tribal Communities"' 64(4) *The Sociological Review* 739, https://smdawes.wordpress.com/2017/01/09/article-introduction-to-michel-maffesolis-from-society-to-tribal-communities.
Mary Douglas (1966) *Purity and Danger: An Analysis of the Concepts of Pollution and Taboo*, Routledge.
Émile Durkheim (1960/1893). *The Division of Labor in Society*, The Free Press.
Ede and Ravenscroft (2003) *Legal Habits: A Brief Sartorial History of Wig, Robe and Gown*, https://legal.edeandravenscroft.co.uk/images/site/Legal_Habits_book.pdf.
Cynthia Fuchs Epstein (1993) *Women in Law*, University of Illinois Press.
John Flood (1983) *Barristers' Clerks: The Law's Middlemen*, Manchester University Press.
——— (2005) 'Socio-Legal Ethnography', in Raza Banakar and Max Travers (eds), *Theory and Method in Socio-Legal Research*, Hart.
John Flood and Andrew Caiger (1993) 'Lawyers and Arbitration: The Juridification of Construction Disputes' 56(3) *Modern Law Review* 412.
John Flood and Morton Hviid (2013) 'The Cab Rank Rule: Its Meaning and Purpose', report for the Legal Services Board, https://research.legalservicesboard.org.uk/wp-content/media/Cab-Rank-Rule_final-2013.pdf.
Stephen Gillers (1989) 'Taking *LA Law* More Seriously' 98 *Yale Law Journal* 1607.
Erving Goffman (1959) *The Presentation of Self in Everyday Life*, Doubleday Anchor Books.
John Heinz and Edward Laumann (1982) *Chicago Lawyers: The Social Structure of the Bar*, American Bar Foundation and Russell Sage.
Darnell Hunt (1999) *O.J. Simpson Facts and Fictions: News Rituals in the Construction of Reality*, Cambridge University Press.
Franz Kafka (2007–19) 'Before the Law', *Franz Kafka online*, www.kafka-online.info/before-the-law.html.
Fiona Kay and Elizabeth Gorman (2008) 'Women in the Legal Profession' *Annual Review of Law and Social Science* 299.
Pascale Krumm (1996) '"A Scandal in Bohemia" and Sherlock Holmes Ultimate Mystery Solved' 39 *English Literature in Transition, 1880–1920* 193.
Stewart Macaulay (1989) 'Popular Legal Culture: An Introduction' 98 *Yale Law Journal* 1545.
Garry Maddox (2017) 'Richard Roxburgh: "Any Day I Don't Hear the Name Charles Waterstreet is Good"', *Sydney Morning Herald*, 27 October, www.smh.com.au/entertainment/tv-and-radio/richard-roxburgh-any-day-i-dont-hear-the-name-charles-waterstreet-is-good-20171027-gz9efk.html.
Leo McKern (n.d.) www.wikiwand.com/en/Leo_McKern.
Leslie Moran (2008) 'Cause Lawyering "English Style": Reading *Rumpole of the Bailey*', in Austin Sarat and Stuart Scheingold (eds), *The Cultural Lives of Cause Lawyers*, Cambridge University Press.
John Mortimer (2001) 'Rumpole and Asylum Seekers', in *Rumpole Rests His Case*, Viking.
——— (2012) *The Collected Stories of Rumpole*, Penguin.
Tim Murphy (2014) 'Simon Roberts Obituary', *The Guardian*, 3 June, www.theguardian.com/science/2014/jun/03/simon-roberts.

Peter John Perry (2011) *Political Corruption in Australia: A Very Wicked Place?*, Routledge.
Robert Post (1987) 'On the Popular Image of the Lawyer: Reflections in a Dark Glass' 75 *California Law Review* 379.
Sean Redmond (2014) 'Suicide by Opera: The Fucking Identity Politics of *Rake*', *CST Online*, 14 March, https://cstonline.net/suicide-by-opera-the-fucking-identity-politics-of-rake-by-sean-redmond.
Geoffrey Robertson (n.d.) www.wikiwand.com/en/Geoffrey_Robertson.
Peter Robson (2017) 'The Portrayal of the Corporate Lawyer on TV: The US and British Models from *LA Law* to *Trust* and *Suits*' 2 *Journal of the Oxford Centre for Socio-Legal Studies* 46.
David Sciulli (2008) 'Revisionism in Sociology of Professions Today: Conceptual Approaches by Larson' 3 *Sociologica, Italian Journal of Sociology Online*, www.rivisteweb.it/issn/1971-8853/issue/196.
Richard Sherwin (2000) *When Law Goes Pop: The Vanishing Line Between Law and Popular Culture*, University of Chicago Press.
C.P. Snow (1950) *The Masters*, Macmillan.
Wendell Steavenson (2015) 'Jonathan Sumption: The Brain of Britain', *The Guardian*, 6 August, www.theguardian.com/law/2015/aug/06/jonathan-sumption-brain-of-britain.
Manfred Steger and Ravi Roy (2010) *Neoliberalism: A Very Short Introduction*, Oxford University Press.
Alan Sykes (2014) *The Whigs and the Politics of Reform: The Rise and Fall of British Liberalism, 1776–1988*, Routledge.
Colin Tatz (1999) 'Genocide in Australia' 1 *Journal of Genocide Research* 315.
William Twining (1994) *Blackstone's Tower: The English Law School*, Sweet & Maxwell.
——— (2002) 'Law Teaching as a Vocation' *Speculum Juris* 161.
Tom Tyler (2006) 'Viewing CSI and the Threshold of Guilt: Managing Truth and Justice in Reality and Fiction' 115 *Yale Law Journal* 1050.
Victoria Law Foundation (2010) *Wigs and Robes: A Lasting Tradition*, www.victorialawfoundation.org.au/sites/default/files/resources/Wigs_and_Robes.pdf.
Cynthia Wang (2018) '*Rake*'s Richard Roxburgh Reveals His Soft Spot for Cleaver Greene: "It's Hard to Let Go"', *TV Week*, 12 September, www.nowtolove.com.au/celebrity/tv/richard-roxburgh-rake-interview-51114.
Michael Zander (n.d.) www.lse.ac.uk/law/people/academic-staff/michael-zander.

Film and television series

Ally McBeal (1997–2002), 20th Century Fox Television (S1–5).
Boston Legal (2004–08), David E. Kelly Productions and 20th Century Fox Television (S1–5).
The Bridge (*Broe/Broen*) (2011–18), Nimbus Films and Filmlance International (S1–8).
The Castle (1997), Rob Sitch, Working Dog Productions.
Get Carmen: The trials of George Carman QC (2002), BBC (telemovie).
The Good Fight (2017–), Scott Free Productions, King Size Productions and CBS Television Studios (S1–).
The Good Wife (2009–2016), Scott Free Productions, King Size Productions, Small Wishes Productions, CBS Television Studios and CBS Productions (S1–7).
Janet King (2013–17), Screentime (S1–3).

Kavanagh QC (1995–2001), Central Television (S1–6).
The Killing (*Forbrydelsen* (*The Crime*)) (2007–12), Danmarks Radio (DR), Norsk Rikskringkasting (NRK), Sveriges Television (SVT) (S1–4).
LA Law (1986–94), 20th Century Fox Television (S1–8).
Line of Duty (2012–), World Productions (S1–).
Rake (2010–18), Essential Media and Entertainment, Blow by Blow Productions, Screen Australia, Australian Broadcasting Corporation, and Easy Tiger Productions (S1–5).
Rumpole of the Bailey (1978–92), BBC and Thames Television (S1–7).
Silk (2011, 2012, 2014), BBC Productions (S1–3).
Spiral (*Engrenages*) (2005–), Canal+, and Son et Lumière (S1–).

Chapter 10

Cleaver Greene

The legal larrikin on Australian screens

Lili Pâquet

Introduction

In the first introduction to Cleaver Greene (Richard Roxburgh), the protagonist of the Australian legal series *Rake*, he is beaten by an apologetic enforcer because of a large gambling debt. In the following domestic scene, his game of backgammon with a beautiful woman, Missy (Adrienne Pickering), is interrupted when the bedside lamps flash, revealing that he is actually in a brothel. The next morning, Cleaver rushes to court to represent himself in a protracted case of tax evasion. Thus, in the first few scenes of *Rake,* Cleaver is shown to break moral codes and, perhaps more shockingly, the law.

In this chapter, I argue that *Rake* challenges an Australian viewership on its admiration of larrikinism, through the subversion of liberal legal moralism. Cleaver is a larrikin lawyer who draws upon Australian myths, causing viewers to confront them through his personal and professional practices – particularly through his trials, which rely on moral liberalism to excuse the bad behaviour of his wealthy clients. Cleaver is a privileged white man who lives in affluent suburbs of Sydney and Canberra and has a respectable occupation as a barrister. At the same time, he is a 'floater' with no permanent chambers or stable home, who squanders his considerable income and the opportunities afforded him by his social position. He is a larrikin, a cultural descendant of Australian convict settlers; he is also a rake, who resembles the idle and spendthrift sons of the English aristocracy. By straddling this boundary, Cleaver forces Australian viewers to confront their cultural ideals and demonstrates how certain privileged white men avoid censure and punishment by performing larrikinism.

Rake was broadcast by the Australian Broadcasting Corporation (ABC) for five seasons and was subsequently made available internationally by the streaming company *Netflix*. The first season (2010) introduces Cleaver as a barrister whose controversial clients include serial bigamists, conservative radio shock-jocks and cannibals. In the second season (2012), Cleaver wastes his chance at redemption, ending the season in prison for conspiracy to murder. He is released early in the third season (2014) and works to rebuild his career, until he is disbarred near the end of the fourth season (2016). The fifth season (2018), supposedly the final one of the series, follows Cleaver's calamitous political career in federal politics. As American lawyer Geoffrey Hazard suggests, the law is written down in the 'medium of verbal symbols rather than through live demonstration or narrative' from which society usually learns.[1] To then represent this written set of regulations through on-screen narratives may more clearly contextualize the opaque workings of the law to viewers. The narratives demonstrate the application of criminal law to various scenarios. In *Rake*, these narratives also reveal the conflicting nature of larrikinism in contemporary Australian culture. While Janet King and other fictional Australian lawyers work to uphold justice, the characters in *Rake* are rarely villains or heroes. Cleaver is a mess of contradictions. He appeals to the ideals of larrikinism in order to defend his clients on controversial liberal grounds, yet his position of privilege deviates from the historical archetype of larrikinism. Cleaver also differs from maverick legal characters such as Horace Rumpole and Judge John Deed because he is not ethical or principled,[2] yet he is rewarded with prestigious positions he neither aspires to nor deserves.

This chapter begins with a history and context of larrikinism in Australian culture and literature, demonstrates how larrikinism is simultaneously celebrated and renounced in *Rake*, then evaluates specific instances in which Cleaver exploits legal moral liberalism in court. The chapter concludes with a reflection on *Rake*'s short-lived adaptation for US audiences.

The Australian myth

Cleaver Greene, the lawyer protagonist of *Rake,* is a combination of the rake-hero and an Australian larrikin. The rake-hero was a character type in English restoration comedies written during the reign of Charles II.[3] As Hume defines the character, 'a rake (short for rakehell) is a *roué*, a licentious or dissolute man. The term carries strong connotations of profligacy, idleness, and waste'.[4] This character type has been divided into sub-categories, including that of the extravagant rake who is impulsive, promiscuous and cheeky.[5] Furthermore,

> the extravagant rake is regarded by other characters in the play with a combination of astonishment and affection. His "wildness" – sexual, financial, or otherwise – is looked on with indulgence by all but the stuffiest of old fathers, and in a good nine cases out of ten he winds up renouncing his former ways and settling down to marriage.[6]

The extravagant rake provides 'carnival release',[7] as reflected in *Rake.* The opening theme music is recognizably Johann Strauss's *Blue Danube Waltz*, but played in an unsteady and frenetic carnivalesque style,[8] while a titular sign attached to a spinning firecracker falls apart and tips over. Non-diegetic carnivalesque music is often played throughout the series, and there are continuous references to the carnival, the circus and clowns. Early on, Missy refers to Cleaver as a clown;[9]

when she writes a book about her experiences as a prostitute and it is adapted into a Hollywood film, Cleaver's counterpart is depicted by Cate Blanchett as a slapstick, clownish drunk;[10] a judge accuses Cleaver of treating court 'like a carnival sideshow';[11] and Cleaver's best friend, Barney (Russell Dykstra), likens his courtroom antics to a circus.[12]

While the rake-hero is an English character type, the Australian variety has developed distinct differences. In his celebrated text, *The Australian Legend,* Russell Ward describes the 'myth' of the archetypal Australian as

> a practical man, rough and ready in his manners and quick to decry any appearance of affectation in others. He is a great improviser . . . He swears hard and consistently, gambles heavily and often, and drinks deeply on occasion.[13]

This myth descends from historical roots in convict transportation and the bushranging activities of the 19th century. English settlers transported their romantic ideas of highway robbery, and Ward writes that:

> In the eyes of the bush-workers, and of a great many other colonists, bushrangers derived added prestige merely from being, so to speak, the professional opponents of the police. It may be doubted whether the police force of any English-speaking country, except Ireland, has ever been more thoroughly unpopular.[14]

The appeal of the larrikin figure in Australia is connected to the nation's particular history as a colonial country, with many Australians in the mid-20th century abandoning the vestiges of 'cultural cringe' to embrace their convict ancestry and revere bushrangers – particularly Ned Kelly. As Dixson suggests, Australians 'tend to return to convictism'[15] in their search for a national identity.

Unlike the British rake-hero, the Australian bushman archetype gains prestige from his working-class status. In *The Fatal Shore,* Robert Hughes investigates the mythologizing of Australia's convict heritage and suggests that the working classes particularly adopted these myths. He argues that 'the system inadvertently produced Australia's first folk heroes, the bushrangers, most of them escaped prisoners. The basic class division of early colonial Australia – guards versus prisoners – lived on as a metaphor of future disputes there'.[16] Convicts escaped in the Australian bush, turning their backs on their British heritage and embracing their new nation.[17] The choice of criminals such as convicts and bushrangers as the folk heroes of Australian cultural myths marked the nation as separate from Britain, 'where the aristocracy set the tone of the nation and its culture'.[18] The difference between English rakes and their Australian counterparts is thus a class distinction. While Australia also has class divisions, television and literature often celebrate the middle and lower class 'Aussie battler'. National public broadcasters purposefully mythologize this cultural fiction, even though Australian series draw many unavoidable comparisons to the screen cultures of the United States and Britain.[19] One evolving difference between the screen cultures appears to be the Australian admiration of larrikins.

Larrikinism: a national cultural narrative

While Ward does not focus specifically on larrikinism in Australian history, the concept grew in prominence in the 19th century alongside the myth of the rough bushman. The term 'larrikin' was imported to Australia from Warwick or Worcester and Cornish,[20] and its first reported use in the media was in the Melbourne newspaper *The Age* in February 1870. In the article, the author described a visit to a jail in which he met larrikins, described as 'ruffians-in-training rather than the genuine article'.[21] In her comprehensive history of larrikinism in Australia, Bellanta explains that the cultural term once described poor urban youths, mostly found in Melbourne, Sydney and Brisbane, who engaged in minor criminal activities.[22] Its original meaning was negative.[23] The term became more popularly adopted following World War I, and Bellanta writes that

> when Australian soldiers branded themselves "diggers" and began celebrating their affinity with larrikins . . . the term started to detach itself from this connection to an unruly street subculture and acquire the positive inflection it still possesses today.[24]

The term thus has roots in a criminal performance. Larrikinism is a rhetorical 'ultimate term' (to borrow Weaver's phrase) that is often used to typify the ideal Australian. It fulfils the notion of a 'charismatic term', which Weaver defines as a word that 'operate[s] independently' of historical meanings through the power of popular consent.[25] The repeated insistence that the larrikin is an Australian archetype can be witnessed through the country's literary history.

Literature – written and on screen – often presents Australian audiences with larrikin protagonists, who provide an Australian angle to the 'primitive rebels'[26] and picaresque protagonists of European literature. In the decades before Federation, the *Bulletin* school of writers created a certain Australian spirit through their protagonists, who were 'the bushman, the larrikin, and the good mate . . . [and] this writing depended on a nostalgia for a disappearing type of Australian man'.[27] C.J. Dennis's bestselling *The Songs of a Sentimental Bloke* (1915) followed a larrikin who reformed himself by marriage to his sweetheart.[28] In another text, *The Moods of Ginger Mick* (1916), Dennis told the tales of a digger larrikin.[29] The big and small screens constitute other media in which the larrikin figure has featured prominently – often as a criminal, as in *Chopper* (2000),[30] *Underbelly* (2008–13)[31] and various Ned Kelly films.

Each of these examples is based on a real case – the *Bulletin* school founded its larrikins in disappearing bushmen, Ginger Mick's antics were grounded in real tales of digger debauchery in Egypt and *Underbelly* and *Chopper* fictionalize real criminal narratives. Likewise, Cleaver is often linked to two real-life 'larrikins': contentious Sydney barrister Charles Waterstreet,[32] who identifies as a larrikin in his memoir,[33] often claims that the character is based on him. Richard Roxburgh vehemently denies these claims, however, particularly following recent scandals in which Waterstreet was accused of sexual harassment.[34] A comparison made less often that might hold more weight is that of Cleaver to Australian politician Cleaver Bunton, who was infamously appointed to fill a vacant Senate position in 1975 against the usual conventions and went on to act independently of both major political parties. Likewise, the fictional Cleaver is unexpectedly voted into the Senate as an independent senator in the finale of the fourth season of the series.

While larrikin literature is often based in reality, the stories are heightened and dramatized as a national cultural narrative. In the case of the ABC, this narrative is subsidized through national policy. Drawing on Anthony D. Smith's writing about the construction of national culture,[35] O'Regan suggests:

> We can usually distinguish between two interrelated aspects of this common national culture: the *national political* – the common political and civic culture involving citizenship and equality before the law – and the *national cultural* – the cultural core of memories, values, customs, myths, symbols, solidarities and significant landscapes shaping 'Australian' identity. Television sustains both kinds of national definitions. If . . . no state can be workable without both a national political and national cultural sense of itself, television matters so much to public policy makers because it is an ongoing forum for national projects and ambitions.[36]

This process of constructing a national culture occurs particularly through narratives, whether in print or on screen. As Elder suggests:

> National narratives are usually based on real historical events – indeed, historical stories and myths are integral parts of 'imagined communities'. . . . Citizens are encouraged to draw on these shared sets of understandings and feelings of what it means to be Australian.[37]

Further, she points out that these narratives take place through real structures, including official policies and laws, and popular journalism, advertising and television.[38] The ABC is editorially independent, mostly funded by the federal government, and has a charter contained in the *Australian Broadcasting Corporation Act* that requires it to broadcast 'programs that contribute to a sense of national identity'.[39] The ABC's 2018 *Annual Report* reveals that 71 per cent of the Australian population engages with ABC publications each week,[40] and 83 per cent of survey respondents 'believe the ABC performs a valuable role in the Australian community'.[41] Popular fictional series by the broadcaster, such as *Mystery Road*, showcase the ABC's offerings for diverse Australians.[42] Seeing ourselves on national television has evolved as an important part of Australian's cultural identity, leading the ABC to fund 'nation-building' series.[43] As O'Regan argues:

> There is no shortage of relations between television and national culture in Australia – identifactory, dramatic, critical, commercial and legislative. Australian content rules are legitimated on the basis that domestically produced television supports national culture.[44]

Into this complex network of Australian policy, culture, media and myth, *Rake* broadcasts particular ideas about white masculinity in contemporary Australia.

Many of these ideas are associated with Cleaver's larrikinism, with all its controversy and cultural significance. He upholds the law through criminal defence, while at the same time he breaks the law (through drug-taking and tax evasion) and disregards both professional ethics and his own personal morals. Throughout the series, he lives in a grungy apartment above the famed Piccolo Bar (named Dario's in the series) in Sydney's red-light district of King's Cross, in the cluttered spare room at his ex-wife's house and in a Canberran townhouse that has an erupting toilet. He has no permanent chambers but is a 'floater'. He also has trouble with family responsibilities, and his son describes him as 'a shit dad' but a 'mate'.[45] Fatherhood is not stereotypically an important part of larrikin life. Elder writes:

> Fatherhood has, over a long period, been represented as being "in crisis" in non-Indigenous Australia. This is not surprising, given that the privileged national narrative centralizes a larrikin, knock-about single man.[46]

Despite his flaws, many Australians are charmed and titillated by Cleaver, whose larrikin behaviour links him to bushranger folk heroes.

Various authors point out the hypocrisy of this kind of folk-hero worship. Julian Burnside, a barrister from Melbourne, questions how Australians can celebrate national values that laud bushrangers like Ned Kelly, but also allow the illegal imprisonment of refugees.[47] Likewise, in his 'Letter from Sydney', New Zealander Martin Edmond notes that:

> the much vaunted larrikinism, the disrespect for authority, the cheerful insolence of many Australians, under pressure subsides and an entirely different demeanour is revealed: anxiety in the face of the power of the law.[48]

Hirst also comments on the contradiction of the larrikin figure with legal realities, suggesting that:

> Australians imagine themselves to be the opposite of obedient. They think of themselves as anti-authority. They love a larrikin. Their most revered national

> hero is a criminal outlaw, the bushranger Ned Kelly. Their unofficial national anthem honours an unemployed vagrant who commits suicide rather than be taken by the police troopers for stealing a sheep.

Yet Hirst argues that, in reality, modern Australians are dutiful.[49] While Hirst is probably correct, the *idea* of larrikinism is celebrated and recognized as an Australian cultural stereotype that is a 'pleasurable and meaningful story'.[50] Thanks to their historical criminality, contemporary 'Australians are now very ready to indulge a larrikin'.[51] This larrikin character adopted by Cleaver is contradictory. He is ultimately forgiven and receives accolades (positions in parliament and the High Court of Australia) because he straddles the boundaries of white privilege and larrikinism.

Lowering the bar: Cleaver's larrikinism

Cleaver's profession in criminal defence links him to historical ideas about larrikins, despite his position of legal power. As journalist John Stanley James described larrikins in 1877,

> the larrikin not only chaffs and annoys the policeman on his beat, but daily crowds the police court, and manifests the liveliest interest in the fate of male or female friends who may be on trial.[52]

This accurately describes Cleaver's actions throughout *Rake*, but his role is professionalized. Although he has social cachet as a barrister, Cleaver is often under an ethical cloud in the law community due to his rakish behaviour. *The Daily Telegraph* newspaper reports on his sleeping with clients,[53] and he breaks professional ethics through his behaviour and dress throughout the series – for instance, he is expelled from events because of his drunkenness. This behaviour links Cleaver to Bellanta's descriptions of early larrikins. As she explains, 'Making trouble at working-class events was another way that groups of larrikins distinguished themselves'.[54] However, unlike Ginger Mick and other early larrikin characters, Cleaver lives and works in privilege. His larrikinism is culturally resonant, rather than class based.

Two events in the series, in which Cleaver is punished for his unethical actions, demonstrate the boundary he straddles between his privileged legal colleagues and his larrikin lifestyle. At the end of Season 2, he fails to legally defeat a con-man in the courtroom, then drunkenly asks an enforcer to scare the con-man, which – through a series of misadventures – concludes with the assassination of the man's elderly neighbour. Cleaver is found guilty of conspiracy to murder and sent to prison for fourteen years with a non-parole period of eight years, of which he serves one year before his conviction is quashed. He is shown to understand his clients from the criminal perspective – indeed, in prison he shares camaraderie with the other prisoners, many of whom he has defended in the past. On the other hand, despite his privileged position as a white man with a highly paid occupation, he is an outsider with his colleagues. In Season 4, he is disgusted that his surprise birthday party is peopled with criminals rather than 'silks',[55] but this is hardly surprising considering that he appears to have more in common with his clients than with his colleagues.

The second time the legal establishment punishes Cleaver is near the end of Season 4; this again demonstrates his contradictory position on the boundary of privilege and larrikinism. After leaving a trial in which his client was unfairly sentenced, Cleaver rants to a reporter about the elderly judge and the justice system. The rant is secretly filmed and broadcast to the public, which leads to the termination of Cleaver's Bar membership. He is astonished that his accurate statements could lead to his termination because he was once suspended for two months for taking cocaine in the court toilets: an ethical violation that was an actual crime.[56] By speaking out against a judge, a white man in an even more favoured position of power than his, Cleaver disconnects himself from the entitled privilege he could enjoy. These two events demonstrate the tension between Cleaver's larrikin performance and his position of power as a barrister.

The ethics of Cleaver as a defence barrister are particularly interesting. While literature sometimes represents the defence of guilty clients as unethical, it is necessary for the successful operation of an adversarial justice system.[57] As Morris writes, laypeople might not understand that guilty clients also deserve representation.[58] Yet there is a special kind of antagonism in the way Cleaver defends those whom no other lawyer will, demonstrating his flexible morality. In some cases, it may appeal to Australian viewers who feel kinship with ancestors transported for petty crimes. In other cases, it may force viewers to confront how larrikin ideals should not always be applied to the law. Viewers are asked to appreciate Cleaver's troubles, but any extended reflection will cause viewers to question cultural myths of larrikinism and class. Cleaver wins an average of 51 per cent of trials, which he says is good when you think that 99 per cent of his clients are guilty,[59] often of crimes that many viewers would consider immoral and offensive.

The tension between Cleaver's roles as a rake and a larrikin are represented through his class, dress and language. As a white male barrister, Cleaver should hold a powerful position, but he is reduced to poverty by his excesses and bad decisions. While he has a much more highly paid position than the larrikin youths of the 19th century, Cleaver rarely has access to his earnings as a result of his own actions. An important characterization of the extravagant rake is 'his indebtedness and the poverty his wild courses have brought upon him'.[60] On the other hand, Cleaver's disdain for snobbery suggests an egalitarian stance. Bellanta argues that the larrikin myth is no longer tied to specific classes, writing that:

> The larrikin myth is all about engaging in a performance of egalitarian Australianness, usually via the exhibition of ocker vernacular and the anti-intellectualism this implies. In its roguish informality, it is also a way to portray oneself as non-conformist, whether or not this bears any relation to everyday realities.[61]

Cleaver is a combination of the rake-hero and the larrikin; he is privileged and spoiled, but also performs a larrikin role.

The tension between Cleaver's dual roles is represented both visually and verbally. As a barrister, Cleaver has a position of power in the law, and yet his non-conformity distances him from that power. Even when he wears his barrister's wig, it sits at a jaunty, haphazard angle. His untidy appearance is often sneered at by colleagues. This mode of dress also has links to historical performances of larrikinism. As Bellanta writes, the archetypal Anzac digger demonstrated his anti-authoritarian stance through sloppy attire that was 'meant to complement his lack of interest in social niceties'.[62] Despite his contrary disregard for pretentions, though, rich clients (particularly men) seek Cleaver's professional services. For example, Season 2 introduces Missy's rich and moralistic fiancé, Joshua Floyd (Martin Henderson).[63] Scenes cut between a speech Floyd gives to the media, in which he refers to Draco (the first legislator of Athens in Ancient Greece), and Cleaver's summation in defence of a man obsessed with areolas. The contrasting scenes highlight how Cleaver linguistically represents his larrikin attitude. When Floyd jokingly commends Cleaver on his summation, Cleaver responds, 'Well, I was going to invoke the ghost of the Athenian, Draco, but it felt – what's the word? – pretentious'. Both despite and because of Cleaver's larrikin attitude, Floyd requests his legal representation. Floyd needs a lawyer 'who's prepared to play outside of the rules. Someone who can say "mammophile" without flinching'.[64] The entire scene demonstrates the performative aspect of larrikin behaviour in modern Australia, as well as its connection to 'mateship'. By performing as a larrikin, even though he occupies a position of privilege, Cleaver is rewarded with a lucrative client. The disjunction between this outcome and the idea of equality can raise questions for ambivalent Australian audiences, who both appreciate and condemn larrikinism.

Rake's continuing popularity may lead to questions about why Cleaver's bad behaviour is appreciated by Australian audiences. Cleaver sleeps with his best friend's wife, takes drugs and is imprisoned and disbarred yet many viewers ultimately forgive him. Their forgiveness could be attributed to his larrikinism. As Bellanta explains:

> To be a larrikin is to be sceptical and irreverent, to knock authority and mock pomposity. . . . To call someone a larrikin is also to excuse their bad behaviour, offering an affectionate slant on their disrespect for social niceties and raucous drunkenness with mates.[65]

Cleaver's morals align him with criminals, but also with the Australian viewers who root for those criminals. In one review, he is described contradictorily as 'an honest rogue'.[66] When Cleaver distances himself from the authority of the legal Bar, he connects with an audience of layperson viewers who may find the (fictional) establishment condescending and un-egalitarian. His disbarment is a final act of separation. While the rake-hero of Restoration dramas was often redeemed through marriage, the larrikin character often shuns the institution as a trap. Cleaver's return to the law after his appalling attempt at politics and swearing in as the new Chief Justice – Australia's highest positioned judicial officer who presides over the High Court – is his character's redemption in the finale of Season 5.[67] His estrangement from ex-wife Wendy (Caroline Brazier) allows her to continue to act as the 'voice of reason' in the series – a fitting role for a therapist. Perhaps, the series seems to suggest, it is time for Australians to divorce themselves from bad behaviour, rather than rewarding it as the stamp of larrikinism.

The larrikin approach to legal liberalism

Three of Cleaver's trials demonstrate how he abuses the ideals of moral liberalism to defend the immoral crimes of affluent white men. The idea of liberalism in legal morality is often attributed to John Stuart Mill's *On Liberty* (1859), in which he states that

> the only purpose for which power can be rightfully exercised over any member of a civilized community, against his will, is to prevent harm to others. His own good, either physical or moral, is not a sufficient warrant.[68]

From Mill's work, many legal scholars have attempted to craft a workable harm principle that would aid the law in protecting its citizens from harm while not overstepping into their autonomy by entering subjective morals into law. As Greenawalt suggests:

> If every unpleasant feeling or negative thought counted as harm, an act might be prohibited because it made some people envious or disturbed them. With such an expansive notion of harm, enforcement of all aspects of morality could be swallowed up as prevention of harm to others.[69]

Many legal scholars agree that moral ills such as lying and cheating should not be punished by criminal law.[70] Joel Feinberg defines liberalism as 'the view that the harm and offense principles, *and only these*, state good and relevant reasons for state coercion by means of the criminal law'.[71] The opposing conservative viewpoint supports 'a social order in which the state is more heavily involved in the regulation of moral behavior'.[72] Harm can constitute many effects, which are not only physical, and contemporary liberals argue that many autonomous arrangements between consenting adults should be illegal.[73]

Feinberg's addition of an offence principle qualifies some occurrences that are not covered by the harm principle, but there is also much dissent about what offences should be criminally punishable. Simpson argues that 'while regulating offense impairs people's liberty, leaving it unchecked sometimes does as well. The law's legitimate purpose in regulating offense, then, derives, from the liberal's core ideal: protecting individual liberty'.[74] To illustrate the wide range of offences that should or should not be criminalized, Feinberg writes a story in *Offense to Others* about a series of offensive acts performed on a public bus. These acts range from the repulsive but unharmful offences of burping and eating vomit to the more outrageous, such as sex acts with animals and desecration of human corpses.[75] Feinberg concludes that his examples demonstrate

> that to suffer such experiences, at least in their extreme forms, is an evil; but that to the normal person (like the reader) such experiences, unpleasant as they are, do not cause or constitute harm.[76]

The offences are supposedly unharmful because a witness of the acts is able to ignore them or leave.[77] Scoccia argues that:

> The problem with a theory that permits criminalization only on the basis of the harm and offense principles is that it is *under-inclusive,* ruling out laws that most liberals believe are justified.[78]

He then goes on to use corpse desecration as an example of a 'free floating evil' that fits into Feinberg's conception of liberal moralism in the law, but that most libertarians would agree should be criminalized. The cannibal case in *Rake*'s inaugural episode demonstrates this kind of trial, but it is prosecuted as murder rather than corpse desecration.

In the episode, Cleaver defends Professor Murray, an economist (performed by Hugo Weaving) on trial for murder after he cannibalized a maritime lawyer, who gave full, legal consent in a video before committing suicide. Cannibalism, it is revealed in the episode, is not illegal in the state of New South Wales, and so the economist is charged with murder. Cleaver jokes that convincing the jury that Professor Murray is not a murderer is easy: 'It's easier than convincing them that an economist is a human being'.[79] Although the video definitively proves that Murray did not commit murder, it seems that he will be imprisoned based on the jury's perception of him as a cold, conceited economist. Consequently, Cleaver finds that he really does need to convince jurors that an economist is a human being. In cross-examination, he questions Murray's failure to predict the global financial crisis and, at this strategic moment of vulnerability, has Murray's estranged wife enter the courtroom. Murray breaks down in tears and confesses how sorry he is to have harmed his wife (who – thinking it was chicken – imbibed human flesh seasoned with garlic, white wine, pepper and a little balsamic) and yells, 'I'd never do anything to hurt her. I didn't mean to hurt anyone. I'm not a killer, I'm an economist!' The jury feels more morally aligned with Cleaver's client following this demonstration of human fallibility, and he is found not guilty.

Another episode of *Rake* focuses on the 'unharmful offence' of having sex with animals,[80] one of the more extreme examples provided by Feinberg. The episode follows the trial of obstetrician Dr Bruce Chandler (played by Sam Neil) after a video is discovered that shows him having sex with the family dog. While H.L.A.

Hart argues that cruelty to animals is not truly an example of legal moralism, as 'the law is here concerned with the *suffering*, albeit only of animals, rather than with the immorality of torturing them',[81] Cleaver's liberal argument references Australian moral philosopher Peter Singer, claims that sex with animals does not necessarily involve harm and argues that Chandler 'didn't hurt anyone or anything'. Further, Cleaver argues that the law is a 'devastating hypocrisy' when humans use animals more harmfully for sport, testing and food. He thus appeals to jury nullification for the crime of animal cruelty – that is, he attempts to persuade the jury to find Chandler innocent because they disagree with the law, despite overwhelming evidence that he has committed the crime. Cleaver's appeal for jury nullification is another example of his contrariness, as the practice is 'openly condemned and surreptitiously fostered',[82] and causes both censure and praise within the legal community.[83] He makes the jury watch the video multiple times, 'frame by frame', until its contents evolve from offensive to boring. In this way, his approach is to counteract the offensiveness of the evidence through familiarization, until it no longer appears so offensive. Although Feinberg includes boredom as an offence, he writes:

> After considering such jolts to sensibility [as the offenses related to shame, revulsion, and morality], it may seem altogether anticlimactic to turn to the offenses [related to boredom . . .] of such a common type that we suffer from it to some degree almost every day of our lives.[84]

Cleaver's tactic of changing an offence of sensibility into a boring one works, and Chandler is found not guilty.

Bigamy is another crime based on moral reasoning that Feinberg argues should not be a criminal felony. He writes that the second marriage should not be legally defined as a marriage, and that – like adultery – laws against bigamy should be repealed.[85] In an episode of *Rake*, Cleaver defends George Dana, a chef accused of bigamy.[86] The problematic core of this crime is whether Dana has caused harm to his wives. The trial appears to be progressing in Cleaver's favour, particularly when the two wives agree that the defendant is an excellent husband and father. The prosecution argues that Dana has no regard for 'the moral laws that underpin our society', while Cleaver points out the liberal view that infidelity is legally preferable, and morality is a 'peculiarly individual matter'. The jurors find Dana guilty; however, the judge finds merit in Cleaver's liberal arguments and hands down a lenient sentence.

These examples demonstrate how Cleaver defends clients who have broken moral codes, and he often wins these cases. The judgement of viewers on his clients' morality is subjective, no matter what shared cultural ideals Australians may have on larrikinism and criminality. As Morawetz argues about legal fiction:

> The critical challenge plays havoc with [conservative and liberal] attitudes by raising the possibility that the moral dimensions of law (and morality

> generally) may depend on the beholder (the reader), that the very nature of legal texts and legal institutions may depend on whether they are seen by winners or losers, and that therefore the very idea that law is the sort of thing about which one can make objective claims rather than offer endless fictions may itself be an illusion.[87]

Indeed, viewers may cringe at the crimes committed by Cleaver's clients and feel that they would be less inclined to find in his favour if they served on the fictional jury. While viewers may find that Cleaver's clients are immoral, and that he (undoubtedly) has an important role in releasing them back into the public domain, it is clear that the reason he can defend these particular cases is because of his own anti-authoritarian, larrikin character. He can say 'mammophile' without flinching. The series asks viewers to make judgements not only on the crimes of Cleaver's clients, but also on his personal and professional actions. Out of the three examples provided here, it is interesting to note that the bigamist was found guilty, whereas the cannibal and the animal abuser were found not guilty because Cleaver appealed to emotion and boredom. These outcomes are unlikely to be replicated in a real Australian courtroom; however, they demonstrate how privileged men like Cleaver use larrikinism and moral liberalism to avoid punishment for their immoral actions.

Conclusion: what is an American larrikin?

Rake cleverly capitalizes on the cultural myths of larrikinism in order to challenge its national audience. As Cunningham argues, 'television is fundamentally a local medium'.[88] Perhaps its distinct Australianness is the reason the series did not translate well across the Pacific in 2014. The US version (starring Greg Kinnear) ran for a single season before its cancellation. Cleaver's larrikin behaviour and questionable morals were watered down in the adaptation – for example, the cannibal episode that opened the Australian series was preceded by three more tame episodes in the American version, to avoid immediate offence.[89] According to show creator Peter Duncan, American screen culture is more idealistic and religiously influenced, and they love heroic protagonists.[90] The idealistic trial series is one audiences have seen before. As Cleaver explains about giving juries idealistic truths, 'Mate, that jury between them would have watched ten thousand episodes of *Law and Order*. They've heard all that shit before'.[91] Avoiding offence dissolves the underlying questions about larrikinism in Australian cultures, a point of difference between Cleaver and other legal protagonists. Lyons argues that *Rake* broadcasts 'a distinctly Australian cultural environment . . . with Cleaver embodying a more nuanced version of the Aussie battler'.[92] Indeed, it is hard to translate the word 'larrikin', with its criminal history and cultural influence, to an American equivalent. That does not mean that citizens of other countries will not appreciate the original. The Australian series is available on the streaming giant Netflix in Australia, New Zealand, the United States, Canada, the United Kingdom, Ireland, the Netherlands and India. While Netflix does not release viewing statistics, it has clearly found an international audience for the Australian version.

ABC television has policy issues around whether to aim for a culturally significant product or to compete in a global commercial market,[93] often brought up in political arguments about privatization. Without policy and funding for the creation of Australian content, there is doubt that much local drama would be written, filmed and distributed. *Rake* aired its fifth season in 2018, coincidentally demonstrating the destructive influence of Cleaver on federal government at the time of yet another leadership spill in Australian federal politics. The toppling of the sign in the series' opening credits was mirrored by the literal implosion of Parliament House in the final episode.[94] The implosion is reminiscent of Bellanta's comments on the longevity of the larrikin figure in Australian culture. As she writes, 'Since it appears to hold a special appeal for white men in their fifties or older, it is a real question whether or not the larrikin myth will remain relevant in the future'.[95] The term was once negative and based on a type of bushman who was already disappearing. Its current connotation as a cultural performance has led some Australians to admire the supposed rebelliousness of men such as Charles Waterstreet, but other Australians are beginning to hold larrikins to account for their actions. If, as Weaver argues, an 'ultimate term' needs popular consent to gain its cultural status, it can also lose that status; however, larrikinism is still deeply entrenched in Australian culture. As Bellanta notes, it has begun to encompass a wider variety of Australians, from a range of ethnic, socio-economic and gender backgrounds.[96] Further, the figure is a myth, perpetuated by policy, literature and cultural and political narratives. For the years that *Rake* has been broadcast on Australia's free-to-air national station, the larrikin figure of Cleaver Greene has confronted viewers with moral questions, which connect to egalitarian and anti-authoritarian national myths. What in the Bob Menzies will Australians do without him on their screens?

Notes

1 Hazard (1995), p 449.
2 See Asimow (2009), particularly chapters by Bergman, pp 177–88; Ross, pp 195–204; and Greenfield, Osborn and Robson, pp 205–16.
3 Hume (1977), p 30.
4 Hume (1977), p 33.
5 Hume (1977), p 38.
6 Hume (1977), p 39.
7 Jordan (1972), pp 87–8.
8 The music is performed by David McCormack, a member of the iconic Australian rock band Custard.
9 *Rake* (2010), S1 Ep 2.
10 *Rake* (2014), S3 Ep 3.
11 *Rake* (2016), S4 Ep 5.
12 *Rake* (2016), S4 Ep 6.
13 Ward (1958), pp 1–2.

14 Ward (1958), pp 136, 144.
15 Dixson (1999), p 112.
16 Hughes (1986), p 158.
17 Hughes (1986), p 243.
18 Elder (2007), p 50.
19 Carter (2002), p 84.
20 Moore (2010), p 106.
21 Bellanta (2012), p 4.
22 Bellanta (2012), p xiv.
23 Moore (2010), p 106.
24 Bellanta (2012), p xv.
25 Weaver (1985), p 227.
26 Hobsbawm (1959).
27 Elder (2007), p 190.
28 Dennis (1915).
29 Dennis (1916); see Hirst (2007), pp 66–8.
30 Dominik (2000) *Chopper*.
31 *Underbelly* (2008–13).
32 Waterstreet has acted as criminal defence in many high-profile cases, including Glen McNamara's murder trial and Evie Amati's recent axe attack in Newtown, Sydney. Artist Nigel Milsom won the Archibald Prize in 2015 with a portrait of Waterstreet, who defended him.
33 Waterstreet (1998).
34 Maddox (2017).
35 Smith (1986), pp 129–39.
36 O'Regan (1993), p 81.
37 Elder (2007), p 25.
38 Elder (2007), p 29.
39 *Australian Broadcasting Corporation Act 1983* (Cth), s 6.
40 Australian Broadcasting Corporation (2018), p 22.
41 Australian Broadcasting Corporation (2018), p 20.
42 *Mystery Road* (2018–).
43 O'Regan (1993), p 8.
44 O'Regan (1993), p 80.
45 *Rake* (2010), S1 Ep 6.
46 Elder (2007), p 86.
47 Burnside (2007), p 15.
48 Carey (2016), p 291.
49 Hirst (2007), p 135.
50 Elder (2007), p 34.
51 Hirst (2007), p 63.
52 Hirst (2007), p 64.
53 *Rake* (2010), S1 Ep 3.
54 Bellanta (2012), p 15.
55 *Rake* (2016), S4 Ep 4.
56 *Rake* (2016), S4 Ep 7.
57 Talbot (2017), pp 25–6.
58 Morris (2013), p 628.
59 *Rake* (2012), S2 Ep 3.
60 Jordan (1972), p 77.
61 Bellanta (2012), p 182.
62 Bellanta (2012), p 172.

63 *Rake* (2012), S2 Ep 4.
64 *Rake* (2012), S2 Ep 4.
65 Bellanta (2012), p xii.
66 Schwartzkoff (2010), para 5.
67 *Rake* (2018), S5 Ep 8.
68 Mill (2011), p 18.
69 Greenawalt (2010), p 468.
70 Carr (2004), p 4.
71 Feinberg (1986), p 3.
72 Hovenkamp (1997), p 1435.
73 Carr (2004), p 8; Hart (1963), p 33.
74 Simpson (2018), p 239.
75 Feinberg (1985), pp 10–13.
76 Feinberg (1985), p 14.
77 Feinberg (1985), p 22.
78 Scoccia (2013), p 515. Original emphasis.
79 *Rake* (2010), S1 Ep 1.
80 *Rake* (2010), S1 Ep 5.
81 Hart (1963), p 34.
82 Duvall (2012), p 412.
83 Fissell (2013); McKnight (2013).
84 Feinberg (1985), p 20.
85 Feinberg (1986), pp 265–6.
86 *Rake* (2010), S1 Ep 3.
87 Morawetz (2010), pp 455–6.
88 Cunningham (2008), p 144.
89 Robert Siegal, Interview with Ben Neutze recorded by *NPR*, 1 May 2014.
90 Idato (2014).
91 *Rake* (2016), S4 Ep 6.
92 Lyons (2016), para 12.
93 Cunningham (2008), p 145.
94 *Rake* (2018), S5 Ep 8.
95 Bellanta (2012), p 188.
96 Bellanta (2012), p 188.

References

Secondary sources

Michael Asimow (ed.) (2009) *Lawyers in Your Living Room! Law on Television*, American Bar Association.

Australian Broadcasting Corporation (2018) *Annual Report Volume 1*, https://about.abc.net.au/wp-content/uploads/2018/10/AP18_Vol1_FINALnew.pdf.

Melissa Bellanta (2012) *Larrikins: A History*, University of Queensland Press.

Julian Burnside (2007) 'Australian Values' 79 *AQ: Australian Quarterly* 15.

Gabrielle Carey (2016) 'On Being Australian: A Provocation' 51 *Griffith Review* 288.

Craig L. Carr (2004) 'Between Virtue and Vice: The Legal Enforcement of Morals' 14 *Kansas Journal of Law and Public Policy* 1.

David Carter (2002) 'Going, Going, Gone? Britishness and Englishness in Contemporary Australian Culture' 169 *Overland* 81.

Stuart Cunningham (2008) *In the Vernacular: A Generation of Australian Culture and Controversy*, University of Queensland Press.
C.J. Dennis (1915) *Songs of a Sentimental Bloke*, Angus & Robertson.
——— (1916) *The Moods of Ginger Mick*, Angus & Robertson.
Miriam Dixson (1999) *The Imaginary Australian: Anglo-Celts and Identity – 1788 to the Present*, UNSW Press.
Keith Duvall (2012) 'The Contradictory Stance on Jury Nullification' 88 *North Dakota Law Review* 409.
Catriona Elder (2007) *Being Australian: Narratives of National Identity*, Allen & Unwin.
Joel Feinberg (1985) *The Moral Limits of the Criminal Law, Vol. 2: Offense to Others*, Oxford University Press.
——— (1986) *The Moral Limits of the Criminal Law, Vol. 3: Harm to Self*, Oxford University Press.
Brenner M. Fissell (2013) 'Jury Nullification and the Rule of Law' 19 *Legal Theory* 217.
Kent Greenawalt (2010) 'Legal Enforcement of Morality', in Dennis Patterson (ed.), *A Companion to Philosophy of Law and Legal Theory*, Blackwell.
H.L.A. Hart (1963) *Law, Liberty, and Morality: The Harry Camp Lectures at Stanford*, Stanford University Press.
Geoffrey C. Hazard Jr (1995) 'Law, Morals, and Ethics' 19 *Southern Illinois Law Journal* 447.
John Hirst (2007) *The Australians: Insiders and Outsiders on the National Character Since 1770*, Black Inc.
E.J. Hobsbawm (1959) *Primitive Rebels: Studies in Archaic Forms of Social Movement in the 19th and 20th Centuries*, Manchester University Press.
H. Hovenkamp (1997) 'Law and Morals in Classical Legal Thought' 82 *Iowa Law Review* 1427.
Robert Hughes (1986) *The Fatal Shore*, Alfred A. Knopf.
Robert D. Hume (1977) 'The Myth of the Rake in Restoration Comedy' 10 *Studies in the Literary Imagination* 25.
Michael Idato (2014) 'Can Our *Rake* Survive the US Culture?', *Sydney Morning Herald*, 5 January, www.smh.com.au/entertainment/tv-and-radio/can-our-rake-survive-the-us-culture-20140104-30aq9.html.
Robert Jordan (1972) 'The Extravagant Rake in Restoration Comedy', in Harold Love (ed.), *Restoration Literature: Critical Approaches*, Methuen.
Siobhan Lyons (2016) 'Bloody Good TV: How *Rake* Changed Australian Television', *The Conversation*, 7 July, https://theconversation.com/bloody-good-tv-how-rake-changed-australian-television-61433.
Garry Maddox (2017) 'Richard Roxburgh: "Any Day I Don't Hear the Name Charles Waterstreet Is Good"', *Sydney Morning Herald*, 27 October, www.smh.com.au/entertainment/tv-and-radio/richard-roxburgh-any-day-i-dont-hear-the-name-charles-waterstreet-is-good-20171027-gz9efk.html.
Aaron McKnight (2013) 'Jury Nullification as a Tool to Balance the Demand of Law and Justice' 4 *Brigham Young University Law Review* 1103.
John Stuart Mill (2011) *On Liberty* (2nd ed.), Project Gutenberg.
Bruce Moore (2010) *What's Their Story? A History of Australian Words*, Oxford University Press.
Thomas Morawetz (2010) 'Law and Literature', in Dennis Patterson (ed.), *A Companion to Philosophy of Law and Legal Theory*, Blackwell.

Grant Morris (2013) 'Devils Down Under: Perceptions of Lawyers' Ethics in New Zealand Fiction' 44 *Victoria University of Wellington Review* 628.
Tom O'Regan (1993) *Australian Television Culture*, Allen & Unwin.
Louis Schwartzkoff (2010) '*Rake*'s Excess', *Sydney Morning Herald*, 1 November, www.smh.com.au/entertainment/tv-and-radio/rakes-excess-20101101-179m8.html.
Danny Scoccia (2013) 'In Defense of "Pure" Legal Moralism' 7 *Criminal Law and Philosophy* 513.
Robert Siegel and Ben Neutze (2014) 'Meanwhile in Australia: A Bawdier, Riskier *Rake*', *NPR*, 1 May, www.npr.org/2014/05/01/308737975/meanwhile-in-australia-a-bawdier-riskier-rake.
Robert Mark Simpson (2018) 'Regulating Offense, Nurturing Offense' 17 *Politics, Philosophy & Economics* 235.
Anthony D. Smith (1986) *The Ethnic Origins of Nations*, Basil Blackwell.
Brian Talbot (2017) 'Replaceable Lawyers and Guilty Defendants' 14 *Journal of Moral Philosophy* 25.
Russel Ward (1958) *The Australian Legend*, Oxford University Press.
Charles Waterstreet (1998) *Precious Bodily Fluids: A Larrikin's Memoir*, Sceptre.
Richard M. Weaver (1985) *The Ethics of Rhetoric*, Hermagoras Press.

Films and television series

Chopper (2000), First Look Pictures.
Mystery Road (2018–), All3Media.
Rake (2010–18), Blow by Blow Productions and Essential Media and Entertainment (S1–5).
Underbelly (2008–13), Art Company and Screentime.

Primary legal sources

Australian Broadcasting Corporation Act 1983 (Cth).

Chapter 11

Eyes wide shut

Homosociality, justice and male rape through an Australian lens

Bruce Baer Arnold

Introduction

This chapter is about mobility, violence and images – on screen and in our minds – of men behaving badly. It offers a dark and queer reading of Australian film and Australian identity. It aims to provide a perspective rather than an exhaustive truth about law, film and social solidarity. The contention is that the depiction in Australian cinema of male-on-male rape offers a lens for understanding masculinity, homosociality and justice within Australia and across the globe. The following pages use that lens for a subversive view of mateship, a male social solidarity that is a supposedly distinctive expression of Australian values. The same lens also offers a view of how Australian films engage with power, justice and silence.

Male rape is a sexualized assault that objectifies the victim and valorizes the perpetrator as powerful and thus either making the rules or outside them. It is a recurring but largely unrecognized feature of the Australian screen. Once looked for, it is evident in such iconic works as *Wake in Fright* (1971),[1] *The Chant of Jimmie Blacksmith* (1978),[2] *Mad Max* (1979)[3] and *Ghosts . . . of the Civil Dead* (1988).[4] Those works often use distinctly Australian landscapes and voices, which are clearly neither of the American West nor the snow-clad forests and rain-swept streets that background 'Nordic Noir'.

The films involve brutality with an Australian accent, which is expressed in an environment in which legal authority is absent, weak or indifferent. That authority is a matter of socially accepted and publicly enforced conventions about rules and remedies. The environment is one in which there are bystanders: the homosocial 'mates' whose deepest emotional relationships are with each other but who remain silent about any expression of their own homoerotic desires. Those bystanders are complicit, contemptuous or even amused by the 'unmanning' of a victim through force or intoxication. The four films discussed in this chapter depict rape as placing the victim – unlike the perpetrator – outside the social solidarity that is central to mateship. The films therefore lack the redemptive ending of noble suffering and triumph over adversity that is a feature of US films such as *The Shawshank Redemption* (1994),[5] *American History X* (1998)[6] and *Midnight Express* (1978).[7]

This chapter suggests that the four films offer a view of male belonging, power, complicity and exclusion that is at odds with the recent Australian celebration of difference in *Priscilla, Queen of the Desert* (1994),[8] *The Sum of Us* (1994)[9] and *Holding the Man* (2015).[10] The view is also at odds with American adventures such as *Deliverance*,[11] where heroic masculinity is sufficiently self-confident to support a male victim. If 'mateship' is a distinctively – albeit increasingly fictive – Australian value, the films offer a dark view of complicity and violence within the sunburnt country, a land of sweeping plains, kangaroos and male eyes that are wide shut to brutality. Those eyes are male because women (and values of empathy) are absent. At a global level, the films tell us something interesting about the anxieties at the heart of manhood and about the efficacy of law where sexual victimization excludes men from justice.

The first part of this chapter considers homosociality as an aspect of the 'Australian character' and 'Australian film'. The second part contextualizes the discussion by considering aspects of male-on-male rape. That sexual assault is an offence that encompasses what has historically been dubbed rape, sodomy, indecency or buggery, but is not restricted to anal penetration.[12] Rape is a matter of power rather than, to adapt a characterization by Keneally, the white phallus.[13] This part notes the challenging nature of data about rape in Australia. It suggests we can fruitfully ask questions about law by looking at cinematic depictions of sexual assault. The third part identifies the depiction of male rape in four films, works that are regarded by Australian audiences or critics as representatively Australian. Those films are examined for insights about masculinity, belonging and law, including a bureaucratic indifference that potentially is universal. The final part provides a conclusion about the performance of power on screen and in real life.

Homosociality and the Australian lens

Is the Australian lens, in engaging with law (most specifically the characterization of male rape and its legal consequences), more than kangaroos, Akubra hats, corrugated iron on the roof of a remote pub or a car chase down a desert highway that could equally be in Arizona or Namibia? If we dub the supposedly unintelligible Australian accent damned by US film critics reviewing *Mad Max*,[14] is the lens mid-Pacific – a lens that is increasingly cosmopolitan rather than parochial and thus not distinctive?[15] Are some of the films an instance of offshore 'ozploitation', reflected in one critic's astringent dismissal of *Wake in Fright* as simply a 'parking space' for a Canadian director and a British star?[16]

One response to that question is that Australian feature film often embodies an ideology of mateship and masculinity.[17] That embodiment valorizes what many Australians choose to conceptualize as 'most Australian', a manifestation of Australian values and relationships that are superior to those of other cultures. The ideology of mateship is gendered, homosocial and populist. It is an ideology in which men often have their most significant, but typically unstated, emotional connection with each other: their mates.[18]

It is an ideology that valorizes particular attributes such as physical strength, resilience, initiative, risk-taking, practicality, competitiveness, drinking and gambling. It is evident in respect for manual labour, awkwardness in interaction with women (in some instances a marked misogyny),[19] disrespect for elites and education, wariness about language,[20] contempt for physical/emotional weakness, acceptance of sexualized humour, advocacy of an egalitarian 'fair go', opposition to 'dobbing' and a perception that life outside cities is at its most authentic. It is an ideology propagated through popular film, through official rhetoric such as Anzac Day and Australia Day speeches,[21] explanations of law,[22] public administration[23] and norms in the day-by-day lives of ordinary men.[24] Robert Hughes noted that it was enshrined in the Australian legend but suggested that in part it was a convict import rather than indigenous. He thus referred to

> Mateship, fatalism, contempt for do-gooders and God-botherers, harsh humour, opportunism, survivors' disdain for introspection, and an attitude to authority in which private resentment mingled with ostensible resignation. . . . They also brought, if men, the phallocracy of tavern and ken, and, if women, a kind of tough passivity, a way of seeing life without expectations.[25]

It is an ideology many men – particularly those in a bureaucratized workplace – find it hard to live up to. It is at odds with the realities of contemporary life, such as the ongoing depopulation of the rural Australia in which the iconic stockman (an individual with the same function as a US cowboy) represents exemplary masculinity. It situates the toughest, roughest, most emotionally distant and most aggressive man as the one most deserving of respect and worthy of emulation. That man will, on occasion, be the most disturbed man among his peers, prepared to unthinkingly enforce his will and impose his desires on his mates. His superiority is not a function of lineage, class or intellect; it is instead a function of the capability to exercise power and the weakness of inhibitions about that exercise.

Australian homosociality is accompanied by uneasiness about the expression of affection towards mates, potentially perceived as an indication of homosexual desire. It is thus appropriate in a moment of emotional exuberance to hug your mates after your team wins the football match or to huddle in a trench for warmth and comfort under existential challenge at Gallipoli or the Somme, two battles enshrined by Australian cinema during the past 90 years.[26]

In the land of mateship, it is not appropriate to kiss, caress or communicate emotional needs unless intoxicated.

Incomprehension, hostility and homophobia are the flipside of Australian homosociality in the bush or on the beaches of Bondi and Gallipoli,[27] with masculinity potentially being asserted through sexual assault that denies the autonomy of a victimized male. Because that assertion is coercive, it cannot be condemned by peers as homosexual. Within the lens of mateship, such assault is a matter of performing or subverting authority rather than a manifestation of a stigmatized sexual affinity. It is about power, not affection or desire.

Rape in front of the lens: power and complicity

Rape is a matter of law and social values. Susan Brownmiller provocatively characterized rape as

> a sexual invasion of the body by force, an incursion into the private, personal inner space without consent . . . [that] constitutes a deliberate violation of emotional, physical and rational integrity and is a hostile degrading act of violence.[28]

Her preoccupation is with gendered relationships. Yet sexual assaults on males, typically but not exclusively by male perpetrators, have a long history in both law and culture.[29] Male rape occurs in Australia.[30] As an expression of power, it can be discerned as universal. It has, for example, been a feature of action by armed forces since at least the time of the Romans, with defeated officers and troops being violated as both a signifier of submission and a 'release' for victors after the battle. It is evident in total institutions such as prisons, with depictions in various national cinemas.[31] It is also evident in migration detention facilities and places of enforced residence by young people – for example, homes operated by religious organizations.

That activity is apparent in studies of victimization,[32] litigation regarding offenders and bystanders,[33] proposals for institutional reform[34] and tropes in popular culture, such as 'don't drop the soap'.[35] Male rape is also increasingly evident in litigation and media accounts of sexualized violence outside those institutions. Changes to social attitudes are reflected in increasing numbers of reports of assaults on gay and straight males, adults or youths, who were attacked while in public places; abused by a partner; or, in what is dubbed 'date rape', involving a casual contact met in a social setting such as a bar or on an online dating platform such as Grindr.[36] Fear of assault has been used to legitimate violence against gay and other men under the so-called homosexual panic defence.[37]

Characterizations of rape in law and in common understandings of what is permissible or wrong have varied considerably over time. In part, that variation reflects historically contingent views of sexual expression and masculinity. The Romans, for example, in valorizing agency, stigmatized the recipient of sexual penetration as 'unmanly'. Late mediaeval and Tudor jurists condemned every participant in 'unnatural vice' as guilty of an abomination, irrespective of consent. They established a crime that was both silenced because it was unnamable but sufficiently capacious to encompass both buggery (at times construed as oral rather than merely anal penetration) and mutual masturbation.

In contemporary Australian courts, journalists, rights advocates, criminologists and others have come to engage with what was traditionally erased from public discourse as too offensive or shameful to be publicly acknowledged and formally reported, whether in court reports or by victims. That engagement reflects both an acknowledgement of crime and changing social values. In law, and increasingly in popular culture, Australians similarly re-vision as assault what in the past was construed as adolescent horseplay.[38] In contemporary Australian law, we have belatedly decriminalized consensual same-sex activity.[39] Consensual activity within Australian prisons, a human right as an aspect of sexual citizenship, is still proscribed as contrary to good discipline.[40] Law is instead properly concerned with questions of physical/psychological injury, disregard of consent and denial of dignity through objectification by a perpetrator of another person for the perpetrator's sexual or other gratification.

In making sense of that gratification, we should acknowledge that the motivation for sexual assault may be as much about power as it is about physical pleasure. Such an expression of power transcends gender and what an offender would identify as the desired partner in intimacy. Judith Butler argues that power works to shape sex and sexuality, determining what are deemed legitimate modes of sexual affinity, sexual acts and sexual relationships.[41] Power provides a language in which some acts are criminal and some, in an echo of the Tudors, are socially unspeakable. That silence is discussed in Moran's *The Homosexual(ity) of Law*.[42] It is illustrated, for example, by the 'rustic sodomite's assault in Tarantino's *Pulp Fiction* (1994)[43] on crime czar Marsellus Wallace (Ving Rhames), a rape that is to remain forever unspoken by both Wallace and witness Butch Coolidge (Bruce Willis), and thereby erased.[44]

In making sense of assault and historical contingency, we should also acknowledge that law has struggled with sexual activity that involves the consensual infliction of physical pain, subjection or humiliation. Such conventionally disruptive activity encompasses S&M,[45] or master/slave role-play, which is sometimes deeply theatrical.[46] It also encompasses the depictions of sexual violence or paraphilia that disturb heteronormative expectations about pleasure and propriety.[47] Law's struggle is evident in the frameworks for regulation of print, broadcast, live theatre, cinema and online dissemination of films. Such frameworks are relevant to the contentions in this chapter because they propagate norms about behaviour and belonging. They also represent a soft power: the state shaping what law is and how it is shown.

The social and legal unspeakability of consensual same-sex activity has resulted in an erasure that deepens the silence in contemporary and historic Australia regarding the rape by males of other males, including adults and minors. The silence is sporadically broken by reports of prosecutions, criminological studies and depictions in Australian film, television and novels. Those depictions are the foundation of this chapter. The official literature regarding the incidence and other aspects of that sexual assault is incoherent. We have acknowledgement that the rape of males occurs in institutional settings, but data is patchy. That is unsurprising, given concerns about liability and wariness on the part of victims and bystanders about reporting. Perforce many scholars, such as the author of this article, draw on research from overseas.[48] Rape outside institutions encompasses non-consensual activity by strangers and intimates. We may infer that its incidence is under-reported, consistent with research regarding under-reporting of assaults on adult and minor females.[49] We may recognize that many perpetrators do not identify as gay.[50] The history noted earlier indicates that some perpetrators may indeed use rape to erase the masculinity of their victims. That erasure is a rewriting of how both victims and bystanders understand the victim's identity within a homosocial setting where being a 'man' is paramount.

One way of both asking and answering questions about law in relation to rape is to look beyond the scholarly literature and interrogate cinematic representations. The Australian feature film canon is diverse, and the following discussion does not purport to be definitive. It instead offers a lens that complements the other views featured in this book.

Four images of law and power

Images of authority, belonging, indifference and acceptance are at the heart of four Australian films featuring male rape. Sexual violence begins George Miller's iconic Australian road movie *Mad Max*, a tale of speed, violence and grotesques that echoes a John Ford Western. In the post-apocalyptic wilderness, Max Rockatansky (Mel Gibson) and sidekick Jim Goose (Steve Bisley) encounter a young 'rev head' couple who have been detained while on the road and sexually assaulted by some of the lawless tribals unavailingly policed by Max as the surviving embodiment of the state. Those tribals are camp versions of the cannibals and child molesters in John Hillcoat's slower speed and psychologically more persuasive *The Road* (2009)[51] or of the First Nations people in Hollywood Westerns.[52]

The homoerotic undertones of *Mad Max* have been astutely analyzed by Johinke, but the rape has not been considered in detail by scholars.[53] Its function is arguably to illustrate that 'anything goes' after the end of civilization as we know it and to provide viewers with a discomforting laugh, given Freud's insight that laughter is often a response to what we find unsettling. For the purpose of this chapter, the incident is suggestive because the sight of the traumatized male victim, running for the horizon with bleeding posterior on display, is regarded by Max and Goose as amusing rather than as something deserving of empathy. As a master craftsman of spills and thrills, Miller then takes us on a high-octane ride that depicts Australia as a place of absence, where law is a matter of the agency exercised by our self-regulated invulnerable and alienated leather-clad hero.[54] It is a given on that journey that Max, as the essential man – the hero against whom all other men when judged are deemed inadequate – may well be overpowered, detained, tortured and scarred but will never be sexually violated. He is a manifestation of both Australian homosociality and pre-colonial hero sagas in which the wronged protagonist exercises exemplary private vengeance against those perpetrators he deems to be outside the law, without regard for any code embraced by members of that 'other'.

Mad Max is a film of surface: kinetic action and Gothic images rather than nuance, unfolding characterization, legal dilemmas and personal conundrums. It presents a world where force and endurance are paramount, a paramountcy that is the law and that was valorized by Carl Schmitt.[55] In the post-apocalyptic state of nature, we are not invited to empathize with victims or indeed recognize victimization and offence. Reparation for harm to the raped male and female partner will be incidental, will be determined by the most powerful and self-accountable actor (in this instance, Max) and will be endorsed by those who lack his charismatic potency. It is a legal world reminiscent of that envisaged by Schmitt, where the struggle is existential, and the saviour is the law, makes the law and is above the law.[56] We cheer the superman in leather and disregard the pain of others – for example, the physical and psychological trauma of the sodomized victim pictured disappearing into the middle distance.

Fred Schepisi's *The Chant of Jimmie Blacksmith* depicts Australia at an epochal time in its legal history: the move towards Federation. The film is a tale of dispossession, anger, injustice and power: power expressed and power sought, including expression through sexual violence. The tale begins with Aboriginal tracker Blacksmith (Tom E. Lewis) assisting senior constable Farrell (Ray Barrett) with the capture of Blacksmith's peer Harry Edwards (Jack Charles). Blacksmith is an obedient servant of the colonial justice system, instrumental in the apprehension of Edwards and dismissive of the captive on the basis that those without power deserve what they get. Blacksmith's identification with his master means that he provides no comfort to the frightened Edwards. The prisoner is subsequently raped and murdered by Farrell (two illegal actions by an individual who embodies the law), with Blacksmith being deaf to the offence and complicitly cleaning the corpse before clearing out of Farrell's service. The 'tidying up' is a manifestation of the erasure evident in several of the films: procedure affirms legitimacy and thereby fosters silence.

That snapshot can be read as a paradigm of the colonial relationship. A corrupt Irish-Australian representative of the imperial state exercises his power on the subservient body of a First Nations person without fear of intervention by Blacksmith as someone who appears to be aware of what is likely to happen to Edwards and who is conscious of the offence as it takes place. Within the frame of this chapter, the incident might more narrowly be construed as emblematic of questions about contemporary justice and masculinity. In disrupting Schepisi's tale of a misjudged drift from injustice to savagery and Blacksmith's death on the gallows, we could revise the incident.[57] It is convenient to found the tale on Blacksmith's ethnicity, but would Farrell restrict his predation to people of colour? Is Farrell's murder of Edwards a matter of disposal of evidence or an expression of guilt about a stigmatized affinity – an affinity whose manifestation in consensual and non-consensual activity alike was at that time a criminal offence? Could we envisage a version in which Blacksmith has agency rather than just being complicit: warning Edwards, reproving Farrell, intervening during the rape, liberating Edwards or even appropriating justice by harming Farrell after the event?

Is Blacksmith's incapacity symptomatic of the denial that is evident in contemporary Australian correctional institutions, discussed next? More broadly, within the context of the recent Royal Commission into Institutional Responses to Child Sexual Abuse[58] and the Australian Defence Abuse Response Taskforce,[59] where generations of authorities disregarded claims made by abused minors, would a Federation-era court have heeded a claim by Edwards? Would Edwards have become the subject of empathy rather than derision, given the persistent belief that 'real men' – the men valorized through hegemonic Australian feature film – do not get raped?

Disquietingly, in thinking about law and identity, could we re-vision Blacksmith as a precursor of the National Socialist *kapo*, an active participant in an assault rather than someone who wants to ignore the crime and avoid the perpetrator? Tragically, some inmates of concentration camps adopted the values and mannerisms of their masters, serving as auxiliaries in crimes against humanity and on occasion pathetically mimicking the attire of the guards.[60] *The Chant of Jimmie Blacksmith* depicts Blacksmith as initially diligently embracing his position in the colonial justice system: wearing the white man's clothes, using Farrell's pejorative language, assimilating the master's values. As someone who is denied agency by virtue of his ethnicity, we might envisage Blacksmith assimilating power by himself assaulting Edwards, given that assault with immunity is a privilege of the powerful and not specific to gender.

One response to such re-visioning is that it is inappropriate because it is outside the filmmaker's intentions[61] or because, as an instance of postmodernism, it relativizes harms and agency. A rejoinder is that law reform is an exercise of the imagination noted by Minow and Spelman:[62] a willingness to conceive of different relationships and reduced harms through legal change. A society that respects the dignity of all people, irrespective of gender, ethnicity and sexual affinity, would not be one in which the disempowered subjects of the law were buggered by representatives of the state while others shielded their eyes and ears from that harm. If film is an exercise of imagination on the part of the author(s) and viewer, so is law reform and writing about law.

The 1971 *Wake in Fright*, set in the Australian outback, is based on Kenneth Cook's novel of the same name.[63] It has been described as 'arguably Australia's greatest feature film'.[64] It depicts the vicissitudes of a young male teacher, an occupation positioned as one deserving of less respect than those involving 'real men' who earn their living through physical labour in rural Australia. That location is salient, given the long-standing cultural values that periodically are invoked by politicians of a conservative bent articulating manual work as more 'authentic', worthy and 'Australian' than labour at a desk or through professional credentials.[65] It is a location to which many Australians pay lip service, but in which increasingly few Australians choose to live. Apart from the absence of amenities, that avoidance is in part a reflection of perceptions of latent lawlessness and abuse by (or incapacity on the part of) law enforcement personnel. Such perceptions are evident in similar locations overseas, with US dramas featuring misadventures involving corrupt sheriffs in the Deep South or Northwest, such as Welles' *Touch of Evil* (1958),[66] Jewison's *In the Heat of the Night* (1967)[67] and Winterbottom's *The Killer Inside Me* (2010).[68]

In *Wake in Fright*, the teacher protagonist (Gary Bond) is misled and exploited by the clannish locals for whom he will always be an outsider before being sexually abused by a drunken ex-doctor (Donald Pleasance). In this nightmare, there is no support from the law, in the person of archetypal 'Aussie' actor Chips Rafferty. Social solidarity among mates means there is no assistance from the townspeople. As with the two onlookers in *Mad Max*, the community is complaisant: indifferent to if not amused by his exploitation. Most chillingly, he is so incapacitated that after an ineffectual escape he ends up returning to the locale in which he was harmed, perhaps to unstated further victimization. He reconciles with his assailant and the locals, no longer dismissive of rural rednecks and their homosociality.

Wake in Fright offers a view of law and masculinity in which social solidarity within the peer group of insiders is fundamental, law is local, abuse of outsiders is endorsed and people whose strength or resilience is deficient are exploited without any consequences to the perpetrators. It is not a dog-eat-dog, all-against-all Hobbesian state of nature; instead, it is a legal culture of silence and assent, in which groups of men look the other way due to fear that they may themselves become victims if they dissent or who look on with approval at the infliction of pain by peers who lack their internal or social restraints. The film offers a bleak view of Australian society as one of little imagination, where there is an inability on the part of bystanders to place themselves in the shoes of the victims and to exercise the moral independence that, as noted earlier, is supposedly a key facet of the Australian character.[69] As such, it may resonate with readers of works such as Christopher Browning's *Ordinary Men*, an account of ethical autonomy and men engaging in repugnant activity in order to remain in step with their peers rather than merely to evade punitive sanctions.[70] *Wake in Fright* can be read as a particularly bleak view of homosociality as a matter of education. Rape educates for belonging. It results in the victim embracing both his rapist and peers, learning his place and learning not to look down on the blokes who were indifferent to the abuse. Being Australian, from that perspective, is a matter of fitting in, embracing punitive social norms. The laconic archetypal Australian has much to be quiet about.

If *Wake in Fright* is grounded in the desolation of remote rural Australia, John Hillcoat's *Ghosts . . . of the Civil Dead* has an interior landscape that is decidedly and chillingly high tech. We see the antiseptic interior of a carceral 'supermax' and the stainless steel of the escalators at Parliament House station – an ironic ascent from the underworld – in Melbourne. *Ghosts . . . of the Civil Dead* lacks the redemptive quality of *The Shawshank Redemption*, *American History X*, *Midnight Express*[71] or *Brubaker* (1980).[72] The central character of *Ghosts . . . of the Civil Dead* is progressively brutalized after incarceration, failing to negotiate interactions with peers who are tougher and more disordered than himself in an environment where correctional staff are as brutal as those peers but clinically detached. This detachment is facilitated by a panoptic architecture and management regime in which the authorities are aware of, but indifferent to, abuses. That is an echo of findings of inquiries into systemic violence in the Victorian, New South Wales and

Queensland prison systems and historic penal colonies such as Norfolk Island.[73] The protagonist (David Field) is raped, scarred and robbed by fellow inmates. Eventually anomic, he is released into the outside community. The viewer infers that his subdued rage against a world responsible for the protagonist's injuries will be unleashed in acts of violence.

The facility's management is complicit in his suffering, like the guards in *Fortune and Men's Eyes* (1971):[74] bored official bystanders observing a gang rape while gawkers enjoy the show, and other inmates a few feet away unconcernedly eat lunch. Indeed, the *Ghosts . . . of the Civil Dead* executives are happy to release a high-risk offender into the community because his next crime will justify their plan to increase revenue through a bigger facility. One message is that crime pays if your business is a containment facility. The embodiment of law as a privately operated correctional facility, a for-profit state-sanctioned jungle, legitimates itself in *Ghosts . . . of the Civil Dead* by creating criminals – that is, those violent males who need containment. The *Ghosts . . . of the Civil Dead* supermax regime brutalizes inmates through a culture in which managers turn a blind eye to the assaults, including sexual violence, which are normative. It is a homosocial culture in which the norms are set by the *Mad Max*–style uber-male: the sociopathic super-predator at the top of the carceral ecosystem. In this instance, the exemplary male is one identified by the supermax managers as an authority figure and accordingly given agency to exercise his will, directly or through subordinates, as long as he does not challenge those executives or their delegates.

Saliently, the institution in *Ghosts . . . of the Civil Dead* is privately operated and profit oriented. It is an expression of the neoliberal zeitgeist in advanced economies that, over the past two decades, has seen privatization of prisons[75] and other public services hitherto regarded as the sole province of the state.[76] It is an institution whose managers share an ideology and performance metrics with peers in similar bodies across the globe.[77] They understand ethical questions through a transnational language of managerialism centred on cost reduction, at odds with the legitimacy derived from liberal democratic corrections facilities as places of reform for offenders who have civil disabilities but retain inalienable rights.[78] In that environment, inmate-on-inmate rape is a matter of accounting, not of human dignity and rights, for *Ghosts*'s civil dead.

Max Weber encapsulated the state as providing a legal framework in which it has a monopoly on determining the legitimate exercise of violence.[79] From that perspective, law in the world of *Ghosts . . . of the Civil Dead* is founded on an acceptance of males enacting authority by engaging in sexual violence against each other – sanctioned violence that harms the victim but is less administratively inconvenient than inmates killing each other. Rape by an individual inmate or gang of inmates may indeed be more feared by potential victims because being sodomized is less heroic, less masculine than being killed in battle, dying an exemplary death in the mode of Maximus (Russell Crowe) in Ridley Scott's *Gladiator* (2000)[80] or the gunfighter in a score of American Westerns and gangster dramas.

If we construe Australian law as a matter of dignity and fostering individual flourishing, the depiction of justice in *Ghosts . . . of the Civil Dead* may be both repugnant and frighteningly close to our fears about the realities of life behind bars, a life that for many viewers and voters is conveniently out of sight and thereby out of mind. We owe a duty to minimize assaults by inmates on each other – people who have a civil disability but are not outside the law. The judgment in *R v Fern* explains:[81]

> This Court, whatever sympathy it may feel for the appellant, has a very serious responsibility to extend what protection it can to persons who are incarcerated by force of law in penal institutions. Those people have no choice about being there; they are sent there by the courts as punishment for their crimes. They are entitled to serve their punishment free of abuse and indignity and interference with their basic rights as human beings. . . . If prisoners can abuse fellow prisoners in the way in which this appellant abused the victim and escape severe punishment, it must expose other prisoners in the system to the risk of being similarly abused and increase their vulnerability to violence and particularly sexual violence at the hands of fellow prisoners. . . . A prisoner is entitled to expect that a sentence will be served according to civilized standards and free from barbaric outrage.[82]

The barbaric outrage is not same-sex activity *per se*. It is instead private appropriation of the law and, by extension, confinement systems in which assault is prevalent but observers are indifferent.[83]

One basis for the comment regarding administrative inconvenience is that although the dead have no voice – and, indeed, have no legal standing – their death may be apparent. Put more simply, they can be identified as discrepancies in a roll call or an audit. They do not speak, but because they are now visible as bodies on the mortuary slab or coronial statistics, someone may speak for them. Historically that has not been the case for most male victims of sexual violence in Australia, the United Kingdom, Ireland, the United States and elsewhere. Those people may choose not to speak for themselves, may not have advocates to speak on their behalf and may speak to deaf ears and averted eyes.

A preceding comment thus noted the persistent disbelief by authorities and others when minors claimed that they had been victimized by clergy, schoolteachers, students, sports coaches, superiors in the armed forces or guardians in residential institutions. That disbelief is evident when those victims have subsequently, as adults, reported the abuse to police, senior clergy and other entities. It coexists with the reluctance of men who have been sexually abused as adults, whether by intimates or strangers or people with whom they are forced to share space, to disclose they have been victimized.[84]

That silence is in part a function of the pervasive cultural values about masculinity noted towards the beginning of this chapter. As entities whose attributes are reified by law (evident in conflation of the legal person with agency and masculinity), men are likely to construe their self-worth and the worth of their peers in terms of physical strength and resilience, independence, acceptance by their cohort and reticence in expressing empathy, fear, pain or affection. Assault is something that is not to be voiced by victims; being victimized and failing to repel the assault is deeply shameful and potentially provokes questions in a heteronormative society regarding whether the victim 'asked for it' and, indeed, enjoyed it.[85] Historically, it has juridically been on occasion unspeakable, with a representative statement by a Tasmanian court in 1832 that merely hearing about victimization, as distinct from its experience by the man who was violated, is too painful to relate:

> The disgusting details of this horrible transaction, must have been exceedingly painful to all those whose avocations compelled them to be auditors thereof, as they are of that revolting nature, which render them utterly unfit to meet the public eye.[86]

An observation from the four films is that bystanders are well aware of the existence of assault but do not talk about it using a language of reparation and law reform, as distinct from tacit endorsement through silence and laughter. There is social solidarity among the mates in the community, prison and justice administration, remembering that mates do not 'dob' or otherwise step out of line. Crucially, there is no empathy for or solidarity with the 'othered' victim.[87] A viewer in search of more than entertainment is required to supply that empathy herself and, drawing on her imagination, to ask how law might cure and prevent such harms.

There is a more disturbing observation from a critical reading of the films. The iconic male in those works is sociopathic rather than collegial, putting himself ahead of lesser men because he is both stronger and uninhibited by the law. He resembles Schmitt's dictator figure, the charismatic individual who embodies the law (potentially a law of the jungle), makes the law (obeyed by and enacted on lesser creatures) and is above the law.[88]

Conclusion

The law in the films discussed in this chapter is a matter of performance and appropriation, of individual agency rather than collective action. It may be sanctioned by 'mates', imprisoned or otherwise. It is not a performance by a delegate of the community on behalf of that community for the flourishing of individuals within the community. It is also a matter of silence, with peers neither speaking out nor coming to the aid of victims, and institutions being complicit in harms of abuse. The depictions of that abuse have an Australian accent, but, as expressions of power and of complaisance by onlookers, they are universal.

This chapter reveals the dark side of mateship – a homosociality in which peers are indifferent to or complicit in sexual assault and authority appropriated by exemplary men is unrestrained by the legal system. The output of the Australian film industry – particularly outside work for arthouse distribution – often features violence. That is unsurprising given that action, and hence violence, sell. Mainstream cinema rarely features non-consensual same-sex activity. Overall, Australian cinema, along with its overseas peers, is a manifestation of sexual erasure. It rarely features any same-sex activity, and when an expression of that affinity is evident, it is typically exceptional rather than something incidental to the lives of a film's characters.

A more challenging response is that the author has cherry-picked genres rather than merely individual works. Preceding paragraphs have, for example, not engaged with questions about the depiction of coercion, authority, identity and violence in domestic and overseas production of gay erotica.[89] Such selectivity is acknowledged, given both the concentration on 'Australian film' and the paucity of scholarly research about Australian gay porn production, much of which appears to feature the bronzed surfers and Snowy Mountains cattlemen we would otherwise expect to see in films about heroic boys at ANZAC Cove, Changi or Bondi Beach.[90]

This chapter began by questioning the 'Australianness' of Australian film and the specificity of the depictions in that cultural work of Australian law. One conclusion might be that recent film is mid-Pacific rather than parochial, aptly construed on occasion as export fodder rather than as a deliberate exercise in nation-building through articulation and affirmation of a desired national character understood as shared values and relationships. In a post-colonial economy, the Australian myth of the rugged bushman has faded:[91] 'Billabong' is now a signifier of board shorts worn by style-conscious young people in a gentler, less hip Australian version of California. The myth we see in *Mad Max* is timeless, an echo of the self-reliant gunslingers affirmed by John Ford and the 'savage' infested badlands in 80 years of Wild West dramas.[92] The carceral wrongs depicted in *Ghosts . . . of the Civil Dead* could equally be located in *Pixote*'s Brazil,[93] in Alcatraz, Attica and chillingly antiseptic French prisons or inferred from a thoughtful reading of Dante, a realm of those who have yielded to bestial appetites and violence or perverted their intellect to fraud or malice against their fellow men.[94]

The four films depict imagined worlds – alas, not too far from our own – in which men perform masculinity by imposing violence on other men, violence that in the snapshots discussed in this chapter may have a sexual character and, accordingly, be more erosive of the victim's self/social identity than the loss of an eye or acquisition of a scar. They are worlds in which other men perform their homosociality by staying in line, displaying a lack of initiative, robustness and ethical integrity that is at odds with the national myth of the rugged independent bloke.[95]

Notes

1 Kotcheff (1971) *Wake in Fright*.
2 Schepisi (1978) *The Chant of Jimmie Blacksmith*.
3 Miller (1979) *Mad Max*.
4 Hillcoat (1988) *Ghosts . . . of the Civil Dead*.

5 Darabont (1994) *The Shawshank Redemption.*
6 Kaye (1998) *American History X.*
7 Parker (1978).
8 Elliot (1994) *The Adventures of Priscilla, Queen of the Desert.*
9 Dowling and Burton (1994) *The Sum of Us.*
10 Armfield (2015) *Holding the Man.*
11 Boorman (1972) *Deliverance.*
12 Graham (2006), p 191.
13 Keneally (1972), p 20. See also Wilson (2007).
14 Dwyer (2018), p 117.
15 Matthews (1984), p 13.
16 Jennings (2009), p 42.
17 Altman (1987), p 163; Dyrenfurth (2015).
18 Hammarén and Johansson (2014), p 1; Sedgwick (1985).
19 Murri (1998), p 69; Jennings (2009), p 40 notes the supposed definition in tradition popular culture of 'the homosexual' as a man who talks to women.
20 West (2000), p 46.
21 Leahy (2007), p 7; McKenna, Simpson and Williams (2001), p 401; Watson (2011).
22 Dodson (2000), p 73; Duggan (2003), p 283; Lindisfarne (2004); Rickett (2005), p 73.
23 Barratt (2004); Collins (2008); Somerfield (2004).
24 Webster (2007), p 1.
25 Hughes (2010), p 175.
26 See, for example, Chauvel (1940) *Forty Thousand Horsemen*; Sims (2010) *Beneath Hill 60*; Weir (1981) *Gallipoli*; Wincer (1987) *The Lighthorsemen.*
27 Featherstone (2008), p 77.
28 Brownmiller (1975), p 422.
29 Jones (2000), p 104.
30 Crome, McCabe and Ford (1999), p 62 offer indicative figures; see also Crome (2006) and, for a perspective on reporting, Naffine (1992), p 756.
31 See *AW* (2004); *R v Guingab* (2011); *R v Fern* (1989). Among the secondary literature, see Brouwer (2014); Heilpern (1998); Malkin (1995).
32 Heilpern (1998).
33 See, for example, Royal Commission (2017).
34 Brouwer (2014).
35 Eigenberg and Baro (2003), p 56.
36 Crown Prosecution Service (2018).
37 Blore (2018), p 159; Braun and Gray (2016), p 91; Sewell (2001), p 47; Statham (1998), p 301.
38 Royal Commission (2017), pp 10–11, 15.
39 Baird (2003), p 3; Berman (2008), p 236.
40 Richardson (2000), p 105; Richters et al. (2012), p 517.
41 Butler (2011), p 18.
42 Moran (2002), p 33.
43 Tarantino (1994) *Pulp Fiction.*
44 Bell (2000), p 550; Kaplan (2014), p 89.
45 *R v Boyea* (1992); *R v McIntosh* (1999); *R v Stein* (2007); *R v Wilson* (1996). Among the secondary literature, see Bennett (2013), p 541; Bronitt (1995), p 59; White (2006), p 167.
46 *R v Brown* (1994); Bell (1995), p 139; White (2006).
47 Kendall (1993), pp 31–2, in embracing anti-pornography arguments advanced by Catherine MacKinnon and Andrea Dworkin, disregards the legitimate pursuit of pleasure by self-possessed adults in a liberal democratic state. For a more nuanced analysis, see Corneau and Van der Meulen (2014).

48 For examples, see Coxell and King (1996); Crome (2006); Kaufman et al (1980); Lowe and Rogers (2017); Naffine (1992); Richters et al. (2012).
49 Lievore (2003).
50 See, for example, Hodge and Canter (1998).
51 Hillcoat (2009) *The Road.*
52 Robertson (2018), p 70.
53 Johinke (2001).
54 Lucas (1998), p 143.
55 McElligott (2014), p 219, quoting Schmitt's 1934 'Der Führer schütz das Recht'.
56 Schmitt (1997), p 27.
57 As examples of re-visioning, see Améry (2018/1978); Leys (1991).
58 Royal Commission into Institutional Responses to Child Sexual Abuse (2017).
59 Australian Defence Abuse Response Taskforce (2016).
60 Wachsmann (2015).
61 Barthes (1977), p 142.
62 Minow and Spelman (1990).
63 Cook (1961).
64 Caterson (2006), p 86.
65 Joyce (2018); Ward (1958).
66 Welles (1958) *Touch of Evil.*
67 Jewison (1967) *In the Heat of the Night.*
68 Winterbottom (2010) *The Killer Inside Me.*
69 Lucas (1998), p 141.
70 Browning (1992).
71 Parker (1978) *Midnight Express.*
72 Rosenberg (1980) *Brubaker.*
73 Peart (2019).
74 Hart (1971) *Fortune and Men's Eyes.*
75 Schichor (1998).
76 Harding (2018).
77 Bottomley and James (1997), p 259.
78 Dolovich (2005), p 437.
79 Weber (1991), pp 77, 78; see also Kletzer (2013), p 272.
80 Scott (2000) *Gladiator.*
81 *R v Fern* (1989), King CJ at 274.
82 Similar statements feature in *R v George* (1981) and *R v Short* (1992).
83 Brouwer (2014); Heilpern (1998).
84 Javaid (2017), p 279.
85 Mitchell, Hirschman and Nagayama Hall (1999), p 369; Prichard (2000). A perspective is provided by Naffine (1992), p 748.
86 *R v Charles* (1832).
87 Smith and Batiuk (1989), p 34.
88 Schmitt (1997), p 27.
89 Kendall (2004), p 94.
90 McKee (1999a, 1999b).
91 Murri (1998), p 68.
92 Robertson (2018), p 68.
93 Babenco (1980) *Pixote: a Lei do Mais Fraco.*
94 MacAllister (2009), p 23.
95 Lucas (1998), p 141; Murri (1998), p 74.

References

Secondary sources

Dennis Altman (1987) 'The Myth of Mateship' 46 *Meanjin* 163.

Jean Améry (1978/2018) *Charles Bovary, Country Doctor: Portrait of a Simple Man*, Adrian Nathan West (trans), New York Review of Books.

Australian Defence Abuse Response Taskforce (2016) *Final Report*, https://apo.org.au/sites/default/files/resource-files/2016/09/apo-nid67232-1205506.pdf.

Barbara Baird (2003) 'Sexual Citizenship in Tasmania: Stories of Gay Law Reform' 17 *Continuum: Journal of Media & Cultural Studies* 3.

Roland Barthes (1977) 'The Death of the Author', in Stephen Heath (trans), *Image, Music, Text*, Hill and Wang.

David Bell (1995) 'Pleasure and Danger: The Paradoxical Spaces of Sexual Citizenship' 14 *Political Geography* 139.

——— (2000) 'Farm Boys and Wild Men: Rurality, Masculinity, and Homosexuality' 65 *Rural Sociology* 547.

Theodore Bennett (2013) 'Sadomasochism Under the *Human Rights (Sexual Conduct) Act 1994*' 35 *Sydney Law Review* 541.

Alan Berman (2008) 'The Repeal of Sodomy Laws in Tasmania in 1997', in Shirleene Robinson (ed.), *Homophobia: An Australian History*, Federation Press.

Kent Blore (2018) '"*Lindsay v The Queen*": Homicide and the Ordinary Person at the Juncture of Race and Sexuality' 39(1) *The Adelaide Law Review* 159.

A. Keith Bottomley and Adrian L. James (1997) 'Evaluating Private Prisons: Comparisons, Competition and Cross-fertilization' 30 *Australian & New Zealand Journal of Criminology* 259.

Kerstin Braun and Anthony Gray (2016) 'Green and Lindsay: Two Steps Forward – Five Steps Back Homosexual Advance Defence – Quo Vadis' 41 *University of Western Australia Law Review* 91.

Simon Bronitt (1995) 'The Right to Sexual Privacy, Sado-masochism and the *Human Rights (Sexual Conduct) Act 1994* (Cth)' 2 *Australian Journal of Human Rights* 59.

G.E. Brouwer (2014) *Investigation into Deaths and Harm in Custody*, Victorian Ombudsman.

Christopher Browning (1992) *Ordinary Men: Reserve Police Battalion 101 and the Final Solution in Poland*, Oxford University Press.

Susan Brownmiller (1975) *Against Our Will*, Bantam.

Judith Butler (2011) *Bodies that Matter: On the Discursive Limits of Sex* (2nd ed.), Routledge.

Simon Caterson (2006) 'The Best Australian Film You've Never Seen' 50 *Quadrant* 86.

Kenneth Cook (1961) *Wake In Fright*, Michael Joseph.

Simon Corneau and Emily Van der Meulen (2014) 'Some Like it Mellow: On Gay Men Complicating Pornography Discourses' 61 *Journal of Homosexuality* 491.

Adrian W. Coxell and Michael B. King (1996) 'Male Victims of Rape and Sexual Abuse' 11 *Sexual and Marital Therapy* 297.

Sarah Crome (2006) *Male Survivors of Sexual Assault and Rape*, Australian Institute of Family Studies.

Sarah Crome, Marita McCabe and Lindsay Ford (1999) 'Male Rape Victims: Fact and Fiction' 73 *Law Institute Journal* 60.

Crown Prosecution Service, England & Wales (2018) 'Man Jailed for Drugging and Raping Men He Met on Grindr', 4 June, www.cps.gov.uk/wessex/news/man-jailed-drugging-and-raping-men-he-met-grindr.

Patrick Dodson (2000) '1999 Vincent Lingiari Memorial Lecture: Until the Chains are Broken' 5 *Australian Indigenous Law Reporter* 73.

Sharon Dolovich (2005) 'State Punishment and Private Prisons' 55 *Duke Law Journal* 437.

Anthony Duggan (2003) 'The Trumping of Mateship: Unconscionability in the High Court of Australia' 39 *Canadian Business Law Journal* 275.

Tessa Dwyer (2018) 'Accented Relations: *Mad Max* on US Screens', in Adrian Danks, Stephen Gaunson and Peter Kunze (eds), *American–Australian Cinema*, Palgrave Macmillan.

Nick Dyrenfurth (2015) *Mateship: A Very Australian History*, Scribe.

Helen Eigenberg and Agnes Baro (2003) 'If You Drop the Soap in the Shower You are on Your Own: Images of Male Rape in Selected Prison Movies' 7 *Sexuality and Culture* 56.

Lisa Featherstone (2008) 'Sex and the Australian Legend: Masculinity and the White Man's Body' 10 *Journal of Australian Colonial History* 73.

Ruth Graham (2006) 'Male Rape and the Careful Construction of the Male Victim' 15 *Social & Legal Studies* 187.

Nils Hammarén and Thomas Johansson (2014) 'Homosociality: In Between Power and Intimacy' 4 *Sage Open* 1.

Richard Harding (2018) *Private Prisons and Public Accountability*, Routledge.

David Heilpern (1998) *Fear or Favour: Sexual Assault of Young Prisoners*, Southern Cross University Press.

Samantha Hodge and David Canter (1998) 'Victims and Perpetrators of Male Sexual Assault' 12 *Journal of Interpersonal Violence* 222.

Robert Hughes (2010) *The Fatal Shore*, Random House.

Aliraza Javaid (2017) 'In the Shadows: Making Sense of Gay Male Rape Victims' Silence, Suffering, and Invisibility' 29 *International Journal of Sexual Health* 279.

Kate Jennings (2009) 'Home Truths: Revisiting *Wake in Fright*', *The Monthly*, July.

Rebecca Johinke (2001) 'Manifestations of Masculinities: *Mad Max* and the Lure of the Forbidden Zone' 25 *Journal of Australian Studies* 118.

Ivor H. Jones (2000) 'Cultural and Historical Aspects of Male Sexual Assault', in Gilliam Mezey and Michael King (eds), *Male Victims of Sexual Assault* (2nd ed.), Oxford University Press.

Barnaby Joyce (2018) *Weatherboard and Iron: Politics, the Bush and Me*, New Holland.

Margo Kaplan (2014) 'Sex-Positive Law' 89 *New York University Law Review* 89.

Arthur Kaufman, Peter Divasto, Rebecca Jackson, Dayron Voorhees and Joan Christy (1980) 'Male Rape Victims: Non-institutionalised Assault' 137 *American Journal of Psychiatry* 221.

Christopher N. Kendall (1993) 'Real Dominant, Real Fun: Gay Male Pornography and the Pursuit of Masculinity' 57 *Saskatchewan Law Review* 21.

——— (2004) 'Gay Male Pornography and Sexual Violence: A Sex Equality Perspective on Gay Male Rape and Partner Abuse' 49 *McGill Law Journal* 877.

Thomas Keneally (1972) *The Chant of Jimmie Blacksmith*, Angus & Robertson.

Christopher Kletzer (2013) 'Primitive Law' 4 *Jurisprudence: An International Journal of Legal and Political Thought* 263.

Peter Leahy (2007) 'Lest We Forget' 4 *Australian Army Journal* 7.
Simon Leys (1991) *The Death of Napoleon*, Allen & Unwin.
Denise Lievore (2003) *Non-reporting and Hidden Recording of Sexual Assault: An International Literature Review*, Commonwealth Office of the Status of Women.
Michelle Lowe and Paul Rogers (2017) 'The Scope of Male Rape: A Selective Review of Research, Policy and Practice' 35 *Aggression and Violent Behavior* 38.
Rose Lucas (1998) 'Dragging it Out: Tales of Masculinity in Australian Cinema from *Crocodile Dundee* to *Priscilla, Queen of the Desert*' 22 *Journal of Australian Studies* 138.
Archibald MacAllister (2009) 'Introduction', in John Ciardi (trans), *Dante Alighieri: The Inferno*, New American Library.
Ian Malkin (1995) 'Tort Law's Role in Preventing Prisoners' Exposure to HIV Infection While in Her Majesty's Custody' 20 *Melbourne University Law Review* 423.
Sue Matthews (1984) *35mm Dreams: Conversations with Five Directors*, Penguin.
Anthony McElligott (2014) *Rethinking the Weimar Republic: Authority and Authoritarianism 1916–1936*, Bloomsbury.
Alan McKee (1999a) 'Australian Gay Porn Videos: The National Identity of Despised Cultural Objects' 2 *The International Journal of Cultural Studies* 178.
——— (1999b) 'Suck on that Mate: Australian Gay Porn Videos', in Deb Verhoeven (ed.), *Twin Peeks: Australian and New Zealand Feature Films*, Damned Publishing.
Mark McKenna, Amelia Simpson and George Williams (2001) 'With Hope in God, the Prime Minister and the Poet: Lessons from the 1999 Referendum on the Preamble' 24 *UNSW Law Journal* 401.
Martha Minow and Elizabeth Spelman (1990) 'In Context' 63 *Southern California Law Review* 1597.
Damon Mitchell, Richard Hirschman and Gordon C. Nagayama Hall (1999) 'Attributions of Victim Responsibility, Pleasure, and Trauma in Male Rape' 36 *Journal of Sex Research* 369.
Leslie Moran (2002) *The Homosexual(ity) of Law*, Routledge.
Linzi Murrie (1998) 'The Australian Legend: Writing Australian Masculinity/Writing "Australian" Masculine' 22 *Journal of Australian Studies* 68.
Ngaire Naffine (1992) 'Windows on the Legal Mind: The Evocation of Rape in Legal Writings' 18 *Melbourne University Law Review* 741.
Mark Peart (2019) 'Sodom Island: Pandaemonium and the Botany Bay of Botany Bay' 28 *Journal of the History of Sexuality* 263.
Jeremy Prichard (2000) 'Manipulable Mores: An Analysis of Prisoner Attitudes to Rape' 12 *Current Issues in Criminal Justice* 198.
Diane Richardson (2000) 'Constructing Sexual Citizenship: Theorizing Sexual Rights' 20 *Critical Social Policy* 105.
Juliet Richters, Tony Butler, Karen Schneider, Lorraine Yap, Kristie Kirkwood, Luke Grant, Alun Richards, Anthony M.A. Smith and Basil Donovan (2012) 'Consensual Sex between Men and Sexual Violence in Australian Prisons' 41 *Archives of Sexual Behavior* 517.
Charles Rickett (2005) 'Unconscionability and Commercial Law' 24 *University of Queensland Law Journal* 73.
Paul Lester Robertson (2018) 'Indians of the Apocalypse: Native Appropriation and Representation in 1980s Dystopic Films and Comic Books' 51 *The Journal of Popular Culture* 68.
Royal Commission into Institutional Responses to Child Sexual Abuse (2017) *Report of Case Study 45: Problematic and Harmful Sexual Behaviours of Children in Schools*, www.childabuseroyalcommission.gov.au/final-report.

Carl Schmitt (1997/1932) *The Concept of the Political*, University of Chicago Press.
Eve Klossowsky Sedgwick (1985) *Men: English Literature and Male Homosocial Desire*, University of California Press.
Jef Sewell (2001) '"I Just Bashed Somebody Up. Don't Worry About It Mum, He's Only a Poof": The "Homosexual Advance Defence" and Discursive Constructions of the "Gay" Victim' 5 *Southern Cross University Law Review* 47.
David Shichor (1998) 'Private Prisons in Perspective: Some Conceptual Issues' 37 *The Howard Journal of Criminal Justice* 82.
Norman E. Smith and Mary Ellen Batiuk (1989) 'Sexual Victimization and Inmate Social Interaction' 69 *The Prison Journal* 29.
Bronwyn Statham (1998) 'The Homosexual Advance Defence: Yeah, I Killed Him, but He Did Worse to Me – *Green v R*' 20 *University of Queensland Law Journal* 301.
Nikolaus Wachsmann (2015) *KL: A History of the Nazi Concentration Camps*, Hachette.
Russell Ward (1958) *The Australian Legend*, Oxford University Press.
Marilyn Watson (2011) 'Remarks of the Hon Marilyn Watson AC Chief Justice of Victoria on the Occasion of the Great Australia Day Breakfast 2011', Parliament House, Melbourne, 26 January.
Max Weber (1991) 'Politics as a Vocation', in Hans Gerth and C. Wright Mills (eds), *From Max Weber: Essays in Sociology* (2nd ed.), Routledge.
Barbara Webster (2007) '"They'd Go Out of Their Way to Cover Up for You": Men and Mateship in the Rockhampton Railway Workshops, 1940s–1980s' 4 *History Australia* 1.
Russell West (2000) '"This is a Man's Country": Masculinity and Australian National Identity in *Crocodile Dundee*', in Russell West and Frank Lay (eds), *Subverting Masculinity: Hegemonic and Alternative Versions of Masculinity in Contemporary Culture*, Rodopi.
Chris White (2006) 'The Spanner Trials and the Changing Law on Sadomasochism in the UK' 50 *Journal of Homosexuality* 167.
Janet Wilson (2007) 'Reconsidering Fred Schepisi's *The Chant of Jimmie Blacksmith* (1978): The Screen Adaptation of Thomas Keneally's Novel (1972)' 1 *Studies in Australasian Cinema* 191.

Primary legal sources

AW [2004] WACIC 46.
Barratt and Military Rehabilitation & Compensation Commission [2004] AATA 1141.
Wayne Edward Collins and Commissioner of Police [2008] NSWIRComm 30.
Lindisfarne R&SLA Sub-branch and Citizens Club Inc a v Buchanan [2004] TASSC 73.
R v Boyea (1992) 156 JPR 505.
R v Brown [1994] 1 AC 212.
R v Charles, Dutches, Going and Glover [1832] TASSupC 40.
R v Fern (1989) 51 SASR 273; 152 LSJS 219; [1989] SASC 1625.
R v George (1981) 4 A Crim R 12.
R v Guingab (2011) VSC 110.
R v McIntosh [1999] VSC 358.
R v Short (1992) QCA 108.
R v Stein (2007) 18 VR 376.
R v Wilson [1996] 3 WLR 125.
Somerfield and Military Rehabilitation & Compensation Commission [2004] AATA 52.

Films

Neil Armfield (2015) *Holding the Man*, Screen Australia.
Hector Babenco (1980) *Pixote: a Lei do Mais Fraco*, HB Films.
John Boorman (1972) *Deliverance*, Elmer Productions.
Charles Chauvel (1940) *Forty Thousand Horsemen*, Famous Feature Films.
Frank Darabont (1994) *The Shawshank Redemption*, Castle Rock Entertainment.
Kevin Dowling and Geoff Burton (1994) *The Sum of Us*, The Samuel Goldwyn Company.
Stephan Elliot (1994) *The Adventures of Priscilla, Queen of the Desert*, Polygram Filmed Entertainment.
Harvey Hart (1971) *Fortune and Men's Eyes*, Cinemex.
John Hillcoat (1988) *Ghosts . . . of the Civil Dead*, NLT Productions.
——— (2009) *The Road*, 2929 Productions.
Norman Jewison (1967) *In the Heat of the Night*, The Mirisch Corporation.
Tony Kaye (1998) *American History X*, New Line Cinema.
Ted Kotcheff (1971) *Wake in Fright*, Group W Films and NLT Productions.
George Miller (1979) *Mad Max*, Kennedy Miller Productions.
Alan Parker (1978) *Midnight Express*, Casablanca FilmWorks.
Stuart Rosenberg (1980) *Brubaker*, 20th Century Fox.
Fred Schepisi (1978) *The Chant of Jimmie Blacksmith*, Hoyts Universal.
Ridley Scott (2000) *Gladiator*, Scott Free Productions.
Jeremy Sims (2010) *Beneath Hill 60*, Lucky Country Productions.
Quentin Tarantino (1994) *Pulp Fiction*, A Band Apart.
Peter Weir (1981) *Gallipoli*, Associated R&R Films.
Orson Welles (1958) *Touch of Evil*, Universal Pictures.
Simon Wincer (1987) *The Lighthorsemen*, South Australian Film Corporation.
Michael Winterbottom (2010) *The Killer Inside Me*, Revolution Films.

Chapter 12

Romper Stomper

A critique of neoliberalism in Australia

Kim D. Weinert

Introduction

When the independent film *Romper Stomper* was released in 1993, its portrayal of a gang of neo-Nazi skinheads in Australia was highly controversial. Much of the anxiety surrounding *Romper Stomper* related to the level of extreme violence and the glorification of 'fight and fuck' that existed within the skinhead subculture.[1] Critical discourse about the film centred on 'narrativizing a dystopian of multiculturalism',[2] which projected a strong message that Australia, as a settler state, has a race problem. Drawing attention to the fault lines in Australian life, *Romper Stomper* highlights the political concepts of power and authority, as well as a socio-legal reality of intolerance and injustice. In teasing out these concepts, the film can be read as a manifestation of Australian political culture that was orientating towards neoliberalism.

I argue that *Romper Stomper* critiques the political values of the neoliberal state by exacerbating the idea of self. My argument is twofold: first, it illustrates how the film is an extreme parody of the self within Australia's neoliberal polity of the 1990s; and second, it challenges the neoliberal assumption that the individual can be saved from society. The chapter begins by discussing *Romper Stomper*'s filmography and its plot. This is followed by a brief outline of the predominant elements of neoliberalism, focusing primarily on the individual as an autonomous, independent and free agent. By drawing on this ideology's principle elements, the chapter then analyzes *Romper Stomper* to highlight the exaggerated self as a critique of neoliberal values, which reveals the truth that the hedonistic neo-free individual cannot be saved from society.

Australia losing its cinematic innocence

Listed as one of the most dangerous films ever made, *Romper Stomper* was a watershed moment in Australian cinema.[3] Australia's leading film critics and cinema savants, Margaret Pomeranz and David Stratton, were at odds regarding how *Romper Stomper* should be received.[4] Despite being banned in numerous countries,[5] Pomeranz declared *Romper Stomper* 'one of the finest films to be made in this country in recent years', whereas Stratton blatantly refused to rate the film, explaining that 'in these volatile times, with racism on the march again all over the world, this is a dangerous film'.[6]

Romper Stomper is a fictional narrative about the exploits and the final demise of a neo-Nazi gang of skinheads in Melbourne's western suburb of Footscray. Commanding his gang of misfits and typical 'good for nothing; dole bludgers' is trenchcoat-wearing Hando (Russell Crowe) and his co-commander (and best mate) Davey (Daniel Pollock).[7] The film's opening scene is the brutal assault and murder of two innocent Vietnamese teenagers at the hands of Hando and his gang.[8] Racial hatred pontificated by Hando in this scene informs an audience of the film's unrelenting xenophobic storyline. Drawing heavily on neo-Nazi ideology and using white supremist and Australian bigotry rhetoric,[9] Hando can be described as a self-empowered alpha-warrior with a modus operandi to be victorious in this Darwinian social struggle with the local Vietnamese community by 'romping and stomping from one fight to the next'.[10]

The film's final scene perhaps best represents the gang's inevitable self-destruction, which is brought about by the tempestuous relationship between the three main characters, Hando, Davey and Gabe (Jacqueline McKenzie).[11] *Romper Stomper* ends with Davey stabbing Hando in the neck with a Nazi youth knife in a desperate effort to stop Hando from drowning Gabe.[12] Hando's blood-curdling death unfolds on a beach overlooked by a busload of hapless Japanese tourists.[13] This ironic ending pulls the audience back into reality; away from all Hando's chaos comes a realization that for all the extreme hatred and living on the margins, Hando's life is invariably hollow – and life seemingly goes on.

Romper Stomper does not make for easy viewing. The film has provided a challenge in locating an agreeable truth from the imagined world of Hando. Critics have discussed the film through its obvious themes of racial violence,[14] hegemonic masculinity,[15] homoeroticism between Hando and Davey[16] and love.[17] Emerging from these reviews is the debate about where *Romper Stomper* fits within the canon of Australian film. Placing *Romper Stomper* comfortably within a single genre of Australian film is not an easy task. It has been argued that the film is an Australian bushranger and outlaw movie,[18] and the fast-paced adrenaline fight sequences are said to be reminiscent of Hong Kong action cinema.[19] Tight shots of characters, filmed in blue tone, fast paced Oi! music and frantic editing does not make *Romper Stomper* your typical 'Australian film'. Forming part of this debate has been the film's portrayal of a white Australian man.

Moving away from the stereotypical and enduring identity of an Australian male, Hando is not a larrikin; nor is he the archetype heroic Australian who successfully overcomes British colonial ties.[20] Instead, *Romper Stomper* lives out British colonialism punctuated by the elements of hypermasculinity and patriarchy to reinforce an Anglo-Celtic identity.[21] Hando's and Davey's skinhead identity is projected through a traditional hegemonic masculinity that allows them to exercise, in a brutal way, an unfettered level of power over women and the local Vietnamese community.[22] The depiction of neo-Nazi ideology coupled with the confronting level of racial violence played out on suburban Australian streets falls within a cinematic tradition closer to *A Clockwork Orange*[23] and *Taxi Driver*.[24] Through this shift away from mystical mediations with the land,[25] *Romper Stomper*'s narrative and characters offered something very different for local and international audiences.[26] Described aptly as 'a kind of cultural acid bath, peeling back layers of collective denial to reveal an unwelcome glimpse of home-grown extremism',[27] the film was a confronting truth for many.

Few critics grasped the nationalistic rhetoric in *Romper Stomper* as a searing true account of events that were broadly happening in Australian society.[28] Attesting to this reality was Wright's explanation for how he came to write the film. Wright became aware of a shift in some of Melbourne's street gangs during the late 1980s. He observed that these gangs had started to take on political ideals that drew inspiration from their European counterparts.[29] Wright said that Australia during the 1990s had

> peaked in terms of social friction or social concerns about a wave of Vietnamese immigration that took place from the end of the Vietnam War on to the early 90s. From the mid 70s to the mid 1990s, a cultural shift took place, but right up until the end of that period there were some nasty reactions and that's what *Romper* the movie depicts. Hando, the character Russell Crowe played, represented the most blatant race-fear mongers still at odds with a changing society. . . . Neo-Nazis, Antifa, ISIS, and other groups have appeared in Australia. They're part of the landscape.[30]

Wright's dystopian portrayal of Australian society was dismissed out of hand by some critics. Tsiolkas and Williams both held the strong view that racial violence by skinheads on suburban Australian streets was nothing but a fantasy that did not reflect the reality of race in Australia.[31] Fast forward 25 years, though, and Wright's film and his reasons for creating *Romper Stomper* have been vindicated.

In late 2018, online streaming service Stan announced that the film was to be rebooted into a six-episode television series.[32] Reaction to the announcement of *Romper Stomper* the television series was the opposite of that of the film's release. Generally, Stan's television series had been welcomed and foreshadowed as a timely reflection of an unsettled reality involving extreme politics and vehement white nationalist groups that fear and target Muslims in modern-day Australia.[33]

Fear of any minority group or outsider has provided a steady basis for public alarm in Australia since Federation.[34] As David Marr has insightfully observed, panic is 'so Australian',[35] and Wright has crafted *Romper Stomper* from a culture of panic. The multitude of violent attacks in the film is an historical reminder of how Australia acts out its ritual of panic. Hando's battle for domination remonstrates an Old World colonial, hierarchal order to society that must be preserved. At the time of *Romper Stomper*'s cinematic release, the High Court of Australia's *Mabo* decision[36] triggered national panic and fear that 'our backyards' were under threat.[37] *Mabo* seriously challenged Australia's Old World conservative order, which Hando and others in Australia were fighting hard to maintain. Attempting to quell this panic was then–Prime Minister Paul Keating, who held the steadfast and optimistic view that *Mabo* provided an opportunity for Australia to redefine itself.[38] No longer desiring to maintain the Old World order, Keating knew how to move Australia forward – and this was to be done by means of economic reform.

Australia's shift towards a new way of governing and organizing civil society was built on neoliberal ideals. Embracing neoliberalism, and specifically the element of individualism, brought about a new paradigm in how we thought about ourselves.[39] Wright's initial reasons for making *Romper Stomper* may not have been about neoliberal ideology, but the film can be read as a foretelling of or warning about the perils of a neoliberal society when a free individual dominates; and moreover, a message that no individual can be saved from society.

How neoliberalism is understood

'Neoliberalism' is a much-debated, ill-defined, over-used and unspecified term.[40] Despite well-intentioned efforts to reach a single, logical and precise meaning, it remains elusive.[41] Described by Mudge as a *sui generis* ideological utopian system born from an historical and intellectual struggle against classic liberalism and the encroaching power of the state in Europe during the 1930s,[42] neoliberalism is a complex and contradictory hegemonic system that is best understood through the ideology's agreed set of elements.

There are three general and predominant elements to the neoliberal doctrine. First is the market where economic growth is guaranteed, and it is the only place where individual freedoms are adequately protected.[43] This socio-economic vision is underpinned by the second element, that free and independent citizens are capable of achieving personal development through sufficient private property ownership.[44] The third element is the idea that private property ownership will free individuals of dominating employers and the arbitrary interference of the state.[45] The individual is the power centre of neoliberal philosophy, so it is important to give more attention to the neoliberal individual in this chapter rather than being side-tracked by the dynamics of market economics.

Neoliberalism makes ontological assumptions about the individual,[46] including that the individual avoids subordination to another.[47] The free and uninhibited individual relies heavily on the tropes of neoliberalism in that they are free to 'shape their own course of action in accordance to their present intentions'.[48] The way an authentic individual pursues their cohesive plan of action of personal betterment starts with the individual thinking from their private space.[49] Drawing from their own and limited knowledge of some circumstance, the individual will employ their skills to exploit recognizable limits and opportunities. In deciding how to follow their planned course of action, the individual will make choices according to their own purpose and morality in human life.[50] The second assumption is that the individual is a rational decision-maker, and no matter what success or failure may arise from the individual's rational choices and self-referential actions, neoliberalism (rather than the state) will teach responsibility.[51]

The teaching of responsibility is framed around the principle that the individual has the responsibility to drive their own destiny.[52] Any consequential misfortunes, tragedies and inequalities may simply be overcome through the individual's efforts to be more competitive.[53] Inherent in this concept is an understanding that the individual bears all the responsibility to be integrated, competitive and adaptive to the market.[54] Beyond any economic benefits that an individual may gain, there is an understanding that neoliberalism promises to always reward an individual for their meritorious efforts to survive away from the disordered state.[55] The common understanding of this ontological individual has always been associated with market activities; however, the non-economic activities undertaken by the individual are also recognized by neoliberalism.[56]

Away from the marketplace, the individual will still continue to make rational decisions and choices, but rather than be influenced by the capitalist market, the individual's decisions are instead shaped by social networks and relationships.[57] Within a social context, neoliberalism denotes that an individual is capable of making transformations, which is attributed to the individual's power and authority.[58] According to Patterson, when the individual has social power and authority, neoliberalism becomes fused onto identity politics, which is how social movements such as nationalist groups are created and grow.[59] This willingness to be affiliated with a social group does oppose the notion of the hegemonic individual within this ideology; however, one of the contradictory aspects of neoliberalism is that an individual is content to reduce their identity to a shared single property or characteristic within a group and give their voice to a dystopian narrative.[60] Social movements of this kind are thought to be inexplicably linked to social class, but neoliberals outrightly reject this by arguing that creating or joining a social movement rests with the individual's power, rationality and freedom to make a decision that are self-referential and self-representational.[61]

Essential to the individual's freedom is the nomocratic role of the state.[62] All efforts by the state are designed to avoid interfering with an individual's pursuit of self, and all political and economic activities of a neoliberal state are aimed at organizing the marketplace around *laissez faire* capitalism.[63] The Reagan administration in the United States, Thatcher's government in the United Kingdom during the 1970s and 1980s and Pinochet's rule in Latin America are examples of governments that moved away from 'big government' traditions to embrace neoliberalism.[64] Articulating neoliberal policy imperatives, Thatcher remarked:

> You know, there's no such thing as society. There are individual men and women and there are families. And no government can do anything except through people, and people must look after themselves first. It is our duty to look after ourselves and then, also, to look after our neighbours.[65]

Australia's progression towards embracing the global 'mega trend' of neoliberalism was incremental.[66]

Prime Minister Bob Hawke lit the neoliberal fuse that transitioned Australia away from big government in the 1980s. The policies of the Hawke-Keating governments encouraged markets to be used in practical ways that would resolve problems associated with the distorted allocation and distribution of resources. The underpinning neoliberal principle in the Hawke-Keating agenda was the resolution of disputes without state involvement.[67] Succeeding Hawke in a party room factional leadership challenge, Paul Keating was faced with a hard-hitting recession in 1991. He navigated Australia through this tough fiscal time by adopting neoliberal economic policies that liberated wages and the finance sector through market deregulation.[68] Beyond economics, Keating acknowledged that individualistic rights and freedoms existed in modern Australia.[69] Contained in this acknowledgement was a strong neoliberal message that the relationship between the individual and the state was about to change and that 'the cosy world of state paternalism'[70] would end.

With the neoliberal foundation laid, John Howard's Liberal-National Coalition government implanted its own brand of this ideology in the mid-1990s. The strategic aim of Howard's neoliberal policy agenda was to improve productivity by opening up new ways for individuals to enter and participate better within the market.[71] Consequently, Australians needed to reorganize their lives to become economically and socially competitive. Howard's direction for a modern Australia was primarily driven by the values of self-responsibility and self-management.[72] Perpetuating all the neoliberal elements, Howard saw that it was his government's responsibility to enhance the liberty, freedom and opportunity of individuals to help themselves.[73] Making the neoliberal individual the centre of the national political agenda changed social relations and behaviours in Australia.[74]

Romper Stomper sits on the Australian cinema landscape in a period that is inexplicitly tied up with a newly defined personal freedom that was cultivated by neoliberal government economic policy. With the state no longer wanting to actively guide and/or protect its citizenry as it once did, the individual was allowed to be free in all aspects of life. The film explores Wright's suspicion about this inspirational notion of negative freedom through an allegory of neo-Nazi identity. The use of neo-Nazi imagery and rhetoric in *Romper Stomper* signifies a recognizable embodiment of national interests that can easily be latched onto when there is nothing else available. Wright's manifestation of Australia's neoliberal polity in the film warns that too much personal freedom is dangerous, for it inevitably brings chaos and injustice. This honest telling of the gritty and dark side of neoliberalism seeks to highlight what happens when the state retreats from our daily lives and to show how the free individual becomes an unrelenting and dangerous force.

Traces of neoliberalism in *Romper Stomper*

Unapologetically, *Romper Stomper* makes no effort to rebalance the horrors of racial violence.[75] Instead, the film underscores Australia's changing political and social life in the 1990s by exaggerating Hando and his gang of misfits. The film's use of pervasive characters links Australia's neoliberal agenda to the general societal feelings of insecurity and vulnerability of the day. Against this backdrop of change, *Romper Stomper* illuminates the emergent cracks in a neoliberal order whereby the free neoliberal self does not always prosper and that modern Australia has not progressed far from its history of extreme racial hatred and violence.

The free neoliberal self

Romper Stomper's cultural receptivity of the individual projected through Hando's life is complex. Hando reflects both Australia's brutal xenophobic past of panic and a new order of personal freedom that requires Hando to organise himself to survive. Living within this new modern notion of freedom, *Romper Stomper* presents a construct of the individual whose actions are shaped by conscious thoughts and emotions that are not always either rational or good. Wright pronounces this by taking the competitive free individual to an extreme level, and it is his flirtation with extremism that highlights the conflated dangers of individualized freedom.

The film engenders a fascination with why Hando and Davey are neo-Nazi skinheads. Avoiding any of the sociological and psychological complexities that may explain this, the film projects Hando and his gang through a stereotypical skinhead identity. Aesthetically resembling this subculture, the gang members wear Doc Martens boots and suspenders and have lots of tattoos and shaved heads. Reflected in this identity is the portrayal of Hando and his skinhead gang as being products of their low socio-economic circumstances. The gang's decision to be skinheads and have neo-Nazi sympathies is driven less by their social position and more by Hando's personal concept of self.

For the neoliberal individual, the concept of self is important, and Hando possesses a strong sense of self. This is evident in his identity, personal choices and actions – despite most of his personal actions being highly disagreeable. Hando's fierce singularity is understood when he explains to Gabe why he 'goes into all of this stuff'.[76] From his private space – his bedroom – Hando's explanation for his violent actions is crudely expressed to Gabe:

> I don't want to be a White Cooley in my own country anymore.
>
> Because rich people and powerful people brought in boat loads of human trash.
>
> Cheap labour.
>
> Gooks mainly.
>
> And there is going to be more.
>
> I want people to know that I am proud of my white history. My white blood.
>
> And one day that might be all that I may have.
>
> And I don't want to go the same way as the fucking Abo.
>
> See that map? That is all the Gook properties in Barkley Street. A few years ago, it was a white area.[77]

Hando's introspection can be seen to propagate a message that Australia's direction towards a market economy will ultimately be defective for him. The fear and hostility shown by Hando in resisting this political-economic shift may well be seen as a cover-up for his own failure to be a competitive agent in the spontaneous market. While Hando would not see himself as a typical victim of neoliberalism, he does use his autonomy to manipulate a victim narrative by launching a witch hunt on the enemy.[78]

In his speech to Gabe, Hando declares the enemy to be the new governing intellectual and fiscal elite (those who have gained some level of social and political influence and power from their prosperity as economic agents), which includes the local Vietnamese community. Declaring the Asian race to be an enemy, Hando is simply reflecting and drawing from a deep historical panic and fear of Asian nations as a basis for the collapse of White Australia.[79] Hando has the free choice to take up this historical 'White Australia' fight, which in his case is motivated by a European legacy that takes on ultra-nationalism, anti-immigration and fascism ideals.[80]

When drawn into the imagined boundaries of Hando's and his gang's way of life, it can be held to be a reconstructed cult of Nazi religiosity and worship. Hando's commitment to and admiration for the Third Reich is clear when he directly reads the following passage from *Mein Kampf*:

> All the noble cultures of the past declined because the purity and vigour of the originally created race faded out. They were compromised by the seed of lesser races, retracted to the works of the superior men. The undeniable reason for their decline was that due to a kind of racial blood poisoning. Racial blood must then be preserved in its purity at all costs.[81]

Despite global condemnation of fascism, Hando's choice to be committed to this regressive movement is unrelenting. He and his skinhead gang are trapped in the nostalgic cult of Hitler worship[82] by reading *Mein Kampf*, having swastika back tattoos and a swastika flag and posters hanging in Hando's bedroom and sharing knowledge of Nazi youth weaponry and Nazi salutes with each other.

Desperate to have something that resembles a national identity, Hando and his Aryan cult have chosen to live by the film's anthem:

> When you see the yellow scum coming up the road, will you turn the other cheek?
> just like a gutless toad or will you stand your scared ground and inform off the bat
> tell him that he is not welcome here and give him several smacks.
> Smack him if he is yellow.
> Smack him if his black.
> Smack him until he fucks off and doesn't come back.
> Smack him in the bollock.

> Smack him in the head. Smack him until it really hurts.
> Smack him until he is dead.[83]

The practice of smacking, romping and stomping by all the skinhead characters in the film directly reflects neo-fascism as a defensive ideology in the tradition of an Aryan cult. Living by fascist beliefs and having a xenophobic and fringe existence are not simply arrived at organically.[84] This observation draws attention to how Hando and his crew are emblematic of historical and rhetorical violence specifically directed at Asians.

Hando's anti-Asian rhetoric and violence reveal his inability to advance himself beyond an early time in Australian society. By pursuing every one of his impulses, Hando is merely continuing national customs of excessive drinking and upholding white patriotism by reciting the commonly known White Australian catchphrase 'this is not your country'.[85] Yet to argue that Hando's unacceptable behaviour is permissible due to his blindly following historical customs is erroneous. Hando's choice to sit outside modern social rules of tolerance and to cause harm to others illustrates an individualized choice and freedom that he is permitted to make for himself away from state guidance and/or interference. These choices are without the need to factor in any utilitarian end for the good. The film shows that individualized freedoms are primarily for self-happiness and self-interest grounded in irrationality and bad faith.

The marketplace

According to neoliberalism, the generous relationship between freedom and autonomy enjoyed by Hando and others is due to the marketplace. The notion of the marketplace is where the contradictions of neoliberalism are most obvious, and *Romper Stomper* goes some way towards highlighting these contradictions and the weakness of this ideology.

Under neoliberal logic, Tiger's (Tony Lee) family and his friends are the successful winners in the marketplace. Although Hando does pay rent for his warehouse, it is Tiger's family and the others in the local Vietnamese community who have capitalized on their skills and available resources by becoming small business owners and operators and acquiring real estate (the Railway Hotel).[86] As the fittest economically, Tiger should be rightly afforded protection from any misfortune, tragedies and inequality yet, as a direct consequence of Hando's choices and actions, *Romper Stomper* reveals that the marketplace does not necessarily guarantee freedoms for a harmonious life – societal order can still be chaotic in the market.

In comparison, Hando is not a typical economic agent, and he could easily be regarded as an economic failure. Instead, Hando illustrates Sen's notion of modern freedom that has Hando judged by his capability set.[87] The capability approach focuses on what Hando is capable of doing, both economically and socially.[88] His acquisition and treatment of property and relationships is only possible due to his ability to simply take. The taking and destroying of all property and relationships with Davey and Gabe show that Hando's capability set gives him the freedom to be competitive. Included in this capability set is his ability to assert power and authority to consume what he wants – and this makes Hando greedy (a trait that is more akin to a neoliberal individual than to a liberal individual in the classic sense).

The neoliberal Australian state

The aggravated projection of the neoliberal state in *Romper Stomper* is manifested in two ways: first in Hando himself and second in the inaction of the state and its agents. The neoliberal shift of 'hollowing out' the nation-state in the film is the noticeable silence of the state by not condemning the numerous occurrences of hate speech or taking any meaningful action to prevent the 'romping and stomping' on the streets of Footscray. Without the purview of the state, Hando is allowed to be free to espouse his fascist ideology and to act on his intolerance to cause harm to Tiger. The film signifies that when the paternalistic state is greatly diminished, there is a gap that is filled by irrational free individuals such as Hando.

Confidently stepping into this gap, Hando reflects an early Australian paternalistic state constructed around hierarchy, ultra-masculinity and anarchy. The extreme violence and crimes committed by Hando (and his gangs) are easily reimagined to be an exercise of coercive state power whereby past wrongdoings by the state against Indigenous Australians and early Asian settlers were beyond reproach. This punitive view of the Australian state is taken further in *Romper Stomper* by Hando rebuffing the neoliberal principle of 'racelessness'. Strongly negating this ideal, the film captures profound racial inequalities within Australia and conveys a sobering belief that Australia is unlikely to ever be a post-racial society.

Romper Stomper as a cultural text is not optimistic about neoliberal governmentality in Australia. The film captures the state's departure from its welfare role through the portrayal of anarchy. It tells in a brutal way that individuals are not stoically rational, but frail. The unremitting vilification, harassment and physical attacks by Hando and his gang are traumatic and frustrating for Tiger and his friends. Without the state in its welfare role to guarantee Tiger's security, he has no choice but to take essential action to protect himself. Tiger's efforts to stop Hando's taunting involve mobilizing his friends and others in the Australian-Vietnamese community to become a stronger combative force. Arming themselves with chains, planks of wood and guns, they bring down the skinheads in a 'by all means' rebellion.[89] Tiger's *coup d'état* is an inevitable counterbalance to the consequences of unconstrained white supremist activities in Australia.

The film makes a *sui generis* case of living in a post-welfare state by illustrating the marked contradictions of neoliberalism. The political engineering of Prime Ministers Keating and Howard for a smaller state and encouraging self-determination and personal autonomy to maximize self-interest obscure Australia's strongly held value of egalitarianism. *Romper Stomper* exacerbates the disastrous social conditions and inequality experienced by Tiger as a stark reminder that the state no longer has an interest in protecting its citizenry – specifically the vulnerable – or the ability to do so.

Beyond the state's role of protecting the vulnerable, *Romper Stomper* is also questioning the state's morality in not taking action to change intolerance. While neoliberal thought accepts that any action by the state is necessary to ensure stability, this argument comes with a caveat that any state's interference through legal constraints does not always achieve the desired outcome of tolerance.[90] This seems to be true in *Romper Stomper* due to the fact that any forceful police action to enforce legislative rules may not have any impact on Hando to cause him to become tolerant and accepting of Tiger.

Nevertheless, *Romper Stomper* is a strong reminder that a state has an underlying special relationship with individuals, as well as with society at large. Although this relationship is complex, the film is an examination of just how far the bounds of the free neoliberal individual should be allowed to go. In an exaggerated way, *Romper Stomper* is an honest telling that the state has a performative function to protect the weak, and if the state is to shrink in this role and function, then only disorder and insecurity will ensue.

Conclusion

Romper Stomper is a decisive cultural rejection of neoliberal ideology. The honesty of the film's narrative makes clear that the deep social and racial issues of Australia's past are a deplorable failure of the state. The aesthetics of these political failings in *Romper Stomper* offer a vacuum to critique Australia's modernity or progressive new world order to reveal an innate sense that the injustices and intolerance will continue to worsen. The film's polarization of the contradictory and pious aspects of neoliberalism exposes the predictable crisis of a new world order in which the individual is not rational and cannot be saved from society. Yet Wright's projection of alarm through crude language and a fast-paced film structure offers a clash of ideological discourses from the New and Old orders that completely displaces Australia's virtue of being a fair and just society.

Notes

1 Slane (1997), p 173.
2 O'Regan (1996), p 152.
3 Anon (1 August 2011) 'The 25 Most Dangerous Movies Ever Made'.
4 Wright (1992), *Romper Stomper*. For 28 years, Australians were entertained by the numerous bickering exchanges, which consisted of Margaret loving a film and David being in total disagreement, and conversely David loving a film and Margaret disagreeing with David's views – there were very few occasions where they both agreed.
5 Upon *Romper Stomper*'s international release, the film was banned in South Korea, Canada and Glasgow. See Aveyard, Moran and Vieth (2018), p 205; Haflidason (2006); Quinn (1993), p 5.

6 Anon (1992c).
7 Daniel Pollock committed suicide at Newtown Station in Sydney shortly after filming *Romper Stomper*. Following Pollock's untimely death, Crowe wrote a song about his friend entitled 'The Night That Davey Hit the Train'. Crowe's song was performed by his band Thirty Odd Foot of Grunts. See Anon (1992a).
8 Wright (1992) *Romper Stomper* 0:54–3:07. The opening scene was actually filmed at Richmond Train Station and not at Footscray Train Station as the film states. Anon (1992b).
9 See Wright (1992) *Romper Stomper* 2:01-2:12, 22:06–24:16, 38:31-38:52, 46:24–46:50.
10 Fried (1993), p 49. See also Wright (1992) *Romper Stomper* 0:54–3:07, 27:35-41-04, 1:17:55–1:18:09.
11 Wright (1992) *Romper Stomper* 1:21:49–1:28:45.
12 Wright (1992) *Romper Stomper* 1:27:56–1:28:00. The Nazi Youth knife was bought by Hando for Davey from Magoo (John Brumpton), who stole the knife from the National War Museum: Wright (1992) *Romper Stomper* 17:35.
13 Wright (1992) *Romper Stomper* 1:28:30–1:29:05.
14 Berry (1993), p 9.
15 Butterss (1998), p 41.
16 Fried (1993), p 50.
17 O'Regan (1996), p 138.
18 Goldsmith (2001), p 117.
19 Paterson (2009).
20 For a small example of select films, see *For the Term of His Natural Life* (1927), *The Adventures of Barry McKenzie* (1972) and *Mad Dog Morgan* (1976).
21 Tsiolkas (February–March 1993), p 47.
22 Butterss (1998), pp 44–5.
23 *A Clockwork Orange* (1971). Writing for *Variety*, David Stratton curtly described *Romper Stomper* as '*A Clockwork Orange* without the intellect'. See Stratton (1992).
24 *Taxi Driver*(1976).
25 See, for example, *Picnic at Hanging Rock* (1975), *Crocodile Dundee* (1986) and *The Man from Snowy River* (1982).
26 Greenberg (1993).
27 Elliott (2017).
28 Butterss (1998), p 45; Quinn (1993), p 6.
29 Gray (2012).
30 Stewart (2018).
31 Tsiolkas (1993), p 47; Williams (1993), p 48.
32 Whitford (2017).
33 Ma (2018); Pidgeon (2017); Quinn (2017a, 2017b). Naturally, the announcement of the film's reboot had some detractors. See also Shad (2017).
34 Cole (2015), p 134.
35 Marr (2001), p 1.
36 *Mabo v Queensland (No. 2)* (1992) 175 CLR 1.
37 Anon (2002).
38 Keating (1993).
39 Edwards (2007), p 20.
40 Hardin (2014), p 199.
41 See Campbell and Pedersen (2001), p 5; Durkheim (2001); Fourcade and Healy (2007), p 287; Hayek (1944); Stiglitz (2008); Walter (1944).
42 Mudge (2008), p 703. The journey of neoliberalism can be traced to the first gathering of the Mont Pelerin Society, where the society's founding member, Friedrich Hayek, organized a meeting in the Swiss Alps on 10 April 1947. The first meeting attracted

elite intellectuals from the subject areas of economics, history and philosophy. Hayek held the strong hope that the Mont Pelerin Societies could be established as an international academy of political philosophy that would refute socialism and, moreover, be a source of influence on political structures through ideas. See Darity (2008), pp 272–3.
43 Turner (2008), p 4; Gall et al. (2011), p 2.
44 Jackson (2016), pp 827–8.
45 McIntosh and Hatcher (2010), p 2.
46 Patterson (2005), p 376.
47 Hayek (2011), p 13.
48 Wrenn (2015), p 1233.
49 Plant (2010), p 8.
50 Plant (2010), pp 8–9.
51 Robbins (1932), p 136.
52 Wrenn (2015), pp 1233–4.
53 Wren (2015), pp 1233–4.
54 Amable (2011), p 15.
55 Nafissi (2000), pp 215–16.
56 Patterson (2005), p 378.
57 Bourdieu (1986), p 379.
58 Lerch et al. (2017), p 39.
59 Patterson (2005), p 379.
60 Patterson (2005), p 379.
61 Patterson (2005), p 379.
62 Plant (2004), p 33.
63 Zafaruliah and Huque (2012), p 21.
64 Sharpe (2009), p 79; Taylor (2006).
65 Anon (2013) *The Guardian*.
66 Prime Minister Paul Keating's privatization framework was advanced by John Howard by corporatizing profitable state entities (e.g. Telstra and Qantas), outsourcing public services and subsidizing the private consumption of public goods to expand markets (such as education and health). Fenna (2013), p 96; Redden (2019), p 7.
67 Pusey (1991), p 14.
68 Collins and Cottle (2010), p 26.
69 Weller and O'Neill (2014), p 112.
70 Tingle (2013), p 27.
71 Aulich and O'Flynn (2007), p 369.
72 Rose and Miller (2008), pp 67–8.
73 Howard (1995).
74 Paul (2006), p 224.
75 Compared with the American skinhead film *American History X* (Kaye 1989), in which white supremacist leader and neo-Nazi Derek Vineyard (Edward Norton) is arrested, prosecuted and imprisoned for the murder of two black Americans. Derek is reformed in jail, and while on parole, he desperately attempts to protect his younger brother, Danny, and prevent him from joining a white supremacist group and a life of violence and crime.
76 Gabe asks this question when looking up from Hando at the portrait of Adolf Hitler and the Nazi flag. Wright (1992) *Romper Stomper* 23:07.
77 Wright (1992) *Romper Stomper* 23:09–24:08.
78 Fekete (2016), p 6.
79 Walker (2003), pp 35–7.
80 It is worth noting that *Romper Stomper* sits alongside numerous Australian films in which savage racial conflict and the assertion of white colonial British values through

authority and power are transfigured on the screen. For just a few of the many white colonial Australian films, see *Jedda* (1995), *The Chant of Jimmie Blacksmith* (1978), *Rabbit-Proof Fence* (2002), *The Cowra Breakout* (1984) and *Australian Rules* (2002).

81 Wright (1992) *Romper Stomper* 25:22:00.
82 Goodrick-Clarke (2001), p 3.
83 Wright (1992) *Romper Stomper* 15:42:00–16:14. This is also known as the 'The Smack Song', composed by John Clifford White. See Screen Australia (1992).
84 Whitsel (2001), p 91.
85 Wright (1992) *Romper Stomper* 2:13.
86 Wright (1992) *Romper Stomper* 26:05–26:30.
87 Sen (2009), p 231.
88 Sen (2009), p 235.
89 Wright (1992) *Romper Stomper* 28:17–42:00.
90 Spong (2001), p 90.

References

Secondary sources

Bruno Amable (2011) 'Morals and Politics in the Ideology of Neo-Liberalism' 9 *Socio-Economic Review* 15.

Anon (1992a) 'Daniel Pollock Biography', *IMDb*, www.imdb.com/name/nm0689646/bio?ref_=nm_ov_bio_sm.

——— (1992b) 'Romper Stomper (1992) – Trivia', *IMDb*, www.imdb.com/title/tt0105275/trivia.

——— (1992c) '*Romper Stomper*: The Movie David Stratton Famously Refused to Rate', *The Movie Show*, SBS, 11 November, www.sbs.com.au/movies/review/romper-stomper-review-movie-david-stratton-famously-refused-rate.

——— (2002) 'I was Wrong on *Mabo*: Kennett', *The Age*, 1 June, www.theage.com.au/national/i-was-wrong-on-mabo-kennett-20020601-gdu9dt.html.

——— (2011) 'The 25 Most Dangerous Movies Ever Made (by Premiere) on IMDb', *IMDb*, 1 August, www.imdb.com/list/ls005175975/.

——— (2013) 'Margaret Thatcher: A Life in Quotes', *The Guardian*, 8 April, www.theguardian.com/politics/2013/apr/08/margaret-thatcher-quotes.

Chris Aulich and Janine O'Flynn (2007) 'John Howard: The Great Privatiser?' 42(2) *Australian Journal of Political Science* 369.

Karina Aveyard, Albert Moran and Errol Vieth (2018) *Historical Dictionary of Australian and New Zealand Cinema* (2nd ed.), Rowman and Littlefield.

Chris Berry (1993) 'More Bangs for Your Buck: Male Sexuality and/or Violence in Recent Australian Films' 13(1) *Artlink* 9.

Pierre Bourdieu (1986) *Distinction: A Social Critique of the Judgement of Taste*, Routledge.

Philp Butterss (1998) 'When Being a Man is all You Got: Masculinity in *Romper Stomper*, *Idiot Box*, *Blackrock* and *The Boys*' 117 *Metro: Media & Education Magazine* 41.

John L. Campbell and Ove K. Pedersen (2001) *The Rise of Neoliberalism and Institutional Analysis*, Princeton University Press.

Mike Cole (2015) *Racism: A Critical Analysis*, Pluto Press.

Joe Collins and Drew Cottle (2010) 'Labor Neoliberalists or Pragmatic Neoliberalists? The Hawke and Keating Governments in Office 1983–96' 98 *Labour History* 26.

William Darity (2008) *International Encyclopaedia of the Social Sciences*, Vol. 5 'Mont Pelerin Society', Macmillan.

Emile Durkheim (2001) *The Elementary Forms of Religious Life*, Oxford University Press.

Lindy Edwards (2007) *How to Argue with an Economist: Reopening Political Debate in Australia* (2nd ed.), Cambridge University Press.

Tim Elliott (2017) 'Geoffrey Wright on His *Romper Stomper* Remake – And Why Donald Trump Inspired Him', *Sydney Morning Herald*, 17 November, www.smh.com.au/lifestyle/geoffrey-wright-on-his-romper-stomper-remake-and-why-donald-trump-inspired-him-20171107-gzgadi.html.

Liz Fekete (2016) 'Flying the Flag for Neoliberalism' 58(3) *Race & Class* 6.

Alan Fenna (2013) 'The Economic Policy Agenda in Australia, 1962–2012' 72(2) *Australian Journal of Public Administration* 96.

Marion Fourcade and Kieran Healy (2007) 'Moral Views of Market Society' 33 *Annual Review of Sociology* 287.

John Fried (1993) '*Romper Stomper*' 20(2) *Cineaste* 49.

Gregor Gall, Adrian Wilkinson and Richard Hurd (eds) (2011), 'Introduction' *The International Handbook of Labour Unions*, Edward Elgar.

Ben Goldsmith (2001) 'All Quiet on the Western Front: Suburban Reverberations in Recent Australia', in Ian Craven (ed.), *Australian Cinema in the 1900s*, Frank Cass.

Nicholas Goodrick-Clarke (2001) *Black Sun: Aryan Cults, Esoteric Nazism and Politics of Identity*, New York University Press.

Richard Gray (2012) 'Exclusive Interview: Geoffrey Wright on 20th Anniversary of *Romper Stomper*', *The Reel Bits.com*, 2 October, https://thereelbits.com/2012/10/02/exclusive-interview-geoffrey-wright-on-20th-anniversary-of-romper-stomper.

James Greenberg (1993) 'The Box Next to Film Clips: Hate from Down Under; Director Geoffrey Wright Survived Death Threats to Make *Romper Stomper* "a Graphic Look at Australian Skinheads"', *Los Angeles Times*, 13 June, http://articles.latimes.com/1993-06-13/entertainment/ca-2554_1_geoffrey-wright.

Almar Haflidason (2006) '*Romper Stomper* DVD (1992)', *BBC*, 19 November, www.bbc.co.uk/films/2000/10/20/romper_stomper_1992_dvd_review.shtml.

Carolyn Hardin (2014) 'Finding the "Neo" in Neoliberalism' 28(2) *Cultural Studies* 199.

Friedrich Hayek (1944) *The Road to Serfdom*, University of Chicago Press.

——— (2011) *The Constitution of Liberty*, University of Chicago Press.

The Honourable John Howard (1995) 'The Role of Government', Speech, Menzies Research Centre, https://australianpolitics.com/1995/06/06/john-howard-headland-speech-role-of-govt.html.

Ben Jackson (2016) 'Currents of Neo-Liberalism: British Political Ideologies and the New Right, c. 1955–1979' 131(551) *English Historical Review* 827.

The Honourable Paul Keating (15 November 1993) '*Mabo*: An Address to the Nation', www.keating.org.au/shop/item/mabo-an-address-to-the-nation-15-november-1993.

Julia Lerch, Patricia Bromley, Francisco O. Ramirez and John W. Meyer (2017) 'The Rise of Individual Agency in Conceptions of Society: Textbooks Worldwide, 1950–2011' 32(1) *International Sociology* 39.

Walter Lippmann (1944) *The Good Society*, Allen & Unwin.

Wenlei Ma (2018) 'The Problem with Controversial Romper Stomper Series', *News.com.au*, 2 January, www.news.com.au/entertainment/tv/tv-shows/the-problem-with-controversial-romper-stomper-series/news-story/57b949705facbb83d54881807b5eb37d.

David Marr (2001) *Panic*, Black Inc.

Wayne V. McIntosh and Laura J. Hatcher (eds) (2010), 'Introduction' *Property Rights and Neoliberalism: Cultural Demands and Legal Actions*, Routledge.

Stephanie Lee Mudge (2008) 'The State of the Art: What is Neo-Liberalism?' 6 *Socio-Economic Review* 703.

Mohammad R. Nafissi (2000) 'The Paradox of Principles: The Dialectics of Hayek's Liberalism' 29(2) *Economy and Society* 215.

Tom O'Regan (1996) *Australian National Cinema*, Routledge.

Lucille Paterson (2009) '*Romper Stomper* (Geoffrey Wright, 1992)' 52 *Senses of Cinema*, http://sensesofcinema.com/2009/key-moments-in-australian-cinema-issue-70-march-2014/romper-stomper-geoffrey-wright-1992.

Thomas C. Patterson (2005) 'The Turn to Agency: Neoliberalism, Individuality, and Subjectivity in Late Twentieth-Century Anglophone Archaeology' 17 *Rethinking Marxism* 376.

Erik Paul (2006) *Little America: Australia, the 51st State*, Pluto Press.

Emily Pidgeon (2017) 'Is this a True Depiction of Australia Today? The New *Romper Stomper* Shows Racist Violence in the Street – as the Series is Condemned as a "Ticking Time Bomb" for Inciting Gangs', *Daily Mail Australia*, 23 December, www.dailymail.co.uk/news/article-5208109/Romper-Stomper-TV-series-ticking-time-bomb-gangs.html.

Raymond Plant (2004) 'Neo-Liberalism and the Theory of the State: From *Wohlfahrtsstaat* to *Rechtsstaat*' 75 *The Political Quarterly* 33.

——— (2010) *The Neo-Liberal State*, Oxford University Press.

Michael Pusey (1991) *Economic Rationalism in Australia*, Cambridge University Press.

Karl Quinn (1993) '*Romper Stomper*' 92 *Metro Magazine: Media & Education Magazine* 5.

——— (2017a) '*Romper Stomper* Holds a Mirror to the Ugly Face of Racism in Australia Today', *Sydney Morning Herald*, 19 December, www.smh.com.au/entertainment/tv-and-radio/romper-stomper-holds-a-mirror-to-the-ugly-face-of-racism-in-australia-today-20171218-h06aqa.html.

——— (2017b) '*Romper Stomper*'s Violent Neo-Nazi Skinheads to Run Riot Again – This Time on TV Stuff', *Stuff*, 1 August, www.stuff.co.nz/entertainment/tv-radio/95306186/romper-stompers-violent-neonazi-skinheads-to-run-riot-again-this-time-on-tv.

Guy Redden (2019) 'John Howard's Investor State: Neoliberalism and the Rise of Inequality in Australia' *Critical Sociology*, doi:10.1177/0896920517745117.

Lionel Robbins (1932) *An Essay on the Nature and Significance of Economic Science*, Macmillan.

Nikolas Rose and Peter Miller (2008) *Governing the Present: Administering Economic, Social and Personal Life*, Polity Press.

Screen Australia (1992) 'The Screen Guide – *Romper Stomper* 1992', *Screen Australia*, www.screenaustralia.gov.au/the-screen-guide/t/romper-stomper-1992/1403.

Amartya Sen (2009) *The Idea of Justice*, Allen Lane.

Saman Shad (2017) '*Romper Stomper*: Why I Won't Be Watching Stan's New TV Series', *ABC News*, 11 August, www.abc.net.au/news/2017-08-11/why-i-wont-be-watching-the-new-romper-stomper/8790934.

Matthew Sharpe (2009) 'Is Neoliberalism a Liberalism, or a Stranger Kind of Bird? On Hayek and Out Discontents' 10 *Critical Horizons* 79.

Andrea Slane (1997) 'Sexy Nazis and Daddy's Girl: Fascism and Sexuality', in Bend Huppauf (ed.), *War Violence and the Modern Condition*, Walter de Gruyter.

Heath Spong (2001) 'Individuality and Freedom: From Aesthetic Individualism to a Modern Approach' 6 *New York University Journal of Law & Liberty* 90.

Red Stewart (2018) 'Exclusive Interview – Filmmaker Geoffrey Wright Talks *Romper Stomper* TV Series, Donald Trump, and Roger Corman Compromises', *Flickering Myth.com*, 21 June, www.flickeringmyth.com/2018/06/exclusive-interview-filmmaker-geoffrey-wright-talks-romper-stomper-tv-series-donald-trump-and-roger-corman-comparisons.
Joseph E. Stiglitz (2008) 'The End of Neo-Liberalism?', *Project Syndicate*, 7 July, www.project-syndicate.org/commentary/the-end-of-neo-liberalism?barrier=accesspaylog.
David Stratton (1992) '*Romper Stomper*', *Variety*, 31 December, https://variety.com/1991/film/reviews/romper-stomper-1200429267.
Marcus Taylor (2006) *From Pinochet to the 'Third Way': Neoliberalism and Social Transformation in Chile*, Pluto Press.
Laura Tingle (2013) *Great Expectations: Government, Entitlement and an Angry Nation*, Black Inc.
Christos Tsiolkas (1993) '*Romper Stomper* – Dad and Dave Go Skinhead: *Romper Stomper* and the Art of Non-Political Cinema', *Arena Magazine*, February–March.
Rachel S. Turner (2008) *Neo-Liberal Ideology – History, Concepts and Policies*, Edinburgh University Press.
David Walker (2003) 'Race Building and Disciplining of White Australia', in Laksiri Jayasuriya, David Walker and Jan Gothard (eds), *Legacies of White Australia: Race, Culture and Nation*, University of Western Australia Press.
Sally Weller and Phillip O'Neill (2014) 'An Argument with Neoliberalism: Australia's Place in a Global Imaginary' 4(2) *Dialogues in Human Geography* 112.
Troy Whitford (2017) '*Romper Stomper* Reboot Is a Compelling Investigation into Australia's Extremist Politics', *ABC News*, 30 December, www.abc.net.au/news/2017-12-30/romper-stomper-stan-russell-crowe-skinheads-neo-nazis/9291716.
Brad Whitsel (2001) 'Ideological Mutation and Millennial Belief in the American Neo-Nazi Movement' 24 *Studies in Conflict & Terrorism* 91.
Evan Williams (1993) 'Strictly Stomper' 1–2 *Quadrant* 48.
Mary V. Wrenn (2015) 'Agency and Neoliberalism' 39 *Cambridge Journal of Economics* 1233.
Habib Zafaruliah and Ahmed Shafiqui Huque (2012) *Managing Developments in a Globalized World: Concepts, Process, Institutions*, Taylor & Francis.

Primary sources

Mabo v Queensland (No. 2) (1992) 175 CLR 1.

Films

Bruce Beresford (1972) *The Adventures of Barry, McKenzie*, Longford Productions.
Charles Chauvel (1995) *Jedda*, Charles Chauvel Productions.
Norman Dawn (1927) *For the Term of His Natural Life*, Australasia Films.
Peter Faiman (1986) *Crocodile Dundee*, Rimfire Films.
Paul Goldman (2002) *Australian Rules*, Tiny Town Productions.
Tony Kaye (1989) *American History X*, New Line Cinema, Savoy Pictures and the Turman-Morrissey Company.
Stanley Kubrick (1971) *A Clockwork Orange*, Polaris Productions.
George T. Miller (1982) *The Man from Snowy River*, Cambridge Productions, Edgeley International and Snow River Investment.

Philippe Mora (1976) *Mad Dog Morgan*, Motion Picture Productions.
Phillip Noyce (2002) *Rabbit-Proof Fence*, Olsen Levy Productions and Rumbalara Films.
Fred Schepisi (1978) *The Chant of Jimmie Blacksmith*, Victorian Film.
Martin Scorsese (1976) *Taxi Driver*, Bill/Phillips Productions/Italo/Judeo Productions.
Peter Weir (1975) *Picnic at Hanging Rock*, Australian Film Commission, British Empire Films and McElroy & McElroy Picnic Productions.
Geoffrey Wright (1992) *Romper Stomper*, Romper Stomper.

Chapter 13

Justice at the end of *Fury Road*

Kieran Tranter

Introduction

After 33 years in the cinematic wilderness, George Miller's reboot of the Mad Max[1] franchise with *Mad Max: Fury Road*[2] (*Fury Road*) was a surprise. While it performed adequately at the box office, with takings of US$378 million,[3] becoming the 20th highest grossing film in 2015, it was better received by the Academy, winning six Oscars with ten nominations.[4] It was a bigger success with critics, many of whom regarded it as one of the best films of the year.[5] Key to its critical success was Miller's reimagining of the high-octane post-apocalyptic Australian desert dystopia as a woman's story.[6] This handbrake U-turn in messaging from the previous films was dramatic, reflective of the spectacular vehicle stunts of the film. As Alexis de Coning notes, the franchise had 'represented a fantasy of masculine power, geared primarily for male consumption',[7] yet with *Fury Road* the projection of men, machines and violence that drove the original trilogy of films (*Mad Max*,[8] *Mad Max 2: The Road Warrior*[9] and *Mad Max: Beyond Thunderdome*)[10] – like the repurposed and reappropriated mid-20th-century vehicles that battle and thunder relentlessly across the films – is changed. *Fury Road* is clearly the end of the road for the men and their form of technological masculinity of the previous films, but, notwithstanding the suggestions of ecological and climate collapse, it is not *the end*. Rather, this chapter argues that, through Furiosa's victory over Immortan Joe (Hugh Keays-Byrne) (with Max's help) and the return to the Citadel, *Fury Road* opens up the possibility of a future free from the violence of men and machines.

The chapter begins by looking back on the Mad Max franchise as a raw and violent representation of men and cars in Australia. It then argues that, in screening this end, *Fury Road* presents a different form of justice – a justice of potential that could be a harbinger of a changed future.

Mad Max, men and cars in Australia

Every two years the tiny Australian town of Silverton, just outside Broken Hill, hosts the Mad Max festival,[11] centred at its *Mad Max 2: The Road Warrior*–themed museum.[12] The town becomes an epicentre for cosplayers and their families to indulge in the aesthetics of the franchise through costumes and vehicles within the landscape of the film.[13] This family-orientated fun time in the outback seems perversely at odds with the S&M costuming, rapes, murders and bloody vivisections depicted in the films. The films are known for the visceral violence of men in motor vehicles hurting and destroying: '*Mad Max* is a film about the collective compulsion to engage in, and applaud, murderous vehicular conduct on the roads'.[14] Given that a founding event in the Mad Max universe is the death of Max's wife and child under the wheels of Toecutter's (played by a much younger Hugh Keays-Byrne) motorcycle,[15] the franchise seems like a strange context for family fun. It is this juxtaposition between the aesthetic and critical legacy of the original films and the family holiday of the Mad Max festival that drives this section of the chapter.

For critics, the original films are nihilistic and destructive, expanding out in several directions like a slow-moving dust cloud. In a dark, voyeuristic manner, the original films exposed the insubstantial nature of Australian settler state masculinity, its death drive with the machine, its alien occupation of another people's land, its need to fabricate foundational myths. The films occupy a liminal space where gratuitous celebration entwines with critique. The original films are an exciting, complicit visualization of various, yet specifically Australian, injustices. Yet at the epicentre of this dusty, enveloping cloud of critique was the car crash.[16]

Cars are everywhere in the Mad Max films. They are driven, chased, crashed. Bits of cars are reappropriated for shelter and for other machines. With the lens focused on the car, the films – even *Mad Max*, where entropic civilization is sliding into the fall – there are movement and mobility. Landscapes flashes by, flat and red and full of dead stationary things – despoiled carcasses of cars, humans and animal life. To be mobile is to live; to stop is to die.[17] However, the films are 'autogeddon', not 'autopia'.[18] The car system, with its global reach of geopolitics of energy, pollution and climate change, is identified as causing the collapse. This is the first of many ironies of the original films: after the car-driven fall, the car retains vitality and necessity.[19]

Furthermore, there is a strong gendered dimension to the screened car use.[20] Men are predominately the drivers of vehicles in the original films, and critics have long identified a profound gendered and sexual orientation to the use and abuse of the car.[21] The violence, destruction and explosive climaxes to the car chases are deeply sexual in a hard, masculine way. There is an intertwining of the male body, as powerful, sexual and damaged, with the physical materiality of the car. There is interchangeability between vehicle and male bodies in the film.[22] This mechanical eros performs and exposes a particular historical truth of Australian roads and car culture. Mad Max captures

> an Australian Gothic feel, characterised by deceptively empty roads where death could await just around the next corner. Max's nightmare is that of every road user and every Australian who has been affected by Australia's road carnage. This hyper-realism associated with death and the roads intersects with viewers' definitions of the relationship between sexuality and space.[23]

Studies of car culture have identified a particular gendered performance associated with cars, driving and gender.[24] Sarah Redshaw uses the phrase 'combustion masculinity' to encapsulate the mechanical eros that critics identify in Mad Max. Redshaw defines combustion masculinity as a violent, invasive drive to subdue machine and world.[25] She identifies combustion masculinity as an extreme expression of male sexuality, involving alternating pressure and release, anticipation of limits and ecstasy of surpassing.[26] It also has a homosocial spectatorship.[27] Combustion masculinity not only involves speed and the surpassing of limits in cars, but also does so spectacularly. It is a form of masculinity that requires the performance to be seen by other men.[28]

The films are deeply ambivalent regarding combustion masculinity. Foremost, the queer tendencies that dwell within combustion masculinity are exposed. The early films seem to be trying too hard to stabilize the heterosexual credentials of combustion masculinity. In *Mad Max*, Max's revenge spree is triggered by the murder of his wife and child. In *The Road Warrior*, the settler community desires to escape to the coast to 'breeeeeed'.[29] In both films, the marauding villains are negatively portrayed as other than heterosexual.[30] At an immediate level, these films – with their evil 'gay baddies' who rape, kill, plunder and destroy – are homophobic. However, as Rebecca Johinke notes,

> Miller establishes Max as a masculine hero, questing to defend the car-driving patriarchy from the threat of menacing gay scoot-jockeys. Interestingly, this heterosexual mission sends him into the Forbidden Zone of homoerotic desire.[31]

In driving and fighting in his modified black and dusty V8 Interceptor, wearing torn black and dusty leathers, Max visually becomes indistinguishable from the other queer road warriors. Further, throughout the films, Max does not find redemption and solace in the arms of women. His friendships are few and entirely with men: Goose (Steve Bisley) in *Mad Max*, the Gyro Captain (Bruce Spence) in *The Road Warrior.* The police captain Labatouche (Jonathan Hardy), trying to maintain order on the raggedy edge of civilization in *Mad Max*, is decidedly camp.[32] Sarah Lochlann Jain identifies that:

> Historically, the car was picked up nearly immediately as a tool to renew a masculinity challenged by industrialization. . . . This assertion of masculinity through technology followed ambivalent tracks. On the one hand, the driver's seat reasserted the male as the family head in control of its destiny. The car became a symbol of paternity – daddy driving the family on around on Sunday. On the other hand, the car provided the male with a means of escape from the family and domesticity – it was the private place that gentlemen could drink, swear, and court.[33]

With its emphasis on men, their bodies and their intertwining with machines, Mad Max follows these ambivalent tracks. There are just too many '"unquiet" look(s) at the screened male'[34] for these to be heteronormative films. Indeed, the ambiguous anxieties of its sexual orientation might explain the number of Mad Max-inspired pornographies in which the films' aesthetics are explicitly positioned as heteronormative.[35] The car's patriarchal and heterosexual credentials are revealed as a performance, a forced manifestation of an underlying technological entwined masculinity that, in its essential tendencies, is not that concerned with women and care, but with being seen driving to the limit by other excited men.[36]

The end expression of this expression/repression conflict in combustion masculinity lies in dissolution and madness. Mel Gibson's Max in the films is 'mad', a mostly mute monad whose self-destruction is only averted by luck and chance. Notwithstanding in-text claims about his redemption, Max does not seem at peace with himself at the conclusions of *The Road Warrior* and *Beyond Thunderdome*. His death wish for a climatic, explosive end in an automobile accident remains unfulfilled. Rather, his final scenes have him hurt and alone on the road in the desert. Max pointedly does not join either settler group. For Katherine Biber, this lost insubstantialness to Max at the conclusion of his battles connects to something distinctly Australian:

> The road in Australian cinema does not lead anywhere. It does not move towards masculine affirmation, nor does it locate freedom. No one ever goes anywhere on the roads. They are a forum, a stage, for the performance of a series of cultural rituals.[37]

Mad Max did not just screen the expression/repression of male sexuality within combustion masculinity but did so in a very specific place. In the filmography of red deserts and blue skies, the kangaroo carcasses, the blue heeler cattle dog, the unique Australian-made 1970s cars and the accents heard, Mad Max screened a particularly Australian iteration of combustion masculinity.[38] Mad Max is specifically a white Australian tale.[39] There are no First Nations Australians or any suggestion of First Nations knowledge and culture of living well in the Australian bush. The only possible indication is the Feral Child in *The Road Warrior*, whose boomerang and features possibly suggests First Nation heritage. The lens capturing the action in Mad Max is a lens located within the settler state. Nothing suggests *terra nullius* more than empty spaces and decayed objects. The Australian landscape is presented as a hostile, dangerous unknown that must be traversed and conquered with machines.[40] It is a space that needs to be made place through technologically augmented white labour in the face of death.

Yet Mad Max does connect combustion masculinity to Australian colonial occupation. *The Road Warrior* has been identified as particularly encoding the role of the car in the settler state, arguing how the film shows the car as an instrument of control over bodies in time and space in a specific, targeted mobile fashion.[41] In this, it articulates the technical imagery that underpinned the ongoing colonialist programme of removing First Nations children from kin and country.[42] The landscape of Mad Max is a post-settler state as much as it is post-apocalyptic.

Before the fall, the car – very possibly Max in the 'Pursuit Specials' of the 'Main Force Patrol' – had already done its job of disappearing the First Nations people. Where the settler state has to engage with a First Nation presence continually through laws and technologies, Mad Max depicts an already 'whited out' Australia ready for conflicted, violent men in machines to claim.

In the absence of any suggestive rival cosmologies, critics regard the films as what can be termed a 'white mythology'.[43] It has been identified as a playing out of the Hobbesian state of nature.[44] The decline of sovereign authority has witnessed the resurgence of the war of all against all.[45] This seems superficially on show in *The Road Warrior* – although, rather than war of all against all, what is witnessed in Papagallo's (Mike Preston) fortified community and Humungus's (Kjell Nilsson) horde is more a 'conservative fantasy'[46] of 'protection societies' coming into conflict over scarce resources.[47] In *Mad Max*, rather than the conflict leading to the re-establishment of Leviathan,[48] the wastelands and battling bikies and vigilante cops better disclose Behemoth,[49] the decomposition of sovereign order by unruly groups.[50] In *Beyond Thunderdome*, nothing particularly 'exceptional' is happening in Bartertown. Rather, in the power struggles of Aunty Entity (Tina Turner) and Master (Angelo Rossitto), there is the everyday intrigue of the palace.[51] Underlying all these representations of the rise, decline and politicking of the state is a violent, individualized humanity. The human as wolf – Hobbes's *homo homini lupus*,[52] represented to a degree by the animal tails adorning some of the bikies – is projected by the first three Mad Max films.

This vision of humans as wolves does disclose an orientation to law. Mad Max vividly presents modernity's law as grounded in essential violence.[53] The cops of the 'Main Force Patrol' of the first film are as violent towards the bikies as the bikies seem to be towards others. Max wantonly rams Nightrider's (Vince Gil) vehicle in the opening chase sequence and goes on to hunt down and extrajudicially execute Toecutter and his gang one by one as his 'madness' seeps in. In a world of wolf-men, law only has a reality through actualities of violence.[54] Law is disconnected from any higher order or justice and is revealed as just a material fact of power to be deployed by the powerful for expedient ends: the securing of scarce resources, the removal of problematic populations, the bloody enforcing of the powerful's preferred order. In this unadorned legal space, the sovereign is revealed as merely the alpha-wolf – the biggest, baddest beast in the pack. This is something to which Miller alludes repeatedly in the look and actions of the lead antagonists, Toecutter, Humungus and Immortan Joe.

This wolfish horizon, where humans violently kill over the scraps of civilization and law is nothing more than the will of the powerful, essentially exhausts the mythic value of the initial Mad Max films. Within this world-view, the only escape and possibility for change is through the hero. Miller has indicated how he was influenced by Joseph Campbell and the monomyth of the hero in his work, and in Mad Max specifically.[55] Through this lens, Max emerges as a blighted hero whose sacrifices rebirth civilization.[56] However, the hero is a conservative figure. The hero restores pre-existing order.[57] Max's 'justice' is pure retribution – the revengeful hunting down of Toecutter's gang in the first film.[58] Max, the white male policeman who becomes a road warrior, seemingly can only bring forth societies doomed to repeat patriarchy, technologically augmented displacement of the First Nations people and despoliation of the environment.[59] Within Campbell's mythology true change, a break with the heroic circle of rise, fall and rise again lies with the trickster.[60] Male Max with his heroic 'madness', machines, fighting and low loquacity can seemingly only ensure a return of the same.[61] Men and machines are still in the lead at the end of *The Road Warrior*. In *Beyond Thunderdome*, notwithstanding Savannah Nix's (Helen Buday) caring, it is still the men with machines – Max, Master and Jedediah the pilot (Bruce Spence)[62] – that lead the plane-wrecked children to Tomorrow-Morrow Land. Tina Turner's 'We Don't Need Another Hero'[63] over the credits in *Beyond Thunderdome* seems a plea for a change from hero men as something to break the cycle, but the substantive focus titillatingly remains on violent men and the conserving justice of their machine use and abuse.

This vision of men, machines and violence has now changed. Australian roads and driving are not the sites for men proving themselves through mangled metal and lives that Miller experienced in the early 1970s as a young trauma surgeon in Australia.[64] The cars and roads have substantially changed. Vehicles are safer and semi-intelligent, increasingly not allowing drivers to perform the tyre-shredding excesses of combustion masculinity.[65] The roads have been re-engineered and remade, with concrete barriers, extra lanes, speed cameras and various other forms of passive and active policing.[66] The gender order that was sustained by motor vehicles – the order preserved by Max's heroics – is being challenged.[67] Women are present as vehicle owners, drivers and purchasers.[68] Indeed, the whole energy economy of automobility is shifting from fossil fuels to electrics.[69] This changed culture can be glimpsed in the material accruements of contemporary Australian automobile culture. A feature that emerged in the mid-2010s was the visual economy of a woman driving an SUV with a decal proclaiming 'My Family', through representations of the family members as stick figures.[70] This strong declaration of road and vehicle use as zones for women and children generated a response from the remnants of combustion masculinity: the affixing of offensive and violent 'My Family' parody stickers. This was a response rooted in defeatist insecurity, a need to resist encroachments into the traditionally male terrain of the road through symbolic violence.[71] Simply put, the road culture that is ambiguously both celebrated and critiqued in the first three films is retreating in the rear-view mirror.

It is this *pastness* of the first three films that might explain the Mad Max festival. There is a nostalgia for an aesthetics and a moment in time, for remembering a particular style of vehicular consumption and being male that is challenged and changing.[72] Nostalgia powerfully repurposes memories in the present.[73] It heals or forgets the hurt and violence. It is a lens that filters the complexities of a lived past to reveal a wellspring of safety and identity for the present. Studies of cosplay have identified the strong twining of nostalgia with the safety of the self within the performance.[74] The Mad Max festival seemingly celebrates the look and feel and excitement of the original films, without taking on-board the toxic masculinity. After 40 years from the first instalment, the festival is pure surface play that has blotted out the violence and injustices that were depicted so graphically in the original films.

It is at this point that the fourth film, *Fury Road*, can be introduced. This film – ambiguously a reboot or a fourth instalment[75] – shares with the Mad Max festival a nostalgia for the aesthetics of the original film. The desert-scape and blue skies are present, although unseasonal rainfall meant the planned filming around Broken Hill had to be moved to the Namibian desert. The pre-1980 cars, including some of the iconic Australian-made 1970s muscle cars of the original films, are again present, stripped, honed and reappropriated. The black leather and salvaged material detritus of suburban consumer capitalism adorn predominately male bodies. Australian accents and well-known Australian actors, such as John Howard (the People Eater) are in evidence throughout – although the two non-Australian leads, Tom Hardy (Max) and Charlize Theron (Imperator Furiosa), adopt a fairly neutral 'global' English accent. *Fury Road* takes the furious kinetic action of the original chase and battle scenes and extends that frenzy of movement to the entire film. There is very little stopping in *Fury Road*, just chase, car-borne battles and the enclosed claustrophobia of bodies in vehicle cabins. Like the Mad Max festival, it is aesthetic nostalgia, reliving the style and energy of the earlier films, particularly through the substantial use of live-action sequences where actual vehicles and stunt people are driving, jumping, falling, crashing and exploding, coupled with restrained – for a contemporary action/adventure film – use of CGI enhancements. There is also a sense of the endurance of white mythology. First Nations Australians and their culture are predominately missing, although Max is now haunted by a First Nations man (Crusoe Kurddal), who is accusing Max of failing to save him. There is a suggestion of the Stolen Generations in Furiosa's narrative of being taken by the big white man, Immortan Joe, as a child. The mashed-up, half-remembered culture within the Citadel emanates from a white teenage suburban combustion masculinity, a Valhalla where deceased heroes go 'McFeasting', drink 'aqua-cola', chant 'V8, V8, V8' and have had their 'kamakrazee' heroics witnessed. In short, the new film recreates the visceral dystopia of the originals; however, it does not recreate the messaging.

At the end of *Fury Road*

The narrative of *Fury Road* is brief. It is not Max's story – although in many ways *The Road Warrior* and *Beyond Thunderdome* are also not Max's stories. *The Road Warrior* is about the survival and endurance of Papagallo's community, with Max as the cowboy heroic interloper. *Beyond Thunderdome* is about the redemption of others – Master, Jedediah and the lost children – again with Max as the heroic catalyst for change. *Fury Road* is even less about Max. The narrative and screen focus is Theron's Imperator Furiosa. It is her story of rebellion, leadership and use of machines and violence more than it is Max's.[76] Indeed, for a portion of the film, Max is gagged and fix-mounted as a 'blood bag' on the bonnet of War Boy Nux's (Nicholas Hoult) pursuit vehicle. The narrative arc of the film concerns Furiosa's betrayal of Immortan Joe, her escape from his Citadel with his harem of 'wives' in his formidable War Rig in search of Furiosa's childhood of a green place. Pursued by Immortan Joe and his sick old men allies, Furiosa connects with her mother's tribe, the Vuvalini, discovers that the green place has now succumbed to ecological devastation and defeats Immortan Joe and his minions to return to the Citadel. Throughout, Max plays the reluctant ally of convenience, his wolfish nature kept in check by Furiosa's more-than-equal skill with machines and violence and their mutual self-interest in preservation against Immortan Joe.

Immediately, the film engages with patriarchy's tenuous basis in the domination of women and reproduction.[77] Whereas Hugh Keays-Byrne's first outing as the lead villain in *Mad Max* had him playing the not-so-closeted Toecutter, his return as Immortan Joe has him as the grotesque patriarch, controlling both precious water and reproduction resources. The film is the story of his fall, losing not only his wives and allies, but also his Citadel and his life. Seemingly, this is the screened end of the road for combustion masculinity. The total car crash on the last page of *his-story*. While the original films reflect the violence and contradictions of 1970s Australian road culture, *Fury Road* suggests that contemporary road culture has mostly overtaken the old men in their now dated, inefficient and polluting V8s. What is also overtaken is the gendered order and the cycle of male heroic redemption.

In contrast to the survivors from *The Road Warrior* and *Beyond Thunderdome* who were led by men to a new home, there is in *Fury Road* a reclaiming of the centre. Furiosa drives and battles back to liberate the Citadel with Immortan Joe's body cooking on the engine of his custom vehicle, the Gigahorse. The symbolism could not be clearer. The lead wife, Splendid Angharad (Rosie Huntington-Whiteley), asks rhetorically midway through the film when the wives are attempting to de-condition the apprehended Nux, 'Then who killed the world?' This phrase has been seized on by critics.[78] But the context of its saying is unmistakable. It was men like Immortan Joe and the battling men of the earlier films, with their mechanistic control and violence, who made the 'Earth . . . sour'.[79]

This could flow directly into a celebration of *Fury Road* as an eco-feminist triumphant road movie. The 'guzzoline'-soaked men and machines finally self-combust, leaving strong women – Furiosa, the wives and the surviving Vuvalini – with a bag of seeds to claim the Citadel. For some critics like Darin Payne, this is the success of *Fury Road*:

> The movie thus works to complicate longstanding gender norms of the 'Hollywood blockbuster', but not via the sorts of countercultural critique typical of art-house cinema and instead as a mainstream embrace of broader shifts in our shared ideological landscape.[80]

The conclusion holds a suggestion of hope for the post-Trump world: women in ascent, the potential for an ecological future and men respectfully in a supporting role.[81] Max, the redeemed male ally, generously tips his head and turns away as Furiosa rises up to the Citadel in the final scene, while Nux, condemned to a half-life with cancerous tumours (the personified Larry and Barry), makes the heroic self-sacrifice with the War Rig in the canyon stranding the remnants of Immortan Joe's forces. This is the screened end of the road for combustion masculinity. Tina Turner's plea in *Beyond Thunderdome* for not needing another hero seemingly is answered in Furiosa. She is not a hero: with her malformed arm and her asexuality,[82] she is much more a trickster[83] who breaks the cosmogonic cycle, opening the potential for something new.[84] Taylor Boulware particularly notes that Furiosa, with her steampunk prosthetic arm, can be seen as an embodied representation of Donna Haraway's trickster icon – the feminist cyborg.[85] Furiosa thus presents the possibility of something other than conquering, consuming and destroying patriarchy.[86]

This reception of the film has not gone uncontested. Laura Martínez-Jiménez, Linan Gálvez-Muñoz and Ángela Solano-Caballero see 'neoliberalism feminism' projected through Furiosa. They locate her within a dangerously regressive tradition that Angela McRobbie identifies as the 'phallic girl':[87]

> The 'phallic girl' shows herself to be fear-less, self-assured and even aggressive, in some cases questioning or rejecting the postfeminist masquerade, while she 'emulates male behaviour as a post-feminist gesture'.[88]

Furiosa triumphs because she out-males the men. She drives the truck, she fixes the truck, she fights and she shoots. When the Bullet Farmer (Richard Carter) is approaching the bogged War Rig in the morass that was the green place, Max fails to shoot out the search light, handing the gun to Furiosa, who succeeds.[89] In Furiosa, old and toxic gender binaries are repackaged for a new generation[90] – masculine values of independence and competition, values desirable in a neoliberal wasteland of economic precariousness of widening inequalities and digital platform gigs.[91] To succeed in the public space of desert and desolation, women must out-battle and out-compete the marauding men. In this world, women who do not emulate men are relegated to passive chattels – the wives or the bloated lactating women at the Citadel. The scantily clad wives are directly established as foremost sexual beings to be used and consumed by the screened males and the male audience.[92] This orientation makes their introductory scene, where they are removing the grisly chastity belts, less emancipatory and more a titillating strip-tease – a declaration of available feminine flesh.[93] Whereas the queer subaltern pervaded the earlier films, threatening and questioning the flimsy heterosexual credentials of combustion masculinity, in *Fury Road* there might be some other-than-normal bodies – Furiosa's malformed arm; Immortan Joe's son Corpus Colossus, played by Australian actor and disability advocate Quentin Kenihan; Nux's tumour growths[94] – but cis-normality seemingly rules in the Citadel and the wastelands. Even the tragically 'mediocre'[95] War Boys, whose meagre lives are framed by Immortan Joe's ideology of salvation through spectacular death, are locked into the conventions of the high-octane masculinity of homosocial competition,[96] but without any suggestion of queer complexities. Indeed, the budding romance between Nux and the wife Capable (Riley Keough) is a heterosexual fairy tale of doomed star-crossed lovers from different stations. A conservative gender normality is seemingly established by *Fury Road* and, with it, a valorization of neoliberal life.

That a Mad Max movie is ambiguous in its messaging is to be expected, given the previous films. That *Fury Road* could be an imagining of the demise of patriarchy and its economy of exploitation of women and the environment and an affirmation of the gendered orientations that sustain patriarchy and neoliberal exploitation[97] reflects the complicities and mixed messaging that have pervaded the franchise from its inception. However, Furiosa's triumph in killing Immortan Joe by ripping his breathing apparatus away in the climax-of-climaxes final fight sequence and her return to claim the origin, the Citadel, with its scarce greenery, water and huddled masses, are originally significant. There is much about Furiosa that suggests phallic girl; however, her motivations are not phallic. She is not fighting for herself or even for her own survival. The adoration given to her by the War Boys in the opening scenes as she is entrusted with the War Rig to undertake what is assumed to be an ordinary supply mission to Gas Town and the Bullet Farm suggests her position as Immortan Joe's 'Imperator' is well established. If her motivation were only to escape and try to find the green place of her childhood, she could have done so before the cataclysmic events of the film. She rebels because she feels a responsibility and concern for the wives and their unborn children.[98] Further, she decides to return to the Citadel, over the other option of riding out into the desert, because it represents the only possibility for the women in her care to have a future. This is very different from Immortan Joe, who ruled for self-gratification and the maintenance of his own power. Her leading is also different from that of the other leaders in the earlier films. Papagallo and Aunty Entity scheme and manipulate for their vision of the greater good: Papagallo in not disclosing to Max the details of the escape plan from the compound and Aunty Entity in manipulating Max to provoke Blaster (Paul Larsson). Furiosa's risks and sacrifices are for others. *Fury Road* is not a conservative story about maintaining power; rather, it is about the certainty of an end – the end of a specific patriarch and the possible ends of a patriarchal worldview involving a cycle of men, machines and violence. It is also a lens to a possible, hopeful, unformed future,[99] which might transcend and replace the specific arrangements of gender and technology that drove itself to extinction in the films.

This is the justice at the end of *Fury Road*: a worldview away from the visceral 'Ozploitation' conclusion of *Mad Max*, which sees a revengeful Max walking back to a much newer, cleaner Interceptor, leaving Johnny the Boy (Tim Burns) manacled to a burning vehicle.[100] That conclusion screened the justice of retribution for the wrongs, a taking in kind for the deaths of Goose, Jessica (Joanne

Samuel), Sprog (Brendan Heath) and the other roadside victims of Toecutter's spree. The ending of *The Road Warrior* and *Beyond Thunderdome* enact the conserving justice of the cosmogonic cycle, with the saving hero allowing a resetting of normal relations but unable to cross into the promised land.[101] The end of *Fury Road* is the possibility of something profoundly different. The road and its movement, and the violence of traversing a ravaged landscape, have come to an end. There is an affirmation of place and not movement in the conclusion of *Fury Road*. The Citadel's store of marauding vehicles and War Boy drivers has been used up. Prior to his death, the People Eater, a parody of audit culture, brought this sense of depletion in his counting the loss of Immortan Joe's assets in the chase to capture Furiosa and the wives. The road – together with the resources to be scavenged or traded between outposts and the need for road warriors battling – is gone. The white Australian horror of immobility that drove the action of the earlier films has been suspended, and rather than a geography of Citadel, wastelands and contested roads, there is the possibility of an inclusive home and a landscape of place to be shared by all.[102]

Whether Furiosa's Citadel does become something new or regresses into Aunty Entity's Bartertown remains unknown – much like the uncertainty around a further Mad Max instalment, given legal action by Miller against Warner Brothers.[103] Yet a possibility that the wolf-men and their orientations might re-manifest does not distract from the justice in the moment of Furiosa's winning. Instead of justice as retribution and the conserving justice of return, it holds within it the possibility of a different future. The cycle is not closed off, doomed to repeat, but gender and technology are uncoupled from the history of Australian combustion masculinity, and a home for dreaming something else has been won. This is a generative justice of potential, of possibilities, freed from the constraining violence of past configurations of gender and technology. This is the justice at the end of *Fury Road*.

Conclusion

This chapter has argued that the Mad Max franchise of four films exceeds obvious readings of justice. The first three films are ambiguous, fondly remembered as a celebration of combustion masculinity in Australia and a critical exposure of its sexual contradictions, its entwining with the settler state and its enactment of the heroic cycle. In the first three films, justice was bloody, exclusionary and conservative. They were lenses capturing men and machines doing fundamental violence. *Fury Road* continues – indeed celebrates – the dystopian aesthetics of the earlier films, but it also retells the post-apocalyptic as a women's story. Furiosa's triumph could witness an end for the configurations of gender and technology that 'killed the world'. This is an indication that the forms of movement, consumption and violence of combustion masculinity are receding in the rear-view mirror. *Fury Road* is not definitive on this: in its aesthetics and heterosexuality, it could suggest resurgent normalities around technology and gender that take away from the victory glow. However, the end of *Fury Road* is not *the* end, but a beginning, anticipating something new that potentially is to come. There is a justice of anticipation and a sense of the possibility for change that is in contrast to the men in the driver's seat in the earlier films.

Notes

1 In this chapter, I am using Mad Max (without italics) to refer to the franchise as a whole. *Mad Max* (with italics) refers to the first film, *The Road Warrior* to the second film (*Mad Max II: The Road Warrior*), *Beyond Thunderdome* to the third film (*Mad Max: Beyond Thunderdome*) and *Fury Road* to the fourth instalment (*Mad Max: Fury Road*). Max (without italics) refers to the titular character.
2 Miller (2015) *Mad Max: Fury Road.*
3 Anon (2015).
4 Anon (2015); Bishop (2016).
5 Fletcher and Primack (2017), p 344. On Australian Mad Max cosplaying as an escape from the urban and metropolitan landscapes of mainstream Australia, see Langsford (2016), p 26.
6 Martinez-Jimenez, Gálvez-Muñoz and Solano-Caballero (2018), p 403; Payne (2017), p 107.
7 De Coning (2016), p 175.
8 Miller (1979) *Mad Max.*
9 Miller (1981) *Mad Max 2: The Road Warrior.*
10 Miller and Ogilvie (1985) *Mad Max: Beyond Thunderdome.*
11 Gooch (2017).
12 Anon (2018).
13 Beeton (2005), pp 24, 56.
14 Biber (2001), p 34.
15 Sharrett (1985); Yar (2015), p 30.
16 Kitson (2003).
17 Johinke (2009), p 313; Simpson (2006).
18 On the rival car futures 'autopia' and 'autogeddon' as proposed by J.G. Ballard, see Wollen (2002), p 10.
19 Payne (2017), p 111; Sharrett (1985), p 84; Tranter (2003), p 69.
20 Du Plooy (2019), pp 414–15.
21 Boulware (2016), p 182; Kitson (2003), p 69.
22 Tranter (2003), p 70.
23 Johinke (2001), p 123 notes omitted.
24 Walker (1998, 1999, 2003); Walker, Butland and Connell (2000).
25 Redshaw (2008), pp 83, 122; Redshaw (2018), p 89.
26 Redshaw (2008), p 122; Tranter and Martin (2013), p 5.
27 Tranter and Martin (2013), p 11.
28 Redshaw (2008), p 81.
29 Falconer (1994), p 37.
30 Johinke (2001), p 121; Morris (1998), p 221.
31 Johinke (2001), p 118.
32 Johinke (2001), pp 119–20.
33 Lochlann Jain (2005), p 195.
34 Biber (2001), p 35.
35 Broderick (1993b).
36 Biber (2001), p 35; Sharrett (1985), p 84.
37 Biber (2001), p 43.

38 Simpson (2006).
39 Morris (1998).
40 Curthoys (1999), p 8.
41 Tranter (2003), pp 70–1.
42 Tranter (2003), pp 76–7.
43 Derrida (1974), p 11; see also Morris (1998); Johinke (2009).
44 Taylor (1984); Tranter (2003), p 69.
45 Yar (2015), p 29.
46 Stratton (1983).
47 Nozick (1974), p 109.
48 Hobbes (2008).
49 Hobbes (1990).
50 Schmitt (1996).
51 Boulware (2016), p 185.
52 Hobbes borrows the phrase from Plautus. Hayward and Kemmelmeier (2007).
53 Derrida (1992).
54 Tranter (2018), pp 63–9.
55 Miller (1999).
56 Barbour (1999); Broderick (1993b), p 378.
57 Campbell (1968), pp 193–237.
58 Yar (2015), p 84.
59 Broderick (1993a); Du Plooy (2019), p 417; Martin (2003), p 55.
60 Tranter (2018), p 12.
61 Morris (1998), p 256.
62 Bruce Spence played the Gyro Captain in *The Road Warrior*, and, although Jedediah was meant to be a different character, there is sufficient ambiguity in the film for fans and critics to suggest that they are the same.
63 Turner (1985) 'We Don't Need Another Hero'.
64 Johinke (2001), p 123; Simpson (2006).
65 Redshaw (2018); Tranter and Martin (2013).
66 Rees (2016).
67 Manderscheid (2018).
68 Doyle and Tranter (2015); Lochlann Jain (2002); Walsh (2008).
69 Dowling and Simpson (2013).
70 Doyle and Tranter (2015); see also Lloyd and Fourt-Wells (2018).
71 Doyle and Tranter (2017), pp 12–14.
72 Tranter and Martin (2013).
73 Boym (2001).
74 Amon (2014); Phillips (2013).
75 Boulware (2016), p 181; Payne (2017).
76 De Coning (2016), p 175.
77 Du Plooy (2019), p 417.
78 Boulware (2016); Hampshire (2017); Klangwisan (2016). It also is one of the slogans the wives had painted on the walls of their dormitory/prison.
79 Miller (2015) *Mad Max: Fury Road* prologue voiceover.
80 Payne (2017), p 107.
81 Payne (2017), pp 114–15.
82 Klangwisan (2016), p 79.
83 The trickster comes in many guises, but two hallmarks are physical deformity and extreme manifestation of sexuality. See Lock (2002).
84 Phelan (1996).
85 Boulware (2016), p 12.

86 Fletcher and Primack (2017), p 344.
87 McRobbie (2007).
88 Martinez-Jimenez, Gálvez-Muñoz and Solano-Caballero (2018), p 413, citing McRobbie (2007), p 733.
89 Boulware (2016), p 15; Du Plooy (2019), p 418; Payne (2017), p 118.
90 Martinez-Jimenez, Gálvez-Muñoz and Solano-Caballero (2018), p 417; Payne (2017), p 122.
91 Pasquale (2016); Shum and Tranter (2017).
92 Martinez-Jimenez, Gálvez-Muñoz and Solano-Caballero (2018), p 413.
93 Du Plooy (2019), p 425.
94 On *Fury Road*'s success regarding 'how conditions of disability could be understood as a non-stigmatized part of life that everyone inevitably experiences', see Fletcher and Primack (2017), p 345.
95 'Mediocre!' is the dismissive term uttered by Immortan Joe and his minions when a War Boy attempts a heroic action only to foolishly die.
96 Boulware (2016), p 7.
97 Payne (2017), p 124.
98 Klangwisan (2016), p 84.
99 Boulware (2016), p 16; Payne (2017), p 117.
100 On the relationship of *Mad Max* with the 'Ozploitation' genre and the utility of such a classification, see Martin (2010); Ryan (2010).
101 Klangwisan (2016).
102 Du Plooy (2019), p 423; Fletcher and Primack (2017), p 346.
103 Scott (2019).

References

Secondary sources

Maria Patrice Amon (2014) 'Performances of Innocence and Deviance in Disney Cosplaying' 17 *Transformative Works Cultures*, https://journal.transformativeworks.org/index.php/twc/article/view/565.

Anon (2015) '2015 Worldwide Grosses', *Box Office Mojo*, www.boxofficemojo.com/yearly/chart/?view2=worldwide&yr=2015.

——— (2018) 'Mad Max Museum', *Silverton: Visit Outback New South Wales*, http://silverton.org.au/mad-max-museum.

Dennis H. Barbour (1999) 'Heroism and Redemption in the Mad Max Trilogy' 27 *Journal of Popular Film Television* 28.

Sue Beeton (2005) *Film-Induced Tourism*, Channel View.

Katherine Biber (2001) 'The Threshold Moment: Masculinity at Home and on the Road in Australian Cinema' 7 *Limina* 26.

Bryan Bishop (2016) '*Mad Max: Fury Road* Wins Most Awards of the Night with Six Oscars', *The Verge*, 29 February, www.theverge.com/2016/2/29/11131218/mad-max-fury-road-most-awards-academy-awards-2016.

Taylor Boulware (2016) '"Who Killed the World?": Building a Feminist Utopia from the Ashes of Toxic Masculinity in *Mad Max: Fury Road*' 1 *Mise-en-scène| The Journal of Film & Visual Narration*, http://journals.sfu.ca/msq/index.php/msq/article/view/11.

Svetlana Boym (2001) *The Future of Nostalgia*, Basic Books.

Mick Broderick (1993a) 'Heroic Apocalypse: Mad Max, Mythology and the Millennium', in Christopher Sharrett (ed.), *Crisis Cinema: The Apocalyptic Idea in Postmodern Narrative Film*, Maisonneuve Press.

——— (1993b) 'Surviving Armageddon: Beyond the Imagination of Disaster' 20 *Science Fiction Studies* 362.

Joseph Campbell (1968) *The Hero with a Thousand Faces* (2nd ed.), Princeton University Press.

Ann Curthoys (1999) 'Expulsion, Exodus and Exile in White Australian Historical Mythology' 23 *Journal of Australian Studies* 1.

Alexis De Coning (2016) 'Recouping Masculinity: Men's Rights Activists: Responses to *Mad Max: Fury Road*' 16 *Feminist Media Studies* 174.

Jacques Derrida (1974) 'White Mythology: Metaphor in the Text of Philosophy' 6 *New Literary History* 5.

——— (1992) 'Force of Law: The "Mystical Foundations of Authority"', in Drucilla Cornell, Michel Rogerfield and David Grey Carlson (eds), *Deconstruction and the Possibility of Justice*, Routledge.

Robyn Dowling and Catherine Simpson (2013) '"Shift: The Way You Move": Reconstituting Automobility' 27 *Continuum* 421.

Kylie Doyle and Kieran Tranter (2015) 'Automobility and "My Family" Stickers' 29 *Continuum* 70.

——— (2017) 'F#CK YOUR FAMILY! The Visual Jurisprudence of Automobility' 30 *International Journal for the Semiotics of Law* 1.

Belinda Du Plooy (2019) '"Hope Is a Mistake, If You Can't Fix What's Broken You Go Insane": A Reading of Gender, (S)Heroism and Redemption in *Mad Max: Fury Road*' 28 *Journal of Gender Studies* 414.

Delia Falconer (1994) '"We Don't Need to Know the Way Home": Selling Australian Space in the Mad Max Trilogy' 27 *Southern Review* 28.

Brandon Fletcher and Alvin J. Primack (2017) 'Driving Toward Disability Rhetorics: Narrative, Crip Theory, and Eco-Ability in Mad Max: Fury Road' 34 *Critical Studies in Media Communication* 344.

Declan Gooch (2017) 'Mad Max Enthusiasts Converge on Silverton in Celebration of Epic Australian Franchise', *ABC News*, 8 March, www.abc.net.au/news/2017-03-08/mad-max-enthusiasts-converge-on-silverton/8336900.

Kathryn Hampshire (2017) '"Who Killed the World?": Monstrous Masculinity and Mad Max' *The Digital Literature Review* 177.

R. David Hayward and Markus Kemmelmeier (2007) 'How Competition is Viewed Across Cultures: A Test of Four Theories' 41 *Cross-Cultural Research* 364.

Thomas Hobbes (1990) *Behemoth or the Long Parliament*, University of Chicago Press.

——— (2008) *Leviathan*, Pearson Longman.

Rebecca Johinke (2001) 'Manifestations of Masculinities: Mad Max and the Lure of the Forbidden Zone' 25 *Journal of Australian Studies* 118.

——— (2009) 'Not Quite *Mad Max:* Brian Trenchard-Smith's *Dead End Drive-In*' 3 *Studies in Australasian Cinema* 309.

Michael Kitson (2003) 'The Great Aussie Car Smash at the End of the World' 31 *Australian Screen Education* 64.

Yael Klangwisan (2016) '*Mad Max Fury Road*: Escaping the Phallic Economy of Exodus' 12 *The Bible Critical Theory*, https://novaojs.newcastle.edu.au/ojsbct/index.php/bct/article/view/648/594.

Claire Margaret Langsford (2016) 'Floating Worlds: Cosplay Photo Shoots and the Creation of Imaginary Cosmopolitan Places' 13 *Sites: A Journal of Social Anthropology Cultural Studies Review* 13.
Mike Lloyd and Sanna Fourt-Wells (2018) 'Stickers on Cars: A Note on "My Family" Decals' 32 *Continuum* 201.
Sarah S. Lochlann Jain (2002) 'Urban Errands: The Meaning of Mobility' 2 *Journal of Consumer Culture* 385.
——— (2005) 'Violent Submission' 61 *Cultural Critique* 186.
Helen Lock (2002) 'Transformations of the Trickster' 18 *Southern Cross Review* 1.
Katharina Manderscheid (2018) 'From the Auto-mobile to the Driven Subject? Discursive Assertions of Mobility Futures' 8 *Transfers* 24.
Adrian Martin (2003) *The Mad Max Movies: Mad Max, Mad Max 2 / The Road Warrior, Mad Max Beyond Thunderdome*, Currency Press.
——— (2010) 'Ozploitation Compared to What? A Challenge to Contemporary Australian Film Studies' 4 *Studies in Australasian Cinema* 9.
Laura Martinez-Jimenez, Lina Gálvez-Muñoz and Ángela Solano-Caballero (2018) 'Neoliberalism Goes Pop and Purple: Postfeminist Empowerment from Beyoncé to Mad Max' 51 *Journal of Popular Culture* 399.
Angela McRobbie (2007) 'Top Girls? Young Women and the Post-Feminist Sexual Contract' 21 *Cultural Studies* 718.
George Miller (1999) 'The Apocalypse and the Pig, or the Hazards of Storytelling', in Raffaele Caputo and Geoff Burton (eds), *Second Take: Australian Film-Makers Talk*, Allen & Unwin.
Meaghan Morris (1998) 'White Panic or *Mad Max* and the Sublime', in Kuan-Hsing Chen (ed.), *Trajectories: Inter-Asian Cultural Studies*, Routledge.
Robert Nozick (1974) *Anarchy, State, and Utopia*, Basic Books.
Frank Pasquale (2016) 'Two Narratives of Platform Capitalism' 35 *Yale Law and Policy Review* 309.
Darin Payne (2017) 'Shifting Gears and Paradigms at the Movies: Masculinity, Automobility, and the Rhetorical Dimensions of *Mad Max: Fury Road*' 40 *Studies in Popular Culture* 102.
Shane Phelan (1996) 'Coyote Politics: Trickster Tales and Feminist Futures' 11 *Hypatia* 130.
Ivan Phillips (2013) 'Frock Coats, Yo-Yos and a Chair with a Panda on It: Nostalgia for the Future in the Life of a *Doctor Who* Fan', in Paul Booth (ed.), *Fan Phenomena*, Intellect.
Sarah Redshaw (2008) *In the Company of Cars: Driving as a Social and Cultural Practice*, Ashgate.
——— (2018) 'Combustion, Hydraulic, and Other Forms of Masculinity: An Essay Exploring Dominant Values and Representations of the Driver in Driverless Technology' 8 *Transfers* 86.
Katherine G. Rees (2016) 'Accelerate, Reverse, or Find the Off Ramp? Future Automobility in the Fragmented American Imagination' 11 *Mobilities* 152.
Mark David Ryan (2010) 'Towards an Understanding of Australian Genre Cinema and Entertainment: Beyond the Limitations of "Ozploitation" Discourse' 24 *Continuum* 843.
Carl Schmitt (1996) *The Leviathan in State Theory of Thomas Hobbes: Meaning and Failure of a Political Symbol*, Greenwood Press.
Ryan Scott (2019) 'Is *Mad Max 5* Finally Starting to Rev Up Its Engines?', *Movie Web*, https://movieweb.com/mad-max-5-production-update-2019.

Christopher Sharrett (1985) 'The Hero as Pastiche: Myth, Male Fantasy and Simulacra in *Mad Max and The Road Warrior*' 13 *Journal of Popular Film and Television* 80.
Annie Shum and Kieran Tranter (2017) 'Seeing, Moving, Catching, Accumulating: *Pokémon GO*, and the Legal Subject' 30 *International Journal for the Semiotics of Law* 477.
Catherine Simpson (2006) 'Antipodean Automobility and Crash: Treachery, Trespass and Transformation of the Open Road' 39–40 *Australian Humanities Review*, http://australianhumanitiesreview.org/2006/09/01/antipodean-automobility-and-crash-treachery-trespass-and-transformation-of-the-open-road.
Jon Stratton (1983) 'What Made Mad Max Popular? The Mythology of a Conservative Fantasy' 9 *Art and Text* 37.
Paul Taylor (1984) 'A Culture of Temporary Culture' 16 *Art & Text* 94.
Kieran Tranter (2003) 'Mad Max: The Car and Australian Governance' 5 *National Identities* 67.
——— (2018) *Living in Technical Legality: Science Fiction and Law as Technology*, University of Edinburgh Press.
Kieran Tranter and Damien Martin (2013) '"The Cutting Edge of Cocking About": *Top Gear*, Automobility and Law' 7 *Law and Humanities* 1.
Linley Walker (1998) 'Under the Bonnet: Car Culture, Technological Dominance and Young Men of the Working Class' 3 *Journal of Interdisciplinary Gender Studies* 23.
——— (1999) 'Hydraulic Sexuality and Hegemonic Masculinity: Young Working-class Men and Car Culture', in Rob White (ed.), *Australian Youth Subcultures: On the Margins and in the Mainstream*, Australian Youth Clearing House.
——— (2003) 'Car Culture, Technological Dominance and Young Men of the Working Class', in Stephen Tomsen and Mike Donaldson (eds), *Male Trouble: Looking at Australian Masculinities*, Pluto Press.
Linley Walker, Dianne Butland and R.W. Connell (2000) 'Boys on the Road: Masculinities, Car Culture, and Road Safety Education' 8 *Journal of Men's Studies* 153.
Margaret Walsh (2008) 'Gendering Mobility: Women, Work and Automobility in the United States' 93 *History* 376.
Peter Wollen (2002) 'Introduction: Cars and Culture', in Joe Kerr (ed.), *Autopia: Cars and Culture*, Reaktion Books.
Majid Yar (2015) *Crime and the Imaginary of Disaster: Post-Apocalyptic Fictions and the Crisis of Social Order*, Palgrave Macmillan.

Films and music

George Miller (1979) *Mad Max*, Roadshow Film Distributors.
——— (1981) *Mad Max 2: The Road Warrior*, Warner Bros.
——— (2015) *Mad Max: Fury Road*, Warner Bros Pictures.
George Miller and George Ogilvie (1985) *Mad Max: Beyond Thunderdome*, Warner Bros.
Tina Turner (1985) 'We Don't Need Another Hero', *Mad Max Beyond Thunderdome: Original Motion Picture Soundtrack*, Capitol.

Chapter 14

Going bunta on Western law

Violent jurisdictions, melodrama and the Australian carceral imaginary in *Wentworth*

Laura Joseph and Honni van Rijswijk

Introduction

Kaz Proctor: I know what you've done. Justice is coming.
Joan Ferguson: I'll put the kettle on.[1]

Representing a uniquely Australian carceral imaginary, the long-running Australian television show Prisoner (1979–86)[2] and its contemporary reimagining, Wentworth (2013–),[3] have attracted large audiences and grown dedicated fanbases worldwide. This chapter explores the phenomenon of these popular Australian carceral imaginaries through a reading of *Wentworth*, arguing that the series stages a radical theory of law that takes on the Western liberal legal imaginary and that viewers, in their passionate engagement with the series, are in part responding to its unique take on questions of power, authority and legitimacy. Taking as a starting point the axiom that state law is never the only law operating in a particular context, we argue that *Wentworth* has worldwide traction partly because the show explicitly stages various iterations of legal pluralities and their outcomes to demonstrate the failure of state law to provide justice.

Like *Prisoner, Wentworth* foregrounds urgent questions of lawfulness and justice. This foregrounding is particularly compelling because these questions of law and justice are examined from radical, marginalized positions (gendered, raced, queered).[4] *Wentworth* departs from *Prisoner* in the show's multiple narratives of complicity that, we argue, thematize the impossibility of escaping violence within the inherently compromised and compromising legacies of colonial pasts and neoliberal modernities. This chapter argues that Australia's particular carceral imaginary, which follows Western traditions of representing hell and underworld narratives, allows a perverse articulation of legal pluralities that are uniquely Australian, while also being of allegorical significance globally.

Wentworth is critically acclaimed and, like its predecessor,[5] popular both domestically and internationally. The show has been sold to 141 countries, remade in 4 countries and, despite being a pay television show (through the subscription-based Australian Foxtel network), won Most Outstanding Drama at both the 2015 and 2018 Logie Awards as well as Most Popular Drama in 2018. *Wentworth* is set in a corrections facility of the same name in modern-day Australia. Although it is an ensemble show, the first four seasons of the show focus on, and are largely focalized through, the character of Bea Smith (Danielle Cormack)[6] as a central protagonist. The first episode of Season 1, 'No Place Like Home', follows protagonist Bea into the correctional centre after her attempted murder of her abusive husband, Harry.[7] The series opens with Bea in a prison van, about to enter prison on remand after being charged. We are with her as her life on the outside ends dramatically and suddenly and the world of the prison opens up before her. Bea is an Australian 'everywoman' – a suburban hairdresser, a wife, a mother, a working-class battler. It is through her viewpoint that the viewer encounters the structural violence of the prison and the wider socio-legal violence it reflects. Like Bea, most of the other characters are either victims of violence and structural injustices that are not recognized by the state, or their vulnerability exposes them to further state violence. As with *Prisoner*,[8] law and violence are explicit themes of *Wentworth*, as are questions of authority. Bea's story arc towards her position as a corrupted 'top dog' explores how she maintains her extra-legal power and how and when her violence is justified to maintain this authority (particularly when it is in direct conflict with the legal authority of the governor). The prison has two separate and competing jurisdictions: the extra-legal jurisdiction of the inmates and the legal jurisdiction of the governor. The show uses this legal plurality to critique neoliberal state law and rehearse a series of juridical alternatives. The show's claims about law and violence are particular to the perverse and compromised agency that emerges from the Australian carceral imaginary.

With its history as a destination for convict transportation, Australia's carceral aspect in the popular imaginary is obvious. However, it is not a case of history creating fiction. The imagination of Australia as a carceral space preceded the historical fact of transportation by many centuries. As a point of collision between classical and Judeo-Christian cosmologies and geographic reality, the antipodes straddle the threshold of imaginary and real spaces.[9] The colonial establishment of the antipodean penal colonies was a manifestation of an older imaginary that equated the bottom of the Earth with hell – a legacy of the pre-Copernican vertical cosmology. Because of their location between these real and imaginary worlds, the antipodes have a relation of proximity to European classical and biblical underworlds: the vertical cosmology of heaven, Earth and hell is superimposed over the globe, and the antipodes and hell share the same position. The choice of the antipodean location as a repository for England's criminals was partly indebted to an imaginary that associated the antipodes with hell – an infernal space of despair and punishment. This is evidenced by pre-modern cosmologies, cartographies and a literary tradition that extends from Dante's inferno to antipodean utopias and dystopias – for example, *Gulliver's Travels* begins, 'Northwest of *Van Diemen's* Land' with the protagonist incarcerated.[10]

The convict transportation to Van Diemen's Land is perhaps the most extreme and literal example of the transposition of association between the antipodes and hell as prison. As Irish Nationalist John Mitchel (1815–1875), who was held in Van Diemen's Land from 1850 to 1853, wrote in his prison journals that the island was 'Dante's Tartarean vision' made real.[11] As hell on Earth, the penal colony of Van Diemen's Land is a manifestation of pre-modern antipodean metaphorics. The Australian penal colonies are explicitly figured as hell in Marcus Clarke's famous novel *For the Term of His Natural Life*. Van Diemen's Land is a 'pit of torment . . . so deep that one could not even see heaven',[12] Port Arthur is 'a den of horrors',[13] 'a deep into which the eye of Heaven did not penetrate',[14] echoing with the 'never ceasing clashing of irons and the eternal click of hammers'.[15]

Wentworth implicitly recalls the power of Australia's infernal carceral imaginary, not only through the logic of its narrative but also through its aesthetics. With its cold chromatic colour scheme and claustrophobic camera angles, the experience of watching *Wentworth* is itself nightmarishly carceral. The consistent use of blues and greens in the filters, lighting and *mise en scène* makes Wentworth Prison a Hades. Visually similar to other contemporary dystopian series such as *The Handmaid's Tale*[16] and *Westworld*,[17] in which the hopelessness of the central characters is emphasized, in *Wentworth* blue filters are applied to both interior and exterior scenes to create a bleak underworld. The sets and costumes also use a blue palette, with the outdoor and indoor walls painted a shade similar to that of the teal tracksuits worn by the inmates, a chromatography that renders the prison cold and Tartarean. *Wentworth* is also firmly placed within the aesthetic and narrative traditions of the Australian carceral underworlds as the plot follows a katabasis, or descent narrative, structure.

In literary criticism, 'katabasis' is the term used to describe a narrative journey to the underworld. Conventionally, katabasis narratives follow a progression of descent (katabasis), inversion and ascent (anabasis). For example, in Dante's *Inferno* – perhaps the most famous katabasis plot – Dante descends further and further into hell, until he reaches Satan. From here, they continue to travel in a direction that Dante believes to be down until they reach the centre of the world. He then finds himself climbing up, and he and Satan emerge finally (at the Earth's antipodes) to see the stars. In *Hell in Contemporary Literature*, Rachel Falconer argues that this tripartite narrative structure functions as a means of unmaking and remaking subjectivity; from the second half of the 20th century, Western literary representations of hell have largely functioned as a space where the subject is unmade and reborn.[18] *Wentworth* is a katabasis narrative in the sense that the first four seasons of the show chart Bea Smith's journey further and further into the underworld, but while *Wentworth* follows the descent and inversion movement of a katabasis narrative, there is no anabasis or ascent in terms of escape from the carceral hell. Bea moves further and further into the hell of Wentworth, earning additional sentences of 12 years for the murder of crime matriarch Jacqueline Holt (Kris McQuade)[19] and then life for the murder of Holt's son, Brayden.[20] While *Wentworth* follows a narrative tradition of katabasis, it also departs from the convention of katabasis narratives as the protagonist never escapes the underworld. Bea does, however, undergo a mini-ascent within the world of Wentworth as she becomes self-realized and socially powerful until she is literally at the top of the prison hierarchy as 'top dog'. Bea overturns the corrupt regime of sadistic Governor Joan 'the Freak' Ferguson (Pamela Rabe), and the carceral underworld of Wentworth offers similar over-turning and progressions for other characters thematized as a victory of their 'agency'.

In many ways, the Australian carceral underworld in *Wentworth* operates paradoxically as a space of agency, where most main characters undergo a transformation towards power and/or self-sufficiency, in contrast to their positions of powerlessness in 'outside' world narratives of liberal law and mainstream society. Wentworth is a 'corrections' facility,[21] designed to rehabilitate prisoners from 'criminal' to 'productive'; however, this linear progression is not the transformation that is emphasized in *Wentworth*. Rather, the carceral is a space in which more interesting and violent structural reversals occur: criminals are heroes; the normally marginalized voices of women, queers, working-class women and women of colour are foregrounded; and formal language is overturned through idiom, profanity and humour – as in the inmates' use of the nickname 'Vinegar Tits'[22] for deputy governor Vera Bennett (Kate Atkinson), for example. The structural violence of the patriarchy, particularly the normalization of certain kinds of domestic and emotional labour, creates perverse sites of agency, as do such articles of domestic machinery as the steam press, the kettle and the sewing machine, which all become instruments of torture used by the inmates to uphold their own law and maintain their power.

By remaining in the compromised space of the carceral underworld, *Wentworth* explicitly draws attention to and rehearses different versions of the violence that maintains law. *Wentworth* is based in realism, and most characters are unremarkable everywoman figures: their lives are circumscribed by both lawful and lawless violence. *Wentworth* draws attention to structural violence and the complicity of liberal law in these structures, but there is no outside to violence – the only 'way out' is death or to be moved to solitary confinement, which constitutes social and mental death. The women are victims of violence, but they are not innocent. Every character is compromised by and complicit in the violence that establishes and maintains prison law – which is also the colonial condition – and the agency and power they have individually and collectively is created and maintained through violence. As Franky Doyle (Nicole da Silva) says of Wentworth Corrections Centre, 'Innocent person? Do we even have any of those?'[23] Within this compromised and inescapable space of complicity, the spectre of 'justice' remains, and it is the question of justice, phrased by the show as 'How and when is violence justified?', that propels the narrative of *Wentworth*.

Legal authority and violence

> You don't run this prison, I do.[24]

The show uses the legal plurality of the prison to critique neoliberal state law and rehearse a series of alternatives, and the show's claims about law and violence are particular to the perverse and compromised agency that emerges from the Australian carceral imaginary. Like its predecessor, *Prisoner*, *Wentworth* makes strong claims about what is lawful and what is unlawful violence, and through the adjudication of this violence asserts new sites of law-making – new jurisdictions. Both shows are examples of pop culture as sites in which law is made, not just reflected and critiqued – pop culture as a site where the collective zeitgeist is thinking through questions such as: What is lawful violence? What is the role of violence in groups asserting their authority? What is legitimate authority in these circumstances?

At key points in *Wentworth*, Bea commits violent acts that she asserts are lawful, and these are the points at which she asserts or reasserts her role as lawful leader. In this way, Bea is asserting a jurisdiction – an authority to adjudicate – over certain harms that liberal law has failed to adjudicate. These include attempting to kill her abusive husband after a long history of his beatings that went unpunished and were even unregistered by liberal law. Her two subsequent murders are also motivated by justice and the rationale of proportionality (what is 'right'). Liberal law fails to recognize so much violence – gendered violence and violence to queer people especially. The harms termed 'domestic violence' are harms that our law and culture have problems even narrating well. Liberal law has proven completely inadequate in adjudicating the violence committed by men towards women, and this violence has mostly been invisible, quotidian and unremarkable, except when it arises under prescribed circumstances and can be crafted into a specific 'event' under liberal law, which operates within the genre of aggressive realism[25] because law asserts that it has an exclusive and unmediated access to the truth. This is particularly the case in Australian law, which has repeatedly denied any form of legal pluralism that would acknowledge continuing Aboriginal sovereignty and law over the territory. In fact, we exist within multiple pluralities, but this is not acknowledged by state law. *Wentworth* self-consciously thematizes its status as representation and employs a number of genres to communicate a legally plural universe. There is liberal, state law, but there is also the legal world of the prisoners, and these two legalities are self-consciously navigated.

Wentworth shows many examples in which the 'victims' of violence that liberal law fails to adjudicate in turn assert their own jurisdictions and judgments, with 'justice' becoming a key term for the prisoners. For example, in Season 2, Maxine Conway (Socrates Otto) stabs her boyfriend with scissors after he cuts her hair.[26] Liberal law would not recognize the extent of the violence committed against Maxine, a trans woman, when her boyfriend 'merely cuts her hair', so Maxine asserts her own jurisdiction. In these ways, *Wentworth* (like movements such as #MeToo) is theorizing law, making law, setting loose into the collective imaginary new genres, narratives and tropes for the adjudication of gendered/queer violence.

Justice is an overt theme of *Wentworth*, and the show uses the carceral space to critique liberal law and to imagine, theorize and test alternate legalities. *Wentworth* is also theorizing law in the context of the limited ways by which liberal law imagines identities, relationships and communities. *Wentworth* sees liberal law for what it is: a mythical promise of equality, fraternity and justice that arose out of the historical specificity of the Enlightenment and its historically specific violent practices of colonialism, racism and sexism. These violent practices cannot be separated out. Liberal law pretends that its justice is ahistorical and eternal and that only its inequalities are historically specific and temporary and can be incrementally reformed out when, in fact, its justice is specifically produced, and its inequalities are 'eternal'. Legal pluralism in *Wentworth* critiques these failures and theorizes alternative models of law-making and authority.

Legal pluralism: beyond liberal law

Liz: Oh, you know the panic button by the front door?
Bea: Yeah.
Liz: Don't ever press it.[27]

Liberal law is an historically specific law, and it is a form of authority that uses violence to assert jurisdiction – violence is innate to its operation (it has its own delineation of lawful/unlawful violence, and its authority turns on these points of interpretation). *Wentworth* is obsessed with the relation of violence to jurisdiction and how this relation produces legal pluralism. The show clearly represents legal pluralism in action and explores the way negotiations between the two legal authorities take place. There are two jurisdictions that are acknowledged by the governors/screws and prisoners alike: one led by the governor and one dictated by the 'top dog', with the two leaders often meeting to negotiate. The significance of the rule of 'no lagging' is jurisdictional. The 'top dog' adjudicates the violence/harms of the prisoners. To lag is to defy that jurisdiction and to end the legal pluralism.

Wentworth stages a spectrum of legal authorities through the different ruling regimes that are asserted by each 'top dog'. Jacqueline 'Jacs' Holt, Franky Doyle, Bea Smith, Kaz Proctor (Tammy MacIntosh) and the Freak all enact a different theory of law through the specific ways in which they use violence to enforce the internal laws of the prison. Wentworth's internal laws are those established among the inmates, such as not lagging and never pressing the panic button. Most violence in Wentworth is lawful in terms of the internal laws, and the transgression of these laws is coded as either abject ('Juicy' Lucy Gambaro, because her unlawful violence is chaotic and based on pleasure) or evil (the Freak, because her unlawful violence is sadistic and Machiavellian). Each 'top dog' has a unique regime grounded in a particular administration of violence. In Season 1, gangster matriarch Jacqueline Holt deploys violence tyrannically to shore up her personal power inside and outside the prison. Once Bea murders Jacs, Franky Doyle takes over. While Franky takes more of an interest in the welfare of the women than Jacs, her use of violence is effectively identical to that of Jacs as she tries to maintain power to protect herself from rivals and maximize the profit of her drug trade. When Bea takes over in Season 3, she articulates an authority that is in the best interests of the women – including an anti-drugs position. She asserts the necessity of lawful violence in running 'her' prison and upholds the established law of 'no lagging'. The nature of legitimate authority is central to Season 4 because Bea's use of violence to maintain law has unjust outcomes, and Kaz Proctor's position is that women should not commit violence against women. Kaz's assertion of feminist democratic rule (for example, the idea that the women are entitled to their right to be 'kept safe' by using the panic button) misses the point that who gets to adjudicate violence is key to who gets jurisdiction over the women. Kaz's philosophy introduces a social chaos to the prison and enables Bea's key rivals, Tina Mercado and the Freak, to undermine her position. Destabilized by the appeal of Kaz's ideology among the women, Bea is caught in a bind in which, even if the use of violence were unjust, not enacting violence as punishment would cede her authority in that she would be asserting her rival's position. Of course, this bind results in an unjust outcome as Bea's infliction of violence as punishment upon the new young inmate Tasha for pressing the panic button leads to Tasha's attempted suicide.[28] It is here that the Freak is able to manipulate Bea's friends Boomer and Doreen to undermine her authority on the basis of the injustice of Bea's rule. Once Bea is forced into breaking the internal law herself (by lagging), she cannot lead and, due in part to Kaz's destabilization of the prison's internal laws, is murdered by the Freak.[29] By Season 6, Kaz acknowledges the failure of her feminist vision of democracy/equality and asserts her leadership through violence, trading the steam press for the sewing machine as her instrument of punishment/violent jurisdiction.[30] She realizes that, in the context of the liberal legal framework in which she is forced to engage, there is no other way.

The significance of genre to *Wentworth*'s legal argument

Wentworth positions itself as fundamentally concerned with questions of law, not only at the level of narrative but also through genre. The genre arcs of each season are themselves an important part of *Wentworth*'s argument. Each season moves from social/legal realism to melodrama and then to sublime endings that draw on tragedy and Gothic horror. The sublime endings each contain moments of both justice and injustice: at the end of the first season, Bea's murder of Jacs Holt;[31] at the end of the second season, Bea's murder of Jacs' son, Braydon;[32] the Freak's killing of Jess Warner at the end of Season 3 and the Gothic fire that burns down half of Wentworth;[33] Bea's death at the end of Season 4,[34] which is simultaneously a tragedy and an act of justice (Bea sacrifices her life to keep the Freak in jail); and the Gothic ending of Season 5, in which Frankie and the Freak escape in coffin-like boxes, and the Freak is buried alive.[35] One question is how law-making maps onto genre: the movement from social realism to melodrama to the sublime of Greek tragedy and Gothic horror. Each season finale is the peak moment in which the questions of justice raised across that season are answered. In each, we see a radical departure from realism. Then we move back to social realism by the beginning of the next season, and with this shift comes a new set of judicial questions. The show's genre of justice is not liberal law's genre, nor is it law's aggressive realism. The possibility of justice, it is suggested, can only be communicated through a radical departure from liberal law's terms of representation. By radically departing from realism, *Wentworth* argues against the acceptance of neoliberal law and liberal law's lie that justice will follow incrementally through more of the same.

As 'modernity's dominant aesthetic form', melodrama 'subtends pervasive cultural narratives reflecting and modelling the modern self from the Enlightenment to the contemporary era' and registers the modern subject's (secular) 'longings for an impossible escape'.[36] Although melodrama has been regarded by many as a conservative genre that tends to reinforce dominant cultures and forms, Monique Rooney argues that this argument ignores melodrama's 'endurance as an aesthetic category that has mutated as it has migrated across time and space', its 'disruptive elements' and 'unpredictability'.[37] As a colonial melodrama set inside a women's prison, *Wentworth* inhabits the agency and creative potential of marginal figures – the criminal, the colonial, the feminine and the queer – to disassemble the Western legal imaginary.

The use of music and the generic possibilities of melodrama as a composite type of storytelling in *Wentworth* are central to the show's assertion of the multiplicity of subjectivity, relationality and law. Popular songs of the late 20th century and early 21st century are key to *Wentworth*'s development of character and theme via the generic possibilities of melodrama. Crucially, in the first episode of each season, a montage of the key characters is set to a song that sets the tone, themes and major conflicts for that season. In 'No Place Like Home',[38] the first episode of Season 1, *Prisoner*'s theme song, 'On the Inside' (Lynne Hamilton),[39] sung intradiegetically by Season 1's villain Jacqueline Holt, both melancholically draws a connection between *Prisoner* and *Wentworth* and ironically marks the show's distance from it in terms of its bleak violence and hopelessness. In 'Born Again',[40] the first episode of Season 2, Gotye's 'Heart's a Mess' (covered by Missy Higgins)[41] underscores the destructive chaos of both Joan 'the Freak' Ferguson's governorship and Bea Smith's obsession with revenge. In 'The Governor's Pleasure',[42] the first episode of Season 3, Imagine Dragons's 'Radioactive'[43] sets up the showdown between Bea and the Freak. In 'First Blood',[44] the first episode of Season 4, the Divinyls' 'Pleasure and Pain'[45] echoes Bea's despair and exhaustion, and finally, in 'Scars',[46] the first episode of Season 5, 'Laura' by Bat for Lashes[47] marks the loss of Bea and the effects of her death on the prison. In her reading of Elizabeth Jolley's novel *The Well*, Rooney draws a connection between Australian melodrama and the Enlightenment melodrama of Rousseau and his move towards a heterogeneous form by 'call[ing] attention to the discrete features of his *mélodrame*'s constituent parts and, in doing so, to offset what he saw as the totalizing effects of French opera's over reliance on harmony'.[48] As drama interspersed with songs, melodrama is the genre of heterogeneity and foregrounds disparate parts that both reflect and technically produce the multiple identities and legalities emphasized by *Wentworth*. Drawing attention to melodrama's mythic origins, Rooney argues further that melodrama is a genre of metamorphosis and describes the Australian carceral imaginary of *The Well* as 'an encrypted imaginary that nevertheless animates [a] fascination with terrestrial death and sub-terrestrial life and its corresponding depiction of a human will to closure or burial that is conditional to a will to transfer, transform and renew'.[49] In *Wentworth*, this tension between the will to closure or burial and transformation resolves tragically as justice is ultimately impossible under the terms of liberal law.

The power of 'Seeing Red', the Season 4 finale, lies not only in the tragedy of Bea's death, but also in the tragic spectacle of the impossibility of justice in the structure of liberal law. While Bea achieves retributive justice against Jacs, Braydon and the Freak, it is at the expense of the loss of her own meaningful life as each act of revenge yields further prison sentences for Bea. Bea's death in Season 4 occurs because she cannot, in the end, achieve justice/retribution against the Freak, or even contain the harm the Freak threatens, within the wider framework of liberal law. Liberal law and the structural violence of gender and class that liberal law supports are too immense for Bea to fight, and throughout Season 4, we see Bea's despair, suicidality and self-harm. Bea is worn down by the particular violence of the prison and the more general, insidious violence of legal/social systems. Bea also can't, in the end, outsmart the Freak, who is a psychopath, but also an educated, upper middle-class woman. The Freak's class is thematized through her clothing, her hobby of fencing and her obsession with opera and classical music. She can afford the best QCs and use liberal legal processes to her tactical advantage, whereas the other prisoners are left with an under-funded legal aid service. In 'Plan Bea', Episode 8 of Season 4, as the Freak prepares to (unsuccessfully) drown Bea, she tells her (and the viewer) that she is really giving Bea a merciful death, preventing a long and meaningless life behind bars: 'There are only two ways in prison to die, Bea. You can fall victim to an attack, left to bleed in some filthy corner, or, far worse – you could grow old . . . your legacy forgotten, just vomiting yourself to death in a barren cell'[50]. There is truth in what the Freak says, and this statement reframes what is happening: there's the particular, heightened and obvious violence that takes place within the prison, but the Freak articulates her actions according to the structural violence within/without, which is not as obvious and yet so much more determinative. Even though Bea finally ensures via her own suicide that the Freak remains in prison for murder – her last words are 'I win' – Bea cannot escape her own structural incarceration. Within this larger framework, the injustice of Bea's position arises because liberal law has failed to hold violent men accountable for violence against women, provoking the violence against Harry that landed Bea in prison in the first place.

Conclusion

> Now I know a place called hell
> 'Wentworth (You Don't Know Me)' by Pleasantville
> (Wentworth theme song)[51]

Hell is a hopeless place. As the words inscribed above the gate to hell warn, 'Abandon all hope, You who enter here'.[52] In Wentworth, there is no hope because there is no way out of the violence that maintains the internal laws of the prison and no escape from the structural violence of the liberal law that circumscribes the women's lives. Yet, from this place of hopelessness and complicity, possibilities emerge through compromise as new forms of kinship and love are generated and themselves generate potential (Doreen's garden, Boomer's workshop, Franky's life on the outside). In her reading of Radiohead's 2003 album *Hail to the Thief (The Gloaming)* as a popular cultural artefact that navigates the complicity of the Western subject within psychic and social structures of violence, Kate Livett suggests that 'It is only the compromised subject who can suggest compromise itself'.[53] From the violent, compromised and compromising space of Wentworth, justice can be imagined as heterogeneous and not homogenizing. By disassembling liberal law from radical, marginalized positions across gender, race, sexuality and class within a radical generic form, *Wentworth* asserts an ethics of multiplicity that, while itself compromised, is contingent and specific and arises from a recognition of difference rather than a punitive response to it. Inscribed throughout the carceral underworld of the show, this ethos is perhaps most clearly captured in the repeated chorus of the opening song 'You don't know me/When I don't know you'.[54]

Notes

1 *Wentworth* (2017), S5 Ep 11.
2 Watson (1979–86).
3 Hannam, Radulovich and Watson (2013–).
4 See Herman (2003) and Millbank (2004) for an analysis of the rhetorical and political functions of queerness in the 'women in prison' genre.
5 *Prisoner* enjoyed massive international popularity; it was the second most popular show in the United States, earning 25 per cent of the audience when premiered there in 1979. In Los Angeles in 1980, the day after the airing of the episode in which lesbian bikie inmate Franky Doyle is shot by police, over 3,000 women bikies attended wakes to mourn her. In Sweden, after the final episode (number 692) aired in the year 2000, the show was screened again because fans held a massive demonstration – the first time this had happened in Sweden. See Zalcock and Robinson (1996) for more details about the show's many fanbases.
6 Bea Smith is one of the many characters transposed from *Prisoner* to *Wentworth*. Zalcock and Robinson (1996) argue that *Prisoner*'s character focus constituted a major generic departure from the 'women in prison' (WIP) films of the 1950s to 1970s, which were far more action based. Bouclin (2009), p 33, argues that *Caged* (Dir. John Cromwell, 1950) marks the beginning of the WIP genre, particularly as the film 'anticipates

feminist intersectional analyses that highlight the fact that choice does not amount to agency when made in the face of unpalatable options'.

7 *Wentworth* (2013), S1 Ep 1.

8 *Prisoner* explicitly dealt with these questions and effected real cultural change by giving a platform to the prison reform movement of the 1970s and 1980s – particularly in terms of the need for rehabilitation after release. One of the main consultants to the show was Sandra Willson, who at that time was the longest-serving female prisoner in New South Wales, 'an unrepentant lesbian' and the focus of a massive community campaign led by the Women Behind Bars collective advocating her release. The characters and storylines of Judy Bryant and Karen Travers were loosely based on Willson, and *Wentworth* was based on her experiences in Mulawa, Sydney's prison for women. Sandra's prison reform campaign is explicitly referenced when Judy Bryant goes to Sydney in episodes 309–313 to visit Sandra Willson (off screen) at Guthrie House, the halfway house for women that she established – the first of its kind in New South Wales.

9 Joseph (2009).

10 Swift (1726), p 22.

11 Mitchel (1918), p 286.

12 Clarke (1874), p 176.

13 Clarke (1874), p 327.

14 Clarke (1874), p 341.

15 Clarke (1874), p 344.

16 Miller *The Handmaid's Tale* (2017–).

17 Nolan and Joy *Westworld* (2016–).

18 Falconer (2005).

19 *Wentworth* (2013), S1 Ep 10.

20 *Wentworth* (2014), S2 Ep 12.

21 'Born Again', the first episode of Season 2, opens with a voiceover by the new governor, Joan Ferguson, emphasizing that the purpose of the facility is 'to correct'.

22 *Wentworth* (2014), S2 Ep 7,

23 *Wentworth* (2014), S2 Ep 4.

24 Repeated line in *Wentworth* (2015), S3, Ep 1.

25 van Rijswijk (2015), p 239.

26 *Wentworth* (2014), S2 Ep 5.

27 *Wentworth* (2013), S1 Ep 1.

28 *Wentworth* (2016), S4 Ep 6.

29 *Wentworth* (2016), S4 Ep 12.

30 *Wentworth* (2018), S6 Ep 1.

31 *Wentworth* (2013), S1 Ep 10.

32 *Wentworth* (2014), S2 Ep 12.

33 *Wentworth* (2015), S3 Ep 12.

34 *Wentworth* (2016), S4 Ep 12.

35 *Wentworth* (2017), S5 Ep 12.

36 Rooney (2015b), p 4.

37 Rooney (2015b), p 1.

38 *Wentworth* (2013), S1 Ep 1.

39 Hamilton (1979).

40 *Wentworth* (2014), S2 Ep 1.

41 Higgins (2012).

42 *Wentworth* (2015), S3 Ep 1.

43 Imagine Dragons (2012).

44 *Wentworth* (2016), S4 Ep 1.

45 Divinyls (1985).
46 *Wentworth* (2017), S5 Ep 1.
47 Bat for Lashes (2012).
48 Rooney (2015a).
49 Rooney (2015a).
50 *Wentworth* (2016), S4 Ep 8.
51 Pleasantville (2013).
52 Dante (2000), III:9.
53 Livett (2007).
54 Pleasantville (2013).

References

Secondary sources

Suzanne Bouclin (2009) 'Women in Prison Movies as Feminist Jurisprudence' 21 *Canadian Journal of Women and the Law* 19.

Rachel Falconer (2005) *Hell in Contemporary Literature: Western Descent Narratives Since 1945*, Edinburgh University Press.

Didi Herman (2003) '"Bad Girls Changed My Life": Homonormativity in a Women's Prison Drama' 20 *Critical Studies in Media Communication* 141.

Laura Joseph (2009) 'Opening the Gates of Hell: Regional Emergences in *Carpentaria* and *Dreamhunter*' 69 *Southerly* 66.

Kate Livett (2007) '"Thieves and Fascists" the Politics of Abjection in Radiohead's *Hail to the Thief* (The Gloaming)' 41 *Australian Humanities Review*, http://australianhumanitiesreview.org/2007/02/01/thieves-and-fascists-the-politics-of-abjection-in-radioheads-hail-to-the-thief-the-gloaming.

Jenni Millbank (2004) 'It's About This: Lesbians, Prison, Desire' 13 *Social and Legal Studies* 155.

Monique Rooney (2015a) 'Mute Eloquence: Elizabeth Jolley's *The Well* as Encrypted Melodrama' 15 *JASAL: Journal of the Association for the Study of Australian Literature*, https://openjournals.library.sydney.edu.au/index.php/JASAL/article/view/9936/9824.

——— (2015b) *Living Screens: Melodrama and Plasticity in Contemporary Film and Television*, Rowman & Littlefield.

Honni van Rijswijk (2015) 'Encountering Law's Harm Through Literary Critique: An Anti-Elegy of Land and Sovereignty' 27 *Law and Literature* 237.

Beverley Zalcock and Jocelyn Robinson (1996) 'Inside *Cell Block H*: Hard Steel and Soft Soap' 9 *Continuum* 88.

Television series, music and literature

Dante Alighieri (1308–1321) *The Inferno* (Trans. Robert and Jean Hollander), Doubleday (ed 2000).

Bat for Lashes (2012) 'Laura'. *The Haunted Man*, Parlophone.

Michael Chapman and Holly Knight (1985) *What a Life!*, Chrysalis.

Marcus Clarke (1874) *For the Term of His Natural Life*, Rowman & Littlefield.

The Divinyls (1985) 'Pleasure and Pain' *What a Life!* Chrysalis.

The Handmaid's Tale (2017–) Daniel Wilson Productions, the Littlefield Company, White Oak Productions and MLM Television (S1–).

Missy Higgins (2012) 'Heart's a Mess' (Gotye cover), *Like A Version: Volume 8*, Triple J.

Imagine Dragons (2012) 'Radioactive' *Interscope*.

John Mitchel (1918) 'Jail Journal, Commenced on Board the *Shearwater* steamer, in Dublin Bay, continued at Spike Island – on board the *Scourge* war steamer – on board the *Dromedary* hulk, Bermuda – on board the *Neptune* convict ship – at Pernambuco – at the Cape of Good Hope (during the anti-convict rebellion) – at Van Diemen's land – at Sydney – at Tahiti – at San Francisco – at Greytown – and concluding at no. 3 pier, North River, New York', M.H. Gill & Son.

Reg Watson *Prisoner* (1979–86) Reg Grundy Organisation (S1–8).

Pleasantville (2013) 'Wentworth (You Don't Know Me)' *Richard Pleasance. Fremantle-Media Australia.*

Jonathan Swift (1726/2003) *Gulliver's Travels*, Penguin.

David Hannam, Lara Radulovich and Reg Watson (creators), *Wentworth* (2013–) Foxtel SoHo (2013–2016) Foxtel Showcase (2017–).

Westworld (2016–18) HBO Entertainment, Kilter Films and Warner Bros Television (S1–2).

Index

www.ingramcontent.com/pod-product-compliance
Ingram Content Group UK Ltd.
Pitfield, Milton Keynes, MK11 3LW, UK
UKHW022012180926
475701UK00003B/331

* 9 7 8 1 0 3 2 2 3 7 2 3 7 *